ADVANCED VISUAL EFFECTS WITH DIRECT3D®

PETER WALSH

THOMSON
*
COURSE TECHNOLOGY
Professional ■ Technical ■ Reference

© 2006 by Thomson Course Technology PTR. All rights reserved. No part of this book may be reproduced or transmitted in any form or by any means, electronic or mechanical, including photocopying, recording, or by any information storage or retrieval system without written permission from Thomson Course Technology PTR, except for the inclusion of brief quotations in a review.

The Thomson Course Technology PTR logo and related trade dress are trademarks of Thomson Course Technology and may not be used without written permission.

Direct3D is a registered trademark of Microsoft Corporation.

All other trademarks are the property of their respective owners.

Important: Thomson Course Technology PTR cannot provide software support. Please contact the appropriate software manufacturer's technical support line or Web site for assistance.

Thomson Course Technology PTR and the author have attempted throughout this book to distinguish proprietary trademarks from descriptive terms by following the capitalization style used by the manufacturer.

Information contained in this book has been obtained by Thomson Course Technology PTR from sources believed to be reliable. However, because of the possibility of human or mechanical error by our sources, Thomson Course Technology PTR, or others, the Publisher does not guarantee the accuracy, adequacy, or completeness of any information and is not responsible for any errors or omissions or the results obtained from use of such information. Readers should be particularly aware of the fact that the Internet is an ever-changing entity. Some facts may have changed since this book went to press.

Educational facilities, companies, and organizations interested in multiple copies or licensing of this book should contact the publisher for quantity discount information. Training manuals, CD-ROMs, and portions of this book are also available individually or can be tailored for specific needs.

ISBN: 1-59200-961-1
Library of Congress Catalog Card Number: 2005929824
Printed in the United States of America
06 07 08 09 10 PH 10 9 8 7 6 5 4 3 2 1

Publisher and General Manager, Thomson Course Technology PTR:
Stacy L. Hiquet

Associate Director of Marketing:
Sarah O'Donnell

Manager of Editorial Services:
Heather Talbot

Marketing Manager:
Jordan Casey

Senior Acquisitions Editor:
Emi Smith

Project/Copy Editor:
Karen A. Gill

Technical Reviewer:
David Franson

PTR Editorial Services Coordinator:
Elizabeth Furbish

Interior Layout Tech:
Shawn Morningstar

Cover Designer:
Mike Tanamachi

Indexer:
Sharon Shock

Proofreader:
Steve Honeywell

Thomson Course Technology PTR,
a division of Thomson Course Technology
25 Thomson Place
Boston, MA 02210
http://www.courseptr.com

Dedicated to Lisa, my beautiful wife.

Acknowledgments

First up, I would like to thank my wife, Lisa, whom I will love forever, for putting up with me for the past year while I wrote this book. Lisa stood by me all the way through the book, and I couldn't have finished it without her.

I'd like to thank Emi Smith for talking me into writing another book. A big thank you to my project editor, Karen Gill, without whom this book would only be useful as a doorstop. I think she'd make a great programmer one day if she ever decides to get out of the publishing industry!

Thanks to all my friends who provided support along the way. Our many nights out helped take my mind off 18 hours a day of programming at work and this book! In particular, I'd like to thank my brother David for his help with optimizing advanced particle systems. Mike Andrews and Mark Robb were a huge help with the chapters on pixel and vertex shaders. Jordana Gold and Catriona McLaren were a great source of inspiration for the chapters on vertex skinned animation and Catmull-Rom splines.

And, of course, I'd like to thank you, the reader of this book. I hope this book is useful to you and that it takes you to the next level of your game development career.

About the Author

Peter Walsh has more than five years of experience writing educational material on interactive entertainment software development. This book is his fifth published title. He has worked for some of the largest and smallest game development and entertainment companies in the world directly and indirectly, including Microsoft Gaming Studios, Activision, Real Time Worlds, Visual Sciences, Nicely Crafted Entertainment, Disney, Warner Bros, and others. He has developed games on the PC, PlayStation, PlayStation 2, GameCube, Xbox, Xbox 360, and numerous handheld devices. Peter currently works as a software engineer for Real Time Worlds in Dundee, Scotland, creating next-generation games for the Xbox 360.

Contents

Introduction xiii

Chapter 1   **The New World** 1
               A Little Information About This Book 4
                   Game Programming Best Practice 4
               Getting Down to Business—Windows 9
                   Creating the Windows Interface 9
                   Creating a Placeholder Game Engine 10
               Starting Up the Direct3D API 16
                   Setting Up Visual Studio .NET to Use DirectX 16
                   Initializing Direct3D 17
                   Creating the Device 19
                   Device Validation 21
               Rendering with Direct3D 22
               Conclusion 23

Chapter 2   **The Programmable Pipeline** 25
               Introduction to Shaders 26
               Effect Files 28
                   Techniques 34
                   Semantics 36
                   HLSL 37
                   Vertex Shaders 37
                   Pixel Shaders 42

viii Contents

	EffectEdit 45
	Integrating Shaders into the Game Engine 47
	The cEffect Class 47
	The cEffectManager Class 55
	DirectInput 60
	Starting DirectInput 62
	The Keyboard Device 63
	The Mouse 65
	Extending Joystick Support 67
	Input Polling and Device Reacquisition 67
	Conclusion 69
Chapter 3	**Pimp My Engine** **71**
	Game Synchronization 72
	Frame Rate Calculation and Display 72
	Game Execution Speed Control 73
	Forcing a Frame Rate 74
	Creating a Camera 77
	Movement and Position 79
	Rotation 80
	Computing the View Matrix 81
	Managing Game Objects 84
	Visual Resources 85
	Managing Visual Resources 93
	An Extensible Game Engine 95
	Writing a Glow Shader 96
	Conclusion 106
Chapter 4	**Particle Systems Part 1—** **Coding and Optimization Techniques** **107**
	The Theory of Particles 108
	Particle Rendering Techniques 110
	Optimization Techniques 112
	Branching 112
	The Mother of All Evil: Float-to-Integer Conversions 113
	Function Inlining 115
	Cache Alignment 116

	Particle System Helpers 119
	Fast Linear Interpolation. 119
	Color Lerping 120
	Generating Random Float Values with Limited Range. 121
	Billboarding 122
	Grid Rendering 126
	Conclusion 130

Chapter 5   **Particle Systems Part 2—Implementation** 133

    The cParticle Class 134
        Updating the Particle 139
    A Particle System 142
        Feature Files. 143
        The Functions of a Particle System. 152
    Creating a Particle System Manager and Library 169
    The Results in Action 174
        Glowing Clouds 175
        Water Stream. 176
        Fire 178
    Conclusion 179

Chapter 6   **Alias Maya API Model Exporters** 181

    The Maya Plug-In Wizard 182
        Reconfiguring the Plug-In Location 189
    The Directed Acyclic Graph and
        Other Interestingly Named Objects 190
        The DAG. 190
        The DG 190
        Dependency Nodes and Function Sets. 190
    The Maya API Naming and Coding Conventions 191
        Naming Conventions. 191
        Coding Conventions 192
    Getting a Direct3D Device 194
    The Maya Plug-In Manager 196
    Export Formats 198
    Writing the Exporter 201
    Conclusion 212

Chapter 7   Applied HLSL—Water 213
- Generating the Media 214
- Tracking Time 214
- Overriding Textures 217
- Cubic Environment Mapping 220
- The Water Shader Step by Step 223
- The Water Shader in Full 227
- Conclusion 232

Chapter 8   Introduction to Vertex Skinned Animation 233
- It's All About Skin and Bones! 234
    - Just What Is a Bone? 237
    - More About Skeletons 238
    - Weights and Indices 240
    - Bringing It All Together 240
- Skinned Animation with Direct3D 242
    - In the Beginning... 243
    - Frames and Mesh Containers 244
    - Working with DirectX 249
    - Loading an Animation 263
    - Updating the Mesh 267
    - Rendering an Animated Mesh 269
- Conclusion 272

Chapter 9   Advanced Animation Techniques 275
- Animation Sequences 276
    - Seamless Blending Between Sequences 282
- An Animated Mesh Manager 285
- Multiple Managed Animated Meshes 289
- Conclusion 291

Chapter 10 Implementing Scripting 293
- All About Scripting 294
    - Scripts in Games 294
- Lua 295
- Glue Code Introduction 297
- Writing Lua Code 298
- Add Lua to Your Project 300

Contents xi

	Programming Glue Code 301
	An Inheritable Scripting Class 304
	Calling Lua Script Functions 315
	Implementing a Scriptable Object 319
	Conclusion 321

Chapter 11   Volumetric Shadowing with Stencil Buffers 323

The Theory of Volumetric Shadowing 324
The Wonderful World of Stencil Buffers 325
Building a Versatile Shadowing System 326
   Adding a Global Light Source 326
   Find Occluded Vertices 328
   Extruding an Occluded Vertex 329
   The Stencil Buffer Rendering Process 332
   Rendering the Shadows to the Frame Buffer 335
   Bringing It All Together 339
Volume Shadow Restrictions 346
Conclusion 366

Chapter 12   Environment Generation 367

Terrain 368
   Loading Assets 370
   Creating the Terrain 372
Rendering the Terrain 380
   DrawPrimitive and DrawPrimitiveUP 382
   The Terrain Shaders 383
Sky Box Techniques 389
   Generating the Sky Box 392
   Rendering the Sky Box 396
Conclusion 399

Chapter 13   Advanced Spline and Route Systems 401

Introduction to Routes 402
   Moving Between Points on a Route 403
   Creating a Route Class 403
   Loading a Route 408
   Debug Rendering a Route 410
   Linear Interpolation 413
   Advanced Catmull-Rom Interpolation 416

		Writing a Route Manager 418
		Putting the Routes into Action 422
		Conclusion 423
Chapter 14	**Xbox 360 Controllers on the PC and Video Playback 425**	
	The Xbox 360 Controller on the PC 426	
		The XInput API. 428
		Coding an XInput Controller Class. 432
		Connecting the Input Manager 436
	Video Output with DirectShow 444	
		The Theory of DirectShow 445
		The cVideoRenderer Class. 446
	Conclusion 457	
Chapter 15	**Putting It All Together** **459**	
	Index **485**	

Introduction

This book is designed to fill a large gap in the computer games market. Plenty of books out there cover introductory material on how to learn game development and how to learn particular APIs. Many books also teach extremely advanced material packed full of complicated language, mathematical algorithms, and so on. This book includes a wide range of exciting, advanced material written in an accessible way.

I'll be taking you on an incredible journey through the world of advanced game development, showing you production-quality and optimized code all the way. You'll learn some of the hottest topics and newest techniques to make your games a step above the rest. And unlike some other books, I'm not going to obfuscate and over-complicate these topics just to make myself look good.

This book is all about the subjects that you are required to know in the game industry. It's a step above the API level and deals with many subjects that every developer should know but for which there are no decent sources of information. It includes subjects like how to implement HLSL shaders into an engine, how to write an advanced particle system, how to develop advanced vertex skinned animations, and how to write exporters for popular 3D programs like Maya. Volumetric shadowing, terrain generation, developing on the PC with an Xbox 360 controller, Catmull-Rom spline systems, scripting, and so on are all advanced topics that you will be asked to implement one day if you are in the industry. If you are not yet in the industry, expect these topics to be asked at your interview. By the end of this book, you'll be unstoppable!

Who This Book Is For

This book is for intermediate to advanced programmers who want to expand their game development knowledge, learn new topics, or just sharpen their skills on subjects they already know a little about. You should be confident about C++ programming and have good game development and graphical programming skills. This book uses DirectX as its API; however, apart from shaders, this book does not directly teach much about DirectX. Instead, I use Direct3D to demonstrate advanced techniques that can be implemented with other languages without too much work. So if you are an OpenGL programmer, you should find most of this book accessible enough if you have cursory DirectX knowledge.

To give you an idea of the target level of this book, I don't spend time discussing the basics of creating a game engine, color channels, the Windows API, and so on. Instead, you'll find a wide range of hot game development topics explained without the jargon. If you can take that kind of pace, this is the book for you.

If you're feeling like you might be able to get the material for this book but are worried it's too advanced, don't forget that I'm on hand to help. If you get stuck anywhere along the way, find a bug, or need some clarification, drop me a line at mrzen@msn.com.

How This Book Is Organized

This book is divided into 15 chapters covering exciting topics in game development. I take you from the beginnings of adding HLSL shader support to your engine all the way to creating the most impressive effects with shaders, with many other topics in between. Here's a short summary of the chapters you'll find in this book.

Chapter 1, "The New World," covers everything you need to know about the code I'll be developing throughout this book. You'll get a quick overview of how the skeleton engine I developed works so that you can understand the code later on. You'll also see how to set up your development environment with the latest version of DirectX and see the settings used to set up Direct3D for rendering.

Chapter 2, "The Programmable Pipeline," introduces you to the terminology of shaders, including vertex shaders, pixel shaders, HLSL, effect files, and more. You'll also learn how data is passed between CPU and GPU. In addition, this chapter has a brief overview of DirectInput so that you can move around the 3D world.

Chapter 3, "Pimp My Engine," demonstrates how to take shaders and effects into the real world. An extensible shader manager, library, and associated code automatically load all the shader effect files from your chosen directory, allowing you to easily and instantly associate a particular shader with a renderable object. You'll also see how to create a visual resource manager and learn how to load and render models using shaders.

Chapter 4, "Particle Systems Part 1—Coding and Optimization Techniques," introduces you to the exciting world of particle systems. You'll learn all about how particle systems work. This chapter has massive coverage of topics like cache alignment for optimization, billboarding, configuring particle systems from text files, and much more.

Chapter 5, "Particle Systems Part 2—Implementation," is all about taking the theory from Chapter 1 and putting it to use in an incredibly advanced configurable particle system. You'll learn how to create incredibly fast particles, particle systems, and a particle system manager and library. You'll learn how to control a particle's velocities, colors, sizes, textures, effect files, and much more.

Chapter 6, "Alias Maya API Model Exporters," covers how to write a C++ plug-in model exporter for the incredibly popular 3D authoring package Alias|Maya. You'll learn everything necessary to write a Maya plug-in using the Maya API. The code allows you to export any Maya model to the DirectX X File format. The code is general enough for you to write the data to any format you wish.

Chapter 7, "Applied HLSL—Water," teaches you about how to put HLSL and shaders to use to create a realistic water effect. You'll learn about using multiple textures in a shader, dynamically modifying texture coordinates, and cubic environment mapping.

Chapter 8, "Introduction to Vertex Skinned Animation," shows you how to build a powerful vertex skinned animation library using D3DX. You'll learn all about bones, joints, skeletons, weights, and animation sets. By the end of this chapter, you'll have an advanced system that's capable of smoothly interpolating and rendering seamless 3D animations.

Chapter 9, "Advanced Animation Techniques," builds on the previous chapter to include advanced animation topics like spawning multiple instances of an animation and playing multiple animation sequences. You'll also see how to seamlessly blend between different animations and how to create an advanced extensible animation system manager.

Chapter 10, "Implementing Scripting," deals with the incredibly important but scarcely covered topic of scripting. This chapter shows how to use the popular Lua scripting language, found in many of the best-selling games, to add advanced scripting support to your game engine. You'll learn all about glue code, passing data to the script, and retrieving it.

Chapter 11, "Volumetric Shadowing with Stencil Buffers," shows you how to render advanced shadows using the technique known as *volumetric shadowing*. You'll see how to use shaders to tell which vertices of a model are in shadow, how to create an extruded shadow model, how to utilize stencil buffers to isolate shadowed regions, and how to use multipass rendering to finalize the shadow onscreen.

Chapter 12, "Environment Generation," shows you how to use shaders with a heightmap terrain generation engine to create perfectly blended and seamless texture coverage. You'll also learn about sky boxes and using spherical environment mapping to create incredibly realistic effects.

Chapter 13, "Advanced Spline and Route Systems," demonstrates how to use linear and Catmull-Rom algorithms to create splines that can control the camera, provide routes for models to follow, or even allow particle systems to fly around. You'll learn about the various interpolation techniques and how to create a file format to represent your splines on disk. Finally, you'll see how to create a route manager to manage all your routes.

Chapter 14, "Xbox 360 Controllers on the PC and Video Playback," shows off two very different but nonetheless useful techniques. The Xbox 360 controller is fully compatible with the PC, and the latest version of the DirectX SDK provides the XInput API for you to use. The first half of this chapter shows you how to set up and control up to four Xbox 360 controllers simultaneously. You'll also learn how to control the rumble motors in the controller. The second half of this chapter demonstrates how to render videos in your game using the DirectShow API. You'll learn how DirectShow uses components and the concept of pins to create a rendering graph capable of loading, decompressing, and playing back your videos with audio.

Chapter 15, "Putting It All Together," discusses a sample application to bring together as many of the book's topics as possible to show off all the techniques learned. It includes seamless generated terrain, animated 3D models, particle systems, volumetric shadows, spline routes, and more. The end result is incredible.

CHAPTER 1

THE NEW WORLD

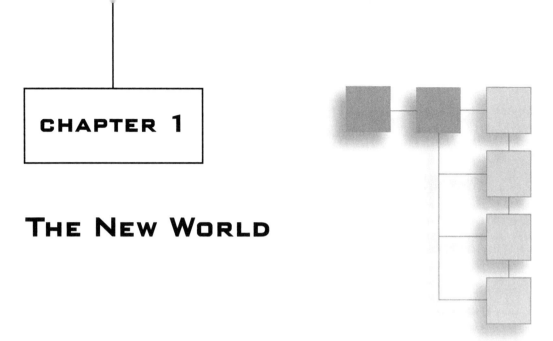

Welcome to *Advanced Visual Effects with Direct3D*! You are about to embark on a journey that will end with your being an expert on the latest techniques for programming games. Whether you want to enter the game industry or are already an industry veteran, this book will turn you into a confident graphics engine programmer, capable of the most amazing effects.

The title of this chapter really does describe current games development. Recently, game development moved into its third great stage. The first stage was when programmers had total control over what they produced and they coded absolutely everything in a game themselves. This stage lasted from the first games many decades ago all the way until the mid-1990s when hardware acceleration became possible. At this stage, game developers lost a lot of control, and they were forced to work with Application Programming Interfaces (APIs) such as DirectX and OpenGL to take advantage of the new processing power available with hardware acceleration. However, this meant being constrained by the API and hardware developers. As the technology grew, so did the learning curve. By DirectX 8.0, game developers were spending their lives in a sea of render states, sampler states, blend modes, and COM. Now in the third great stage, control is being passed back to developers. We can now write exactly what we want to run on 3D accelerators to create the most amazing real-time effects ever seen. The only downside, of course, is that the level of complication has again risen exponentially. By the end of this book, you will look down at the mere mortals around you who do not have the knowledge of the programmable pipeline and laugh heartily at your own magnificence. Maybe that's going a little too far, but you'll certainly be pushing the envelope of graphics development!

This book is designed for experienced programmers who have a working knowledge of DirectX or OpenGL. This chapter covers the following topics:

- What the Windows API is, and how it interacts with the game engine. Don't worry, you'll hardly even know it's there.
- How the game engine used in this book works. You'll also see an overview of it in skeleton format, ready to be fleshed out in the next chapter.
- How to get a real-time message pump working.
- How to set up Visual Studio .NET to use DirectX.
- Which programming practice to use when developing interactive entertainment.
- How to set up Direct3D for windowed and full-screen rendering.

The majority of this chapter should be a review of DirectX concepts so that you understand the placement of code in the rest of this book. This book is about hardcore game programming, so I'm not going spend much time on getting Direct3D set up. You'll find loads of books out there on that topic.

And I do mean hardcore! Check out Figures 1.1 through 1.3, which show what you'll be able to achieve by the end of this book.

Figure 1.1
Volumetric shadows cast in real time and calculated in a vertex shader.

Figure 1.2
Advanced particle systems with billboarding implemented with shaders.

Figure 1.3
Real-time vertex skinned animation.

With that in mind, let's get rolling!

A Little Information About This Book

The majority of this book covers advanced game programming topics. The unfortunate side effect of this is that most of the topics covered require a heavy-duty game engine to be created already. Most game programming books spend their time discussing the creation of a game engine. This book attempts the task in one chapter, so there is plenty of space left over for everything else to be crammed in! Because this book is meant for experienced programmers, most topics are here just to give you an idea of how it all works.

Many game development books take the easy way out and display code that is not up to scratch for a final project, is not properly commented, doesn't do error checking, works only in special cases, and so on. To have gotten this far, you must have read other programming books, so you know the score. This book is going to, as far as possible, show production-quality code that you can plug in to your existing projects with minimal problems. The only feature it lacks is hardcore optimization, which is project specific and makes it much harder to understand the code. Wherever possible, optimization tips will be pointed out along the way.

Game Programming Best Practice

Obviously, you didn't buy this book to learn the best way to program in general; however, you might discover some methods in this book's code that you are not currently using. Because game development projects are now enormous in scale, it is important that you adopt the majority of these techniques if you are not already doing so.

Namespaces

Namespaces group a variety of objects, variables, globals, enumerations, and everything else you can think of under a single heading that you can refer to using the scope resolution operator. This gets around the problem known as *polluting the global namespace*, which happens all the time in large projects. As an example, say that you are working on a multimillion-line piece of software. You decide to write a texture resource manager and a little piece of code, like this:

```
const int MAX_OBJECTS = 25;
```

Now, this would be fine, but your colleague in the 3D rendering department has just written a mesh manager with the following code in it:

```
const int MAX_OBJECTS = 32;
```

See the problem? Which one are you supposed to use? By enclosing all the texture code in a namespace like this

```
namespace TextureManager
{
    const int MAX_OBJECTS = 25;
}
```

and over in the mesh rendering code

```
namespace MeshManager
{
    const int MAX_OBJECTS = 32;
}
```

you can refer to `TextureManager::MAX_OBJECTS` when you want the texture manager and `MeshManager::MAX_OBJECTS` when you want to use meshes. This might seem trivial, but on larger projects, it will save you an enormous amount of messing around. Namespaces really improve the readability of your code.

#defines

Do not use `#defines` for constants. They offer absolutely no benefits over using constant definitions, and they can't be included inside namespaces. It's as simple as this:

```
#define MAX_AI_PLAYERS 10
```

Here's the new improved version:

```
const unsigned int MAX_AI_PLAYERS = 10;
```

With that simple change, you now have a value that can be type-checked, included in a namespace, and debugged easily!

Platform-Independent Variables

This will save you untold hours when your next project becomes an overnight best seller and you get a call in the morning with some suit saying, "Hey, wouldn't it be great if this game ran on the Xbox 2?!" Here's a little problem for you: The Xbox 2 uses wide character strings by default, so that blows all your string handling code out of the water, not to mention causing a million other problems. Or how about developing on the PlayStation 1, which doesn't even support proper floating point operations?

The only solution to these and related problems is to run through every line of code in every file and replace all the `chars` with something else and all the `floats` with `ints`. Sound like fun? The solution is to define independent macros for your variable types from the start and use them in place of the standard types. These are the definitions used in this book:

```
#define indInt              int
#define indUInt             unsigned int
#define indReal32           float
#define indByte             unsigned char
#define indChar             char
#define indUChar            unsigned char
#define indWord             unsigned short
#define indDWord            unsigned long
#define indShort            short
#define indUShort           unsigned short
#define indLong             long
#define indULong            unsigned long
#define indBool             bool
#define indString           char*
```

So you can now use `indInt` in place of `int`. That way if the size of `int` suddenly changes from 32 bits to 64 bits, as is extremely likely, there is only one place in your code that you'll need to change. The *ind*, by the way, stands for independent.

Singletons

Singletons are useful for ensuring that certain objects exist only once. For example, you probably only want one instance of your game engine running per process, and you probably don't want more than one sound manager. A singleton creates an object on its first access and returns the same object on future accesses. If there is an attempt to create the object a second time, it is overridden invisibly, and the first object is returned. Singletons are used throughout the code in this book. Look at the following object:

```
class cResourceManager
{
public:
    cResourceManager(void);
    ~cResourceManager(void);
```

```
public:
    static cResourceManager* getInstance();

protected:
    static cResourceManager *ms_pResourceManager;
    static indBool     ms_InstanceFlag;
};
```

To turn this object into a singleton, you must make the following changes:

1. Make the constructor `private`. This ensures that the object cannot be created outside of itself. That is, the object can only create itself. If you try to create the object manually, you will get a compilation error because the constructor is private.

2. Add a `static` member pointer that points to itself in the class:

   ```
   static cResourceManager *ms_pResourceManager;
   ```

3. Add a `static` flag to tell whether the object has been created yet:

   ```
   static indBool     ms_InstanceFlag;
   ```

4. Add a `public static` function to return the `static` pointer:

   ```
   cResourceManager* cResourceManager::getInstance()
   {
       if(!ms_InstanceFlag)
       {
           ms_pResourceManager = new cResourceManager();
           ms_InstanceFlag = true;
           return ms_pResourceManager;
       }
       else
       {
           return ms_pResourceManager;
       }
   }
   ```

5. Finally, add the `static` member access functions to the implementation:

   ```
   bool cResourceManager::ms_InstanceFlag = false;
   cResourceManager* cResourceManager::ms_pResourceManager = NULL;
   ```

Here's the result:

```
class cResourceManager
{
private:
    cResourceManager(void);
public:
    ~cResourceManager(void);
public:
    static cResourceManager* getInstance();
    .
    .
    .
protected:
    static cResourceManager *ms_pResourceManager;
    static indBool     ms_InstanceFlag;
};
```

Now you can access all the code in this class by typing the following:

```
cResourceManager::getInstance->CallSomeFunction();
```

Most programmers find it annoying to keep typing the class name and `GetInstance()`, so they add a `#define` like this:

```
#define RESOURCEMANAGER cResourceManager::getInstance()
```

Now you can access all the methods of the singleton object much more easily:

```
RESOURCEMANAGER->CallSomeFunction();
```

Error Handling

This is extremely important and should not be left to the last minute. Throughout the code, the `assert()` function forces a breakpoint whenever something fails. You pass this function any expression that you hope is `true`. If the value ever turns out to be `false`, a big message box pops up on your screen and brings you directly to the point of failure in the debugger. However, never put code to be executed inside a call to `assert()`, because it will be excluded from a release build. As an example, here is what you should do:

```
Object* pNewObject = new cObject;
assert(pObject != NULL);
```

However, this is really bad:

```
assert(Render() != false);
```

When the previous line is compiled in a release build, it is compiled to NULL, and you end up with a big friendly black screen in front of you. Most programmers are aware of this, but I mention it because a couple of weeks ago, a programmer with more than 15 years of experience working on triple-A games made this very error in code, and it took an incredible amount of time to track down the problem.

I think that's about it for the guidelines, although I'll mention a few more as we proceed. You can find some excellent books, such as *Code Complete*, that describe the best ways to program. If you're working on a big project, or you plan to, you'll be missing out if you don't take the opportunity to learn this type of stuff!

Getting Down to Business—Windows

This is the part every programmer hates when starting a new project. You have all these great ideas for a game in your head, and you can't wait to get started. The only thing stopping you is that great big brick wall that everyone loves to bang their head against, the Win32 API. Luckily, you don't have to deal with it that much anymore for games, because DirectX is pretty independent from the rest of Windows, and there is a handy wizard to create the boring old functions like WinMain(), WndProc(), and so on.

Creating the Windows Interface

The first step taken in creating the game engine in this book was to invoke the new project wizard from Visual Studio .NET 2003. Let's start by firing up Visual Studio and selecting File, New Project. This brings up the New Project dialog box, as shown in Figure 1.4.

Select the standard Win32 Project, fill in what you would like to call your project, press OK, and then press Finish in the next dialog box. Visual Studio has automatically created a new project for you that contains, among other things, a windowed application (don't worry, there is no MFC!) with menu support, precompiled headers, resources, and everything else you would normally spend a good hour or so perusing MSDN for. That means the foundation Windows API is taken care of. Let's turn it into a game engine!

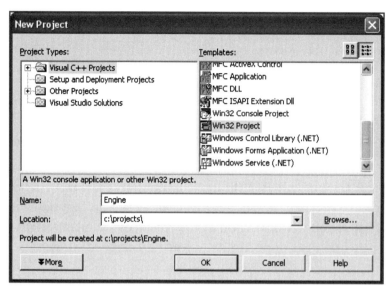

Figure 1.4
The New Project dialog box. Select the standard Win32 Project.

Creating a Placeholder Game Engine

There can't be much of a game without a central engine to control everything. To this end, a new class was added to the project called cEngine. This is the basis of what will become an advanced engine by the end of this book. For now, however, it has to start as a simple singleton with three extra functions:

```
namespace Graphics
{
    const indUInt DEFAULT_SCREEN_WIDTH = 640;
    const indUInt DEFAULT_SCREEN_HEIGHT = 480;
    const indReal32 DEFAULT_GAME_FPS = 60.0f;

    class cGameEngine
    {

    // Functions
    public:
        virtual ~cGameEngine();

    private:
        cGameEngine();
```

```
public:
    bool        Start(HWND hWnd, HINSTANCE hInstance);
    int         Run();
    bool        Shutdown();

    static cGameEngine* getInstance()

protected:
    HWND                m_hMainWnd;
    HINSTANCE           m_hInstance;
    static bool         ms_InstanceFlag;
    static              cGameEngine *ms_pEngine;

};
}
```

As you can see, it is currently just an empty class. (And it's created in its own namespace! I practice what I preach!) The three highlighted functions are pretty self-explanatory. `Start()` is called on application startup to begin the initialization process. All other game initialization is called from this function. `Run()` is called every tick and does all the per-frame work, such as checking for input, rendering, and so on. Finally, `Shutdown()` is called when the game is ready to leave. It is responsible for shutting down and releasing all the resources that the game uses.

Connecting the Win32 API to the Game Engine

We need to make a number of changes to the default Win32 implementation file that Visual Studio created for us to make it work with the game. The most important of these is changing the message pump from being a stalling function to one that works well with games. By default, your application sits around doing nothing if no new windows messages are available. Obviously, this is no good for a real-time game because there is no time for sitting around waiting for messages; your application should be spitting out high-quality pixels at the speed of light! To this end, look at the default `WinMain()` that is created for you:

```
int APIENTRY WinMain(HINSTANCE hInstance,
                     HINSTANCE hPrevInstance,
                     LPTSTR    lpCmdLine,
                     int       nCmdShow)
{
```

```
    // TODO: Place code here.
    MSG msg;
    HACCEL hAccelTable;

    // Initialize global strings
    LoadString(hInstance, IDS_APP_TITLE, szTitle, MAX_LOADSTRING);
    LoadString(hInstance, IDC_ENGINE, szWindowClass, MAX_LOADSTRING);
    MyRegisterClass(hInstance);

    // Perform application initialization:
    if (!InitInstance (hInstance, nCmdShow))
    {
        return FALSE;
    }
    hAccelTable = LoadAccelerators(hInstance, (LPCTSTR)IDC_ENGINE);

    // Main message loop:
    while (GetMessage(&msg, NULL, 0, 0))
    {
        if (!TranslateAccelerator(msg.hwnd, hAccelTable, &msg))
        {
            TranslateMessage(&msg);
            DispatchMessage(&msg);
        }
    }

    return (int) msg.wParam;
}
```

The bold section of code is the message pump, which you should be familiar with if you have done Windows game development in the past. Now look at the modified version, which is real-time game friendly:

```
int APIENTRY WinMain(HINSTANCE hInstance,
                     HINSTANCE hPrevInstance,
                     LPSTR     lpCmdLine,
                     int       nCmdShow)
{
    MSG msg;
    HACCEL hAccelTable;

    // Initialize global strings
    LoadString(hInstance, IDS_APP_TITLE, szTitle, MAX_LOADSTRING);
```

```
    LoadString(hInstance, IDC_ENGINE, szWindowClass, MAX_LOADSTRING);
    RegisterClass(hInstance);

    HWND hWnd;

    // Perform application initialization:
    if (!InitInstance (hInstance, nCmdShow, hWnd))
    {
        return FALSE;
    }

    hAccelTable = LoadAccelerators(hInstance, (LPCTSTR)IDC_ENGINE);

    if(!GAMEENGINE->Start(hWnd, hInstance))
    {
        // Failed to start game engine
        assert(0);
        OutputDebugString("Failed to start the game!\n");
        return -1;
    }

    do
    {
        if (PeekMessage(&msg, NULL, 0, 0, PM_REMOVE))
        {
            if (msg.message == WM_QUIT)
                break;

            TranslateMessage(&msg);
            DispatchMessage(&msg);
        }
        else
        {
            GAMEENGINE->Run();
        }
    }
    while (true);

    return GAMEENGINE->Shutdown();
}
```

The `WinMain()` function has a new call to start up the game engine, run it whenever there are no messages coming in (which is almost always), and shut it down if a `WM_QUIT` message arrives. And that is almost all there is to it! So far, you've barely had to write a single Win32 call! All you need to do now is modify the window creation code to ensure optimal performance.

Creating a High-Performance Window

There isn't much to this. By default, Windows creates the application as if it were a dinosaur like Microsoft Word, which is not what we want. The default Windows creation function, `InitInstance()`, looks like this:

```
BOOL InitInstance(HINSTANCE hInstance, int nCmdShow)
{
   HWND hWnd;

   hInst = hInstance; // Store instance handle in our global variable

   hWnd = CreateWindow(szWindowClass, szTitle, WS_OVERLAPPEDWINDOW,
      CW_USEDEFAULT, 0, CW_USEDEFAULT, 0, NULL, NULL, hInstance, NULL);

   if (!hWnd)
   {
      return FALSE;
   }

   ShowWindow(hWnd, nCmdShow);
   UpdateWindow(hWnd);

   return TRUE;
}
```

With a little game magic poured on, the function changes to look like this:

```
BOOL InitInstance(HINSTANCE hInstance, int nCmdShow, HWND& hWnd)
{
   hInst = hInstance; // Store instance handle in our global variable

   hWnd = CreateWindow(szWindowClass, szTitle, WS_OVERLAPPEDWINDOW,
      CW_USEDEFAULT, CW_USEDEFAULT,
      Graphics::DEFAULT_SCREEN_WIDTH,
      Graphics::DEFAULT_SCREEN_HEIGHT,
      GetDesktopWindow(), NULL, hInstance, NULL);
```

```
    if (!hWnd)
    {
       return FALSE;
    }

    ShowWindow(hWnd, nCmdShow);
    UpdateWindow(hWnd);

    return true;
}
```

There's not too much to change here. Basically, just make sure the window is created with the same width and height as the render target later on when the Direct3D device is created. By having the window and render target the same size, there is much less need to resize the output every frame when in windowed mode. It's generally a good idea to use windowed mode during development so that debug messages work properly. Also, the parent window is set to the desktop, which is generally a good idea for full-screen development.

The next and final step is to change the MyRegisterClass() function to maximize performance. By default, Visual Studio creates the following function for you:

```
ATOM MyRegisterClass(HINSTANCE hInstance)
{
    WNDCLASSEX wcex;

    wcex.cbSize         = sizeof(WNDCLASSEX);

    wcex.style          = CS_HREDRAW | CS_VREDRAW;
    wcex.lpfnWndProc    = (WNDPROC)WndProc;
    wcex.cbClsExtra     = 0;
    wcex.cbWndExtra     = 0;
    wcex.hInstance      = hInstance;
    wcex.hIcon          = LoadIcon(hInstance, (LPCTSTR)IDI_ENGINE);
    wcex.hCursor        = LoadCursor(NULL, IDC_ARROW);
    wcex.hbrBackground  = (HBRUSH)(COLOR_WINDOW+1);
    wcex.lpszMenuName   = (LPCTSTR)IDC_ENGINE;
    wcex.lpszClassName  = szWindowClass;
    wcex.hIconSm        = LoadIcon(wcex.hInstance, (LPCTSTR)IDI_SMALL);

    return RegisterClassEx(&wcex);
}
```

Just one line in this function needs to be changed. By default, the window style is set to redraw (aka send a `WM_PAINT` message) whenever the horizontal or vertical size of the window changes. Because we don't give a rat's banana about window painting, we don't need to bother with `WM_PAINT` messages. Instead, we should change this line to allocate the main window with its own device context so that it doesn't need to spend time getting one from Windows all the time. The new line is as follows:

```
wcex.style           = CS_CLASSDC;
```

And that's it! Apart from a little bit of spring cleaning, we won't have to deal with the Windows API again for the rest of this book!

Starting Up the Direct3D API

Now for a little fun with setting up the Direct3D interface. The guys over at Microsoft really deserve an award for DirectX 9.0. In the past, it took *a lot* of work to get Direct3D up and running. It brought me to tears on many occasions. However, these days Direct3D is almost as simple as OpenGL to get started.

> **Note**
>
> As a little aside, if you are wondering what the best API is to use, please extend your left hand in front of you making a fist. Now extend one index finger and point it toward the roof. That is the number of massively successful game engines written with OpenGL. Please now look out your window and count the number of blades of grass you can see. That is the number of massively successful DirectX games that have been written. You decide!

Setting Up Visual Studio .NET to Use DirectX

There are now only three steps to setting up Direct3D: create a Direct3D object, fill in a `D3DPRESENT_PARAMETERS` structure, and make a call to `IDirect3D::CreateDevice()`. Before covering that, let's look at how to make sure Visual Studio is set up to use Direct3D without compile or link errors. All we need to do is ensure the following:

- Place the following directories into your include directories list, found in Tools, Options, Projects, VC++ Directories, Include Files.

```
X:\DXSDK Install Path\Include
```

- Place the following directories into your library directories list:

    `X:\DXSDK Install Path\Lib`

- Add the following library files to Project, Settings, Linker, Input, Additional Dependencies:

    `dxguid.lib`
    `dinput8.lib`
    `winmm.lib`
    `d3dx9.lib`
    `d3d9.lib`

Initializing Direct3D

Back to the code. New functions were added to the `cEngine` class to start up Direct3D, which are called from the main `Start()` function. These functions are `InitializeGraphics()`, which fills out the presentation parameter's structure, and `CreateDevice()`, which uses the structure to create the actual device. The following settings create the device:

```
indBool cGameEngine::InitializeGraphics()
{
    if(NULL == (m_pDirect3D = Direct3DCreate9(D3D_SDK_VERSION)))
        return false;

    if(m_bFullscreen)
    {
        // Render target width and height
        m_D3DPresentParams.BackBufferWidth = m_ScreenWidth;
        m_D3DPresentParams.BackBufferHeight = m_ScreenHeight;
        // 32-bit render target with alpha
        m_D3DPresentParams.BackBufferFormat = D3DFMT_A8R8G8B8;
        // Just one back buffer
        m_D3DPresentParams.BackBufferCount = 1;
        // No multisampling, as it's not supported by many cards
        m_D3DPresentParams.MultiSampleType = D3DMULTISAMPLE_NONE;
        m_D3DPresentParams.MultiSampleQuality = 0;
        // Discard the back buffer at the end of every frame
        m_D3DPresentParams.SwapEffect = D3DSWAPEFFECT_DISCARD;
        // Rendering window handle
        m_D3DPresentParams.hDeviceWindow = m_hMainWnd;
```

```
            // Full screen mode
            m_D3DPresentParams.Windowed = FALSE;
            // Have Direct3D create a depth and stencil buffer automatically
            m_D3DPresentParams.EnableAutoDepthStencil = 1;
            // 24-bit depth buffer with 8-bit stencil buffer
            m_D3DPresentParams.AutoDepthStencilFormat = D3DFMT_D24S8;
            // Discard the depth and stencil buffer at the end of every frame
            m_D3DPresentParams.Flags = D3DPRESENTFLAG_DISCARD_DEPTHSTENCIL;
            // Default refresh rate
            m_D3DPresentParams.FullScreen_RefreshRateInHz = 0;
            // Display the frame as soon as possible
            m_D3DPresentParams.PresentationInterval =
                                                D3DPRESENT_INTERVAL_ IMMEDIATE;
        }
        else
        {
            m_D3DPresentParams.BackBufferWidth = m_ScreenWidth;
            m_D3DPresentParams.BackBufferHeight = m_ScreenHeight;
            // Unknown format, which is the same as the current desktop setting
            m_D3DPresentParams.BackBufferFormat = D3DFMT_UNKNOWN;
            m_D3DPresentParams.BackBufferCount = 1;
            m_D3DPresentParams.MultiSampleType = D3DMULTISAMPLE_NONE;
            m_D3DPresentParams.MultiSampleQuality = 0;
            m_D3DPresentParams.SwapEffect = D3DSWAPEFFECT_DISCARD;
            m_D3DPresentParams.hDeviceWindow = m_hMainWnd;
            // Windowed rather than full screen
            m_D3DPresentParams.Windowed = TRUE;
            m_D3DPresentParams.EnableAutoDepthStencil = 1;
            m_D3DPresentParams.AutoDepthStencilFormat = D3DFMT_D24S8;
            m_D3DPresentParams.Flags = D3DPRESENTFLAG_DISCARD_DEPTHSTENCIL;
            m_D3DPresentParams.FullScreen_RefreshRateInHz = 0;
            m_D3DPresentParams.PresentationInterval =
D3DPRESENT_INTERVAL_IMMEDIATE;
        }

        CreateDevice();

        // Init default render states

        // Disable lighting until we add some lights
        m_pDevice->SetRenderState(D3DRS_LIGHTING, 0);
```

```cpp
    // Set the texture sampler states to linear blending to remove jaggies
    m_pDevice->SetSamplerState(0, D3DSAMP_MINFILTER, D3DTEXF_LINEAR);
    m_pDevice->SetSamplerState(0, D3DSAMP_MAGFILTER, D3DTEXF_LINEAR);
    m_pDevice->SetSamplerState(0, D3DSAMP_MIPFILTER, D3DTEXF_LINEAR);

    return true;
}
```

These settings should work for the majority of graphics cards. If they don't work for yours, it's probably time to invest in some new hardware, because most of the code in this book is devoted to cutting-edge features, rather than supporting legacy hardware. You can find numerous introductory books that cover this startup material in more detail if you have not come across this before.

Creating the Device

The code to create the device is in a separate function from the code that fills out the presentation parameters so that the device can be re-created quickly during runtime if necessary. The presentation parameters are unlikely to change, so you don't need to reset them every time.

```cpp
indBool cGameEngine::CreateDevice()
{
    HRESULT hr = m_pDirect3D->CreateDevice(D3DADAPTER_DEFAULT, D3DDEVTYPE_HAL,
            m_hMainWnd,
                            D3DCREATE_HARDWARE_VERTEXPROCESSING,
                            &m_D3DPresentParams, &m_pDevice);
    if(FAILED(hr))
    {
        OutputDebugString("Failed to create hardware direct3d device");
        HRESULT hr = m_pDirect3D->CreateDevice(
                D3DADAPTER_DEFAULT, D3DDEVTYPE_HAL, m_hMainWnd,
                D3DCREATE_MIXED_VERTEXPROCESSING,
                &m_D3DPresentParams, &m_pDevice);
        if(FAILED(hr))
        {
            OutputDebugString("Failed to create mixed direct3d device");
            HRESULT hr = m_pDirect3D>CreateDevice(D3DADAPTER_DEFAULT,
                D3DDEVTYPE_HAL, m_hMainWnd,
                D3DCREATE_SOFTWARE_VERTEXPROCESSING,
                &m_D3DPresentParams, &m_pDevice);
            if(FAILED(hr))
```

```
            {
                OutputDebugString("Failed to create software direct3d device");
                assert(0);
                Quit();
                return false;
            }
        }
    }
    return true;
}
```

As you can see, the function attempts to create a hardware device by default. If that fails, a mixed mode device is attempted, followed by a software-only device, which is slow. If none can be created, an `assert` is thrown, and the game ends. It's useless to start without a device.

And that's all the setup code you need. You're ready to start rendering with Direct3D. Just before that, let's take a quick look at the shutdown code. All COM objects should be released with the SAFE_RELEASE() macro, which is defined like this:

```
template<class TYPE>

inline void SAFE_RELEASE(TYPE*& pObj)
{
    if (pObj != NULL)
    {
        pObj->Release();
        pObj = NULL;
    }
    else
    {
        //assert(0);   // Enable this to catch errant releases
        OutputDebugString(_T("Release called on NULL interface ptr\n"));
    }
}
```

At the moment, the shutdown function is pretty bare, but it will be filled out later on. As far as possible, you should release COM objects in reverse order to the way they were created. This prevents any reference counting problems. To shut down the engine, the following code will do for now:

```
indBool cGameEngine::Shutdown()
{
    SAFE_RELEASE(m_pDevice);
    SAFE_RELEASE(m_pDirect3D);

    return true;
}
```

Device Validation

As you are no doubt aware, the Direct3D device can be lost at any time if the user decides to change the application focus or another application goes full screen. To make sure the device you are using is okay, you need to call the ValidateDevice() function every frame to ensure that it's valid. If it's invalid, you need to re-create it:

```
indBool cGameEngine::ValidateDevice()
{
    assert(m_pDevice);
    HRESULT deviceState = m_pDevice->TestCooperativeLevel();

    if(deviceState == D3D_OK)
        return true;

    if(deviceState == D3DERR_DRIVERINTERNALERROR)
    {
        assert(0);
        Quit();
    }

    if(deviceState == D3DERR_DEVICENOTRESET)
    {
        SAFE_RELEASE(m_pDevice);
        CreateDevice();
        return true;
    }

    return false;
}
```

Rendering with Direct3D

Now we're starting to get somewhere. Windows is set up and handling messages, Direct3D is initialized, validation is organized, and the engine can shut down cleanly. All that is needed now is a little rendering code, which usually involves the following steps with Direct3D:

1. Call `IDirect3DDevice::BeginScene()`.

2. Clear the render target, the depth buffer, and the stencil buffer with `IDirect3DDevice::Clear()`.

3. Render all objects.

4. Call `IDirect3DDevice::EndScene()`.

5. Present the render target to the primary surface with `IDirect3DDevice::Present()`.

With that in mind, three new functions are added to the engine: `PreRender()` for once-per-frame scene initialization, `Render()` to render all scene data, and `PostRender()` for once-per-frame cleanup tasks. Here is the skeleton code that will be fleshed out later, all of which is called from the main `Run()` function:

```
indInt cGameEngine::Run()
{
    if(!ValidateDevice())
        return 0;

    PreRender();
    Render();
    PostRender();

    return true;
}

indBool cGameEngine::PreRender()
{
    m_pDevice->BeginScene();

    m_pDevice->Clear( 0,
                      NULL, D3DCLEAR_TARGET | D3DCLEAR_ZBUFFER | D3DCLEAR_STENCIL,
        D3DCOLOR_XRGB(0,0,100), 1.0f, 0 );
```

```
    return true;
}

indBool cGameEngine::Render()
{
    // Render scene
    return true;
}

indBool cGameEngine::PostRender()
{
    m_pDevice->EndScene();
    m_pDevice->Present(0,0,0,0);

    return true;
}
```

These three rendering functions are the real meat and potatoes of the game engine, and I'll be referring to them a lot.

Conclusion

That's our entire game engine laid out in skeleton format ready to hang game code off of. Not bad for one chapter! In this chapter, you learned about the following:

- What the Windows API is, and how it interacts with the game engine. Don't worry, you'll hardly even know it's there.

- How the game engine used in this book works. You'll also see an overview of it in skeleton format, ready to be fleshed out in the next chapter.

- How to get a real-time message pump working.

- How to set up Visual Studio .NET to use DirectX.

- Which programming practice to use when developing interactive entertainment.

- How to set up Direct3D for windowed and full-screen rendering.

Now get ready for the next chapter, where you will learn how to turn this skeleton into something a bit more useful!

CHAPTER 2

THE PROGRAMMABLE PIPELINE

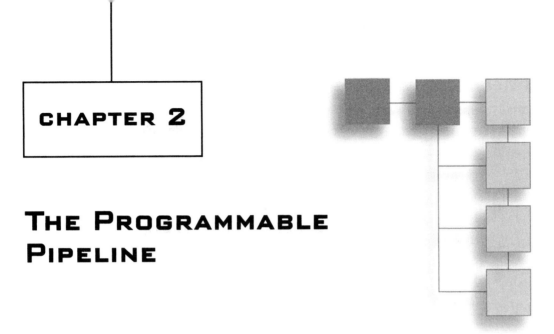

This chapter is all about modern game development with the programmable pipeline. The programmable pipeline will soon be the only way to develop games, so it is vital that you have a good understanding of everything involved. Most programmers take one look at shaders and become instantly puzzled because they are such a world away from traditional DirectX games development. With that in mind, this chapter is going to turn you into a shader wizard. I'll be covering the following topics:

- What exactly shaders, effect files, the HLSL, and all the new-fangled terminology actually means
- Examples of shaders and what they can be used for
- Connecting your game engine to use shaders
- Using DirectInput to get input into your game

Introduction to Shaders

I really don't like the word *shader* because shaders do far more than just darken pixels. Shaders are binary programs that execute on the *Graphics Processing Unit*, or GPU. The GPU is the 3D accelerated chip on your graphics card that you previously had to interact with through Direct3D render states and vertex buffers. In traditional programming, the rendering cycle usually went something like this:

1. Get next vertex buffer full of data.

2. Set up the render states on the graphics card.

3. Send the vertex buffer to the GPU to be rendered.

4. Repeat until rendering of all objects in this frame is complete.

That was fine back in the 1990s when there wasn't much processing power around. However, as graphics cards got better and more advanced, the number of render states and other settings increased dramatically. Render states effectively became the *materials* for rendering objects. For example, you could have a shiny material that needed 15 render states to be set, or a high specular material that needed 8 render states to be set up. However, materials are something that artists should be thinking about, not programmers. Because render states are an API-only implementation, it became a chore to set up code to make render states more accessible. That was the first main problem: It was too hard to just have a material on disk in a file called `shiny.material` or something similar.

The second main problem was the amount of effort it took to generate advanced effects with render states. The more render states there were to expose new functionality, the more complicated rendering became, until it reached its current state, which is just silly.

Finally, the DirectX render state API started to become a bottleneck both to hardware developers and programmers. The hardware developers couldn't develop new features until Microsoft shipped a new version of DirectX, and the programmers couldn't write the effects they wanted; they were forced to use whatever Microsoft and the hardware developers had managed to agree on.

The solution? Open up the GPU and let the software developers write their own effects directly on the graphics hardware. This is where the fun starts. At last, it's unnecessary to wait for hardware developers to release new cards or Microsoft to update the API. Programmers can now write directly to the GPU and execute binary programs in parallel with the main CPU!

Let's learn a little more about these GPU programs. The first thing to note about them is that they are called *shaders*, and there are two main types of them: *vertex shaders* and *pixel shaders*. Shaders used to be written in complex and hard-to-maintain assembly language. Luckily, however, there is a new language called the *High Level Shader Language* (HLSL) that is almost C/C++, which makes it a lot easier. Trust me, you do not want to try to write, debug, and maintain an assembly language shader. They are a nightmare. However, just so you know what they look like, see the following code:

```
dcl_position v0;
dcl_blendweight v1;
dcl_blendindices v2;
dcl_normal v3;
dcl_texcoord0 v4;

//Compensate for lack of UBYTE4 on Geforce3
mul r1,v2.zyxw,c0.wwww
//mul r1,v2,c0.wwww


//Set 1
mov a0.x,r1.x
m4x3 r4.xyz,v0,c[a0.x + 9];
m3x3 r5.xyz,v3,c[a0.x + 9];

//Compute position
mov r4.w,c0.x
m4x4 oPos,r4,c2

//Normalize normals
dp3 r5.w, r5, r5;
rsq r5.w, r5.w;
mul r5, r5, r5.w;

; Do the lighting calculation
dp3 r1.x, r5, c1      ; normal dot light
lit r1, r1
mul r0, r1.y, c8      ; Multiply with diffuse
add r0, r0, c7        ; Add in ambient
```

```
min oD0, r0, c0.x      ; clamp if > 1
mov oD1, c0.zzzz       ; output specular

; Copy texture coordinate
mov oT0, v4
```

That, believe it or not, is vertex shader code from the DirectX sample application that is used to do vertex skinning. I won't bother going into the details of this program because nobody uses this anymore. There are hardly any programs left based on assembly, and if you come across any being used, you should really convert them to High Level Shader Language (HLSL) to improve maintainability. The only time you might need to work in assembly is if you are a true Jedi master and you want to hand-code a shader to improve performance.

Effect Files

A lot of books and tutorials dive straight into explaining shaders without giving you an idea of the bigger picture. The actual shaders you will write will be held in what are known as effect files. An *effect file* is a text file with an .fx extension. It is generally accepted best practice to use one effect file per material you are using. So you could have an effect file called shiny.fx or bump_map.fx, for example.

An effect file holds together a lot of information that will make your life easier as a visual effect programmer. Look at the following example of an effect file before I explain what they are. This is the default simple.fx file that ships with the DirectX Software Development Kit (SDK):

```
//
// Simple Lighting Model
// Copyright (c) Microsoft Corporation. All rights reserved.
//
// Note: This effect file works with EffectEdit.
//

string XFile = "tiger\\tiger.x";    // model
int    BCLR  = 0xff202080;          // background

// light direction (view space)
float3 lightDir < string UIDirectional = "Light Direction"; > = {0.577, -0.577, 0.577};
```

```
// light intensity
float4 I_a = { 0.1f, 0.1f, 0.1f, 1.0f };    // ambient
float4 I_d = { 1.0f, 1.0f, 1.0f, 1.0f };    // diffuse
float4 I_s = { 1.0f, 1.0f, 1.0f, 1.0f };    // specular

// material reflectivity
float4 k_a : MATERIALAMBIENT = { 1.0f, 1.0f, 1.0f, 1.0f };    // ambient
float4 k_d : MATERIALDIFFUSE = { 1.0f, 1.0f, 1.0f, 1.0f };    // diffuse
float4 k_s : MATERIALSPECULAR= { 1.0f, 1.0f, 1.0f, 1.0f };    // specular
float  n   : MATERIALPOWER = 32.0f;                            // power

// texture
texture Tex0 < string name = "tiger\\tiger.bmp"; >;

// transformations
float4x4 World      : WORLD;
float4x4 View       : VIEW;
float4x4 Projection : PROJECTION;

struct VS_OUTPUT
{
    float4 Pos  : POSITION;
    float4 Diff : COLOR0;
    float4 Spec : COLOR1;
    float2 Tex  : TEXCOORD0;
};

VS_OUTPUT VS(
    float3 Pos  : POSITION,
    float3 Norm : NORMAL,
    float2 Tex  : TEXCOORD0)
{
    VS_OUTPUT Out = (VS_OUTPUT)0;

    float3 L = -lightDir;

    float4x4 WorldView = mul(World, View);

    float3 P = mul(float4(Pos, 1), (float4x3)WorldView);   // position
    float3 N = normalize(mul(Norm, (float3x3)WorldView));  // normal
```

```
    float3 R = normalize(2 * dot(N, L) * N - L);       // reflection vector
    float3 V = -normalize(P);                          // view direction

    Out.Pos  = mul(float4(P, 1), Projection);          // position
    Out.Diff = I_a * k_a + I_d * k_d * max(0, dot(N, L));  // diffuse + ambient
    Out.Spec = I_s * k_s * pow(max(0, dot(R, V)), n/4);    // specular
    Out.Tex  = Tex;

    return Out;
}

sampler Sampler = sampler_state
{
    Texture   = (Tex0);
    MipFilter = LINEAR;
    MinFilter = LINEAR;
    MagFilter = LINEAR;
};

float4 PS(
    float4 Diff : COLOR0,
    float4 Spec : COLOR1,
    float2 Tex  : TEXCOORD0) : COLOR
{
    return tex2D(Sampler, Tex) * Diff + Spec;
}

technique TVertexAndPixelShader
{
    pass P0
    {
        // shaders
        VertexShader = compile vs_1_1 VS();
        PixelShader  = compile ps_1_1 PS();
    }
}

technique TVertexShaderOnly
{
    pass P0
    {
        // lighting
```

```
            Lighting       = FALSE;
            SpecularEnable = TRUE;

            // samplers
            Sampler[0] = (Sampler);

            // texture stages
            ColorOp[0]   = MODULATE;
            ColorArg1[0] = TEXTURE;
            ColorArg2[0] = DIFFUSE;
            AlphaOp[0]   = MODULATE;
            AlphaArg1[0] = TEXTURE;
            AlphaArg2[0] = DIFFUSE;

            ColorOp[1]   = DISABLE;
            AlphaOp[1]   = DISABLE;

            // shaders
            VertexShader = compile vs_1_1 VS();
            PixelShader  = NULL;
        }
}

technique TNoShader
{
    pass P0
    {
        // transforms
        WorldTransform[0]   = (World);
        ViewTransform       = (View);
        ProjectionTransform = (Projection);

        // material
        MaterialAmbient  = (k_a);
        MaterialDiffuse  = (k_d);
        MaterialSpecular = (k_s);
        MaterialPower    = (n);

        // lighting
        LightType[0]    = DIRECTIONAL;
        LightAmbient[0] = (I_a);
        LightDiffuse[0] = (I_d);
```

```
            LightSpecular[0]  = (I_s);
            LightDirection[0] = (lightDir);
            LightRange[0]     = 100000.0f;

            LightEnable[0] = TRUE;
            Lighting       = TRUE;
            SpecularEnable = TRUE;

            // samplers
            Sampler[0] = (Sampler);

            // texture stages
            ColorOp[0]   = MODULATE;
            ColorArg1[0] = TEXTURE;
            ColorArg2[0] = DIFFUSE;
            AlphaOp[0]   = MODULATE;
            AlphaArg1[0] = TEXTURE;
            AlphaArg2[0] = DIFFUSE;

            ColorOp[1]   = DISABLE;
            AlphaOp[1]   = DISABLE;

            // shaders
            VertexShader = NULL;
            PixelShader  = NULL;
        }
    }
```

That might look a little confusing, but it actually makes a lot of sense when you figure it out. As you can see, there is a lot of stuff that looks like C/C++. So what's in this file? At the top of the file is the following:

```
string XFile = "tiger\\tiger.x";     // model
int    BCLR  = 0xff202080;           // background

// light direction (view space)
float3 lightDir < string UIDirectional = "Light Direction"; > = {0.577, -0.577, 0.577};

// light intensity
float4 I_a = { 0.1f, 0.1f, 0.1f, 1.0f };    // ambient
float4 I_d = { 1.0f, 1.0f, 1.0f, 1.0f };    // diffuse
float4 I_s = { 1.0f, 1.0f, 1.0f, 1.0f };    // specular
```

```
// material reflectivity
float4 k_a : MATERIALAMBIENT = { 1.0f, 1.0f, 1.0f, 1.0f };    // ambient
float4 k_d : MATERIALDIFFUSE = { 1.0f, 1.0f, 1.0f, 1.0f };    // diffuse
float4 k_s : MATERIALSPECULAR= { 1.0f, 1.0f, 1.0f, 1.0f };    // specular
float  n   : MATERIALPOWER = 32.0f;                           // power
```

These global variable declarations are called semantics. A *semantic* is how you pass data through to your shaders. I'll talk more about these later in this chapter. Next in the file we have the vertex shader, which looks like this:

```
VS_OUTPUT VS(
    float3 Pos  : POSITION,
    float3 Norm : NORMAL,
    float2 Tex  : TEXCOORD0)
{
    VS_OUTPUT Out = (VS_OUTPUT)0;

    float3 L = -lightDir;

    float4x4 WorldView = mul(World, View);

    float3 P = mul(float4(Pos, 1), (float4x3)WorldView);     // position
    float3 N = normalize(mul(Norm, (float3x3)WorldView));    // normal

    float3 R = normalize(2 * dot(N, L) * N - L);             // reflection vector
    float3 V = -normalize(P);                                // view direction

    Out.Pos  = mul(float4(P, 1), Projection);                // position
    Out.Diff = I_a * k_a + I_d * k_d * max(0, dot(N, L));    // diffuse + ambient
    Out.Spec = I_s * k_s * pow(max(0, dot(R, V)), n/4);      // specular
    Out.Tex  = Tex;

    return Out;
}
```

Don't worry too much about how vertex shaders work just now, because I'll be going over them in detail in the next section. Following in the effect file, you can see the pixel shader:

```
float4 PS(
    float4 Diff : COLOR0,
    float4 Spec : COLOR1,
    float2 Tex  : TEXCOORD0) : COLOR
```

```
{
    return tex2D(Sampler, Tex) * Diff + Spec;
}
```

Finally, the real magic of the effect file is contained in techniques. Look at it more closely:

```
technique TVertexAndPixelShader
{
    pass P0
    {
        // shaders
        VertexShader = compile vs_1_1 VS();
        PixelShader  = compile ps_1_1 PS();
    }
}
```

Techniques

If you've programmed DirectX before, you know what a nightmare it is trying to program the latest graphical techniques for end users with hardware that might or might not support what you are writing. You end up with piles of code wasting time checking device capabilities to see if the graphics hardware supports a particular operation. Techniques give you a way to get rid of all that code and just write the effect you want.

So what exactly is a technique? It's basically a list of commands that take the place of render states. You can now keep your material settings separate from your source code, which is a major bonus. What's great is that you can program multiple techniques for the same visual effect to target different levels of a user's hardware, and DirectX will *automatically* pick the technique that will work on the graphics card being used. That's a nice feature!

Caution

To make automatic fallback work, you must write techniques in best-to-worst order. I'll show you this later in the chapter.

So, for example, you could write one technique for old cards that don't support shaders, a second for cards that only support vertex shaders, and a third for cards that support both vertex and pixel shaders. Other additions could be support for the latest pixel shader versions. That's why using them in code is great, because you know there will always be at least one technique for even the oldest PCs to fall back on. You don't need to check endless lists of device capabilities. Of course, it still is important to ensure that you pick a good list of features to use in each technique.

Look at this technique and see if you can tell what it's doing:

```
technique TVertexShaderOnly
{
    pass P0
    {
        // lighting
        Lighting       = FALSE;
        SpecularEnable = TRUE;

        // samplers
        Sampler[0] = (Sampler);

        // texture stages
        ColorOp[0]   = MODULATE;
        ColorArg1[0] = TEXTURE;
        ColorArg2[0] = DIFFUSE;
        AlphaOp[0]   = MODULATE;
        AlphaArg1[0] = TEXTURE;
        AlphaArg2[0] = DIFFUSE;

        ColorOp[1]   = DISABLE;
        AlphaOp[1]   = DISABLE;

        // shaders
        VertexShader = compile vs_1_1 VS();
        PixelShader  = NULL;
    }
}
```

If you look closely, you will see that the settings are, in fact, good old render states without the **D3DRS** prefix. So instead of writing in C++ code:

```
m_pDevice->SetRenderState(D3DRS_LIGHTING, false);
```

You can simply write in the effect technique:

```
Lighting = false;
```

Effect files are generally not case sensitive outside of the shaders, so you can write the render states any way you like. We'll see techniques in action shortly.

Semantics

A *semantic* is just a fancy name for a special variable. Semantics let you send data from your application to the shaders before using them. You could, for instance, pass through the current world matrix for your object that is being rendered. Under the surface, DirectX passes data through to the GPU and shader using constant registers, which are basically small slots in the GPU that can hold data. There are 256 vertex shader registers and 8 pixel shader registers. Each register holds a `float4`, which is basically a vector of four `float`s:

```
struct register
{
    float x,y,z,w;
}
struct register
{
    float r,g,b,a;    // Red, Green, Blue, Alpha Transparency
}
```

As you can see, a register can contain either color data or position data, but not both at the same time. This will make more sense in just a few paragraphs. Think a little about the size of constant registers. If you pass a `float4` through to a shader, it takes up one register. If you pass a 4×4 matrix through, it will take up four registers. Registers are numbered c0 to c255, and you can refer to them this way. However, it is much more interesting to use C-style variable names when writing shaders, because this style makes it much more readable.

A semantic is simply a variable name used in place of a register constant. You define a semantic just like a normal C variable, except it is followed by a colon (:) and then the keyword `register` followed by the register number like this:

```
float4 someData : register(c0);
```

You can now refer to c0 anywhere in the effect file using the variable name `someData`. You can also bypass register allocation altogether and let the API figure it out for you, but this is not always a good idea. You're bound to come across this later on, so check out how it works:

```
float4 k_a : MATERIALAMBIENT = { 1.0f, 1.0f, 1.0f, 1.0f };    // ambient
```

In this example, a new global `float4` variable, called k_a, is defined. It is attached to the semantic called `MATERIALAMBIENT` and given an initial default value. This default value is what will be used if you don't set the register to be anything from your code. Notice that no register is defined, and `MATERIALAMBIENT` takes its place. In C++, you can set semantic variables by using the string name of the semantic, so using the register is useless.

HLSL

HLSL is a fantastic new way to write shaders without involving yourself in the tedium of assembly language. HLSL is a C-like language that makes it much simpler to write shaders. The language is readable and improves on C with its nifty features like constructors, which are stolen from C++. HLSL has new variable types, such as `float4`, which is just a vector of `float` values, and `float4x4`, which is used for a 4×4 matrix. Many new types are available, but listing them all now would just over-complicate things. I'll point out the necessary information as we start going through shaders line by line.

Vertex Shaders

Vertex shaders are amazingly valuable. You can use them to modify vertices on the fly during rendering. They cannot create new or delete current vertices, but they can edit the properties of any vertex, such as its color, position, and texture coordinates. A vertex shader runs once for every vertex in a vertex buffer just before it is rendered. The process runs a little like this:

1. Get the next model to render, and send the vertex buffer to Direct3D.

2. Set up the vertex shader (and pixel shader if needed) for the current object.

3. *Dispatch* the shader (that is, pass data through its semantics).

4. Run the vertex shader for every vertex in the vertex buffer.

5. Run the pixel shader for every pixel that the object takes up onscreen.

6. Repeat until all objects are rendered.

A vertex shader completely replaces the standard transformation pipeline. That means *you* are responsible for everything that DirectX used to do, including applying the world, view, and projection matrices, calculating the lighting, and setting the texture coordinates. Some of this might already be set up in the data you are using, as in the case of a model loaded from disk, which already has its texture coordinates set. In this case, you are simply passing data through the shader without modifying it.

You can think of a vertex shader as part of a pipeline. It sucks a vertex out of the vertex buffer, plays around with its data, and then spits it out the other end ready for the pixel shader to play with.

> **Note**
>
> When using vertex shaders, it's common to define **float3**s and other variable types as a *vector* of three floats. This doesn't necessarily have to be a vector as in coordinate systems, and you can read this like a normal **struct** or **array in C++**.

A Minimal Vertex Shader

At the very least, a vertex shader will generally perform the following steps:

1. Translate the vertex position from *local space* to *world space* to *view space* to final *projection space*.

2. Calculate the final vertex color based on lighting and other information.

3. Setup the texture coordinates

4. Set the specular lighting values.

There's no point in putting it off any longer. Let's look at your first HLSL vertex shader and walk through it to see how it works. From the **simple.fx** file that ships with DirectX, the following is the shader:

```
VS_OUTPUT VS(
    float3 Pos  : POSITION,
    float3 Norm : NORMAL,
    float2 Tex  : TEXCOORD0)
{
    VS_OUTPUT Out = (VS_OUTPUT)0;

    float3 L = -lightDir;
```

```
    float4x4 WorldView = mul(World, View);

    float3 P = mul(float4(Pos, 1), (float4x3)WorldView);   // position (view space)
    float3 N = normalize(mul(Norm, (float3x3)WorldView));  // normal (view space)

    float3 R = normalize(2 * dot(N, L) * N - L);           // reflection vector
(view space)
    float3 V = -normalize(P);                              // view direction
(view space)

    Out.Pos  = mul(float4(P, 1), Projection);              // position (projected)
    Out.Diff = I_a * k_a + I_d * k_d * max(0, dot(N, L));  // diffuse + ambient
    Out.Spec = I_s * k_s * pow(max(0, dot(R, V)), n/4);    // specular
    Out.Tex  = Tex;

    return Out;
}
```

The Function Declaration

So what is going on here? Let's go through it line by line. As you can see, it looks a little bit like a C function. The first few lines are the actual function definition:

```
VS_OUTPUT VS(
    float3 Pos  : POSITION,
    float3 Norm : NORMAL,
    float2 Tex  : TEXCOORD0)
{
```

If this were a C function, it would be a standard function called **VS()** that takes three parameters and returns a **VS_OUTPUT**. The parameters it takes are semantics that are bound to data coming from the vertex buffer. In this case, this function **VS** is interested in the position, normal, and texture coordinates of the vertices.

What about the return value? Well, this was defined slightly earlier in the file and looks like this:

```
struct VS_OUTPUT
{
    float4 Pos  : POSITION;
    float4 Diff : COLOR0;
    float4 Spec : COLOR1;
    float2 Tex  : TEXCOORD0;
};
```

Notice that it's a simple C-style struct with four semantic members for the position, diffuse color, specular color, and texture coordinates. Using the analogy of the pipe again, this shader will take as input the position, normal, and texture coordinates of the vertex, and will output final position, colors, and texture coordinates of the vertex. Make sense so far?

The Code

Next up is this line:

```
VS_OUTPUT Out = (VS_OUTPUT)0;
```

Before the function returns a **VS_OUTPUT** structure, you need to declare this in the shader. Don't worry about variable scope or anything like that here. This is the structure that will be filled with data to send to the pixel shader.

Here's the next line:

```
float3 L = -lightDir;
```

This is simply defining a **float3** (which is a structure containing **float**s) that is set to be equal to the light direction. The light direction is a global semantic variable that would be set up by your program (which I'll show you soon) before the shader was started. This line simply makes a copy of the light direction and reverses it. (The global is a constant register, and you cannot change it from within the vertex shader.)

And then we come to this:

```
float4x4 WorldView = mul(World, View);
```

This is fairly easy, right? A new 4×4 matrix is defined called **WorldView**. The world and view matrices were passed through separately to the shader, so at this point they are both multiplied together using the **mul** intrinsic. An *intrinsic* is a built-in helper function that is part of HLSL. In this case, **mul** multiplies two 4×4 matrices, but you can use it for almost any purpose, such as multiplying a vector by a matrix. The next line looks like this:

```
float3 P = mul(float4(Pos, 1), (float4x3)WorldView);   // position (view space)
float3 N = normalize(mul(Norm, (float3x3)WorldView));  // normal (view space)
```

Remember that shaders replace the standard pipeline, and you are now responsible for everything that happens. The first line of this example is accomplishing a few things. First, it multiplies the position, **Pos**, by the **WorldView** matrix. The result is then copied into **P** for use later on. Then the vertex normal is transformed into view space, normalized, and stored in **N** for later use. The position is transformed from local space so that it looks correct onscreen. The normal is important for lighting calculations.

To be able to calculate specular lighting later on, we need to calculate the view direction and reflection vector. The view direction is simple. Because we are in view space, we are at location (0,0,0) looking down the z axis. The view direction is simply the reverse position of the vertex.

```
float3 R = normalize(2 * dot(N, L) * N - L);        // reflection vector (view space)
float3 V = -normalize(P);                            // view direction (view space)
```

To calculate the reflection vector, we need the following formula:

```
NdotL = Dot product of normal and light direction.
Reflection = 2 * NdotL * (Normal - Light Direction);
```

Finally, we come to outputting the final position of the vector. To do this, we multiply **P**, which is in view space, by the projection matrix:

```
Out.Pos  = mul(float4(P, 1), Projection);           // position (projected)
```

This puts our vertex at the correct position, ready to be rendered by the pixel shader. Next, we need to calculate the diffuse color of the vertex. This involves a little bit more math. Most programmers don't bother to remember it and just copy and paste it as needed. We can calculate the diffuse color using this formula:

```
Final Diffuse = Ambient Light Color * Ambient Material Color +
    Diffuse Light Color * Diffuse Material Color *
    whichever is bigger (0 or NdotL).
```

which basically says, "Add the ambient color to (the diffuse color multiplied by the light intensity)." In HLSL code, it looks like this:

```
Out.Diff = I_a * k_a + I_d * k_d * max(0, dot(N, L)); // diffuse + ambient
```

Next, we need to calculate the specular color of the vertex. This is the highlight you get from shiny surfaces if you are looking at an angle that directly reflects the light from the light source. The formula for this is as follows:

RdotV = (reflection vector) dot product (the view direction)

Specular level = whichever is bigger (0 or RdotV) raised to the power of the intensity you want it to be

In HLSL, it would look like this:

Out.Spec = I_s * k_s * pow(max(0, dot(R, V)), n/4);   // specular

We are not actually changing any of the texture coordinates, so we can simply pass through the texture coordinates as they come in:

```
Out.Tex  = Tex;
```

Finally, the completed structure is returned full of data for the pixel shader to work with:

```
    return Out;
}
```

And that is all there is to a vertex shader. Every other shader you see will be some variation of this form. In fact, some of them vary an incredible amount, but we'll cover all that later in this book. For now, be happy that you are starting to come to grips with all this programmable pipeline stuff!

Pixel Shaders

Pixel shaders are invoked for every pixel of an object that is rendered to screen. As you can probably imagine, this means they are called a lot. For an average frame in a 800×600 rendering window with 300 percent overdraw, that means the pixel shader is being run 1,440,000 times per frame, which in a 60-frame-per-second game would be 86,400,000 executions per second! Therefore, there are far more restrictions on pixel shaders, and they need to be *very* fast.

Pixel shaders usually have two main jobs:

- Sample a texture at the required texture coordinates
- Combine the texture color with the light color and spit it back out to screen

This basically means that pixel shaders get the texture for the pixel they are in and mix it with the lighting color figured out in the vertex shader. They are capable of far more than this, but in our simple example, that is all that needs to be done.

```
float4 PS(
    float4 Diff : COLOR0,
    float4 Spec : COLOR1,
    float2 Tex  : TEXCOORD0) : COLOR
{
    return tex2D(Sampler, Tex) * Diff + Spec;
}
```

As you can see in this case, the pixel shader returns a `float4`. Pixel shaders *always* return a `float4` because it is a color, and the return value is what ends onscreen. In this case, the `float4` has red, green, blue, and alpha components, which define the final color that will rendered to the screen.

This pixel shader, `PS()`, takes three parameters as input, which you might recognize as the output from the vertex shader. This shader takes the diffuse color, the specular color, and the texture coordinates of the vertex. You can see there is not very much code to it, and this is how you want your pixel shaders—with as little code as humanly possible. You might wonder how the values passed to the pixel shader are calculated since they are done per-vertex in the pixel shader. Well, all the values from each vertex output are automatically computed as interpolated vertex buffer output values. So if vertex 1 has texture coordinates of (0,0) and vertex 2 has texture coordinates of (1,1), if you are rendering a pixel halfway across, it will automatically have interpolated texture coordinates of (0.5,0.5).

The code does exactly what it's supposed to. It reads in the texture coordinate with the `tex2D()` intrinsic, which takes a sampler and texture coordinates as input. A *sampler* is simply a description of how Direct3D should sample (that is, read from) a texture. In this case, the sampler looks like this:

```
sampler Sampler = sampler_state
{
    Texture   = (Tex0);
    MipFilter = LINEAR;
    MinFilter = LINEAR;
    MagFilter = LINEAR;
};
```

This sampler sets up sampler states to use linear filtering to help smooth out the texture being read from. `MipFilter` is the filter to use when blurring between levels of a mipmap. `MinFilter` is the sampler to use when the texture is too far away and the texture's pixels are smaller than the screen's pixels and filtering needs to be used to prevent shimmering. `MagFilter` is used when the texture is close and the texture's pixels are far larger than screen pixels and filtering is used to reduce the jaggy of the image. *Linear filtering*, also known as *bilinear filtering*, improves sample quality by actually sampling five separate parts of the texture and averaging them together to reduce the visual artifacts mentioned before. The sampler samples the requested pixel above the pixel, below the pixel, to the left of the pixel, and to the right of the pixel to get the final average. The visual improvement is astounding. Check out Figures 2.1 and 2.2 to see the differences.

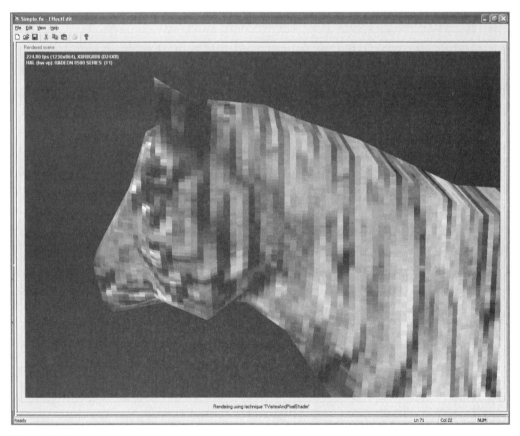

Figure 2.1
Point texture sampling results in jaggy pixels.

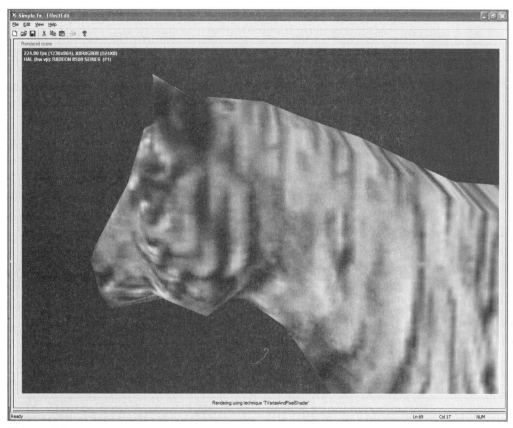

Figure 2.2
Linear sampling vastly improves the image quality.

So `tex2D()` has returned the color of the texture at the requested coordinate. This is then mixed with the specular and diffuse colors, and the result is returned. After the pixel shader, a few hardware operations are performed (such as alpha blending the pixel color with the frame buffer if necessary) and then the result is written to screen.

EffectEdit

Using effect files can take a lot of time after you start working with them on more complicated projects. That's why it's a good idea to know what tools are available to help you. You can obtain some tools from the graphics cards manufacturers like ATI and nVidia, but I recommend just sticking with the simple tools that come with DirectX. The other tools generally won't help you much, and they have their own little "features" that try to get you tied into using one particular type of hardware.

One of the best tools that comes with DirectX is called EffectEdit. This program is useful for testing your effect files and shaders before running them in your game. It's particularly useful when working on large projects that take a long time to start up. You don't want to waste time checking to see if your effect will even run by firing up your game. Just copy it into EffectEdit, and any errors pop in front of you. Check out Figure 2.3 to see what EffectEdit looks like.

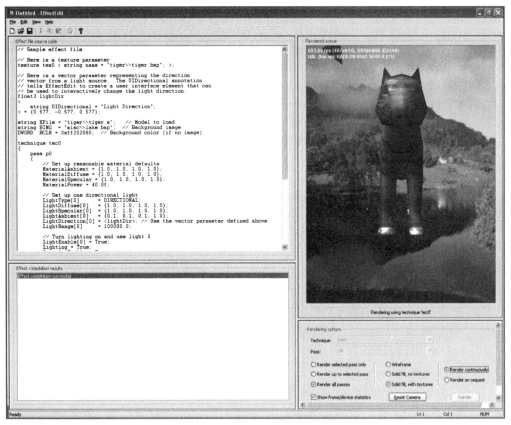

Figure 2.3
EffectEdit—a useful tool for testing your shaders.

EffectEdit lets you select a particular technique to use, and any changes you make update immediately onscreen. There are a number of preset semantics it can pass through to your shader for testing. For a full list of these, select Help, About.

Now would be a really good time to run EffectEdit and play around with the `simple.fx` file that I explained previously. You can find the `simple.fx` file in your SDK directory.

Integrating Shaders into the Game Engine

Now comes the interesting part. So far this chapter has been mostly theory, but now I'm going to show you how to get this stuff integrated into an actual engine. The best way to do this is to have an effect library that loads and compiles all the effect files at startup. Then you can select the technique you want at runtime and dispatch it prior to rendering your object.

To use effects, perform the following tasks:

1. Write the actual effect file, including the vertex shader, pixel shader, techniques, and semantics.

2. Load the effect file with D3DX, and compile it into a usable form.

3. Select the technique you want to render with.

4. Fill the shader with data.

5. Render the object.

6. Release the shader when you are finished with it, usually during shutdown.

Now let's look at these steps in a little more detail.

The cEffect Class

The first class we need is one to wrap an effect file into a nice, easy-to-manage object. This is called `cEffect`, and it is quite useful. Simply pass it a file name on construction, and it loads the file, compiles it, and creates an effect ready for you to use. The `cEffect` class is designed to be inherited from so that you can override the dispatch method to pass any custom data you need to your shader. Look at the class definition:

```cpp
class cEffect
{
public:
    cEffect(indString filename, indUInt newID);
    ~cEffect();

// Functions
public:
    LPD3DXEFFECT GetEffect()
    {
        assert(m_pD3DEffect != 0);
        return m_pD3DEffect;
    }

    void Begin(indUInt& numPasses);
    void End();
    void BeginPass(indUInt passIndex);
    void EndPass();

    indString GetFilename()
    {
        return &m_FileName[0];
    }

    indUInt GetUniqueID()
    {
        return m_UniqueID;
    }

    LPD3DXEFFECT GetD3DEffect()
    {
        assert(m_pD3DEffect);
        return m_pD3DEffect;
    }

    void SetTransforms(D3DXMATRIX& world, D3DXMATRIX& view, D3DXMATRIX& proj)
    {
        m_matWorld = world;
        m_matView = view;
        m_matProj = proj;
    }

    virtual indBool Dispatch();
```

```
protected:

// Variables
public:
    char m_FileName[MAX_PATH];

protected:
    LPD3DXEFFECT m_pD3DEffect;
    indUInt m_UniqueID;

    D3DXMATRIX   m_matWorld,
            m_matView,
            m_matProj;
};
```

This is a bare-bones class used to create an effect. You've already seen how to write an effect in the previous section, so let's look at the other steps that I mentioned.

Loading an Effect File with D3DX

For this engine, I've made a simple **cEffect** class that handles all the loading and compiling for you so that after it's written, you'll never have to worry about this code again if you keep it modular enough. Let's look at the constructor of the class, which takes two parameters: a file name and a unique ID. Here is the whole function, before I go through it step by step.

```
cEffect::cEffect(indString filename, indUInt newID)
{
    D3DXMatrixIdentity(&m_matWorld);
    D3DXMatrixIdentity(&m_matView);
    D3DXMatrixIdentity(&m_matProj);

    strcpy(m_FileName, filename);
    char newpath[MAX_PATH] = "effects\\";
    if(strlen(filename) + strlen(newpath) < MAX_PATH)
            strcat(newpath, filename);
    else
    {
        assert(0); // Path too long
        return;
    }
```

```
    LPD3DXBUFFER compileErrors = 0;
    D3DXCreateEffectFromFile(Graphics::cGameEngine::getInstance()->GetDevice(),
        newpath, 0, 0, 0, 0, &m_pD3DEffect, &compileErrors);
    if(compileErrors)
    {
        assert(0);
        OutputDebugString((indString)compileErrors->GetBufferPointer());
    }

    D3DXHANDLE hBestTechnique;
    m_pD3DEffect->FindNextValidTechnique(NULL,&hBestTechnique);
    if(!hBestTechnique)
    {
        OutputDebugString("Unable to find valid technique");
        assert(0);
    }

    m_UniqueID = newID;
}
```

Now let's look at that constructor in a little more detail:

```
cEffect::cEffect(indString filename, indUInt newID)
{
```

The file name is obviously the name of the effect file you want to load. However, the unique ID parameter is kind of interesting. If you are running a large game with a lot of game objects, you could be switching effects a lot—as in tens of thousands of times per frame. Doing a string compare search on every effect file would take forever, though. With the unique ID system, you only have to string compare once and store the ID for use later, which is a lot faster. There is also an effect manager, discussed later in this chapter, that creates the unique IDs for you so that you can be sure they are actually unique!

At a minimum, every effect file should be able to set the world, view, and projection matrices. These are the only three parameters that the base effect class sets by default for now. When you derive your own classes from cEffect, you can override the constructor and Dispatch() methods to initialize your own extra data. For now, we just have to set up the matrices to default values:

```
D3DXMatrixIdentity(&m_matWorld);
D3DXMatrixIdentity(&m_matView);
D3DXMatrixIdentity(&m_matProj);
```

I like to keep all my effects in their own subfolder of my project called **effects**. The next piece of code adds the string **"effects\"** to whatever file name you pass through so that it looks in the correct directory for the file.

```
strcpy(m_FileName, filename);
char newpath[MAX_PATH] = "effects\\";
if(strlen(filename) + strlen(newpath) < MAX_PATH)
    strcat(newpath, filename);
else
{
    assert(0); // Path too long
    return;
}
```

The file and path are ready to actually load and compile the effect with D3DX.

```
LPD3DXBUFFER compileErrors = 0;
D3DXCreateEffectFromFile(Graphics::cGameEngine::getInstance()->GetDevice(),
    newpath, 0, 0, 0, 0, &m_pD3DEffect, &compileErrors);
if(compileErrors)
{
    assert(0);
    OutputDebugString((indString)compileErrors->GetBufferPointer());
}
```

So, what is happening here, you might ask. First of all, a `D3DXBUFFER` is declared. Direct3DX uses these buffers for all sorts of tasks, but in this case, it holds any compile errors that occur when it tries to compile your effect. You can simply cast the buffer pointer of this object to a `char*` and output it to your desired debug window of choice to see what went wrong. This is amazingly useful when you are trying to figure out why an effect file will not load. Next, the effect is loaded with `D3DXCreateEffectFromFile()`. This fills your effect pointer with a new effect if everything goes okay, or it sets it to NULL and fills out the compile errors for you. If you'd like to see errors in your file before you get this far, I highly recommend just copying and pasting the effect file into EffectEdit to see how it works, because it will show you these errors in its output window. Always output errors somewhere; otherwise, you won't know why your game doesn't start if you make an error.

Selecting the Best Technique

You can select the best technique in two ways: the easy way and the hard way. The hard way involves looking over all the requirements of your technique and checking the device caps for each one until you find one that works. The easy way is to let DirectX do it for you. There is a truly kick-ass function called **ID3DXEffect::FindNextValidTechnique()** whose job it is to find the first available technique that will work with the current hardware. Sounds nice, you might say. But keep listening… If you ensure that you write your techniques in best-to-worse order, Direct3D *automatically* tries every technique until it finds the one that will work best! And this is all the code it takes:

```
D3DXHANDLE hBestTechnique;
m_pD3DEffect->FindNextValidTechnique(NULL,&hBestTechnique);
if(!hBestTechnique)
{
    OutputDebugString("Unable to find valid technique");
    assert(0);
}

    m_UniqueID = newID;
}
```

So, say you're running a really old PC, and this function is called on the **simple.fx** that we looked at a little earlier. D3DX first checks the technique **TPixelAndVertexShader**, but it fails because the graphics card doesn't support pixel shaders. It then moves on to check **TVertexShaderOnly**, but this also fails because the graphics card doesn't support vertex shaders. Finally, D3DX tries **TNoShader**, because this has only basic requirements and no shaders. And all of this is done without your having to think about it. Fantastic!

The titles of the techniques can be anything you like, and DirectX will automatically pick the correct one. I stuck with the default DirectX titles because they make it obvious which technique is for which configuration. You could call them **Beavis** and **Butthead** if you like, and they will still work perfectly well, although your boss might have some questions if it's in production code.

Shutting Down Effect Files

Effect files are easy to maintain. As with most things in Direct3D, it is simply a matter of releasing the COM interface pointer and setting it to **NULL**, or using the handy **SAFE_RELEASE()** macro in its place, as in this code:

```
cEffect::~cEffect()
{
    SAFE_RELEASE(m_pD3DEffect);
}
```

Rendering with Effect Files

Rendering with shaders and effect files is very different from the old fixed function pipeline. Previously, you were probably used to rendering by setting up the render states, calling something like `GraphicObject->Render()`, and finally setting the states back again.

Some major differences distinguish effect files from shaders, because the render states are all done ahead of time in the techniques, the effect files automatically reset the render states for you after your rendering, and rendering can take multiple passes.

Caution

Actually, they often *do not* get set back correctly, so it's best to write every render state you are going to rely on to some safe default value. After testing the shadowing code later in this book, I came back to test other code only to find it was also shadowing unexpectedly.

Because of this, you need to follow these steps to render:

1. Tell Direct3D that we are about to start rendering with an effect by calling `ID3DXEffect::Begin()`. This function returns the number of passes that this technique takes to render with.

2. For every pass, call `ID3DXEffect::BeginPass()`.

3. Render the object for every pass.

4. At the end of every pass, call `ID3DXEffect::EndPass()`.

5. At the end of all passes, call `ID3DXEffect::End()`.

Note

The word *pass* in the previous list might be something you have not come across before. A *pass* is another word for a full render of the object. On older graphics cards, the hardware was occasionally not powerful enough to achieve a particular rendering effect. The solution was to split your effect into multiple passes so that advanced effects could still be achieved on old hardware. As you can imagine, having multiple passes is really slow and eats up all your graphics card's fill rate capacity, so it's best avoided where possible.

I've wrapped all this up in the **cEffect** class to give a clean interface to it. Notice the simplicity of the code:

```
void cEffect::Begin(indUInt& numPasses)
{
    assert(m_pD3DEffect);
    m_pD3DEffect->Begin(&numPasses, D3DXFX_DONOTSAVESTATE);
}

void cEffect::End()
{
    assert(m_pD3DEffect);
    m_pD3DEffect->End();
}

void cEffect::BeginPass(indUInt passIndex)
{
    assert(m_pD3DEffect);
    m_pD3DEffect->BeginPass(passIndex);
}

void cEffect::EndPass()
{
    assert(m_pD3DEffect);
    m_pD3DEffect->EndPass();
}
```

Dispatching Data to Shaders

The most important thing to do next is to learn how to send data to the shader. This is done with the **Dispatch()** method, and as I mentioned before, it will be overridden later for more advanced effects. For now, it just needs to send off the matrices. At this point, this function uses string names to identify semantics in the effect file:

```
indBool cEffect::Dispatch()
{
    m_pD3DEffect->SetMatrix("World", &m_matWorld);
    m_pD3DEffect->SetMatrix("View", &m_matView);
    m_pD3DEffect->SetMatrix("Projection", &m_matProj);

    return true;
}
```

The method uses the `ID3DXEffect::SetMatrix()` function to set the matrices. This function takes a handle, or string, of the matrix that you want to set along with a pointer to the actual matrix. This function is part of a family of functions for setting different types of variables, such as floats and vectors, which you'll see a lot of later in the book.

The cEffectManager Class

Having a single effect is great, but a real implementation has tens or possibly hundreds of different materials and effects, so what we really need is an easy way to look after these effects. With that in mind, I've put together a class called **cEffectManager**. It's a simple manager class that performs the following functions:

- Initialization and shutdown of all effect-related resources
- The ability to find and return an effect by name or handle
- Creation of unique IDs for identifying different effects quickly
- Automatic loading of all the effect files from a directory on startup

Here is the class definition that handles all that work:

```
class cEffectManager
{
public:
    cEffectManager(void);
    ~cEffectManager(void);

// Functions
public:
    static cEffectManager* getInstance();
    bool Start();
    bool Shutdown();

    indUInt FindEffect(indString name);
    cEffect* GetEffect(indUInt uniqueID);

protected:
    indUInt CreateUniqueID()
    {
        return m_UniqueID++;
    }
```

```
// Variables
public:

protected:
    static cEffectManager  *ms_pEffectManager;
    HINSTANCE              m_hInstance;
    static bool            ms_InstanceFlag;

    std::vector <cEffect*> m_vecEffects;
    indUInt                m_UniqueID;
};
```

There is not much to it at the moment, but we'll be adding more to it later in this book. For now, it works well and does everything we need it to. Now let's look in more details at the functionality that this class implements.

Initialization and Shutdown

There is not much to initialize at the moment, but the constructor is kind of interesting. This initializes the unique ID counter with 231980. You can initialize this with anything you want, but I tend to use something noteworthy like when I was born, which was March 2, 1980 for those of you who want to send me something nice for my birthday! That way, no matter what manager I am using, I can immediately tell when debugging if it has been incremented yet. You could also just use 0, but that's not particularly interesting, and it's a value that could show up by chance in code anyway.

```
cEffectManager::cEffectManager()
{
    // private constructor
    m_UniqueID = 231980; // Increment this magic number for every new ID required
}

cEffectManager::~cEffectManager()
{
    Shutdown();
}
bool cEffectManager::Shutdown()
{
    for(indUInt i = 0 ; i < m_vecEffects.size() ; i++)
    {
        delete m_vecEffects[i];
```

```
    }
    m_vecEffects.clear();
    return true;
}
```

Because all the **cEffects** are held in a **vector**, the shutdown code simply runs through the **vector** and deletes all the members.

Finding Effects

You need to be able to find and use effects easily after they are loaded. It's also important that the way effects are referred to is as human readable as possible to make debugging simpler. Consequently, I usually like to have game objects reference effects by their file name.

However, it's slow to perform a string compare every time you need an effect, which could be thousands of times per frame. So the best solution is to store the effect name in your objects and refer to it that way the first time. Then for every other access, you can just store the unique ID of the effect and use that from that point forward. Because the unique ID is assigned at runtime, it could be different every time the game is run. By using a string name, we can fix the ID automatically the first time it is called:

```
indUInt cEffectManager::FindEffect(indString name)
{
    for(indUInt i = 0 ; i < m_vecEffects.size() ; i++)
    {
        char* newname = m_vecEffects[i]->GetFilename();
        if(!strnicmp(m_vecEffects[i]->GetFilename(), name, strlen(name)))
            return m_vecEffects[i]->GetUniqueID();
    }

    return 0;
}
```

As you can see, the function runs through the vector and compares the file names of the loaded effects with the parameter that is passed to the function. When one is found, the function returns the ID of the effect, which can be used in the next function to access the effect more quickly:

```
cEffect* cEffectManager::GetEffect(indUInt uniqueID)
{
```

```
    for(indUInt i = 0 ; i < m_vecEffects.size() ; i++)
    {
        if(m_vecEffects[i]->GetUniqueID() == uniqueID)
            return m_vecEffects[i];
    }

    return NULL;
}
```

This function returns the effect with the matching ID. If you find in your implementation that the search code is slowing down your execution, you can replace the unique ID with the actual index of the effect in the vector. So you can refer to each effect using its index directly, eliminating the need to search through every item in the vector.

Unique IDs

Creating a unique ID is simple and self-explanatory, as the following code demonstrates:

```
indUInt CreateUniqueID()
{
    return m_UniqueID++;
}
```

Incrementing the unique ID means that you will never get the same ID unless you happen to overflow the **unsigned** integer holder. That's impossible, because you would, on 32-bit systems, run out of addressable memory before this happened!

Loading Effects from Disk

The most useful aspect of the **cEffectManager** is that it is able to automatically load all effect files from a particular directory. It does this with the Win32 functions **FindFirstFile()** and **FindNextFile()**. Here's the code:

```
bool cEffectManager::Start()
{
    WIN32_FIND_DATA FileData;
    HANDLE hSearch;
    char szDirPath[] = "effects\\";
    BOOL fFinished = FALSE;
```

```
hSearch = FindFirstFile("effects\\*.fx", &FileData);
if (hSearch == INVALID_HANDLE_VALUE)
{
    OutputDebugString("No .FX files found.\n");
}

while (!fFinished)
{
    cEffect* pNewEffect = new cEffect(FileData.cFileName, CreateUniqueID());
    assert(pNewEffect);
    m_vecEffects.push_back(pNewEffect);

    if (!FindNextFile(hSearch, &FileData))
    {
        if (GetLastError() == ERROR_NO_MORE_FILES)
        {
            fFinished = TRUE;
        }
        else
        {
            OutputDebugString("Couldn't find next file.\n");
        }
    }
}

// Close the search handle.
FindClose(hSearch);

return true;
}
```

This function instructs Windows to return the first file with the .fx extension found in the **effects** subfolder of the current folder, which is where the game is executing from. This file is then loaded and compiled into a usable **cEffect**. The process is continued for all other effect files in that directory. And that is all there is to integrating effects into your game engine. I'll show you effects in action in the next chapter, but for now, let's look at advancing the game engine with a little input to help us move around.

DirectInput

Obviously you didn't buy this book just to learn about DirectInput, so I'm not going to spend a huge amount of time explaining it. This section is mainly an overview so that you know how the input code works and you can treat it pretty much as a black box that "just works." Input is important for viewing some techniques later on in this book, so it's important to cover this material, at least peripherally.

DirectInput is really simple to work with if you are just sticking to the standard mouse and keyboard, and there is a fair amount of good information in the SDK documentation if you need more help. So let's get started!

The `cInputManager` object handles all input for the game. This class is responsible for acquiring data from the input devices, processing the input, and calling the appropriate parts of the game engine to deal with the input. At the moment, the class supports only simple input (there is no buffered input) that is polled every frame. The class also supports only the mouse and keyboard by default, but I've left placeholder code available for you to extend later if you want to add joystick support. There are numerous tutorials on the Internet about how to do this; check out http://www.gamedev.net for starters.

The input manager needs to perform the following functions:

- Initialize and shut down all input devices
- Poll the devices for input every frame
- Reacquire the devices if they are lost to another application
- Process input and call other parts of the game to deal with the input

Here is the class definition for `cInputManager`:

```
class cInputManager
{
private:
    cInputManager(void);
public:
    ~cInputManager(void);

// Functions
public:
    static cInputManager* getInstance();
```

```cpp
    indBool Start();
    indBool Run();
    indBool Shutdown();

    indBool isMouseButtonDown(indUInt buttonIndex)
    {
        return (m_MouseData.rgbButtons[buttonIndex] & 0x80) ? true : false;
    }

    indBool isKeyDown(indUInt buttonIndex)
    {
        return (m_KeyboardBuffer[buttonIndex] & 0x80) ? true : false;
    }
protected:
    indBool StartKeyboard();
    indBool StartMouse();
    indBool StartJoystick();
    void ProcessInput();

// Variables
public:
    enum mouseButtons
    {
        PRIMARY_BUTTON = 0,        // usually left
        SECONDARY_BUTTON = 1,      // usually right
        TERTIARY_BUTTON = 2        // usually middle scroll button
    };

protected:
    static cInputManager *ms_pInputManager;
    static bool           ms_InstanceFlag;

    LPDIRECTINPUT8        m_pDirectInput;
    LPDIRECTINPUTDEVICE8  m_pKeyboardDevice;
    LPDIRECTINPUTDEVICE8  m_pMouseDevice;
    LPDIRECTINPUTDEVICE8  m_pJoystickDevice;

    indByte               m_KeyboardBuffer[256];
    DIMOUSESTATE          m_MouseData;

};
```

Now let's look at this functionality in a little more detail.

Starting DirectInput

This is the main initialization function of the class:

```
indBool cInputManager::Start()
{
    HRESULT hr = S_OK;

    hr = DirectInput8Create(GAMEENGINE->GetInstanceHandle(), 0x0800,
            IID_IDirectInput8, (void**)&m_pDirectInput, NULL);
    if(FAILED(hr))
    {
        OutputDebugString("Failed to start DirectInput");
        assert(0);
        return false;
    }

    assert(m_pDirectInput);

    if(!StartKeyboard())
    {
        OutputDebugString("Failed to start Keyboard device");
        assert(0);
        return false;
    }

    if(!StartMouse())
    {
        OutputDebugString("No mouse found\n");
        return true;
    }

    if(!StartJoystick())
    {
        OutputDebugString("No Joysticks found\n");
        return true;
    }

    ShowCursor(false);

    return true;
}
```

As demonstrated here, the code is simple. It just starts up DirectInput using the DirectInput8Create() function, which takes as parameters the application **hInstance**, the DirectInput version number, and a pointer to the DirectInput object to be created. Following successful creation, each of the input devices is created. The keyboard throws an **assert** if it cannot start. It's vital that it works, and the other input types just output some debug information.

The Keyboard Device

Creating the keyboard is also quite simple. As with all input devices in DirectInput, you must perform these steps before using the device:

1. Create a device to represent the object.

2. Set the data format of the device. This lets DirectInput know how to send the data to you.

3. Set the cooperative level of the device. This allows you to force input only to your application or share it with others.

4. Acquire the device. If the device is lost later on, you must reacquire it.

The code to do all this looks a little like this:

```
indBool cInputManager::StartKeyboard()
{
    assert(m_pDirectInput);

    HRESULT hr = S_OK;
    hr = m_pDirectInput->CreateDevice(GUID_SysKeyboard, &m_pKeyboardDevice, 0);
    if(FAILED(hr))
    {
        OutputDebugString("Failed to create keyboard input device");
        assert(0);
        return false;
    }

    assert(m_pKeyboardDevice);

    hr = m_pKeyboardDevice->SetDataFormat(&c_dfDIKeyboard);
    if(FAILED(hr))
    {
```

```
            OutputDebugString("Failed to set keyboard data format");
            assert(0);
            return false;
        }

        hr = m_pKeyboardDevice->SetCooperativeLevel(GAMEENGINE->GetMainWnd(),
            DISCL_FOREGROUND | DISCL_NONEXCLUSIVE);
        if(FAILED(hr))
        {
            OutputDebugString("Failed to set keyboard cooperative level");
            assert(0);
            return false;
        }

        hr = m_pKeyboardDevice->Acquire();
        if(FAILED(hr))
        {
            OutputDebugString("Failed to acquire keyboard");
            assert(0);
            return false;
        }

        return true;
    }
```

If all that completes successfully, you have a working keyboard device that you can get data from. You can find the keyboard state by polling the device, which for the keyboard, returns a buffer filled with 256 bytes of information. Each byte represents the state of a particular key. If the high bit of the byte is set, the key is down. So later on during a tick of the game, the following code is executed:

```
m_pKeyboardDevice->GetDeviceState(sizeof(m_KeyboardBuffer), &m_KeyboardBuffer);
```

Then you can check whether a key is down using this code:

```
if(m_MouseData.rgbButtons[buttonIndex] & 0x80)
    … button is down.
```

It's far more convenient to have this as a function than to have to type it every time you want to check the status of a key. That's why I wrote this code into a handy member function:

```
indBool isKeyDown(indUInt buttonIndex)
{
```

```
    return (m_KeyboardBuffer[buttonIndex] & 0x80) ? true : false;
}
```

Easy peasy. Now let's get the mouse going. Again, it is the same process.

The Mouse

Look at this code that starts up the mouse device. It is almost the same process as for the keyboard:

```
indBool cInputManager::StartMouse()
{
    assert(m_pDirectInput);

    HRESULT hr = S_OK;

    hr = m_pDirectInput->CreateDevice(GUID_SysMouse, &m_pMouseDevice, NULL);
    if(FAILED(hr))
    {
        OutputDebugString("Failed to create mouse device\n");
        return false;
    }

    hr = m_pMouseDevice->SetDataFormat(&c_dfDIMouse);
    if(FAILED(hr))
    {
        OutputDebugString("Failed to set mouse data format\n");
        return false;
    }

    hr = m_pMouseDevice->SetCooperativeLevel(GAMEENGINE->GetMainWnd(),
            DISCL_EXCLUSIVE | DISCL_FOREGROUND);
    if(FAILED(hr))
    {
        OutputDebugString("Failed to set mouse cooperative level");
        return false;
    }

    hr = m_pMouseDevice->Acquire();
    if(FAILED(hr))
    {
        OutputDebugString("Unable to acquire mouse");
            return false;
```

        }

        return true;

}

Like I said, the code for the keyboard and mouse is similar. The main difference is that the data format is different. This time, the data format is set to be **c_dfDIMouse**, which tells DirectInput that you expect the data to be given to you inside a **DIMOUSESTATE** structure, which looks like this:

```
typedef struct DIMOUSESTATE {
    LONG lX;
    LONG lY;
    LONG lZ;
    BYTE rgbButtons[4];
} DIMOUSESTATE, *LPDIMOUSESTATE;
```

This is a simple structure that contains all the information you will ever need from a standard mouse. The **lX** and **lY** parameters contain the position of the mouse in screen coordinates. Depending on the mode the device is in, these will either be in absolute or relative units. By default, the mode is relative; however, you can change this if you want by looking up the documentation for **IDirectInputDevice8::SetProperty()**. I'm happy to have the coordinates relative, so I don't need to change it. Also, it's easy to add absolute coordinates to the input manager—simply add the relative coordinates every frame! The **lZ** is kind of interesting. It contains the coordinate values of the third axis, which is typically the wheel. Finally, **rgbButtons** contains the status of up to four mouse buttons.

To fill this structure with data, just use the following:

```
m_pMouseDevice->Poll();
m_pMouseDevice->GetDeviceState(sizeof(m_MouseData), &m_MouseData);
```

This fills in the structure, and you read directly from the position members to get their data or use the following code to check the button status:

```
        enum mouseButtons
        {
            PRIMARY_BUTTON = 0,      // usually left mouse button
            SECONDARY_BUTTON = 1,    // usually right mouse button
            TERTIARY_BUTTON = 2      // usually middle scroll button
        };
```

```
indBool isMouseButtonDown(indUInt buttonIndex)
{
    return (m_MouseData.rgbButtons[buttonIndex] & 0x80) ? true : false;
}
```

I defined some enumerations for the buttons. It is best practice to refer to mouse buttons as *primary* and *secondary* rather than *left/right* to ensure that your code works well for lefties who switch their buttons around. If you are left handed, it's good so that your code works with righties who switch their buttons around.

Extending Joystick Support

I've added an extra function that currently does nothing, but you can extend it if you wish to add support for joysticks. Check out the tutorials in the SDK or the Internet on how to do this, because it is similar to the mouse and keyboard. The function looks like this for now:

```
indBool cInputManager::StartJoystick()
{
    return true;
}
```

Input Polling and Device Reacquisition

Okay, now we're starting to get somewhere! We just need to get the data from the devices and start using it. However, there is one more possibility that we need to discuss to make our program bombproof. It is possible and highly likely for the user to use another program at the same time as ours, and in doing so, lose direct access to the input devices. This situation is referred to as *losing* a device. If you have a lost device, you cannot get input from it until you *reacquire* it. Reacquiring a device is simple. You just need to call the **IDirect3DDevice::Acquire()**, which doesn't take parameters. With that in mind, examine the following function, which is executed once per tick:

```
indBool cInputManager::Run()
{
    HRESULT hr = S_OK;

    assert(m_pKeyboardDevice);
    assert(m_pMouseDevice);
```

```
    hr = m_pKeyboardDevice->GetDeviceState(sizeof(m_KeyboardBuffer),
&m_KeyboardBuffer);
    if(FAILED(hr))
    {
        m_pKeyboardDevice->Acquire();
    }

    hr = m_pMouseDevice->Poll();
    if(FAILED(hr))
    {
        m_pMouseDevice->Acquire();
        m_pMouseDevice->Poll();
    }

    hr = m_pMouseDevice->GetDeviceState(sizeof(m_MouseData), &m_MouseData);

    ProcessInput();

    return true;
}
```

I've highlighted the important bits of code. Notice the penultimate line, which calls **ProcessInput()**. This function is called to use the actual new data from the input devices to do something. It's good practice to keep the code that gets the current device state separate from the code that operates on that information:

```
void cInputManager::ProcessInput()
{
    assert(m_KeyboardBuffer);

    if(isKeyDown(DIK_ESCAPE))
        GAMEENGINE->Quit();

    .
    .   // Other input processing code
    .
}
```

At the moment, the only code needed is to quit the game if the Esc key is pressed. Notice the **DIK_ESCAPE** identifier. You can find a DirectInput key identifier for every key on the keyboard. Look at **dinput.h** if you want to see the rest of the identifiers. They are currently located around line 2,032 in the file.

And that, ladies and gents, is all there is to getting input through DirectInput. After it's written, you shouldn't really need to deal with DirectInput much. That will be the case for this book, even though we will be adding a lot of code to the `ProcessInput()` function.

Conclusion

This chapter has been a real roller coaster. You now have a solid foundation of a lot of new information. You will soon be a master of all this information that I introduced in this chapter:

- Effect files and how they streamline material creation
- Techniques and how they encapsulate render states
- How to have Direct3D do the hard work and automatically select the best available technique for you
- Semantics and how to pass data through to shaders
- How to write your first pixel and vertex shaders
- DirectInput and how to retrieve data from the mouse and keyboard

But that is only the beginning! Turn the page and discover the brave new world of game synchronization, camera creation, visual resource management, creation of a pixel shader to automatically glow around your objects, and much more!

CHAPTER 3

PIMP MY ENGINE

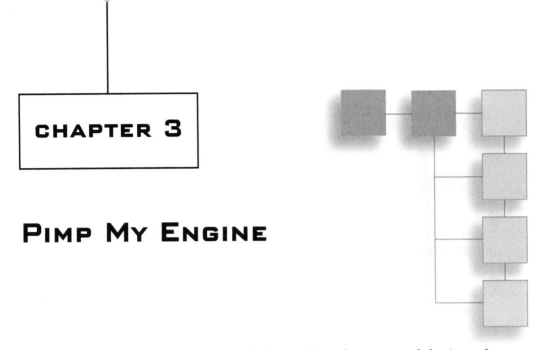

This chapter is going to get seriously jiggy. Now that most of the introductory material is covered, we can start looking at some hardcore coding. In this chapter, I'm going to fill your neural net with all this:

- Game synchronization, including FPS output and ensuring that your engine runs at the correct speed no matter what the actual execution rate is

- Creation of a camera class to encapsulate the view matrix and allow you to explore the 3D world

- Creation of a visual resource object that will represent all the objects in your game, including their associated materials, textures, and shaders

- A real-life look at shaders in action, including how to program a glow shader

Let's roll…

Game Synchronization

There are three good reasons to spend time on game synchronization. First, you need frames per second output so that you can accurately profile the overall speed of your game without the hassle of using a profiler like Intel vTune. Second, you need to ensure that your game is fully playable no matter what the actual frame rate is. For example, if your game is executing at 250 frames per second on one PC, you don't want the characters to move twice as fast on another PC if it is running at 500 frames per second. You want the characters moving at the same speed, but more smoothly. Third, it can be useful to be able to force the frame rate to a particular number, such as 30, so you can calculate whether the game is playable enough at lower frame rates.

Let's start by looking at the first of these issues, which is calculating the actual frame rate.

Frame Rate Calculation and Display

This is really simple. All you need to do is increment a counter every frame and check how much time has passed. If the amount of time that has passed is greater than 1 second, simply output the counter as the FPS and reset it to 0. I've defined a frame rate holder in the main engine class that looks like this:

```
indReal32    m_FrameRate;
DWORD        m_LastFrameTime;
```

These are initialized to 0 during construction. I also added another function called `Synchronization()` that is called every tick and is in charge of everything related to timing. Here is how it looks with just the frame rate counting code in it:

```
void cGameEngine::Synchronization()
{
    static DWORD frameCount = 0;
    frameCount++;

        if(m_LastFrameTime == 0)
    {
        m_LastFrameTime = timeGetTime();
        return;
    }

    DWORD currentFrameTime = timeGetTime();
```

```
    if(currentFrameTime - m_LastFrameTime > 1000)
    {
        indChar newWindowText[256];
        sprintf(newWindowText, "%s - [%i] FPS", m_AppName, frameCount);
        m_FrameRate = (indReal32)frameCount;
        SetWindowText(m_hMainWnd, newWindowText);

        frameCount = 0;
        m_LastFrameTime = currentFrameTime;
    }
}
```

This function starts by incrementing the frame counter. Because it is called every frame, this is the number of frames that have occurred since the last frame rate update. If the last frame time is 0, it must be because this is the first run; therefore, it is initialized with the current time. The function then returns immediately because there is no point in calculating the frame rate for the first frame, as the time delta will be 0.

Then the current time is compared to the time of the last frame rate update. If it is more than 1,000 milliseconds, which is 1 second, we can update the frame rate. I've found the best place to put the frame rate is in the actual title of the window, which is easy with the SetWindowText() Win32 API function. As you can see, a string is created, filled with frame rate, and output to the window title. Finally, the counters are reset ready for the next frame. That was easy. Let's look at something more interesting: making the game run at the correct speed no matter what the frame rate is.

Game Execution Speed Control

If you think about it, this shouldn't be that hard. The result we want is for all game updates—including AI, physics, sound, and everything else—to execute at exactly the correct time no matter what frame rate the game is actually displaying at. So what is needed for this? Well, what we need is to define a base playable rate for the game, such as 60 frames per second. This can be any value you want, but for this game I've chosen 60 Frames per Second (FPS). Now what we need to do is track what speed the game is actually running at and figure out the difference, otherwise known as the *time delta*. The time delta is computed by dividing the actual frame rate by the desired, or base rate.

So if the base rate is 60 FPS but the game is actually running at 120 FPS, the time delta will result in 2.0. If the game is running at 30 FPS, the delta will 0.5. And if the game is running as we want it, the delta will be 1.0. Are you seeing what I'm seeing? If we divide any operation by the delta, it automatically adjusts to the prevailing actual rate. So continuing the previous example, say that the mouse was moved and we wanted to move the camera 1.0 units forward. If the game is running at 120 FPS, we divide 1.0 / 2.0 and get 0.5 units, which is correct. The game is running twice as fast, so we only want the camera to move half as far. If the game is crawling at 30 frames per second and the delta is 0.5, then 1.0 / 0.5 = 2.0. The game is running at half speed, so the camera should move twice as far. As you can see, this works for all values and can be plugged into every time-sensitive routine to make every run synchronized.

The additions to code to make this work are minor. The following variable is added to the class declaration:

```
const indReal32 DEFAULT_GAME_FPS = 60.0f;
…
indReal32    m_TimeDelta;
…
inline float GetTimeDelta()
{
    return m_TimeDelta;
}
```

And in the actual `Synchronization()` function, the code to compute the delta needs to be added:

```
m_TimeDelta = (float)m_FrameRate / DEFAULT_GAME_FPS;
```

And that is all there is to that. A lot of people think that speed control is a really hard topic and implement all sorts of ridiculous solutions, like forcing the game to a particular frame rate, calling update functions more often as the frame drops, or just ignoring the problem and hoping nobody notices. Really, the solution is simple! Of course, for testing, sometimes you want to force a particular frame rate, so let's look at that now.

Forcing a Frame Rate

This is really useful when you are programming advanced input and you want to check the look and feel of your game on a variety of end user machines. Rather than buying a load of old machines, it is much easier just to add control to your engine to force execution at particular frame rates. This is much easier to implement than it sounds.

To achieve this functionality, you need to check the amount of time that would normally pass in milliseconds for the forced frame rate. For example, if you wanted to force the frame rate to 60 FPS, you could calculate the number of milliseconds per frame by dividing 1,000 by the desired frame rate, which in this case would be 1,000 / 60 = 16.66 milliseconds. This is only for rough estimation, by the way, as the code I use for calculating the time uses the Win32 function timeGetTime(), which has varying time resolution. The lower the frame rate you are trying to force, the better it works. If you want to force higher rates, you might want to replace this code to use the QueryPerformanceCounter() functions, which are incredibly accurate. After you have the desired milliseconds per frame, the rest is easy.

You just have to calculate how much time has passed since the last frame. If less time has passed than the desired rate, you simply wait until time passes before proceeding with the rest of the frame. Check out the code added to the Synchronization() function:

```
DWORD currentFrameTime = timeGetTime();

if(m_bForceFrameRate)
{
    static indUInt lastCall = 0;
    indUInt millisecs = 1000 / m_ForcedFrameRate;
    while(currentFrameTime - lastCall < millisecs)
    {
        Sleep(millisecs-(currentFrameTime - lastCall));
        currentFrameTime = timeGetTime();
    }

    lastCall = timeGetTime();
}
```

Notice the call to the Sleep() function. Windows multitasking isn't exactly great at the *pre-emptive* aspect of multitasking when your code is stuck in a tight loop, as in this case. The Sleep() function tells Windows to stall your thread for a desired number of milliseconds while it gets on with other housekeeping. Pass to Sleep() the number of milliseconds until the next frame should execute, and

Windows will not return control to your application until this happens. Simple! So now the entire time control function looks like this:

```
void cGameEngine::Synchronization()
{
    if(m_LastFrameTime == 0)
    {
        m_LastFrameTime = timeGetTime();
        return;
    }

    DWORD currentFrameTime = timeGetTime();

    if(m_bForceFrameRate)
    {
        static indUInt lastCall = 0;
        indUInt millisecs = 1000 / m_ForcedFrameRate;
        while(currentFrameTime - lastCall < millisecs)
        {
            Sleep(millisecs-(currentFrameTime - lastCall));
            currentFrameTime = timeGetTime();
        }

        lastCall = timeGetTime();
    }

    static DWORD frameCount = 0;
    frameCount++;

    if(currentFrameTime - m_LastFrameTime > 1000)
    {
        m_TimeDelta = (float)m_FrameRate / DEFAULT_GAME_FPS;
        indChar newWindowText[256];
        sprintf(newWindowText, "%s - [%i, %f] FPS", m_AppName, frameCount, m_TimeDelta);
        m_FrameRate = (indReal32)frameCount;
        SetWindowText(m_hMainWnd, newWindowText);

        frameCount = 0;
        m_LastFrameTime = currentFrameTime;
    }
}
```

Creating a Camera

Using a camera class to control the view is an absolute necessity in any modern game. You can't just mess around with the view matrix all the time! A camera class usually controls everything to do with viewing the scene, including tracking the player or other objects, moving to certain locations, controlling field of view, and a million other things. For this chapter, we are going to implement a simple camera that can be used to move around the world within first-person-shooter style.

Let's start by looking at the camera class declaration before I explain everything to give you an idea of how everything fits together:

```
class cCamera
{
      private:
        cCamera(void);
    public:
        ~cCamera(void);

    // Functions:
    public:
        indBool Start();
        indBool Run();
        indBool Shutdown();

        static cCamera* getInstance();

        void SetVelocity(D3DXVECTOR3& newVelocity)
        {
            m_CameraVelocity = newVelocity;
        }

        D3DXVECTOR3 GetVelocity()
        {
            return m_CameraVelocity;
        }

        void SetPosition(D3DXVECTOR3& newVelocity)
        {
            m_CameraPos = newVelocity;
        }
```

```cpp
    D3DXVECTOR3 GetPosition()
    {
        return m_CameraPos;
    }

    void SetAngularVelocity(D3DXVECTOR3& newAngularVelocity)
    {
        m_AngularVelocity = newAngularVelocity;
    }

    D3DXVECTOR3 GetAngularVelocity()
    {
        return m_AngularVelocity;
    }

    D3DXMATRIX& GetViewMatrix()
    {
        return m_matView;
    }

    D3DXMATRIX& GetProjectionMatrix()
    {
        return m_matProj;
    }

    void Reset()
    {
        D3DXMatrixIdentity(&m_matView);

        m_CameraUp = D3DXVECTOR3(0.0f, 1.0f, 0.0f);
        m_CameraLookAt = D3DXVECTOR3(0.0f, 0.0f, 1.0f);
        m_CameraPos = D3DXVECTOR3(0.0f, 0.0f, -3.0f);
        m_CameraRight = D3DXVECTOR3(1.0f, 0.0f, 0.0f);

        m_CameraVelocity = D3DXVECTOR3(0.0f, 0.0f, 0.0f);
        m_AngularVelocity = D3DXVECTOR3(0.0f, 0.0f, 0.0f);
    }

protected:
```

```
    // Data
    public:

    protected:
        D3DXVECTOR3      m_CameraUp;
        D3DXVECTOR3      m_CameraRight;
        D3DXVECTOR3 m_CameraLookAt;
        D3DXVECTOR3 m_CameraPos;

        D3DXVECTOR3 m_CameraVelocity;
        D3DXVECTOR3      m_AngularVelocity;

        static cCamera *ms_pCameraManager;
        static bool            ms_InstanceFlag;

        D3DXMATRIX      m_matView;
        D3DXMATRIX      m_matProj;
};
```

There is not much to it at the moment, but it is still worth running through how it works. Notice that for simplicity I've added the projection matrix to the camera. Now let's check out this class in a little more detail.

Movement and Position

Positioning the camera to a particular location is quite simple—you just need to call `cCamera::SetPosition()`. This function sets the position of the camera, which is set into the camera's view matrix every tick. Moving the camera somewhere, as opposed to forcing it to a position and skipping everywhere in between, is kind of interesting. Basically what we want to do is give the camera a velocity. Then we can add the velocity to the position of the camera every frame.

So if the camera starts out at (0,0,0) and we want it to move down the z axis every frame by 1.0 unit, we have to set the velocity to (0,0,1). Then the camera will continue in that direction by that amount automatically every frame. What is really useful about this kind of setup is that you can directly hook the relative movement of the mouse to the camera velocity, and the camera will move directly where you want it. So if the user pushes the mouse forward, its relative movement is in fact its velocity, which can be set into the camera. When the mouse is not moving, the velocity is 0, automatically stopping the camera. You get the picture?

The code to handle all this is extremely simple:

```
void SetVelocity(D3DXVECTOR3& newVelocity)
{
    m_CameraVelocity = newVelocity;
}

D3DXVECTOR3 GetVelocity()
{
    return m_CameraVelocity;
}

void SetPosition(D3DXVECTOR3& newPos)
{
    m_CameraPos = newPos;
}

D3DXVECTOR3 GetPosition()
{
    return m_CameraPos;
}
```

Rotation

Rotation of the camera is necessary if you want to look anywhere except down the z axis! To achieve rotation of the camera, you need an approach similar to the approach used for the movement and position of the camera. For rotation, rather than store velocity, we need to store what is known as *angular velocity*. This is the rate at which an object spins around each axis.

Again, this value can be added each frame to the actual rotation of the frame to produce easily controllable rotations. The code is really simple:

```
void SetAngularVelocity(D3DXVECTOR3& newAngularVelocity)
{
    m_AngularVelocity = newAngularVelocity;
}

D3DXVECTOR3 GetAngularVelocity()
{
    return m_AngularVelocity;
}
```

The real magic happens in the `Run()` function, which uses this information to compute the view matrix, which I'll get to next.

Computing the View Matrix

Computing the view matrix from the position, velocity, directional vectors, and angular velocities is a little math intensive. However, the good news is that after it's written, you don't need to look at it again unless you are doing more advanced camera work. Let's examine the code:

```
indBool cCamera::Run()
{
    D3DXMATRIX matPitch, matRoll, matYaw;

    // Update the x position
    m_CameraPos.x += m_CameraVelocity.x * m_CameraRight.x;
    m_CameraPos.y += m_CameraVelocity.x * m_CameraRight.y;
    m_CameraPos.z += m_CameraVelocity.x * m_CameraRight.z;

    // Update the y position
    m_CameraPos.x += m_CameraVelocity.y * m_CameraUp.x;
    m_CameraPos.y += m_CameraVelocity.y * m_CameraUp.y;
    m_CameraPos.z += m_CameraVelocity.y * m_CameraUp.z;

    // Update the z position
    m_CameraPos.x += m_CameraVelocity.z * m_CameraLookAt.x;
    m_CameraPos.y += m_CameraVelocity.z * m_CameraLookAt.y;
    m_CameraPos.z += m_CameraVelocity.z * m_CameraLookAt.z;

    // Normalize and regenerate the look, right, and up vectors
    D3DXVec3Normalize( &m_CameraLookAt, &m_CameraLookAt );
    D3DXVec3Cross( &m_CameraRight, &m_CameraUp, &m_CameraLookAt );
    D3DXVec3Normalize( &m_CameraRight, &m_CameraRight );
    D3DXVec3Cross( &m_CameraUp, &m_CameraLookAt, &m_CameraRight );
    D3DXVec3Normalize( &m_CameraUp, &m_CameraUp );

    // Set up the x-axis rotation
    D3DXMatrixRotationAxis( &matPitch, &m_CameraRight, m_AngularVelocity.x );
    D3DXVec3TransformCoord( &m_CameraLookAt, &m_CameraLookAt, &matPitch );
    D3DXVec3TransformCoord( &m_CameraUp, &m_CameraUp, &matPitch );
```

```
    // Set up the y-axis rotation
    D3DXMatrixRotationAxis( &matYaw, &m_CameraUp, m_AngularVelocity.y );
    D3DXVec3TransformCoord( &m_CameraLookAt, &m_CameraLookAt, &matYaw );
    D3DXVec3TransformCoord( &m_CameraRight, &m_CameraRight, &matYaw );

    // Set up the z-axis rotation
    D3DXMatrixRotationAxis( &matRoll, &m_CameraLookAt, m_AngularVelocity.z );
    D3DXVec3TransformCoord( &m_CameraRight, &m_CameraRight, &matRoll );
    D3DXVec3TransformCoord( &m_CameraUp, &m_CameraUp, &matRoll );

    // Fill in the view matrix
    m_matView(0,0) = m_CameraRight.x;
    m_matView(0,1) = m_CameraUp.x;
    m_matView(0,2) = m_CameraLookAt.x;

    m_matView(1,0) = m_CameraRight.y;
    m_matView(1,1) = m_CameraUp.y;
    m_matView(1,2) = m_CameraLookAt.y;

    m_matView(2,0) = m_CameraRight.z;
    m_matView(2,1) = m_CameraUp.z;
    m_matView(2,2) = m_CameraLookAt.z;

    m_matView(3,0) = - D3DXVec3Dot( &m_CameraPos, &m_CameraRight );
    m_matView(3,1) = - D3DXVec3Dot( &m_CameraPos, &m_CameraUp );
    m_matView(3,2) = - D3DXVec3Dot( &m_CameraPos, &m_CameraLookAt );

    return true;
}
```

What the heck is all that about? Let's look in a little more detail at what is going on here because if you haven't written a camera system before, it is only a matter of time before you do! There aren't many 3D games out there without a camera. First, the matrices for the pitch, roll, and yaw of the camera are defined:

`D3DXMATRIX matPitch, matRoll, matYaw;`

The *pitch* is the rotation around the x axis, the *roll* is the rotation around the y axis, and the *yaw* is the rotation around the z axis. Mark this page now so that you remember where it is in two months when you want to know which is which!

Next up, we need to find the location of the camera:

```
// Update the x position
m_CameraPos.x += m_CameraVelocity.x * m_CameraRight.x;
m_CameraPos.y += m_CameraVelocity.x * m_CameraRight.y;
m_CameraPos.z += m_CameraVelocity.x * m_CameraRight.z;

// Update the y position
m_CameraPos.x += m_CameraVelocity.y * m_CameraUp.x;
m_CameraPos.y += m_CameraVelocity.y * m_CameraUp.y;
m_CameraPos.z += m_CameraVelocity.y * m_CameraUp.z;

// Update the z position
m_CameraPos.x += m_CameraVelocity.z * m_CameraLookAt.x;
m_CameraPos.y += m_CameraVelocity.z * m_CameraLookAt.y;
m_CameraPos.z += m_CameraVelocity.z * m_CameraLookAt.z;
```

This is what I talked about previously. The position of the camera is the same as it was the last tick except the velocity is added to it. Simple? Simple. The next bit of code is interesting; it recomputes the look, right, and up vectors every tick to ensure that they are not going out of alignment. Accumulated floating point inaccuracies cause these vectors to drift with time, so it's important to reset them every so often like this:

```
// Normalize and regenerate the look, right, and up vectors
D3DXVec3Normalize( &m_CameraLookAt, &m_CameraLookAt );
D3DXVec3Cross( &m_CameraRight, &m_CameraUp, &m_CameraLookAt );
D3DXVec3Normalize( &m_CameraRight, &m_CameraRight );
D3DXVec3Cross( &m_CameraUp, &m_CameraLookAt, &m_CameraRight );
D3DXVec3Normalize( &m_CameraUp, &m_CameraUp );
```

Next we need to figure out the orientation of the camera. We can do that with this code:

```
// Set up the x-axis rotation
D3DXMatrixRotationAxis( &matPitch, &m_CameraRight, m_AngularVelocity.x );
D3DXVec3TransformCoord( &m_CameraLookAt, &m_CameraLookAt, &matPitch );
D3DXVec3TransformCoord( &m_CameraUp, &m_CameraUp, &matPitch );

// Set up the y-axis rotation
D3DXMatrixRotationAxis( &matYaw, &m_CameraUp, m_AngularVelocity.y );
D3DXVec3TransformCoord( &m_CameraLookAt, &m_CameraLookAt, &matYaw );
D3DXVec3TransformCoord( &m_CameraRight, &m_CameraRight, &matYaw );
```

```
// Set up the z-axis rotation
D3DXMatrixRotationAxis( &matRoll, &m_CameraLookAt, m_AngularVelocity.z );
D3DXVec3TransformCoord( &m_CameraRight, &m_CameraRight, &matRoll );
D3DXVec3TransformCoord( &m_CameraUp, &m_CameraUp, &matRoll );
```

The rotation around the axis is computed by using the function `D3DXMatrixRotationAxis()`. This function takes a vector describing an axis and a rotation around that axis and computes a rotation matrix from them. This process is repeated for all three axes to generate the three rotation matrices. Now we come to the important part—assimilating all this stuff into a single view matrix:

```
// Fill in the view matrix
m_matView(0,0) = m_CameraRight.x;
m_matView(0,1) = m_CameraUp.x;
m_matView(0,2) = m_CameraLookAt.x;

m_matView(1,0) = m_CameraRight.y;
m_matView(1,1) = m_CameraUp.y;
m_matView(1,2) = m_CameraLookAt.y;

m_matView(2,0) = m_CameraRight.z;
m_matView(2,1) = m_CameraUp.z;
m_matView(2,2) = m_CameraLookAt.z;

m_matView(3,0) = - D3DXVec3Dot( &m_CameraPos, &m_CameraRight );
m_matView(3,1) = - D3DXVec3Dot( &m_CameraPos, &m_CameraUp );
m_matView(3,2) = - D3DXVec3Dot( &m_CameraPos, &m_CameraLookAt );
```

As you can see, each part of the view matrix is filled in with the corresponding computed matrix from earlier in the function. Now that that's over, you'll never have to look at it again! Well, for a while anyway! Now let's leave cameras for a little while and look at the next biggest part of a 3D game: renderable objects.

Managing Game Objects

If you don't manage every object in your game, you're looking at a world of pain. In simple demos, it's fine to load a model from disk and refer to it by a pointer to the model; however, after you get into the real world of game development, you'll find that quickly becomes unbelievably inefficient.

What you want is for a few manager classes to automatically load all the assets for a particular level on startup. These assets, which include textures, effects, materials, sounds, and models, should only be loaded for the actual level of the game you are dealing with. Loading them all will eventually suck up all your memory unless you are working on a very small title. After the assets are loaded, they should be *instantiable* into the game. That is, there should be only one version of an asset loaded at a time and only an instance of it should be added to the game. So, for example, you could have a monster dragon model loaded into memory, and every time it is used throughout the level, that same model is instanced, or rendered, in every place the model should be. So the model is only in memory once, but five versions of it are displayed.

Various renderable objects, such as particle systems, are rendered in completely different ways to 3D models. However, it is extremely useful to allow the same manager to control all types of renderable objects. Therefore, any manager system should be as generic as possible and allow its children to render themselves as they choose, with overridable functions. For the engine, I've put together a class called cVisualResource to represent each object and a manager called cResourceManager to look after all of these objects. Let's look at them in more detail now.

Visual Resources

The most common visual resource we will be using is that of a mesh, so let's look at implementing one of those first. A 3D model is made up of a number of separate objects that need to be managed by the visual resource class that represents them. These separate parts include the mesh, the textures that are applied to the mesh, the materials, and, of course, the effects. Read through the following code, which shows the visual resource class in action:

```
class cVisualResource
{
public:
    cVisualResource(indString filename, indUInt uniqueID);
    ~cVisualResource(void);

// Functions
public:
    indBool Start();
    indBool Render();
```

```
        indBool Shutdown();
protected:

// Data
public:

protected:
    indUInt                 m_UniqueID;
    LPD3DXMESH              m_pMesh;
    DWORD                   m_NumMeshMaterials;
    LPDIRECT3DTEXTURE9*     m_pMeshTextures;
    D3DMATERIAL9*           m_pMeshMaterials;
    indUInt                 m_EffectID;

    D3DXMATRIX              m_matWorld;
};
```

This class is simple at the moment. It includes member variables to hold the unique ID of the object, along with all the parts I mentioned before. All these values are initialized in the constructor of the object, which takes the file name of an X file to load along with the unique ID to use for the object.

Loading Visual Resources

Let's look at that constructor now:

```
cVisualResource::cVisualResource(indString filename, indUInt uniqueID)
{
    m_pMesh = 0;
    m_NumMeshMaterials = 0;
    m_pMeshTextures = 0;
    m_pMeshMaterials = 0;
    m_EffectID = 0;

    D3DXMatrixIdentity(&m_matWorld);

    m_UniqueID = uniqueID;

    HRESULT hr = S_OK;
    LPD3DXBUFFER pMeshMaterialBuffer = 0;

    char fullpath[256] = "media\\";
    strcat(&fullpath[0], filename);
```

```cpp
    hr = D3DXLoadMeshFromX(fullpath, 0, GAMEENGINE->GetDevice(),
        0, &pMeshMaterialBuffer, 0, &m_NumMeshMaterials, &m_pMesh);
    if(FAILED(hr))
    {
        OutputDebugString("Failed to load mesh\n");
        assert(0);
    }

    strcpy(fullpath, "media\\\0");

    m_pMeshTextures = new LPDIRECT3DTEXTURE9[m_NumMeshMaterials];
    m_pMeshMaterials = new D3DMATERIAL9[m_NumMeshMaterials];

    D3DXMATERIAL* pD3DXMaterials = (D3DXMATERIAL*)pMeshMaterialBuffer->GetBufferPointer();

    for(indUInt i = 0 ; i < m_NumMeshMaterials ; i++)
    {
        m_pMeshMaterials[i] = pD3DXMaterials[i].MatD3D;
        m_pMeshMaterials[i].Ambient = pD3DXMaterials[i].MatD3D.Diffuse;

        strcat(&fullpath[0], pD3DXMaterials[i].pTextureFilename);

        hr = D3DXCreateTextureFromFileEx(GAMEENGINE->GetDevice(), fullpath,
            D3DX_DEFAULT, D3DX_DEFAULT,
            D3DX_DEFAULT, 0, D3DFMT_FROM_FILE,
                    D3DPOOL_DEFAULT, D3DX_FILTER_TRIANGLE,
            D3DX_FILTER_TRIANGLE, 0, 0, 0, &m_pMeshTextures[i]);
        if(FAILED(hr))
        {
            assert(0);
            OutputDebugString("Failed to load mesh texture");
            m_pMeshTextures[i] = NULL;
        }

        strcpy(fullpath, "media\\\0");
    }
    SAFE_RELEASE(pMeshMaterialBuffer);

    m_EffectID = EFFECTMANAGER->FindEffect("default.fx");
}
```

Can you see what's going on? The function starts with some housekeeping, like initializing all the member variables to 0 and setting the default world matrix to an identity matrix. Then the unique ID is saved for later use. After that, the path to the file to load is changed to include the media\ prefix because that is a good place to keep all your assets. You can change this line to be whatever you would like as long as it matches where you resources actually are.

Then the real meat 'n' potatoes gets called, which is D3DXLoadMeshFromX(). This function takes a file name to load and fills in a material buffer and a new mesh object:

```
hr = D3DXLoadMeshFromX(fullpath, 0, GAMEENGINE->GetDevice(),
        0, &pMeshMaterialBuffer, 0, &m_NumMeshMaterials, &m_pMesh);
if(FAILED(hr))
{
    OutputDebugString("Failed to load mesh\n");
    assert(0);
}
```

Check out the fifth parameter; this is an ID3DXBuffer buffer object that we saw before when we dealt with compiling shaders. Back then, a buffer was used to store error messages if the compile failed. Here it is used to hold materials. It is a versatile object that is used all over the D3D eXtensions library.

After D3DXLoadMeshFromX() is called, we have three pieces of information: a buffer full of materials, the number of materials in that buffer, and a mesh object. So what needs to be done to turn those objects into something we can render onscreen? First we need to extract all the materials from the buffer. If you look closely, you will find that the mesh material buffer contains a big array of D3DXMATERIAL structures, which look like this:

```
typedef struct D3DXMATERIAL {
    D3DMATERIAL9 MatD3D;
    LPSTR pTextureFilename;
} D3DXMATERIAL;
```

The first part of this structure is the D3DMATERIAL9 structure, which contains all the different types of coloring information. The substructure looks like this, in case you haven't seen it before:

```
typedef struct _D3DMATERIAL9 {
    D3DCOLORVALUE Diffuse;
    D3DCOLORVALUE Ambient;
```

```
    D3DCOLORVALUE Specular;
    D3DCOLORVALUE Emissive;
    float Power;
} D3DMATERIAL9;
```

Now that we know what's in the buffer, let's work on getting it converted into something more useful. We know how many materials there are from the original load function, so we need to create new structures to hold the material data for each material, like this:

```
m_pMeshTextures = new LPDIRECT3DTEXTURE9[m_NumMeshMaterials];
m_pMeshMaterials = new D3DMATERIAL9[m_NumMeshMaterials];
```

Don't forget to delete these when you are finished. Next we need to get a pointer to the data inside the buffer. This is done with the ID3DXBuffer::GetBufferPointer() function, which returns a void pointer to the contents of the buffer. This pointer needs to be cast to the correct type of pointer for us to use it. That's where this comes in:

```
D3DXMATERIAL* pD3DXMaterials = (D3DXMATERIAL*)pMeshMaterialBuffer->GetBufferPointer();
```

Now we need to loop through every one of the materials, extract and load the texture name and the materials, and save them. The textures are loaded with the D3DXCreateTextureFromFileEx() function, which takes way too many parameters but ends up loading the texture for us and giving us a pointer to it. Check out the loop code again:

```
for(indUInt i = 0 ; i < m_NumMeshMaterials ; i++)
{
    m_pMeshMaterials[i] = pD3DXMaterials[i].MatD3D;
    m_pMeshMaterials[i].Ambient = pD3DXMaterials[i].MatD3D.Diffuse;

    strcat(&fullpath[0], pD3DXMaterials[i].pTextureFilename);

    hr = D3DXCreateTextureFromFileEx(GAMEENGINE->GetDevice(), fullpath,
        D3DX_DEFAULT, D3DX_DEFAULT,
        D3DX_DEFAULT, 0, D3DFMT_FROM_FILE,
            D3DPOOL_DEFAULT, D3DX_FILTER_TRIANGLE,
        D3DX_FILTER_TRIANGLE, 0, 0, 0, &m_pMeshTextures[i]);
    if(FAILED(hr))
    {
        assert(0);
        OutputDebugString("Failed to load mesh texture");
```

```
            m_pMeshTextures[i] = NULL;
    }

    strcpy(fullpath, "media\\\0");
}
```

Notice that the ambient light color is set to be the same as the diffuse color. By default, the ambient color is set to black, which isn't normally what you want it to be. Instead, overwrite it with the diffuse color to give a nice light color to the model. You can override this code with your own if you like.

Finally, the visual resource has its effect set to the default effect. It is a good idea to have a default effect lying around in memory that you can fall back on if there are no other effects available or if the one you are trying to use is failing. A lot of developers like to make the default effect render their object in some weird color like bright pink to highlight any problems in the loading code.

Rendering Visual Resources

Rendering, amazingly, is quite simple and actually makes a lot of sense. What you need is to loop through each separate material on the object and render that. Rendering involves setting up the effect files like you saw in the previous chapter and rendering as many passes as it takes to complete each technique. Check out the code:

```
indBool cVisualResource::Render()
{
    VisualEffects::cEffect* pCurrentEffect = EFFECTMANAGER->GetEffect(m_EffectID);

    pCurrentEffect->SetTransforms(
        m_matWorld, CAMERA->GetViewMatrix(), CAMERA->GetProjectionMatrix());
    pCurrentEffect->Dispatch();

    indUInt numPasses = 0;
    pCurrentEffect->Begin(numPasses);

    for(indUInt passCount = 0 ; passCount < numPasses ; passCount++)
    {
        pCurrentEffect->BeginPass(passCount);
        for(indUInt i = 0 ; i < m_NumMeshMaterials ; i++)
        {
            GAMEENGINE->GetDevice()->SetTexture(0, m_pMeshTextures[i]);
```

```
            GAMEENGINE->GetDevice()->SetMaterial(&m_pMeshMaterials[i]);
            m_pMesh->DrawSubset(i);
        }
        pCurrentEffect->EndPass();
    }

    pCurrentEffect->End();

    return true;
}
```

Can you see what's going on? First I get a pointer to the effect used for this visual resource so that I can work with it. Then I set up the transforms in the effect before it is sent to the graphics card with the `Dispatch()` function:

```
VisualEffects::cEffect* pCurrentEffect = EFFECTMANAGER->GetEffect(m_EffectID);

pCurrentEffect->SetTransforms(
    m_matWorld, CAMERA->GetViewMatrix(), CAMERA->GetProjectionMatrix());
pCurrentEffect->Dispatch();
```

Next we need to figure out how many passes this render is going to take and loop for every pass:

```
indUInt numPasses = 0;
pCurrentEffect->Begin(numPasses);

for(indUInt passCount = 0 ; passCount < numPasses ; passCount++)
{
```

Then we call `BeginPass()` so that Direct3D knows to initialize all the render states for this pass. Finally, we can render the object. But remember that it is made of different materials, so we need to render each of them separately!

```
pCurrentEffect->BeginPass(passCount);
for(indUInt i = 0 ; i < m_NumMeshMaterials ; i++)
{
    GAMEENGINE->GetDevice()->SetTexture(0, m_pMeshTextures[i]);
    GAMEENGINE->GetDevice()->SetMaterial(&m_pMeshMaterials[i]);
    m_pMesh->DrawSubset(i);
}
pCurrentEffect->EndPass();
```

We're almost there. There's just a little housekeeping to do involving telling Direct3D that we are done rendering and then returning true to let the calling function know that everything went all right.:

```
    pCurrentEffect->End();

    return true;
}
```

That is basically all there is to rendering visual resources. We'll come back and look at extending this code later in the book when we deal with more advanced topics.

Shutting Down Visual Resources

This is an area that deserves a little attention because there are so many different parts that go into a visual resource. What we need to do is run through everything and release all the resources used by the mesh, textures, and materials. Here's the code:

```
indBool cVisualResource::Shutdown()
{
    SAFE_RELEASE(m_pMesh);

    if(m_pMeshTextures)
    {
        for(indUInt i = 0 ; i < m_NumMeshMaterials ; i++)
            SAFE_RELEASE(m_pMeshTextures[i]);

        delete[] m_pMeshTextures;
        m_pMeshTextures = 0;
    }

    if(m_pMeshMaterials)
    {
        delete[] m_pMeshMaterials;
        m_pMeshMaterials = 0;
    }
    return true;
}
```

This function is called automatically from the destructor, so you never have to worry about leaving resources hanging around and leaking memory.

Managing Visual Resources

Having a visual resource class is great, but what happens when you reach that amazing point in your game development when you want to have two objects onscreen at the same time? Well, you need a manager, that's what! With that in mind, I've taken the liberty of writing the cResourceManager class, which looks after a vector of visual resources. Check out the code, which is a simple wrapper class:

```
class cResourceManager
{
private:
    cResourceManager(void);
public:
    ~cResourceManager(void);

// Functions
public:
    static cResourceManager* getInstance();

    indBool Start();
    indBool RenderAll();
    indBool Shutdown();

    static indUInt GenerateUniqueID()
    {
        return m_UniqueID++;
    }

    void AddVisualResource(cVisualResource* pNewResource);

protected:

// Data
public:

protected:
    static cResourceManager *ms_pResourceManager;
    static indBool     ms_InstanceFlag;

    std::vector <cVisualResource*> m_vecVisualResources;

    static indUInt m_UniqueID;
};
```

The source code is even simpler. At the moment, there are functions to create unique IDs, add resources to the vector, clean up, and render. It is almost identical code to what you saw in the effect manager. Check out the implementation code:

```
cResourceManager* cResourceManager::getInstance()
{
    if(!ms_InstanceFlag)
    {
        ms_pResourceManager = new cResourceManager();
        ms_InstanceFlag = true;
        return ms_pResourceManager;
    }
    else
    {
        return ms_pResourceManager;
    }
}

cResourceManager::cResourceManager(void)
{
    // Private constructor
    m_UniqueID = 231980;
}

cResourceManager::~cResourceManager(void)
{
    Shutdown();
}

indBool cResourceManager::Start()
{
    return true;
}

indBool cResourceManager::RenderAll()
{
    for(indUInt i = 0 ; i < m_vecVisualResources.size() ; i++)
    {
        m_vecVisualResources[i]->Render();
    }
```

```
        return true;
}
indBool cResourceManager::Shutdown()
{
    for(indUInt i = 0 ; i < m_vecVisualResources.size() ; i++)
    {
        delete m_vecVisualResources[i];
    }

    m_vecVisualResources.clear();

    return true;
}

void cResourceManager::AddVisualResource(cVisualResource* pNewResource)
{
    assert(pNewResource);
    m_vecVisualResources.push_back(pNewResource);
}
```

I've bolded the important bits of code for you to look at closely. I'm sure it's nothing you haven't seen before, but it's good to get an idea of how all this stuff fits together.

An Extensible Game Engine

We have reached an exciting point now. Everything that we need to start work on some really great stuff is now in place. I recommend opening the projects in Visual Studio now and looking at how everything fits together. If you execute the code, you should see something like Figure 3.1.

You should notice a lot of the functionality I've talked about in the past few chapters, such as the loaded 3D model, the frame rate output at the top of the screen, the ability to move around with the mouse, and, of course, the rendered model using effect files. Now that we've reached this point, I want to show you just how easy it is to play around with new effect files. To this end, let's see if we can change the effect so that it adds a nice glow outline around the character.

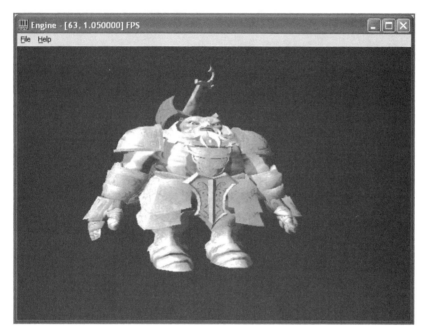

Figure 3.1
The engine in action.

Writing a Glow Shader

You'll be amazed at how easy this is. Before we look at the code, let's set out exactly what I'm talking about. Basically we want to render the object as standard and then render a second pass that creates a sharp glowing outline around the character. Let's look at the current vertex and pixel shader we are using in default.fx.

```
VS_OUTPUT VS(
        float3 Pos  : POSITION,
        float3 Norm : NORMAL,
        float2 Tex  : TEXCOORD0)
{
    VS_OUTPUT Out = (VS_OUTPUT)0;

    float3 L = -lightDir;

    float4x4 WorldView = mul(World, View);

    float3 P = mul(float4(Pos, 1), (float4x3)WorldView);  // position (view space)
    float3 N = normalize(mul(Norm, (float3x3)WorldView)); // normal (view space)
```

```
    float3 R = normalize(2 * dot(N, L) * N - L);       // reflection vector (view space)
    float3 V = -normalize(P);                          // view direction (view space)

    Out.Pos  = mul(float4(P, 1), Projection);          // position (projected)
    Out.Diff = I_a * k_a + I_d * k_d * max(0, dot(N, L)); // diffuse + ambient
    Out.Spec = I_s * k_s * pow(max(0, dot(R, V)), n/4);   // specular
    Out.Tex  = Tex;

    return Out;
}

float4 PS(
    float4 Diff : COLOR0,
    float4 Spec : COLOR1,
    float2 Tex  : TEXCOORD0) : COLOR
{
    return tex2D(Sampler, Tex) * Diff + Spec;
}
```

The technique for using the pixel and vertex shaders looks like this:

```
technique TVertexAndPixelShader
{
    pass P0
    {
        // shaders
        VertexShader = compile vs_1_1 VS();
        PixelShader  = compile ps_1_1 PS();
    }
}
```

What we want to do is add a new shader called VS_GLOW that is a copy of the first vertex shader and call this as a second pass. Let's look at the new shader now and see what is different:

```
VS_OUTPUT VS_GLOW(
    float3 Pos  : POSITION,
    float3 Norm : NORMAL,
    float2 Tex  : TEXCOORD0)
{
    VS_OUTPUT Out = (VS_OUTPUT)0;
```

```
    float3 L = -lightDir;

    float4x4 WorldView = mul(World, View);

    float3 P = mul(float4(Pos, 1), (float4x3)WorldView);  // position (view space)
    float3 N = normalize(mul(Norm, (float3x3)WorldView)); // normal (view space)

    P += N * 0.015; // Extend glow

    float3 R = normalize(2 * dot(N, L) * N - L);          // reflection vector
(view space)
    float3 V = -normalize(P);                             // view direction
(view space)

    Out.Pos  = mul(float4(P, 1), Projection);             // position (projected)
    Out.Diff = float4(1,0,0,0.6); // diffuse + ambient
    Out.Tex  = Tex;

    return Out;
}
```

First up, do you see anything different? The main change is the first bolded line. Let's think about what this does. It's taking the position and adding the normal multiplied by 0.015. What the heck does that do? Well, if you think about it, a properly constructed model has its normals facing outward, as in Figure 3.2.

If you add the normal to the position, you are effectively moving the vertex along the normal vector, in effect blowing up the model like a balloon. This is exactly what we want, but moving it the full length of the normal is too much, even though the normal is normalized. We need to make it much smaller. In this case, I've chosen a value of 0.015f.

We have inflated the model slightly larger than the original. This allows us to render the model normally with the first pass and then the inflated version in the second pass. However, in the second pass, we can turn on alpha blending to make it glow. You also might notice in the changed vertex shader above that no specular lighting is being set. We don't need to calculate specular light because the second pass is semitransparent. It's a waste of time to compute it in this case. The vertex shader also forces the diffuse color to be bright red with 60 percent opacity. To take advantage of this reduced computation shader, we need a new pixel shader.

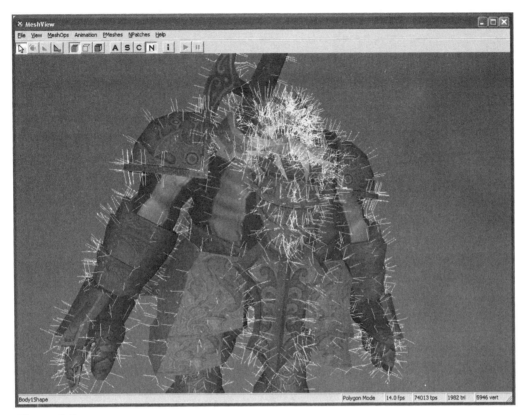

Figure 3.2
Normals almost always point outward from a model.

Look at this:

```
float4 PS_GLOW( float4 Diff : COLOR0) : COLOR
{
    return Diff;
}
```

I don't think it's possible to get a simpler shader than that! It just returns the diffuse color that was computed in the vertex shader! Now there are only a few steps left to make this work. We need to modify the technique to use two passes instead of just one and set up the alpha blending:

```
technique TVertexAndPixelShader
{
    pass P0
    {
```

```
            VertexShader = compile vs_1_1 VS();
            PixelShader  = compile ps_1_1 PS();
    }

    pass P1
    {
            AlphaBlendEnable = true;
            srcblend = srcalpha;
            destblend = one;
            cullmode = none;
            zwriteenable=false;

            VertexShader = compile vs_1_1 VS_GLOW();
        PixelShader  = compile ps_1_1 PS_GLOW();
    }
}
```

See the bold changes? The original pass stays the same as before. The new pass starts by setting up the render states to enable alpha blending and turning off the z writing. The alpha blending states tell the graphics card to multiply the source alpha by 1 to create a glow effect. The z writing is disabled to ensure that the rendering takes place without any z-fighting or flickering and gives a smoother look. Check out Figure 3.3 to see the results.

The entire new shader looks like this:

```
string XFile = "dwarf.x";   // model
int    BCLR  = 0xff202080;                // background

// light direction (view space)
float3 lightDir < string UIDirectional = "Light Direction"; > = {0.577, -0.577, 0.577};

// light intensity
float4 I_a = { 0.1f, 0.1f, 0.1f, 1.0f };    // ambient
float4 I_d = { 1.0f, 1.0f, 1.0f, 1.0f };    // diffuse
float4 I_s = { 1.0f, 1.0f, 1.0f, 1.0f };    // specular

// material reflectivity
float4 k_a : MATERIALAMBIENT = { 1.0f, 1.0f, 1.0f, 1.0f };    // ambient
float4 k_d : MATERIALDIFFUSE = { 1.0f, 1.0f, 1.0f, 1.0f };    // diffuse
float4 k_s : MATERIALSPECULAR= { 1.0f, 1.0f, 1.0f, 1.0f };    // specular
float  n   : MATERIALPOWER = 32.0f;                           // power
```

Figure 3.3
The glow technique in action!

```
// texture
texture Tex0 < string name = "tiger\\tiger.bmp"; >;

// transformations
float4x4 World      : WORLD;
float4x4 View       : VIEW;
float4x4 Projection : PROJECTION;

struct VS_OUTPUT
{
    float4 Pos  : POSITION;
    float4 Diff : COLOR0;
    float4 Spec : COLOR1;
    float2 Tex  : TEXCOORD0;
};

VS_OUTPUT VS(
    float3 Pos  : POSITION,
    float3 Norm : NORMAL,
    float2 Tex  : TEXCOORD0)
{
    VS_OUTPUT Out = (VS_OUTPUT)0;

    float3 L = -lightDir;

    float4x4 WorldView = mul(World, View);

    float3 P = mul(float4(Pos, 1), (float4x3)WorldView);    // position (view space)
    float3 N = normalize(mul(Norm, (float3x3)WorldView));   // normal (view space)

    float3 R = normalize(2 * dot(N, L) * N - L);            // reflection vector (view space)
    float3 V = -normalize(P);                               // view direction (view space)

    Out.Pos  = mul(float4(P, 1), Projection);               // position (projected)
    Out.Diff = I_a * k_a + I_d * k_d * max(0, dot(N, L));   // diffuse + ambient
    Out.Spec = I_s * k_s * pow(max(0, dot(R, V)), n/4);     // specular
    Out.Tex  = Tex;

    return Out;
}
```

```hlsl
VS_OUTPUT VS_GLOW(
    float3 Pos  : POSITION,
    float3 Norm : NORMAL,
    float2 Tex  : TEXCOORD0)
{
    VS_OUTPUT Out = (VS_OUTPUT)0;

    float3 L = -lightDir;

    float4x4 WorldView = mul(World, View);

    float3 P = mul(float4(Pos, 1), (float4x3)WorldView);   // position (view space)
    float3 N = normalize(mul(Norm, (float3x3)WorldView));  // normal (view space)

    P += N * 0.020;

    float3 R = normalize(2 * dot(N, L) * N - L);           // reflection vector (view space)
    float3 V = -normalize(P);                              // view direction (view space)

    Out.Pos  = mul(float4(P, 1), Projection);              // position (projected)
    Out.Diff = float4(0.5,0,0,0.6); // diffuse + ambient
    Out.Tex  = Tex;

    return Out;
}

sampler Sampler = sampler_state
{
    Texture   = (Tex0);
    MipFilter = LINEAR;
    MinFilter = LINEAR;
    MagFilter = LINEAR;
};

float4 PS(
    float4 Diff : COLOR0,
    float4 Spec : COLOR1,
    float2 Tex  : TEXCOORD0) : COLOR
{
    return tex2D(Sampler, Tex) * Diff + Spec;
}
```

```
float4 PS_GLOW(float4 Diff : COLOR0) : COLOR
{
    return Diff;
}

technique TVertexAndPixelShader
{
    pass P0
    {
        VertexShader = compile vs_1_1 VS();
        PixelShader  = compile ps_1_1 PS();
    }

    pass P1
    {
        AlphaBlendEnable = true;
        srcblend = srcalpha;
        destblend = one;
        cullmode = none;

        zwriteenable=false;
        VertexShader = compile vs_1_1 VS_GLOW();
        PixelShader  = compile ps_1_1 PS_GLOW();
    }
}

technique TVertexShaderOnly
{
    pass P0
    {
        // lighting
        Lighting       = FALSE;
        SpecularEnable = TRUE;

        // samplers
        Sampler[0] = (Sampler);

        // texture stages
        ColorOp[0]   = MODULATE;
        ColorArg1[0] = TEXTURE;
        ColorArg2[0] = DIFFUSE;
        AlphaOp[0]   = MODULATE;
```

```
            AlphaArg1[0] = TEXTURE;
            AlphaArg2[0] = DIFFUSE;

            ColorOp[1]   = DISABLE;
            AlphaOp[1]   = DISABLE;

            // shaders
            VertexShader = compile vs_1_1 VS();
            PixelShader  = NULL;
        }
    }

    technique TNoShader
    {
        pass P0
        {
            // transforms
            WorldTransform[0]  = (World);
            ViewTransform      = (View);
            ProjectionTransform = (Projection);

            // material
            MaterialAmbient  = (k_a);
            MaterialDiffuse  = (k_d);
            MaterialSpecular = (k_s);
            MaterialPower    = (n);

            // lighting
            LightType[0]      = DIRECTIONAL;
            LightAmbient[0]   = (I_a);
            LightDiffuse[0]   = (I_d);
            LightSpecular[0]  = (I_s);
            LightDirection[0] = (lightDir);
            LightRange[0]     = 100000.0f;

            LightEnable[0] = TRUE;
            Lighting       = TRUE;
            SpecularEnable = TRUE;

            // samplers
            Sampler[0] = (Sampler);
```

```
        // texture stages
        ColorOp[0]   = MODULATE;
        ColorArg1[0] = TEXTURE;
        ColorArg2[0] = DIFFUSE;
        AlphaOp[0]   = MODULATE;
        AlphaArg1[0] = TEXTURE;
        AlphaArg2[0] = DIFFUSE;

        ColorOp[1]   = DISABLE;
        AlphaOp[1]   = DISABLE;

        // shaders
        VertexShader = NULL;
        PixelShader  = NULL;
    }
}
```

And that is all there is to it! I'm sure you'll agree that this was a gentle introduction to creating effects with shaders. Well, the introduction is over, and it's time to sort the men from the T1000s and the women from the TXs. Later in this book, you'll learn seriously amazing techniques for water, fire, smoke, and everything else you can think of!

Conclusion

In this chapter, you learned about cool techniques like the following:

- Game synchronization, including FPS output and ensuring that your engine runs at the correct speed no matter what the actual execution rate is

- Creating a camera class to encapsulate the view matrix and allow you to explore the 3D world

- Creating a visual resource object that will represent all the objects in your game, including their associated materials, textures, and shaders

- A real-life look at shaders in action, including how to program a glow shader

In the next chapter, we are going to look at how to use shaders to create real-time volumetric shadows that will blow your mind!

CHAPTER 4

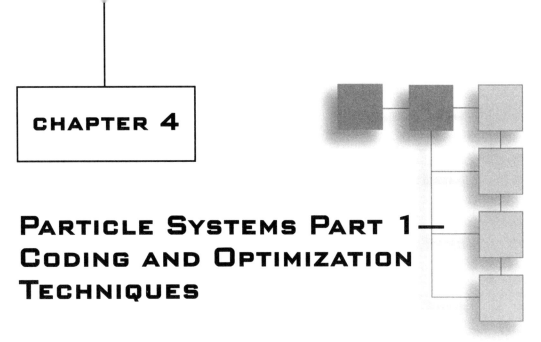

Particle Systems Part 1— Coding and Optimization Techniques

Now that we have a nice little extensible game engine put together, it's time to mod it up a little bit with a flashy particle system. Particle systems are great for modeling everything under the sun that moves dynamically, such as water, smoke, explosions, clouds, snow, rain, you name it. The key to particle systems is *emergent behavior*. The whole is greater than the sum of the parts.

Particle systems work by applying simple rules to a number of particles. Each particle follows these simple rules for its lifespan. When you create hundreds or thousands of particles that follow these rules, the effect can be quite stunning. Some systems, such as clouds, require only a few particles, whereas systems such as waterfalls require thousands.

After game designers learn what particle systems can do, they go a little nuts and suddenly start putting them everywhere they can think of. That makes our jobs as game programmers all that more difficult because the systems have to be ridiculously efficient. I'm going to show you some great optimizations in this chapter to make a particle system blazingly fast. To give you an idea of how important optimizations are, listen to this. On my first pass of the system in this chapter, I wrote it without any thought about optimizations to get a baseline. The result was a great particle system, but with 500 particles, it only ran at 50 Frames per Second (FPS). After a little tweaking here and there, it can now comfortably run 10,000 particles at 350 FPS!

So in this chapter, I'm going to cover the following:

- Particle systems theory
- Coding for multithreading
- Billboarding
- Grid rendering
- Developing an efficient particle
- Blazingly fast particle processing and rendering
- Cache alignment issues
- Configuring particle systems with feature files
- Using macros to speed up feature additions
- Optimizations including cache lines, inline assembly, branching, arrays, fast `float` to `int` conversions, and much more!

Let's get started!

The Theory of Particles

The particle system I'm going to show you in this chapter is extremely fast, extremely customizable, and easy to work with. To get a good idea of particle systems, let's look at them in action. Check out Figure 4.1, which shows a screen shot from the finished system.

Let's get the terminology straight for starters. A *particle* is a rendered quad, which can have any of the following properties:

- Velocity
- Acceleration
- Mass
- Color
- Texture
- Lifespan

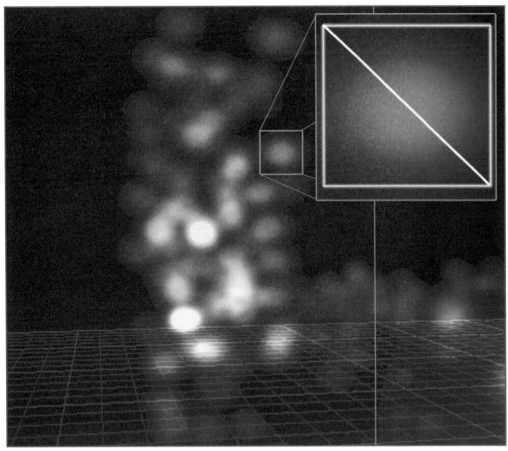

Figure 4.1
Particle systems close up. A particle is a quad made of two triangles.

A particle can have an infinite number of properties, but amazingly, these six are generally enough for almost every effect you can imagine. I'll teach you about other techniques at the end of this chapter if you want to extend the system yourself.

Looking at Figure 4.1 again, you can see a particle system in action. A *particle system* is simply a collection of particles that all have the same rules that guide them. You might have one particle system to represent a fire, another for an explosion, and another for a waterfall. The key to particle systems is that they are *instanciable*. That is, you only have to define the particle system once, and then you can simply create them on the fly whenever and wherever you want in your game. In other words, you can define your particle system for an explosion once, and every time there is an explosion, a new particle system is spawned at the location of the explosion.

Particle systems are responsible for creating their child particles and then killing them when they are due to expire. A particle system sets up all the properties of its child particles when they are created. The particle then acts according to the rules that the particle system has given it until it dies.

Particles need to have an absolute minimum of data in them because they are created so often. For this system, which I'll show you in a moment, a particle will be roughly 128 bytes in size. This might sound small, but think of this in a large 5,000-particle system. That is 640K. Dump four of those into a level, and you have more than 2.5 megs of particles. Size does matter!

Particle Rendering Techniques

There are four main ways to render particles. I'm going to discuss all of them so that you can make good decisions if you ever have to implement your own particle system from scratch. The wrong decision at the outset can cause a lot of pain later on. In fact, this is exactly what happened to me in my first attempt to write a particle system at a company I worked for many years ago. Let's review them in order of complexity.

Untextured Primitives

This is how particles were rendered in the early 3D days before there was enough processing power to use texture polygons (more on that shortly). An untextured primitive is just a colored point, line, or triangle that is rendered for each particle. This is what was used to make some of the explosions in *Quake 1*. This method of rendering is still useful in modern particle systems for techniques such as rain or sparks. There is no support for this in the particle system in this chapter, but it is not difficult to override the rendering function to provide this functionality yourself.

Point Sprites

This is how the particle systems used to be done in the old days. A 2D texture contained the texture that was used for the particle, and it was simply blitted to the back buffer at different locations for each particle. This system can be quite fast, but it has a lot of drawbacks because it is implemented entirely in 2D. You have to manually scale the particles, which can be quite time consuming if you want to give any appreciation of depth. Also, unless you want to put in a lot of processor time, you can't rotate or scale the particles easily on the fly. Point sprites *are* usable, and I have created particle systems in the past based on this method. In fact, DirectX has built-in hardware support for point sprites, which is very useful. At one point during development, the requirements for the point sprite system changed in the middle of development, which meant I had to change it mid-stride to use textured polygons. It was not a simple change, so I don't recommend using this approach unless you thoroughly investigate it first. Point sprites are not used for the particle system in this book.

Note

In case you haven't come across the term before, *blit* is a term in computer graphics that means to copy an image from one location to another in memory. The name comes from the *BitBLT* machine code instruction used in the original Xerox Alto computer.

Textured Quads

These are the meat and potatoes of any modern particle system. They render faster than point sprites with 3D acceleration, and they make advanced effects like scaling and rotation simple. The only downside is that you need a little extra code to make sure that each particle always faces the camera, which uses a technique called *billboarding*. I'll discuss this a little later in the chapter. Texture quads are simple. They are just two triangles stuck together to make a quad, with the particle's texture overlaid on top. The color of the vertices of the quad determines the color of the texture. I'll be discussing this method throughout this chapter.

Particle Objects

This is the next step forward in particle systems, and it is possible to extend the particle system in this chapter to use this technique. In this case the particles, rather than being textured polygons, are full 3D objects! It extends what particle systems can be used for to things like birds and animals. Imagine that you set up some slightly more complicated flocking behavior for each particle. Then at each particle's location, you can render an animation bird, rather than just a textured quad. The effect is fantastic!

Optimization Techniques

Before we go on to particles, I want to cover optimization techniques that are used in the code to remove any confusion that might have arisen had you not seen this material first. These techniques are useful in almost all situations, not just for particle systems, so keep them in mind during development. The following sections cover the top performance killers in performance applications, so be sure to root them out of your own code!

Branching

Modern CPUs hate branching because they are pipelined. A *branch* is any part of your code that causes the CPU to make a decision and change code direction based on a result. This includes loops, if statements, and non-inlined function calls, among other things. A modern CPU is pipelined, which means it is chopped into sections that execute different code simultaneously. To keep this pipe fed at full speed, it is vital that the processor has all available code in its local cache. Accessing from main memory is notoriously slow compared to cache.

Every time you make an if statement, you are branching your code off to some new location. This stalls the processor while the fetch logic gets the new branched code out of memory. During this period, every stage of the CPU pipeline is stalled, which leads to a massive slowdown and wasted ticks. That's not what we want! To avoid this situation, the processor tries to predict, before the branch is processed, which way the branch will go. If it predicts correctly, the speedup is enormous. However, if the processor gets it wrong, the result is a massive stall. So the key with programming hardcore code is to avoid branching wherever possible. You have probably coded something like this before and thought it was okay:

```
if(someVariable1 != 0 && someVariable2 != 0)       // Prevent division by 0
    someVariable3 = someVariable1 / someVariable2;
```

This is fine for normal programming because you obviously don't want a division by 0. However, having a load of branches like that deep inside a loop would be a killer. Imagine a 2,000-particle system being executed. There could be an additional 12,000 branches per frame if there were a few systems instanced! The solution? Well, if extreme accuracy doesn't matter that much (as in particle systems), why not just do this:

```
const indReal32 indReal32_DIV0_DELTA = 0.000001f;
```

```
#define NO_DIV_0(x) (x + indReal32_DIV0_DELTA)

someVariable3 = NO_DIV_0(someVariable1) / NO_DIV_0(someVariable2);
```

A `float` is accurate to six decimal places, so just add the tiniest float to the variable. It's an extra addition, but this is much faster than doing an `if` compare in a deep loop.

Similarly, check out this code:

```
if(m_LifeTimeElapsed > m_LifeSpan)
    m_bDead = true;
```

This is a branch that would have to be executed to every particle in every frame, which is a killer. Is there a way around it? How about this instead:

```
m_bDead = (m_LifeTimeElapsed > m_LifeSpan);
```

That's much faster! No more branches!

This one might surprise you:

```
D3DXVECTOR newVector;
```

Spot the branch? D3DXVECTOR3 is a C++ object, which means that on creation, the CPU has to branch off to its constructor. Allocating numerous objects on the stack can impact performance. Fix it like this:

```
static D3DXVECTOR newVector;
```

That way, the new class is created only once on startup, and the same memory is used throughout the life of the program. Only use this technique when the variable is not meant to remember its value between calls. That is, you plan to overwrite its value on every call.

Your mission is to avoid branches in deep loops!

The Mother of All Evil: Float-to-Integer Conversions

Pick up any modern real-time program and run it through vTune or any other profiler, and I will put money that the function at the top of the list of CPU usage is `_ftol`. I almost dare not speak its evil name. It sends shivers down my spine. Not many people know that this is a way to absolutely murder your performance:

```
float someFloat = 3.0f;
int someInt = (int)someFloat;
```

How innocent does that look? The first time I heard about this evil monster, I was amazed. But it's true—converting a float to an integer is among the worst performance wreckers on an Intel CPU. Why? Good question. It all has to do with rounding and truncation.

To be compliant with a bunch of organizations that have too many letters in their names, like IEEE and ANSI, the Intel CPU has what is called a *truncation* and a *round* to convert from a float to an int and maintain the standard. The problem is that the truncation part is insanely slow because it flushes the *entire* CPU pipeline. That means every stage of the pipeline that is currently processing is stopped and has to restart, resulting in hundreds of lost ticks. The actual code that does the conversion uses an evil assembly instruction called _ftol. That is why that monster always ends up at the top of the profiler lists. Every time you call _ftol, you are converting your Pentium to an 8086! What's the solution?

Well, it just so happens that there is another CPU instruction, with the somewhat dubious name of fistp. It's our savior. It does away with most of the truncation and rounds the float to an int in a single instruction, which can literally lead to a 1000 percent performance improvement over _ftol. The problem is that the compiler doesn't generate this instruction automatically. You can get the compiler to do this globally, but that's not a good idea because there are some accuracy issues with the new method that you wouldn't want used for your entire program. So instead, we have to write it as inline assembly. Check out the code. It's simple, even if you haven't used inline assembler before.

```
static inline DWORD ConvertFloatToDWORDFast(const indReal32 incomingFloat)
{
    static DWORD outgoingDWORD;

    __asm
    {
        fld        incomingFloat          // load up the float to convert
        lea        eax, outgoingDWORD     // load up the outgoing integer
        fistp      dword ptr[eax]         // fistp that puppy all the way home
    }

    return outgoingDWORD;
}
/// Example
DWORD result = ConvertFloatToDWORDFast(22.0f);
```

`fistp` is so fast that I can barely get the text to stay in one place on this page. Notice that it is declared `inline` for speed. I'll discuss this in a moment. You might be wondering why this is such an issue in graphics programming. Well, I'll tell you. You do most of your color work in `D3DXCOLOR`, which is a four-float structure with a `float` representing every color component. However, the GPU does all its work in `D3DCOLORS`, which is a 32-bit integer with 8 bits for each color component. Every time you transfer a colored vertex to the GPU, you are using the evil `_ftol`! If you are rendering 50,000 triangles per frame, that is at least 600,000 calls (50,000 triangles by 3 vertices each by 4 color components each) per second to that performance-sapping instruction. Check out this little speed demon:

```
static inline D3DCOLOR ConvertD3DXCOLORToD3DCOLORFast(D3DXCOLOR& color)
{
    return D3DCOLOR_ARGB(
        ConvertFloatToDWORDFast(color.a * 255.0f),
        ConvertFloatToDWORDFast(color.r * 255.0f),
        ConvertFloatToDWORDFast(color.g * 255.0f),
        ConvertFloatToDWORDFast(color.b * 255.0f));
}
```

Can you say, "More than half a million fewer calls to _ftol!?"

Function Inlining

This is vitally important for performance functions. Every time you make a function call like this

```
bool IsDead = IsDead()
```

the compiler has to go through several steps. First it has to spend a while saving the current stack for the current function you are in. The stack contains all the registers, parameters, and other data necessary to run a function. Then it has to *branch* off in code to wherever the new function is and set up a new stack. Then it executes the code in the function and pops the stack before copying back the return value and restoring the original stack. This is a limited example, but as you can see, calling a function involves a lot of overhead.

You can use a technique for small functions called *inlining*. This replaces a function call with the actual code from the function in its place, thereby avoiding the function call altogether. For example, compare the following examples:

```cpp
// Not inlined
bool IsDead()
{
    return m_bIsDead;
}
.
.
.
void UpdateParticle()
{
    .
    . //Other code
    .
    bool bDead = IsDead();    // Slow function call!
}

// Inlined
inline bool IsDead()
{
    return m_bIsDead;
}

// Compiles to:
void UpdateParticle()
{
    .
    . //Other code
    .
    bool bDead = (m_bIsDead); // Fast! No function call
}
```

This could lead to a massive performance improvement in deep loops.

Cache Alignment

The Pentium loves to have its variables aligned to particular boundaries. A lot of CPUs, such as the PowerPC, can almost fall over and die on nonaligned data. The Pentium CPU can handle it, but slowly. The Pentium CPU is a 32-bit CPU, which means that it feeds on chunks of data that are 4 bytes long. If you have a variable stored in memory that starts on a byte that is not a multiple of 4, the CPU doesn't like it. If it is not a multiple of 2, the CPU *really* doesn't like it. The CPU has to spend time manipulating the data to access its contents. It also makes it hard to efficiently cache the data in Level 1 or 2 cache. The moral of the story is to always align your variables in performance code. I'll get to how to do this in a moment.

First you might want to think about how a variable becomes unaligned. Study the following code:

```
UINT code = 0;
```

That is your bog standard 4-byte, 32-bit variable that the compiler will happily align for you. But what about this code:

```
struct particle
{
    char letter;      // 1 byte                  // 1 bytes
    UINT code;        // Misaligned!             // 4 bytes
                                                 //--------
                                                 // 5 bytes
}
```

The first `char` member is one byte long, which means that the second member, code, crosses the cache line. It now lives in bytes 2, 3, 4, 5. In effect, the processor has to perform these actions to access the UINT:

1. Fetch the first 4 bytes of data.

2. Zero out byte 1.

3. Shift bytes 2, 3, and 4 down one byte.

4. Fetch the next four bytes of data.

5. Zero out bytes 2, 3, and 4.

6. Shift byte 1 into byte 4 of the other DWORD.

7. Work with the data.

As you can see, this is a complete mess for the CPU. You can help it by rearranging the data so that the UINT comes first and then adding extra padding to the structure to make sure it is cache aligned:

Chapter 4 ■ Particle Systems Part 1—Coding and Optimization Techniques

```
struct particle
{
    UINT code;      // First four bytes aligned        // 4 bytes
    char letter;    // 1 byte                          // 1 byte
    char unusedPadding[3];   // fills up unused space  // 3 bytes
                             //-------
                             // 8 bytes! perfect
}
```

Rearranging the contents like this provides a massive speed boost to any program. You can also use an alternative to make the compiler align the structure without adding the padding, using the compiler directive _declspec align.

__declspec align

This ugly duckling is useful for getting the compiler to automatically align your data to a specific byte value to improve performance. Just specify it before the actual variable that you want to declare, like this:

```
__declspec(align(x)) variable declaration;    // x = alignment
```

Or, for a more real-world declaration using a class, check out this fragment, which would declare a class and align it to 4-byte intervals:

```
__declspec(align(4)) class cParticle
{
    .
    .     // other code and data
    .
};
```

The actual name used for that is a bit rubbish because it doesn't read well. Best practice is to replace it with a macro so that when someone comes across your code, he knows what it does. The double underscore before the identifier indicates that it is Microsoft Visual C++ specific. So if you are working a project with a bunch of PS2 programmers who have just finished working with some GNU C++ variant, they might not immediately recognize it. If you replace it with a macro, its meaning becomes immediately apparent:

```
#define CACHE_ALIGN(x) __declspec(align(x))
```

Now you can align your performance classes easily:

```
CACHE_ALIGN(4) class cParticle
{
.
.    // other code and data
.
};
```

Particle System Helpers

There are a few tasks with particle systems that are used a lot, so it's helpful to get them put together into functions and make them as fast as possible using the techniques described previously. These tasks include linear interpolation, generating random values between two limits, and color lerping. (See the next section to learn all about lerping.) Don't worry if you have not come across these terms before, because I'm going to go over them now.

Fast Linear Interpolation

Linear interpolation, or *lerping* for short, is used all over particle systems. It means to change the blend between two values based on a value that changes. For instance, you could have an initial size of a particle equal to 1.0 and the final size equal to 2.0. The initial size means the size of the particle when it is first spawned, and the final size means the size when the particle ends its life. What we want is for the particle's size to change evenly over its lifetime. Interpolation is actually a lot simpler than it sounds and can be achieved with only one multiply and two adds. The algorithm looks like this:

```
Result = firstValue + (interpolateValue * (secondValue - firstValue));
```

The interpolated value ranges between 0.0 and 1.0. You can implement this quickly in code like this:

```
inline indReal32 Interpolate(indReal32 value1, indReal32 value2, indReal32 percent)
{
    return value1 + (percent * (value2 - value1));
}
```

This code is fast because it's only a few simple instructions. It's all contained in an inlined function which, of course, directly inserts the code into the calling origin, so there is no branching. It's important to be able to implement tight inner functions like this in assembly language if the need arises. Check out the same function that follows written in inline assembler:

```
inline indReal32 Interpolate(indReal32 value1, indReal32 value2, indReal32 percent)
{
    // return value1 + (percent * (value2 - value1));
    __asm
    {
        fld  dword ptr[value2];          // load value2
        fsub dword ptr[value1];          // subtract value1   .ie (value2 -
                                         // value1) from before
        fmul dword ptr[percent];         // multiply by percent. ie (percent *
                                         // (value2 - value1)
        fadd dword ptr[value1];          // add value 1. compiler will automatically
                                         // return
    }
}
```

There is no advantage in this particular function to using inline assembly. In fact, that code is exactly what the compiler produces from the original C++ code before. I'm just showing you so that you get used to converting C++ into assembler for hand-crafted code.

Color Lerping

Color lerping is similar to interpolation except that it applies specifically to colors. Colors take longer to interpolate because they are made up of four components: red, green, blue, and of course alpha. Each of these must be interpolated individually to achieve the final desired code. Direct3D provides a function to do this for us called D3DXColorLerp(). This function has the following prototype:

```
D3DXCOLOR *D3DXColorLerp(D3DXCOLOR *pOut,
         CONST D3DXCOLOR *pC1, CONST D3DXCOLOR *pC2, FLOAT s);
```

D3DXColorLerp() looks just like our Interpolate() function except that it takes colors rather than float values. However, the function also takes pointers as input, which can be slow in some circumstances. However, why use a D3DX function when we can do it with our own? Here is how to interpolate D3DXCOLOR using our interpolate function:

```
m_CurrentColor.r = Interpolate(m_StartColor.r, m_EndColor.r, percentComplete);
m_CurrentColor.g = Interpolate(m_StartColor.g, m_EndColor.g, percentComplete);
m_CurrentColor.b = Interpolate(m_StartColor.b, m_EndColor.b, percentComplete);
m_CurrentColor.a = Interpolate(m_StartColor.a, m_EndColor.a, percentComplete);
```

That's a much better way to do it.

Generating Random Float Values with Limited Range

Often with particle systems, you want to generate some random values that are strictly between two ranges. For instance, you might want to have your particles between 1.0 and 2.0 units to make them look a little more random, rather than just have all particles created with the same size.

The code to do this relies on the `rand()` function which, of course, produces a random integer between the range of 0 and 32,767. However, we want a floating point value between any range of numbers, so a little conversion is required. The code to do this works a little like this:

1. Pass in the two values, `val1` and `val2`, that you want to create a random value between.

2. Generate a random value with the `rand()` function.

3. Divide the random value by the maximum value that `rand()` will produce, which is 32,767.

4. The result of this division is a `float` value in the range of 0.0 to 1.0.

5. Subtract `val1` from `val2` and multiply it by this random number.

6. Add the result to `val1`.

In code, it looks a little like this:

```
inline indReal32 CalculateRandomValueBetween(indReal32 lowerValue, indReal32 higherValue)
{
#ifdef _DEBUG
    if(lowerValue > higherValue)
    {
        assert(0);
    }
```

```
#endif // _DEBUG

    return      lowerValue +
                ((indReal32)((indReal32)rand() / (indReal32)RAND_MAX) *
                (indReal32)((higherValue) - (lowerValue)));
}
```

You might notice the `int` to `float` conversion going on here and wonder if it is slow. In fact, it is not. Only `float` to `int` conversions are slow, not the other way around.

Billboarding

Billboarding is important for particle systems that use texture polygons because particles are effectively just flat squares with a texture on top of them. That means that if the viewer looks at them at an angle, they will look silly and totally ruin the intended effect. Check out Figure 4.2, which demonstrates the problem.

What we want is for the particles to face the camera no matter which way the camera is facing. This requires us to rotate the particles every frame to make sure they are perpendicular to the look-at vector, as in Figure 4.3.

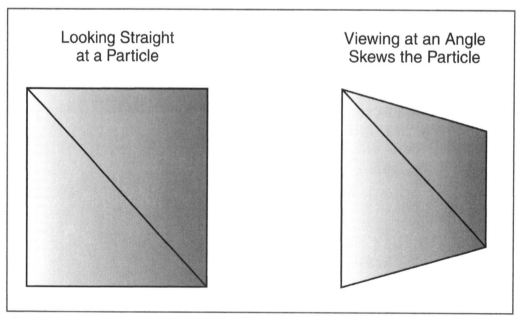

Figure 4.2
Billboarding.

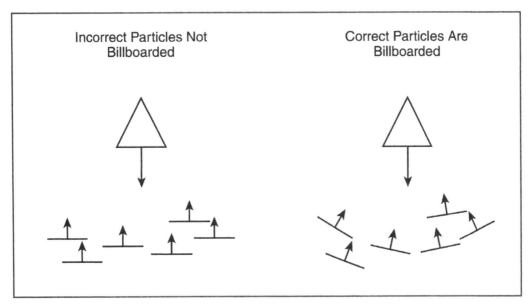

Figure 4.3
Birds-eye view comparison of billboarded and non-billboarded polygons.

Billboarding can be simple if you do it correctly and a complete pain if it goes wrong. Check out these steps.

1. Calculate the camera-to-particle vector by subtracting the world space particle position from the world space camera position. To billboard, we need to have the particles rendered perpendicular to this vector.

2. Next, work out a vector that is perpendicular to the vector just calculated. This is quite easy, because we know the up vector is (0,1,0) since the positive Y axis is always up. So all we have to do is calculate the cross product of the cam-to-particle vector with the up vector. The result is a vector that is perpendicular to the camera's look-at vector. We can use this vector to work out the boundaries of the particle quad.

3. Normalize the perpendicular vector to give it a length of 1.0, and then multiply it by half the size that you want the particle to be. Because the particle quad will be extended away from the particle position in both directions, we only want to go half the distance in either direction to create the full particle.

4. The particle is created from four vertices that are used to create two triangles. To find vertex 1, follow the perpendicular to the left of the particle. Then move X units up (based on the size of the particle). To find vertex 2, follow the vector to the right of the particle and again move up by the size of the particle, and so on until all the vertices are defined. You now have a billboarded particle!

Look at the code that does this. First we need to get the particle position and camera position:

```
particlePos = m_pParticleArray[i].GetPosition();
camPos = CAMERA->GetPosition();
```

Then we need to work out the vector from the camera to the particle:

```
camToParticleVec = m_PositionInitial - camPos;
```

This vector needs to be normalized so that it is only 1 unit long:

```
D3DXVec3Normalize(&camToParticleVec, &camToParticleVec);
```

Now we can cross this vector with the up vector to work out the perpendicular vector:

```
D3DXVec3Cross(&rightVec, &camToParticleVec, &upVec);
D3DXVec3Normalize(&rightVec, &rightVec);
```

After renormalizing the vector, we need to multiply it by the size of the particle so that the quad is created at the correct size:

```
particleSize = m_pParticleArray[i].GetSize();
rightVec *= particleSize;
```

Now we can work out where the left and right sides of the particle are:

```
leftSide  = (particlePos - rightVec);
rightSide = (particlePos + rightVec);
```

That is all we need to work out all the vertices! Check out the code that follows, which fills a vertex buffer with the particle vertices:

```
pVertices[currentVertex].position.x = leftSide.x;
pVertices[currentVertex].position.y = leftSide.y + particleSize;
pVertices[currentVertex].position.z = leftSide.z;
pVertices[currentVertex].color = curParticleColor;
pVertices[currentVertex].tx = 0.0f;
```

```
pVertices[currentVertex].ty = 0.0f;

currentVertex++;

pVertices[currentVertex].position.x = rightSide.x;
pVertices[currentVertex].position.y = rightSide.y + particleSize;
pVertices[currentVertex].position.z = rightSide.z;
pVertices[currentVertex].color = curParticleColor;
pVertices[currentVertex].tx = 1.0f;
pVertices[currentVertex].ty = 0.0f;

currentVertex++;

pVertices[currentVertex].position.x = rightSide.x;
pVertices[currentVertex].position.y = rightSide.y - particleSize;
pVertices[currentVertex].position.z = rightSide.z;
pVertices[currentVertex].color = curParticleColor;
pVertices[currentVertex].tx = 1.0f;
pVertices[currentVertex].ty = 1.0f;

currentVertex++;

pVertices[currentVertex].position.x = rightSide.x;
pVertices[currentVertex].position.y = rightSide.y - particleSize;
pVertices[currentVertex].position.z = rightSide.z;
pVertices[currentVertex].color = curParticleColor;
pVertices[currentVertex].tx = 1.0f;
pVertices[currentVertex].ty = 1.0f;

currentVertex++;

pVertices[currentVertex].position.x = leftSide.x;
pVertices[currentVertex].position.y = leftSide.y - particleSize;
pVertices[currentVertex].position.z = leftSide.z;
pVertices[currentVertex].color = curParticleColor;
pVertices[currentVertex].tx = 0.0f;
pVertices[currentVertex].ty = 1.0f;

currentVertex++;

pVertices[currentVertex].position.x = leftSide.x;
pVertices[currentVertex].position.y = leftSide.y + particleSize;
```

```
pVertices[currentVertex].position.z = leftSide.z;
pVertices[currentVertex].color = curParticleColor;
pVertices[currentVertex].tx = 0.0f;
pVertices[currentVertex].ty = 0.0f;

currentVertex++;
```

Don't worry about the other stuff going on there just yet. It's just important to understand how the vertex positions are being calculated.

Grid Rendering

While developing the particle system for this chapter, I was struck by how difficult it was to tell if the particles were behaving exactly the way I wanted them to because there is so much movement that there was nothing else to compare them to onscreen. Previously, I had always developed systems inside a live game, rather than just on a blank canvas. To help my brain see what was going on, I developed a grid rendering system. Check out Figure 4.4 to see how a grid can give you a much better sense of perspective.

Although you can't see it in the picture, the grid is mainly gray with colored axes. There is an industry standard to coloring the axes particular colors, which you might not have come across before. The x, y, and z axes are *always* rendered red, green, and blue, respectively. This is because it instantly allows you to orient yourself in the world just by checking the color of the axis. When you think of axes, you always think of the order x, y, and then z, right? And colors always in the order red, green, and then blue? Now by color, you can immediately associate a line with an axis. See red? It must be x. See blue? It must be z. It's a real time saver, and I highly recommend that you adopt this technique.

The grid requires just two functions: `cGameEngine::InitGrid()`, which calculates all the vertices and fills in the vertex buffer, and `cGameEngine::RenderGrid()`, which displays the grid onscreen. The grid should be the first thing rendered so that all other objects are rendered on top of it. It is important that you calculate the grid vertices on startup rather than every frame; otherwise, you are just wasting CPU cycles.

Check out the initialization function that follows. It starts by creating a standard vertex buffer and filling it with vertices. Note that 206 vertices are rendered. This is because the gray grid has 100 lines in the x plane and 100 lines in the y plane. Then an additional 3 lines (with two vertices each) for the origin axes makes 206.

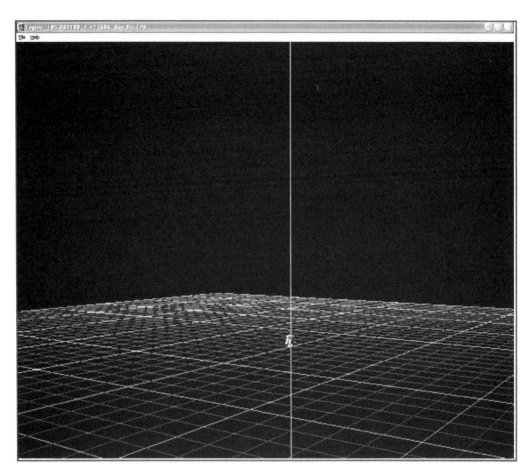

Figure 4.4
Grid rendering.

Here's the code:

```
indBool cGameEngine::InitGrid()
{
    UINT length = sizeof(GRID_VERTEX) * 206;

    m_pDevice->CreateVertexBuffer(
        length, D3DUSAGE_WRITEONLY,
            GRID_VERTEXFORMAT, D3DPOOL_MANAGED, &m_pGridVB, 0);

    if(!m_pGridVB)
        return false;
```

```cpp
GRID_VERTEX* pGridData = 0;
m_pGridVB->Lock(0,0, (void**)&pGridData, 0);

D3DXCOLOR currentColor;
D3DXCOLOR smallGridColor(0.4f, 0.4f, 0.4f, 1.0f);
D3DXCOLOR largeGridColor(0.2f, 0.2f, 0.2f, 1.0f);
D3DXCOLOR originColorX(1.0f, 0.0f, 0.0f, 1.0f);
D3DXCOLOR originColorY(0.0f, 1.0f, 0.0f, 1.0f);
D3DXCOLOR originColorZ(0.0f, 0.0f, 1.0f, 1.0f);

int gridSize = 100;
int halfGrid = gridSize / 2;
float gridExtent = (float)halfGrid;

UINT vertexCount = 0;

// Fill in the x axis
for(int i = 0 ; i < 101 ; i+=2)
{
    float x;

    x = (float)i - 50.0f;

    if(i == halfGrid)
        currentColor = originColorX;
    else if(i % 5)
        currentColor = largeGridColor;
    else
        currentColor = smallGridColor;

    pGridData[vertexCount].color = (DWORD)currentColor;
    pGridData[vertexCount].position = D3DXVECTOR3(-gridExtent, 0.0f, x);

    ++vertexCount;

    pGridData[vertexCount].color = (DWORD)currentColor;
    pGridData[vertexCount].position = D3DXVECTOR3(gridExtent, 0.0f, x);

    ++vertexCount;
}

// Fill in the y axis
for(int i = 0 ; i < 101 ; i+=2)
```

```
    {
        float y;

        y = (float)i - 50.0f;

        if(i == halfGrid)
            currentColor = originColorZ;
        else if(i % 5)
            currentColor = largeGridColor;
        else
            currentColor = smallGridColor;

        pGridData[vertexCount].color = (DWORD)currentColor;
        pGridData[vertexCount].position = D3DXVECTOR3(y, 0.0f, -gridExtent);

        ++vertexCount;

        pGridData[vertexCount].color = (DWORD)currentColor;
        pGridData[vertexCount].position = D3DXVECTOR3(y, 0.0f, gridExtent);

        ++vertexCount;
    }

    pGridData[vertexCount].color = originColorY;
    pGridData[vertexCount].position = D3DXVECTOR3(0.0f, -gridExtent, 0.0f);

    ++vertexCount;

    pGridData[vertexCount].color = originColorY;
    pGridData[vertexCount].position = D3DXVECTOR3(0.0f, gridExtent, 0.0f);

    m_pGridVB->Unlock();

    return true;
}
```

The rendering code should look familiar to you because it is almost identical to the code used to render visual resources in Chapter 3. Check it out:

```
indBool cGameEngine::RenderGrid()
{
    D3DXMATRIX worldMat;
    D3DXMatrixIdentity(&worldMat);
```

```
        GAMEENGINE->GetDevice()->SetStreamSource(0, m_pGridVB, 0, sizeof(GRID_VERTEX));

        VisualEffects::cEffect* pCurrentEffect = EFFECTMANAGER->GetEffect(m_GridEffectID);

        pCurrentEffect->SetTransforms(
            worldMat, CAMERA->GetViewMatrix(), CAMERA->GetProjectionMatrix());
        pCurrentEffect->Dispatch();

        indUInt numPasses = 0;
        pCurrentEffect->Begin(numPasses);

        GAMEENGINE->GetDevice()->SetFVF(GRID_VERTEXFORMAT);

        for(indUInt passCount = 0 ; passCount < numPasses ; passCount++)
        {
            pCurrentEffect->BeginPass(passCount);

            GAMEENGINE->GetDevice()->SetTexture(0, 0);
            m_pDevice->DrawPrimitive(D3DPT_LINELIST, 0, 103);

            pCurrentEffect->EndPass();
        }

        pCurrentEffect->End();

        GAMEENGINE->GetDevice()->SetTexture(0, 0);

        return true;
}
```

Conclusion

That's all the grunt work out of the way. We've covered a lot of stuff in this chapter to build a good framework to put the particle system on top of. Specifically, we discussed the following:

- Particle systems theory
- Coding for multithreading
- Billboarding
- Grid rendering

- Developing an efficient particle
- Blazingly fast particle processing and rendering
- Cache alignment issues
- Configuring particle systems with feature files
- Using macros to speed up feature additions
- Optimizations including cache lines, inline assembly, branching, arrays, fast `float` to `int` conversions, and much more

Check out the next chapter, where we will finalize an amazing particle system to woo your players with.

CHAPTER 5

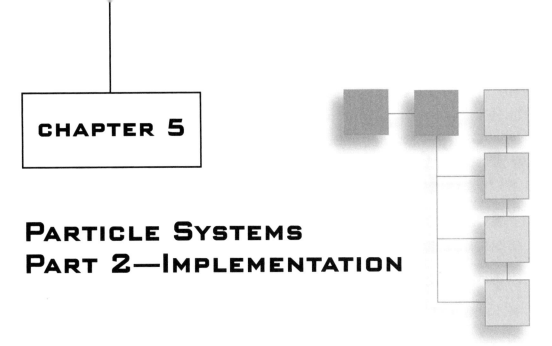

PARTICLE SYSTEMS
PART 2—IMPLEMENTATION

Continuing from the foundation built in the previous chapter, this chapter proceeds to show you how to implement an actual particle system from the ground up. You'll learn all the practicalities of implementing a particle system, including these:

- The physics of particles
- Emitters
- Controlling the emission rate of particles
- What to do at the end of a particle's life
- Grouping particles into a system
- Grouping particle systems under a manager
- Instantiating multiple systems from a particle system library

And, of course, we'll cover much more than that. Let's start at the bottom with a humble particle and work our way up.

The cParticle Class

The `cParticle` class is designed to represent a single particle in a particle system. Thinking about everything in Chapter 4, we want our particle to have the following characteristics:

- Have a minimum amount of data to keep down memory requirements
- Be as efficient as humanly (or cyberly) possible
- Be cache aligned
- Have a lifespan defined in milliseconds
- Know how far through its life it is
- Have a start size, a finish size, and a current size that is in some way interpolated between these two values
- Have mass so that it is affected by gravity
- Be able to record when it has reached the end of its life and has died
- Have a current position where it can be rendered
- Have a velocity that affects the position over time
- Have an acceleration that affects the velocity over time
- Have a start and end color and a current color that is interpolated between the two values

As you will soon discover, a particle is a pretty limited object. It only tracks its current state; that is, it only remembers its own properties and not anything to do with other particles in the system. The real magic happens in the actual particle system, which handles the majority of the computation. We want the particle to be as lightweight as possible because it will be duplicated so many times. Look at this code, which shows the particle members:

```
class cParticle
{
    .
    .
    .
```

```
// Other code
.
.
.
protected:

D3DXCOLOR m_StartColor;              // 16
D3DXCOLOR m_EndColor;                // 16
D3DXCOLOR m_CurrentColor;            // 16

D3DXVECTOR3 m_Position;              // 12
D3DXVECTOR3 m_Velocity;              // 12
D3DXVECTOR3 m_Acceleration;          // 12

indReal32 m_LifeTimeElapsed;         // 4
indReal32 m_LifeSpan;                // 4

indReal32 m_SizeStart;               // 4
indReal32 m_SizeEnd;                 // 4
indReal32 m_CurrentSize;             // 4

indReal32 m_Mass;                    // 4
                                     // ---
                                     // 108    // 4 byte aligned

//BYTE padding[x];                   // Not needed, as particle is 4 byte aligned
};
```

It's a pretty lightweight class; it really only contains members describing its appearance and behavior. Let's look at these in a little more detail.

- **m_StartColor**—The color that the particle will be when it is created
- **m_EndColor**—The color of the particle when it reaches the end of its life
- **m_CurrentColor**—The current interpolated color of the particle
- **m_Position**—The current position of the particle
- **m_Velocity**—The velocity of the particle, which is added to the position on every update

- **m_Acceleration**—The acceleration of the particle, which is added to the velocity on every update

- **m_LifeTimeElapsed**—The number of milliseconds elapsed since this particle was created

- **m_LifeSpan**—The amount of time that this particle will live for

- **m_SizeStart**—The size of the particle when it is created

- **m_SizeEnd**—The size of the particle when it dies

- **m_CurrentSize**—The current interpolated size of the particle

- **m_Mass**—The mass of the particle, or how much it is influenced by gravity

This is the entire particle class with all the property setting functions included:

```
CACHE_ALIGN class cParticle
{
public:
    cParticle(cParticleSystem* pParent);
    cParticle();
    ~cParticle(void);

    indBool Shutdown();

    inline void Run(indReal32 lastFrameDuration, indReal32 delta);

    inline indReal32 Interpolate(indReal32 value1, indReal32 value2, indReal32 percent)
    {
        //return value1 + (percent * (value2 - value1));
        __asm
        {
            fld  dword ptr[value2];
            fsub dword ptr[value1];
            fmul dword ptr[percent];
            fadd dword ptr[value1];
        }
    }
```

```cpp
    inline void SetPosition(D3DXVECTOR3& newPos)
    {
        m_Position = newPos;
    }

    inline void SetVelocity(D3DXVECTOR3& newVel)
    {
        m_Velocity = newVel;
    }

    inline void SetAcceleration(D3DXVECTOR3& newAcc)
    {
        m_Acceleration = newAcc;
    }

    inline indBool IsDead()
    {
        return (indBool)(m_LifeTimeElapsed > m_LifeSpan);
    }

    inline void SetDead(indBool bDead)
    {
        if(!bDead)
        {
            m_LifeTimeElapsed = 0.0f;
        }
        else
        {
            m_LifeTimeElapsed = m_LifeSpan + 0.1f;
        }
    }

    inline void SetLifeSpan(indReal32 milliseconds)
    {
        m_LifeTimeElapsed = 0.0f;
        m_LifeSpan = milliseconds;
    }

    inline void Start()
    {
        // Add any initialization code here
    }
```

Chapter 5 ■ Particle Systems Part 2—Implementation

```cpp
        inline D3DXVECTOR3 GetPosition()
        {
            return m_Position;
        }

        inline D3DXCOLOR& GetColor()
        {
            return m_CurrentColor;
        }

        inline indReal32 GetSize()
        {
            return m_CurrentSize;
        }

        inline void SetSize(indReal32 newSizeStart, indReal32 newSizeEnd)
        {
            m_SizeStart = newSizeStart;
            m_CurrentSize = newSizeStart;
            m_SizeEnd = newSizeEnd;
        }

        inline void SetStartColor(D3DXCOLOR& newColor)
        {
            m_StartColor = newColor;
            m_CurrentColor = m_StartColor;
        }

        inline void SetEndColor(D3DXCOLOR& newColor)
        {
            m_EndColor = newColor;
        }

        inline void SetMass(indReal32 newMass)
        {
            m_Mass = newMass;
        }

    protected:

        D3DXCOLOR m_StartColor;                 // 16
        D3DXCOLOR m_EndColor;                   // 16
        D3DXCOLOR m_CurrentColor;               // 16
```

The cParticle Class

```
D3DXVECTOR3 m_Position;              // 12
D3DXVECTOR3 m_Velocity;              // 12
D3DXVECTOR3 m_Acceleration;          // 12

indReal32 m_LifeTimeElapsed;         // 4
indReal32 m_LifeSpan;                // 4

indReal32 m_SizeStart;               // 4
indReal32 m_SizeEnd;                 // 4
indReal32 m_CurrentSize;             // 4

indReal32 m_Mass;                    // 4
                                     // ---
                                     // 108         // 4 byte aligned

//BYTE padding[x];                   // Not needed, as particle is 4 byte
                                     // aligned.

}; // end class
```

As you can see, there is nothing too complicated about this class yet. Let's look at how some of the properties are updated.

Updating the Particle

The updating code of the particle needs to be extremely efficient because it is so repetitive. Whatever can be updated less than every update should be removed and executed in the particle system code, rather than duplicated in the cParticle class. The particle update code is responsible for updating the properties of the particle that change with time. At rendering time, each particle updates its properties before they are read back to produce a big vertex buffer to blast to the screen.

Check out the code:

```
inline void cParticle::Run(indReal32 lastFrameDuration, indReal32 delta)
{
    static indReal32 fractionSecond;
    static indReal32 percentComplete;
    static indReal32 tempDelta;

    m_LifeTimeElapsed += lastFrameDuration;
    percentComplete = NO_DIV_0(m_LifeTimeElapsed) / NO_DIV_0(m_LifeSpan);
```

```
    fractionSecond = NO_DIV_0(lastFrameDuration) / 1000.0f;
    m_Acceleration.y += g_Gravity * (fractionSecond * fractionSecond) * m_Mass;

    m_CurrentSize = Interpolate(m_SizeStart, m_SizeEnd, percentComplete);

    m_CurrentColor.r = Interpolate(m_StartColor.r, m_EndColor.r, percentComplete);
    m_CurrentColor.g = Interpolate(m_StartColor.g, m_EndColor.g, percentComplete);
    m_CurrentColor.b = Interpolate(m_StartColor.b, m_EndColor.b, percentComplete);
    m_CurrentColor.a = Interpolate(m_StartColor.a, m_EndColor.a, percentComplete);

    tempDelta = NO_DIV_0(delta);

    m_Velocity.x += NO_DIV_0(m_Acceleration.x) / tempDelta;
    m_Velocity.y += NO_DIV_0(m_Acceleration.y) / tempDelta;
    m_Velocity.z += NO_DIV_0(m_Acceleration.z) / tempDelta;

    m_Position.x += NO_DIV_0(m_Velocity.x) / tempDelta;
    m_Position.y += NO_DIV_0(m_Velocity.y) / tempDelta;
    m_Position.z += NO_DIV_0(m_Velocity.z) / tempDelta;

}
```

The function starts with a bunch of static variable declarations. This function is going to be called a lot, so declaring variables on the fly would waste a lot of time. Declare them static, and the CPU will know they are in the same piece of memory for every execution. This means it is far more likely the data will be cached, leading to a big performance improvement.

Then the function moves on to figure out how far through its life the particle is, which it calculates by dividing the elapsed time by the life span of the particle. Notice the NO_DIV_0 tags around the functions. As I discussed earlier, branching is incredibly slow. Therefore, the following code would be incredibly slow to have in this function:

```
if(m_LifeTimeElapsed != 0 && m_LifeSpan != 0)
    percentComplete = NO_DIV_0(m_LifeTimeElapsed) / NO_DIV_0(m_LifeSpan);
```

That adds in two compares, an AND, and a branch, all to make sure a division by zero does not occur. Because there are divides all over this function, the performance penalty would not be acceptable. The accuracy doesn't matter much for particle systems, so we can add a tiny number to the value to force it to almost never be 0 with this macro:

```
const indReal32 indReal32_DIV0_DELTA = 0.000001f;
#define NO_DIV_0(x) (x + indReal32_DIV0_DELTA)
```

A float is accurate to about six decimal places, so 0.000001f is the smallest possible value that can be added to the original. For larger values, the addition will simply round to 0.0f and will not have an impact because there is not enough floating point resolution to include it. The rest of the function continues in a similar way updating each of the member variables.

The only other code in this class is housekeeping code:

```
cParticle::cParticle()
{
    m_Position = D3DXVECTOR3(0,0,0);
    m_Velocity = D3DXVECTOR3(0,0,0);
    m_Acceleration = D3DXVECTOR3(0,0,0);

    m_LifeSpan = 1000.0f;
    m_LifeTimeElapsed = m_LifeSpan + 0.1f; // Start off dead

    m_Mass = 0.0f;
    m_SizeStart = 1.0f;
    m_SizeEnd = 1.0f;
    m_CurrentSize = m_SizeStart;

    m_StartColor = D3DXCOLOR(1,1,1,1);
    m_EndColor = D3DXCOLOR(0,0,1,1);
    m_CurrentColor = m_StartColor;


}

cParticle::~cParticle(void)
{
    Shutdown();
}

indBool cParticle::Shutdown()
{
    return true;
}
```

A Particle System

A particle system contains all the brains to look after the creation, termination, rendering, and resetting of particles. The base of a particle system is simply a collection of particles. However, there are many things to take into consideration when creating a particle system, the most important of which is *external design.*

The most obvious way to create some new particle system might be to create a general particle system class and then inherit all the new, more advanced particle systems from this base class, with each more advanced system implementing its own storage and rendering code. Much as this sounds like the right idea, it is wrong, as I discovered the hard way a few years ago. Particle systems are great to play with, but it's highly unlikely that you, the programmer, are going to be implementing the actual particle systems used in the game if you work in a commercial company.

That's because, as we all know, artists, designers, and art managers can never be satisfied. They constantly want little additions here, a little color tweak there, a new texture here, a little more movement there, and so on *ad nauseam.* If you implement your particle system in code, you are letting yourself in for eternal pain and damnation because the unending art requests will never, *ever*, stop. Wouldn't it be easier if you could just tell the artists, "If you don't like it, fix it yourself? I'm not going to sit here and constantly recompile the code just because you can't make up your mind!" The solution is to make your particle system *configurable.*

The key to any advanced particle system is to have each system described in an external text file that can be edited on the fly and that designers can read. In fact, an even better implementation is to have the system be able to load in the new particle system files while the game is running. So if a designer wants to change the color of a particle, he can do it and immediately see the results onscreen!

That is exactly what our particle system is going to do, and it is a lot easier than it sounds to implement. Check out the particle system file in Figure 5.1, which is one that is actually used for the system in this game engine. I call these files *particle system feature files* because they include all the features of your particle system that the designers can customize.

Don't worry about what all that means just yet. Just bask in the glory that by the end of this chapter, you will have an incredible particle system that can be contained within a single text file!

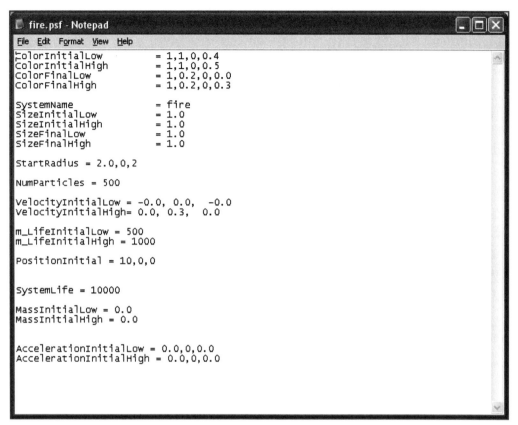

Figure 5.1
A feature file in Notepad.

Feature Files

The problem with feature files is that they require an awful lot of code in an awful lot of places, and adding new features can be a pain. Here's why:

- A function needs to be written to parse the feature files. This means there needs to be a function to handle every command in the feature file.

- There needs to be a function definition for every feature command in the class header file.

- There needs to be a function actually written in the implementation file to parse the particular feature command.

- There needs to be a table of commands containing all the particle feature commands that the command parser can read from.

- There needs to be a member variable to hold the value set by every feature.

That's five places that code needs to be duplicated for every command! Obviously, we need to do what we can to minimize the amount of code that is duplicated to reduce the chance of errors getting in.

The Bigger Picture

Before we get bogged down in the implementation of parsing feature files, let's take a case study of a single variable to watch the process. Let's use a nice simple one like a command to specify the number of particles in the system. Let's call this command NumParticles and have it act as an integer. We add the command to our feature file in Figure 5.2.

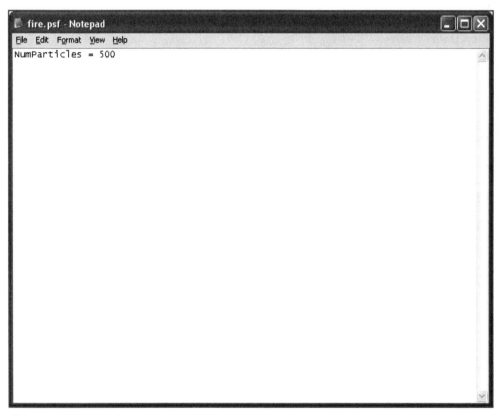

Figure 5.2
The new NumParticles command.

A Particle System

Now we need to parse this command. We'd better build a table of commands that we are going to have in the particle feature file:

```
// In the class definition
.
.
.
struct featureList
{
    const TCHAR*    feature;
        indBool     (cParticleSystem::*featureHandler)(const indChar* parameters);
};
.
.
.
const indUInt MAX_FEATURES = 100;
.
.
.
static featureList m_sFeatureList[MAX_FEATURES];
.
.
.
// In the class implementation
featureList cParticleSystem::m_sFeatureList[MAX_FEATURES] = {
{
    // Feature command string, feature parses
    { NumParicles,       &cParticleSystem::FeatureHandler_NumParticles},
    {0,          0}};
}
```

See how it works? A static member structure is declared that contains a string and a function pointer. The string contains the feature name, such as "NumParticles", and the function contains a pointer to the function that handles the parsing of that command. So all the parsing function has to do is read the current command and then compare it to each one in the structure. When it finds a match, it fires off the function to parse that particular command. Simple? Simple. Let's look at the parsing function now:

```
bool cParticleSystem::ParseFeatureFile(const indChar* featureFile)
{
    FILE* pFile = fopen(featureFile, "r");
```

```
if(!pFile)
{
    OutputDebugString("ERROR opening particle system feature file\n");
    assert(0);
    return false;
}

indChar inputString[512];
while(fgets(inputString, 512, pFile))
{
    indUInt count = 0;
    while(m_sFeatureList[count].feature != 0)
    {
        // See if the feature matches the current one in the structure.
        indChar* pFeature = strstr(inputString, m_sFeatureList[count].feature);

        if(pFeature)
        {
            indChar* pParameters = (strchr(pFeature, '='));
            if(!pParameters)
                assert(0); // Invalid file structure

            pParameters++;

            bool bSuccess = (this->*m_sFeatureList[count].featureHandler)
(pParameters);
            if(!bSuccess)
                assert(0);   // feature execute failed

            break;
        }

        count++;
    }
}

fclose(pFile);
pFile = 0;

for(indUInt i = 0 ; i < m_NumParticles ; i++)
{
```

```
        m_pParticleArray[i].Start();
        ResetParticle(m_pParticleArray[i]);
    }

    return false;
}
```

I've bolded the important lines. Basically, this function just reads the current line and checks whether it matches command help in the particle table. If it finds a match, it fires off the parsing command for that command. Incidentally, the reason we need a separate parser for each command is because each command could have wildly different data. One might contain one float, the next a series of three ints, the next a string. There would be no point trying to put it all in one function, because it would be a little unwieldy. The command parser for "NumParticles" looks like this:

```
// In the header file
.
.
.
indBool FeatureHandler_NumParticles(const TCHAR* featureParams);
.
.
.
// Implementation
indBool cParticleSystem::FeatureHandler_NumParticles(const TCHAR* featureParams)
{
    indUInt inputValue;
    int result = sscanf(featureParams, "%i", &inputValue);
    if(result == EOF)
        return false;
    m_NumParticles = inputValue;
}
```

Now you've seen the journey that the data goes through from a particle feature file to the actual variable that controls it. If you're thinking that is a whole lot of code to add for each particle feature command, you're right. You probably also realized that each handler is doing almost the same thing, just with different forms of data. We can make this a lot more elegant with some good use of macros. The next section shows how to make the feature system more elegant.

A More Elegant Configurable Particle System

Adding all that code to all those different places is a bit of a nightmare. Let's see how we can tidy it up. First up is the feature handler definition in the class definition, which until now has looked like this:

```
indBool FeatureHandler_NumParticles(const TCHAR* featureParams);
```

We shouldn't have to write all that for every feature we want to parse. A little macro like this makes it a lot more readable:

```
#define FEATURE_HANDLER(x) indBool FeatureHandler_##x(const TCHAR* featureParams);
```

This macro takes any identifier as an argument and creates a function declaration for you. The ## identifier tells the preprocessor to include the identifier as part of the code. This is opposed to the single #, which tells the preprocessor to convert the identifier to a string. Now you can add handlers to the header file much more cleanly:

```
FEATURE_HANDLER(SystemName);
FEATURE_HANDLER(SizeInitialLow);
FEATURE_HANDLER(SizeInitialHigh);
FEATURE_HANDLER(SizeFinalLow);
FEATURE_HANDLER(SizeFinalHigh);
FEATURE_HANDLER(ColorInitialLow);
FEATURE_HANDLER(ColorInitialHigh);
FEATURE_HANDLER(ColorFinalLow);
FEATURE_HANDLER(ColorFinalHigh);
FEATURE_HANDLER(MassInitialLow);
FEATURE_HANDLER(MassInitialHigh);
FEATURE_HANDLER(LifeInitialLow);
FEATURE_HANDLER(LifeInitialHigh);
FEATURE_HANDLER(VelocityInitialLow);
FEATURE_HANDLER(VelocityInitialHigh);
FEATURE_HANDLER(AccelerationInitialLow);
FEATURE_HANDLER(AccelerationInitialHigh);
FEATURE_HANDLER(PositionInitial);
FEATURE_HANDLER(NumParticles);
FEATURE_HANDLER(StartRadius);
FEATURE_HANDLER(SystemLife);
FEATURE_HANDLER(EmitRate);
```

I think you'll agree that is a lot cleaner. Next up to fix is that awful table used to hold the commands and parse function pointers. Up until now, it has looked like this:

```
featureList cParticleSystem::m_sFeatureList[MAX_FEATURES] = {
{
    // Feature command string, feature parses
    { NumParicles,    &cParticleSystem::FeatureHandler_NumParticles},
    { FeatureName,    &cParticleSystem::FeatureHandler_FeatureHandler},
    { FeatureName,    &cParticleSystem::FeatureHandler_FeatureHandler},
    { FeatureName,    &cParticleSystem::FeatureHandler_FeatureHandler},
    { FeatureName,    &cParticleSystem::FeatureHandler_FeatureHandler},
    { FeatureName,    &cParticleSystem::FeatureHandler_FeatureHandler},
    {0,        0}};
}
```

That's a bit horrible. A few additional macros can clean it up a lot:

```
#define BEGIN_FEATURE_DECLARATION \
        featureList cParticleSystem::m_sFeatureList[MAX_FEATURES] = {
#define FEATURE_DECLARE(x) { #x,    &cParticleSystem::FeatureHandler_##x}
#define END_FEATURE_DECLARATION ,{ 0,0}};
```

This allows us to add features much more cleanly:

```
BEGIN_FEATURE_DECLARATION

    FEATURE_DECLARE(SystemName),
    FEATURE_DECLARE(SizeInitialLow),
    FEATURE_DECLARE(SizeInitialHigh),
    FEATURE_DECLARE(SizeFinalLow),
    FEATURE_DECLARE(SizeFinalHigh),
    FEATURE_DECLARE(ColorInitialLow),
    FEATURE_DECLARE(ColorInitialHigh),
    FEATURE_DECLARE(ColorFinalLow),
    FEATURE_DECLARE(ColorFinalHigh),
    FEATURE_DECLARE(LifeInitialLow),
    FEATURE_DECLARE(LifeInitialHigh),
    FEATURE_DECLARE(MassInitialLow),
    FEATURE_DECLARE(MassInitialHigh),
    FEATURE_DECLARE(VelocityInitialLow),
    FEATURE_DECLARE(VelocityInitialHigh),
    FEATURE_DECLARE(AccelerationInitialLow),
    FEATURE_DECLARE(AccelerationInitialHigh),
```

```
        FEATURE_DECLARE(PositionInitial),
        FEATURE_DECLARE(NumParticles),
        FEATURE_DECLARE(StartRadius),
        FEATURE_DECLARE(SystemLife),
        FEATURE_DECLARE(EmitRate)

END_FEATURE_DECLARATION
```

Now we just need to take care of the implementation parser. As you saw before, a typical implementation parser looks like this:

```
indBool cParticleSystem::FeatureHandler_NumParticles(const TCHAR* featureParams)
{
        indUInt inputValue;
        int result = sscanf(featureParams, "%i", &inputValue);
        if(result == EOF)
                return false;
        m_NumParticles = inputValue;
}
```

Although it's small, we don't want to have to duplicate all this code every time we add a new feature. Check out these macros:

```
#define SCAN_FEATURE_UINT1(y)                           \
                                                        \
        indUInt inputValue;                             \
        int result = sscanf(featureParams, "%i", &inputValue);  \
    if(result == EOF)                                   \
        return false;                                   \
    y = inputValue;                                     \
        return true;

#define SCAN_FEATURE_FLOAT1(y)                          \
                                \
indReal32 inputValue;                           \
int result = sscanf(featureParams, "%f", &inputValue);  \
if(result == EOF)                               \
    return false;                               \
y = inputValue;                                 \
return true;

#define SCAN_FEATURE_STRING(y)                          \
                                \
indChar inputString[MAX_PATH];                          \
```

```
int result = sscanf(featureParams, "%s", &inputString);    \
if(result == EOF)                                          \
    return false;                                          \
strcpy(y, inputString);                                    \
return true;

#define SCAN_FEATURE_RGBA(y)                                        \
                                                                    \
indReal32 r, g, b, a;                                               \
int result = sscanf(featureParams, "%f, %f, %f, %f", &r, &g, &b, &a);  \
if(result == EOF)                                                   \
    return false;                                                   \
y.r = r; y.g = g; y.b = b; y.a = a;                                 \
return true;

#define SCAN_FEATURE_VECTOR3(a)                              \
                                                             \
indReal32 x1, y1, z1;                                        \
int result = sscanf(featureParams, "%f, %f, %f", &x1, &y1, &z1);\
if(result == EOF)                                            \
    return false;                                            \
a.x = x1; a.y = y1; a.z = z1;                                \
return true;
```

Using these macros, it's now exceedingly simple to add a feature parser to the implementation file. Check these out:

```
FEATURE_IMPLEMENT(SystemName)

    SCAN_FEATURE_STRING(m_SystemName)

END_FEATURE

FEATURE_IMPLEMENT(SizeInitialLow)

    SCAN_FEATURE_FLOAT1(m_SizeInitialLow);

END_FEATURE

FEATURE_IMPLEMENT(SizeInitialHigh)

    SCAN_FEATURE_FLOAT1(m_SizeInitialHigh);

END_FEATURE
```

It is now incredibly simple to add new features to your particle system file. As an example, let's look at adding a new command handler to set the system name so that you can tell the various particle systems apart when debugging. Just do the following:

1. Add a member variable to the header file and initialize it in the constructor if you want:

   ```
   indChar m_SystemName[MAX_PATH];
   ```

2. Add a declaration to the class definition:

   ```
   FEATURE_HANDLER(SystemName);
   ```

3. Add a new handler declaration to the structure:

   ```
   FEATURE_DECLARE(SystemName),
   ```

4. Add a parser function to the implementation file:

   ```
   FEATURE_IMPLEMENT(SystemName)
        SCAN_FEATURE_STRING(m_SystemName)
   END_FEATURE
   ```

I think you'll agree that's pretty slick! For every feature you want to add, there are only six lines of code thanks to the macros. This makes extending your particle system easy. Think of a new feature, add it, and have it working in seconds!

The Functions of a Particle System

Okay, now let's get down to the actual details of running a particle system. A particle system needs to look after a number of situations, including these:

- **Creation**—When the system is created initially, it needs to create all its particle children and initialize them to default states.

- **Execution**—Every time the system is updated, it needs to update each of the particle's positions. Dead particles need to be removed, and new ones created.

- **Rendering**—All the settings looked after by the particles need to be turned into something useful, packaged into a vertex buffer, and fired off to the graphics card for rendering.

- **Shutdown**—All the particles and other resources need to be terminated.

I'll go through each of these areas in turn to give you a good understanding of how it all works.

Storing Particles

Let's start by looking at how particles are stored. You might think, "Hey, particles have random, finite lives; they need to be killed and created regularly. This sounds like the perfect data set for a linked list!" That thinking is downright wrong! If you think about it, what is a linked list? It's a collection of objects in various locations in memory that contain pointers showing how to find the next item in the list. Translated into English, a linked list is incredibly inefficient, cannot be cached, and reduces your particle system to the speed of a tortoise on valium. Because each new particle is linked to some disparate and remote region of memory, the CPU doesn't have a chance of caching them, and has to rely on the slow, high-latency memory bus to get the data. Every particle will involve an L1 cache miss, an L2 cache miss, a stall, and probably a flush before the CPU gets the data. Then it has to do it all over again for the next particle. The solution is to have all the particles right beside each other in memory. Then the CPU can cache all the particles and zip through them at the speed of light. The particles are stored in the cParticleSystem class like this:

```
CACHE_ALIGN cParticle* m_pParticleArray;
```

When the particle system reads in how many particles there will be from the feature file, it allocates all the memory for the particles in one big chunk like this:

```
FEATURE_IMPLEMENT(NumParticles)

    SCAN_FEATURE_UINT1_EXTRA(m_NumParticles);

    if(m_pParticleArray)
    {
        delete[] m_pParticleArray;
    }

    m_pParticleArray = new cParticle[m_NumParticles];
    if(!m_pParticleArray)
    {
        assert(0);
    }
```

```
    return true;
```

END_FEATURE

Make sense? Cool. Now let's see how this puppy works.

Particle Creation

The `cParticleSystem` is started with a call to the `cParticleSystem::Start()` function. This function should be called after the system has parsed a feature file. The function is responsible for setting all the initial values of the system and allocating any resources, such as vertex buffers, that are needed to run. Check out the code:

```
bool cParticleSystem::Start()
{
    QueryPerformanceCounter((LARGE_INTEGER*)&m_LastParticleEmitTime);
    HRESULT hr = D3DXCreateTextureFromFileEx(
            GAMEENGINE->GetDevice(), "media\\particle_blob.tga",
        D3DX_DEFAULT, D3DX_DEFAULT,
        D3DX_DEFAULT, 0, D3DFMT_FROM_FILE, D3DPOOL_MANAGED, D3DTEXF_LINEAR,
        D3DTEXF_LINEAR, 0, 0, 0, &m_pTexture);
    if(FAILED(hr))
    {
        assert(0);
        return false;
    }

    indUInt length = sizeof(PARTICLE_VERTEX) * m_NumParticles * 6;

    GAMEENGINE->GetDevice()->CreateVertexBuffer(
    length, D3DUSAGE_WRITEONLY,
        PARTICLE_VERTEXFORMAT,
        D3DPOOL_MANAGED, &m_pSystemVertexBuffer, 0);

    m_EffectID = EFFECTMANAGER->FindEffect("default_particle.fx");

    return true;
}
```

Notice that the function starts by getting the frequency of the CPU clock for timing. Then the function loads its default texture, which you can change if you like, or add a feature to specify it. After that, the function creates the actual vertex buffer, which will be used for rendering. The size of the vertex buffer is calculated as the size of the particle vertex (more on that in a moment) multiplied by the number of particles, by six. This is because there are size vertices per vertex (that is, for the two triangles). Finally, the default particle effect is loaded. You can change this, too. In fact, I'm sure if you extend the system you might have individual effect files for each type of particle system.

Incidentally, the particle vertex FVF used for rendering is this:

```
struct PARTICLE_VERTEX
{
    D3DXVECTOR3 position;
    DWORD color;
    indReal32 tx, ty;
};
const DWORD PARTICLE_VERTEXFORMAT =
        D3DFVF_XYZ | D3DFVF_DIFFUSE | D3DFVF_TEX1;
```

As you can see, it's a simple vertex with just the particle position, color, and texture coordinates specified.

Particle System Execution

Execution of the particle system occurs once per frame. During this time a number of things must happen. First, all the data for each particle has to be updated. Secondly the data for each particle needs to be molded into a vertex buffer, and finally the vertex buffer needs to be sent to the graphics card for rendering. Let's look at this code now, which is handled by cParticleSystem::Run().

```
bool cParticleSystem::Run()
{
    indInt64 currentCount = 0;
    indInt64 freq = 0;

    QueryPerformanceFrequency((LARGE_INTEGER*)&freq);
    QueryPerformanceCounter((LARGE_INTEGER*)&currentCount);

    UpdatePosition();

    PARTICLE_VERTEX* pVertices = 0;
    m_pSystemVertexBuffer->Lock(0, 0, (void**)&pVertices, 0);
    indUInt currentVertex = 0;
```

```
indReal32 lastframeDur = GAMEENGINE->GetLastFrameDurationMS();
indReal32 delta = GAMEENGINE->GetTimeDelta();

D3DXVECTOR3 particlePos(0,0,0);
D3DXVECTOR3 camPos(0,0,0);
D3DXVECTOR3 upVec(0,1,0);
D3DXVECTOR3 rightVec(1,0,0);
D3DXVECTOR3 camToParticleVec(0,0,0);
D3DXVECTOR3 leftSide, rightSide;
D3DCOLOR curParticleColor;

indReal32 particleSize = 0;

for(int i = m_NumParticles-1 ; i > -1 ; --i)
{
    if(m_pParticleArray[i].IsDead())
    {
        float millisecondsPerParticle = 1000.0f / m_EmitRate;

        double timeDiff = (double)((long double)currentCount -
                    (long double)m_LastParticleEmitTime) /
                (long double)freq;

        if((float)(timeDiff*1000.0) >= millisecondsPerParticle)
        {
            ResetParticle(m_pParticleArray[i]);
            QueryPerformanceCounter(
                (LARGE_INTEGER*)&m_LastParticleEmitTime);
        }

        continue;
    }

    m_pParticleArray[i].Run(lastframeDur, delta);

        curParticleColor =
            ConvertD3DXCOLORToD3DCOLORFast(m_pParticleArray[i].
            GetColor());
    m_PositionInitial = m_EmitterPosition;
    // Billboard the particles so they always face the camera
        particlePos = m_pParticleArray[i].GetPosition();
    camPos = CAMERA->GetPosition();
```

```cpp
camToParticleVec = m_PositionInitial - camPos;
D3DXVec3Normalize(&camToParticleVec, &camToParticleVec);
D3DXVec3Cross(&rightVec, &camToParticleVec, &upVec);
D3DXVec3Normalize(&rightVec, &rightVec);

particleSize = m_pParticleArray[i].GetSize();
rightVec *= particleSize;

leftSide  = (particlePos - rightVec);
rightSide = (particlePos + rightVec);

// Fill in the vertex buffer
pVertices[currentVertex].position.x = leftSide.x;
pVertices[currentVertex].position.y = leftSide.y + particleSize;
pVertices[currentVertex].position.z = leftSide.z;
pVertices[currentVertex].color = curParticleColor;
pVertices[currentVertex].tx = 0.0f;
pVertices[currentVertex].ty = 0.0f;

currentVertex++;

pVertices[currentVertex].position.x = rightSide.x;
pVertices[currentVertex].position.y = rightSide.y + particleSize;
pVertices[currentVertex].position.z = rightSide.z;
pVertices[currentVertex].color = curParticleColor;
pVertices[currentVertex].tx = 1.0f;
pVertices[currentVertex].ty = 0.0f;

currentVertex++;

pVertices[currentVertex].position.x = rightSide.x;
pVertices[currentVertex].position.y = rightSide.y - particleSize;
pVertices[currentVertex].position.z = rightSide.z;
pVertices[currentVertex].color = curParticleColor;
pVertices[currentVertex].tx = 1.0f;
pVertices[currentVertex].ty = 1.0f;

currentVertex++;

pVertices[currentVertex].position.x = rightSide.x;
pVertices[currentVertex].position.y = rightSide.y - particleSize;
pVertices[currentVertex].position.z = rightSide.z;
```

```
            pVertices[currentVertex].color = curParticleColor;
            pVertices[currentVertex].tx = 1.0f;
            pVertices[currentVertex].ty = 1.0f;

            currentVertex++;

            pVertices[currentVertex].position.x = leftSide.x;
            pVertices[currentVertex].position.y = leftSide.y - particleSize;
            pVertices[currentVertex].position.z = leftSide.z;
            pVertices[currentVertex].color = curParticleColor;
            pVertices[currentVertex].tx = 0.0f;
            pVertices[currentVertex].ty = 1.0f;

            currentVertex++;

            pVertices[currentVertex].position.x = leftSide.x;
            pVertices[currentVertex].position.y = leftSide.y + particleSize;
            pVertices[currentVertex].position.z = leftSide.z;
            pVertices[currentVertex].color = curParticleColor;
            pVertices[currentVertex].tx = 0.0f;
            pVertices[currentVertex].ty = 0.0f;

            currentVertex++;
        }

        m_pSystemVertexBuffer->Unlock();

        Render();

        return true;
    }
```

The function starts by getting the frequency and current count for the CPU counters. This works out the emission rate (more on this soon). Then the UpdatePosition() function is called. This is a virtual function that you can plug with any code you want but for now doesn't do anything. It is for moving the emitter location, which is where new particles are created.

The function then goes on to lock the entire vertex buffer, because we will be overwriting all of it. Then a lot of variables are declared, which are mostly used for billboarding the particles. After that, we enter a loop that goes through every particle. The loop starts with this code, which controls the emission rate:

```
for(int i = m_NumParticles-1 ; i > -1 ; --i)
{
    if(m_pParticleArray[i].IsDead())
    {
        float millisecondsPerParticle = 1000.0f / m_EmitRate;

        double timeDiff = (double)((long double)currentCount -
                    (long double)m_LastParticleEmitTime) / (long double)freq;

        if((float)(timeDiff*1000.0) >= millisecondsPerParticle)
        {
            ResetParticle(m_pParticleArray[i]);

                    QueryPerformanceCounter((LARGE_INTEGER*)&m_LastParti-
                cleEmitTime);
        }

        continue;
    }
```
.
.
.

The first thing to notice is the way the loop is laid out. Loops actually execute slightly faster with decrements, hence the backward loop. Also notice the --i. Amazingly, this is faster than i--. It's not a massive speedup, but every little bit helps!

Anyway... back to the loop, which starts by checking whether the particle is dead. This part of the code emits a new particle only if enough time has passed since the last particle was emitted. Otherwise, you get this annoying pulsing effect in which all your particles are created at the same time. If not enough time has passed, the loop is moved to the next particle, which continues until enough time has passed to emit a new particle. The cool thing is that no time is wasted if not enough time has passed—the system just carries on processing the existing particles in the meantime. Notice the ResetParticle() call, which has been bolded. This is a heavy-duty function that we'll be looking at shortly. It has a lot of code for setting up new particles properly.

Next up, the code runs the current particle so that it can update its internal states:

```
m_pParticleArray[i].Run(lastframeDur, delta);
```

It passes in the time it took the previous frame to execute, and how off the frame rate is from what we want it to be. This is so that the particle doesn't have to calculate this stuff itself, and so that the particle knows to run at the correct speed.

Now we need to extract the particle's color and convert it from a D3DXCOLOR, which is four floats, to a D3DCOLOR, which is a single DWORD. Remember that this uses the incredibly slow _ftol microcode by default. We want to override this with our own implementation, which is much faster:

```
curParticleColor = ConvertD3DXCOLORToD3DCOLORFast(m_pParticleArray[i].GetColor());
```

Next, the code moves on to billboard the particles so that they are always facing the camera. Sometimes you might want to avoid this behavior, such as for high stratus clouds that you might want to face downward. Just stick in a new feature command that modifies this code for the behavior you want:

```
particlePos = m_pParticleArray[i].GetPosition();
camPos = CAMERA->GetPosition();

camToParticleVec = m_PositionInitial - camPos;
D3DXVec3Normalize(&camToParticleVec, &camToParticleVec);
D3DXVec3Cross(&rightVec, &camToParticleVec, &upVec);
D3DXVec3Normalize(&rightVec, &rightVec);

particleSize = m_pParticleArray[i].GetSize();
rightVec *= particleSize;

leftSide  = (particlePos - rightVec);
rightSide = (particlePos + rightVec);
```

And that's about it! All that's left is to chuck the particle's quads into the vertex buffer, unlock the buffer, and render it!

```
            pVertices[currentVertex].position.x = leftSide.x;
            pVertices[currentVertex].position.y = leftSide.y + particleSize;
            pVertices[currentVertex].position.z = leftSide.z;
            pVertices[currentVertex].color = curParticleColor;
            pVertices[currentVertex].tx = 0.0f;
            pVertices[currentVertex].ty = 0.0f;

            currentVertex++;
```

```
        pVertices[currentVertex].position.x = rightSide.x;
        pVertices[currentVertex].position.y = rightSide.y + particleSize;
pVertices[currentVertex].position.z = rightSide.z;
pVertices[currentVertex].color = curParticleColor;
pVertices[currentVertex].tx = 1.0f;
pVertices[currentVertex].ty = 0.0f;

currentVertex++;

pVertices[currentVertex].position.x = rightSide.x;
pVertices[currentVertex].position.y = rightSide.y - particleSize;
pVertices[currentVertex].position.z = rightSide.z;
pVertices[currentVertex].color = curParticleColor;
pVertices[currentVertex].tx = 1.0f;
pVertices[currentVertex].ty = 1.0f;

currentVertex++;

pVertices[currentVertex].position.x = rightSide.x;
pVertices[currentVertex].position.y = rightSide.y - particleSize;
pVertices[currentVertex].position.z = rightSide.z;
pVertices[currentVertex].color = curParticleColor;
pVertices[currentVertex].tx = 1.0f;
pVertices[currentVertex].ty = 1.0f;

currentVertex++;

pVertices[currentVertex].position.x = leftSide.x;
pVertices[currentVertex].position.y = leftSide.y - particleSize;
pVertices[currentVertex].position.z = leftSide.z;
pVertices[currentVertex].color = curParticleColor;
pVertices[currentVertex].tx = 0.0f;
pVertices[currentVertex].ty = 1.0f;

currentVertex++;

pVertices[currentVertex].position.x = leftSide.x;
pVertices[currentVertex].position.y = leftSide.y + particleSize;
pVertices[currentVertex].position.z = leftSide.z;
pVertices[currentVertex].color = curParticleColor;
pVertices[currentVertex].tx = 0.0f;
pVertices[currentVertex].ty = 0.0f;
```

```
            currentVertex++;
        }

        m_pSystemVertexBuffer->Unlock();

        Render();

        return true;
}
```

Resetting Particles

As I mentioned earlier, all particles start out dead. This ensures that they can be created at the correct position during the first execution loop. It also enables us to control the emission rate. If you had set an emission limit of 100 particles per second, and there were 1,000 particles in the system, you obviously want that limit to stay in effect from the moment the particle system is created. Hence, the particles start out dead.

The Run() function starts and notices that the particle is dead; therefore, it calls the ResetParticle() function. This function is the daddy of the particle system because it has all the logic to turn the properties of the particle system into a real-life particle. Let's look at the function before I run through it:

```
void cParticleSystem::ResetParticle(cParticle& particle)
{
    particle.Start();

    D3DXVECTOR3 startRange(0,0,0);
    startRange.x = CalculateRandomValueBetween(-m_StartRadius.x, m_StartRadius.x);
    startRange.y = CalculateRandomValueBetween(-m_StartRadius.y, m_StartRadius.y);
    startRange.z = CalculateRandomValueBetween(-m_StartRadius.z, m_StartRadius.z);

    m_PositionInitial.x += startRange.x;
    m_PositionInitial.y += startRange.y;
    m_PositionInitial.z += startRange.z;

    particle.SetPosition(m_PositionInitial);
    particle.SetDead(false);

    // Calculate velocity
    D3DXVECTOR3 velocity;
```

```
    velocity.x = CalculateRandomValueBetween(m_VelocityInitialLow.x,
m_VelocityInitialHigh.x);
    velocity.y = CalculateRandomValueBetween(m_VelocityInitialLow.y,
m_VelocityInitialHigh.y);
    velocity.z = CalculateRandomValueBetween(m_VelocityInitialLow.z,
m_VelocityInitialHigh.z);
    particle.SetVelocity(velocity);

    static D3DXVECTOR3 acceleration;
    acceleration.x =
            CalculateRandomValueBetween(m_AccelerationInitialLow.x,
       m_AccelerationInitialHigh.x);
    acceleration.y =
            CalculateRandomValueBetween(m_AccelerationInitialLow.y,
       m_AccelerationInitialHigh.y);
    acceleration.z =
            CalculateRandomValueBetween(m_AccelerationInitialLow.z,
       m_AccelerationInitialHigh.z);
    particle.SetAcceleration(acceleration);

    static indReal32 life;
    life = CalculateRandomValueBetween(m_LifeInitialLow, m_LifeInitialHigh);
    particle.SetLifeSpan(life);

    static indReal32 mass;
    mass = CalculateRandomValueBetween(m_MassInitialLow, m_MassInitialHigh);
    particle.SetMass(mass);

    static D3DXCOLOR startColor;
    static D3DXCOLOR endColor;
    startColor.r = CalculateRandomValueBetween(m_ColorInitialLow.r,
m_ColorInitialHigh.r);
    startColor.g = CalculateRandomValueBetween(m_ColorInitialLow.g,
m_ColorInitialHigh.g);
    startColor.b = CalculateRandomValueBetween(m_ColorInitialLow.b,
m_ColorInitialHigh.b);
    startColor.a = CalculateRandomValueBetween(m_ColorInitialLow.a,
m_ColorInitialHigh.a);
    particle.SetStartColor(startColor);

    endColor.r = CalculateRandomValueBetween(m_ColorFinalLow.r, m_ColorFinalHigh.r);
    endColor.g = CalculateRandomValueBetween(m_ColorFinalLow.g, m_ColorFinalHigh.g);
```

```
endColor.b = CalculateRandomValueBetween(m_ColorFinalLow.b, m_ColorFinalHigh.b);
endColor.a = CalculateRandomValueBetween(m_ColorFinalLow.a, m_ColorFinalHigh.a);
particle.SetEndColor(endColor);

static indReal32 startSize;
static indReal32 endSize;
startSize = CalculateRandomValueBetween(m_SizeInitialLow, m_SizeInitialHigh);
endSize = CalculateRandomValueBetween(m_SizeFinalLow, m_SizeFinalHigh);
particle.SetSize(startSize, endSize);
}
```

It might look like a fair amount of code, but it's really pretty simple. Remember that this function is called every time a particle dies. That can be quite often, so it also needs to be pretty fast! Let's look at what is going on more closely. The function starts by calling the particle's Start() function.

`particle.Start();`

At the moment, this function doesn't actually do anything, but you can override if you need to and add any new functionality to it. Next, we set up the initial position at which the particle will be created. This requires a little extra work. Due to the rate at which particles are created, if we were to create every particle at the exact emitter location, you would see visible bands between particles as they moved. This is particularly annoying for fast-moving particles. On the other hand, sometimes we want to create particles over a large area, such as with particle systems that represent snow storms or rain. To fix the problems with banding and allow large area particle systems, I added a feature called StartRadius, which sets the area within which a particle will be created in relation to the actual emitter position. Check out the code:

```
D3DXVECTOR3 startRange(0,0,0);
startRange.x = CalculateRandomValueBetween(-m_StartRadius.x, m_StartRadius.x);
startRange.y = CalculateRandomValueBetween(-m_StartRadius.y, m_StartRadius.y);
startRange.z = CalculateRandomValueBetween(-m_StartRadius.z, m_StartRadius.z);

m_PositionInitial.x += startRange.x;
m_PositionInitial.y += startRange.y;
m_PositionInitial.z += startRange.z;

particle.SetPosition(m_PositionInitial);
particle.SetDead(false);
```

Next up, we need to set the velocity of the particle. Usually you want the velocity of the particles to be quite random; otherwise, they look like rubbish. To this end, there are four feature commands to set the range of the particle velocity. They are spelled out here:

- **VelocityInitialLow**—Sets the lowest range value that the velocity will be when the particle is created.

- **VelocityInitialHigh**—Sets the highest range value that the velocity will be when the particle is created. The initial velocity will be somewhere between VelocityInitalLow and VelocityInitialHigh.

- **VelocityFinalLow**—The lowest range of the velocity for the particle when it dies.

- **VelocityFinalHigh**—The highest range of the velocity for the particle when it dies. As with the initial values, the final velocity will be somewhere between these two values.

This allows us to choose a random value for the initial velocity within a range of values and a final velocity that will be random within a range of values. The actual velocity of the particle will linearly interpolate between these values over the life of the particle. Here is the code to create the values:

```
static D3DXVECTOR3 velocity;
velocity.x = CalculateRandomValueBetween(m_VelocityInitialLow.x,
m_VelocityInitialHigh.x);
velocity.y = CalculateRandomValueBetween(m_VelocityInitialLow.y,
m_VelocityInitialHigh.y);
velocity.z = CalculateRandomValueBetween(m_VelocityInitialLow.z,
m_VelocityInitialHigh.z);
particle.SetVelocity(velocity);
```

It's a pretty neat way of putting a lot of randomness into your particles while still exercising control over how distributed the random values will be. It is the same situation with the acceleration, except this time there is only a single acceleration value because it's rare to need to change acceleration over time unless you are modeling particularly complex particle systems:

```
static D3DXVECTOR3 acceleration;
acceleration.x = CalculateRandomValueBetween(m_AccelerationInitialLow.x,
m_AccelerationInitialHigh.x);
```

```
acceleration.y = CalculateRandomValueBetween(m_AccelerationInitialLow.y,
m_AccelerationInitialHigh.y);
acceleration.z = CalculateRandomValueBetween(m_AccelerationInitialLow.z,
m_AccelerationInitialHigh.z);
particle.SetAcceleration(acceleration);
```

Next up, we select the random value for the length of the particle's life. Again, this uses range-bounding functions to keep the particle's random life value within set limits:

```
static indReal32 life;
life = CalculateRandomValueBetween(m_LifeInitialLow, m_LifeInitialHigh);
particle.SetLifeSpan(life);

static indReal32 mass;
mass = CalculateRandomValueBetween(m_MassInitialLow, m_MassInitialHigh);
particle.SetMass(mass);
```

The pattern continues for choosing the colors and sizes of the particles:

```
static D3DXCOLOR startColor;
static D3DXCOLOR endColor;
startColor.r = CalculateRandomValueBetween(m_ColorInitialLow.r,
m_ColorInitialHigh.r);
startColor.g = CalculateRandomValueBetween(m_ColorInitialLow.g,
m_ColorInitialHigh.g);
startColor.b = CalculateRandomValueBetween(m_ColorInitialLow.b,
m_ColorInitialHigh.b);
startColor.a = CalculateRandomValueBetween(m_ColorInitialLow.a,
m_ColorInitialHigh.a);
particle.SetStartColor(startColor);

endColor.r = CalculateRandomValueBetween(m_ColorFinalLow.r, m_ColorFinalHigh.r);
endColor.g = CalculateRandomValueBetween(m_ColorFinalLow.g, m_ColorFinalHigh.g);
endColor.b = CalculateRandomValueBetween(m_ColorFinalLow.b, m_ColorFinalHigh.b);
endColor.a = CalculateRandomValueBetween(m_ColorFinalLow.a, m_ColorFinalHigh.a);
particle.SetEndColor(endColor);

static indReal32 startSize;
static indReal32 endSize;
startSize = CalculateRandomValueBetween(m_SizeInitialLow, m_SizeInitialHigh);
endSize = CalculateRandomValueBetween(m_SizeFinalLow, m_SizeFinalHigh);
particle.SetSize(startSize, endSize);
```

And that's it! The particle is now initialized and ready to be rendered, which I'll show you now.

Rendering the System

Okay, now we are starting to get somewhere. We have a great configurable particle system, and all the particles are created, initialized, filled into a vertex buffer, and ready for rendering. Next up we need to tell Direct3D about the vertex buffer, set up the shader, and blast it to the screen. The remaining code, you'll be happy to hear, is really pretty simple, and you've seen it before. Check it out:

```
bool cParticleSystem::Render()
{
    GAMEENGINE->GetDevice()->SetRenderState(D3DRS_CULLMODE, D3DCULL_NONE);
    GAMEENGINE->GetDevice()->SetRenderState(D3DRS_LIGHTING, FALSE);
    GAMEENGINE->GetDevice()->SetFVF(PARTICLE_VERTEXFORMAT);
    GAMEENGINE->GetDevice()->SetStreamSource(0,
             m_pSystemVertexBuffer, 0, sizeof(PARTICLE_VERTEX));

    GAMEENGINE->GetDevice()->SetRenderState(D3DRS_ZENABLE, FALSE);

    VisualEffects::cEffect* pCurrentEffect;

    if(!GAMEENGINE->IsWireframe())
    {
        pCurrentEffect = EFFECTMANAGER->GetEffect(m_EffectID);
    }
    else
    {
        indUInt effectID = EFFECTMANAGER->FindEffect("debugging.fx");
        pCurrentEffect = EFFECTMANAGER->GetEffect(effectID);
    }

    D3DXMATRIX world;
    D3DXMatrixIdentity(&world);
    pCurrentEffect->SetTransforms(
        world, CAMERA->GetViewMatrix(), CAMERA->GetProjectionMatrix());
    pCurrentEffect->Dispatch();

    indUInt numPasses = 0;
    pCurrentEffect->Begin(numPasses);
```

```
        for(indUInt passCount = 0 ; passCount < numPasses ; passCount++)
        {
            pCurrentEffect->BeginPass(passCount);

            GAMEENGINE->GetDevice()->SetTexture(0, GetTexture());
            GAMEENGINE->GetDevice()->DrawPrimitive(
                        D3DPT_TRIANGLELIST, 0, m_NumParticles);

            pCurrentEffect->EndPass();
        }

        pCurrentEffect->End();
        return true;
}
```

This function is similar to code used previously for the grid and visual resources. There are a few differences, however. First, there are a few render states that are set. These can also be added to the .fx file if you prefer. The first render state is to turn off culling. *Culling*, as you know, removes triangles that are facing the wrong way and are invisible. However, we are billboarding our particles, so they will always be visible. Therefore, the cull check is a waste of time. Next, I turned off lighting, because particles usually are not lit by light-sources in the game. Finally, the render state is set to disable z buffering for particles. Particles are usually so fast, and there are so many of them, that we can't even tell if they are rendered in the wrong order. So why not get the speed improvement by disabling the Z check?

Next up is a little bit of code I added to aid debugging. If the W key is pressed, it turns on wireframe debug mode. Look at Figure 5.3 to see wireframe rendering in action. This allows you to see the particles rendered in their native wireframe without all the other effects turned on, which can help pinpoint bugs:

```
if(!GAMEENGINE->IsWireframe())
{
    pCurrentEffect = EFFECTMANAGER->GetEffect(m_EffectID);
}
else
{
    indUInt effectID = EFFECTMANAGER->FindEffect("debugging.fx");
    pCurrentEffect = EFFECTMANAGER->GetEffect(effectID);
}
```

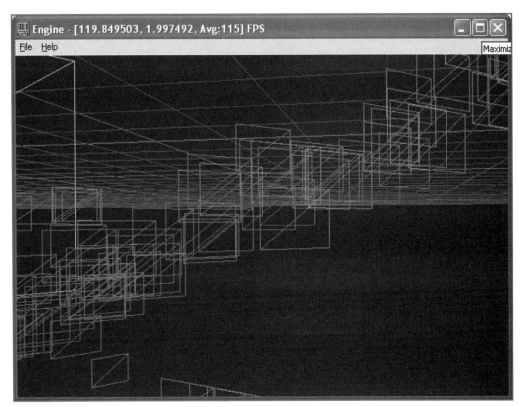

Figure 5.3
Wireframe rendering.

The remaining code just sets up the textures and shoots the vertex buffer to the screen. Hey! We now have one kick-ass particle system. But wait a minute. You can't get by with just one particle system, can you? Heck no, you can't! What we need next is a particle system library and manager!

Creating a Particle System Manager and Library

Having a single particle system is one thing, but what we want is a (breathe in now) *dynamically instanciable configurable particle system* (exhale)! What does that mean? Well, I'll tell you. What we want is for our particles to be described by particle feature files, like I showed you before. So, for every particle system file, we want to load that and add it to a particle system library. Then during gameplay, we want to be able to instance each of these systems whenever and wherever we want.

Think about it a little more…. Say that you had a particle system for fire. You'd create a particle system by describing it in a .psf file on disk. Then during the game's loading, you'd create the particle system and add it to the library of particle systems. Then every time an explosion went off, you'd instance the particle system to be visible in the game at the location of the explosion. Therefore, you can create as many copies of the fire particle system as you need and instance them into particular locations in the game. Then when the particle systems exceed their lifetimes, they are automatically removed from the scene.

That would be pretty easy to implement. All we'd need would be a cParticleSystemManager class that wraps two linked lists. The first list would contain all the particle systems in a library, and the second would contain all the instanced systems from the library that are currently active in the scene. Particle systems are referred to by their name, so it's important to give each one a unique identifier with the SystemName command in the .psf file.

It would also be necessary for the particle system to be able to be reloaded at runtime. To this end, I've added code to reparse all the particle system files and the instanced versions when the R key is pressed. Check out the class definition:

```
class cParticleSystemManager
{

    public:
        virtual ~cParticleSystemManager();
    private:
        cParticleSystemManager();

public:
    static cParticleSystemManager* getInstance();

    indBool Start();
    indBool Run();
    indBool Shutdown();

    void ReparseAll()
    {
        for (PARTICLE_SYSTEMS::iterator itPS = m_ParticleSystemsInstances.begin();
            itPS != m_ParticleSystemsInstances.end(); ++itPS)
        {
            (*itPS)->ReparseFeatureFile();
```

```
        }

        for (PARTICLE_SYSTEMS::iterator itPS = m_ParticleSystemsLibrary.begin();
            itPS != m_ParticleSystemsLibrary.end(); ++itPS)
        {
            (*itPS)->ReparseFeatureFile();
        }
    }

    indBool SpawnSystemInstance(char* name, D3DXVECTOR3& location)
    {
        cParticleSystem* pLibrarySystem = 0;

        for (PARTICLE_SYSTEMS::iterator itPS = m_ParticleSystemsLibrary.begin();
            itPS != m_ParticleSystemsLibrary.end(); ++itPS)
        {
            if(_stricmp((*itPS)->GetName(), name)==0 )
            {
                pLibrarySystem = (*itPS);
            }
        }

        if(!pLibrarySystem)
            return false;

        cParticleSystem* pNewSystem = new cParticleSystem(*pLibrarySystem);
        if(!pNewSystem)
            return false;

        pNewSystem->Start();
        pNewSystem->SetEmitterPosition(location);

        m_ParticleSystemsInstances.push_back(pNewSystem);

        return true;
    }

protected:
```

```
        static indBool          ms_InstanceFlag;
        static                  cParticleSystemManager *ms_pParticleManager;

        typedef std::list<cParticleSystem*> PARTICLE_SYSTEMS;
        PARTICLE_SYSTEMS m_ParticleSystemsLibrary;
        PARTICLE_SYSTEMS m_ParticleSystemsInstances;
};
```

As you can see, the code is a pretty straightforward encapsulation of the standard library std::list class. Here is the source code. Watch out for the function that loads all the .psf files from disk:

```
indBool cParticleSystemManager::ms_InstanceFlag = false;
cParticleSystemManager* cParticleSystemManager::ms_pParticleManager = NULL;

cParticleSystemManager* cParticleSystemManager::getInstance()
{
    if(!ms_InstanceFlag)
    {
        ms_pParticleManager = new cParticleSystemManager();
        ms_InstanceFlag = true;
        return ms_pParticleManager;
    }
    else
    {
        return ms_pParticleManager;
    }
}

cParticleSystemManager::cParticleSystemManager(void)
{
}

cParticleSystemManager::~cParticleSystemManager(void)
{
}


indBool cParticleSystemManager::Start()
{
    WIN32_FIND_DATA FileData;
    HANDLE hSearch;
    indBool fFinished = FALSE;
```

```
    hSearch = FindFirstFile("particles\\*.psf", &FileData);
    if (hSearch == INVALID_HANDLE_VALUE)
    {
        OutputDebugString("No .PSF files found.\n");
    }

    while (!fFinished)
    {
        indChar filename[MAX_PATH] = "particles\\";
        strcat(filename, FileData.cFileName);
        cParticleSystem* pNewSystem = new cParticleSystem(filename);
        pNewSystem->Start();
        m_ParticleSystemsLibrary.push_back(pNewSystem);

        if (!FindNextFile(hSearch, &FileData))
        {
            if (GetLastError() == ERROR_NO_MORE_FILES)
            {
                fFinished = TRUE;
            }
            else
            {
                OutputDebugString("Couldn't find next file.\n");
            }
        }
    }

    return true;
}

indBool cParticleSystemManager::Run()
{
    for (PARTICLE_SYSTEMS::iterator itPS = m_ParticleSystemsInstances.begin();
        itPS != m_ParticleSystemsInstances.end(); ++itPS)
    {
        if((*itPS)->IsSystemDead())
        {
            itPS = m_ParticleSystemsInstances.erase(itPS);
        }
    }
```

```
    for (PARTICLE_SYSTEMS::iterator itPS = m_ParticleSystemsInstances.begin();
        itPS != m_ParticleSystemsInstances.end(); ++itPS)
    {
        (*itPS)->Run();
    }

    return true;
}

indBool cParticleSystemManager::Shutdown()
{

    for (PARTICLE_SYSTEMS::iterator itPS = m_ParticleSystemsLibrary.begin();
        itPS != m_ParticleSystemsLibrary.end(); ++itPS)
    {
        delete (*itPS);
    }

    for (PARTICLE_SYSTEMS::iterator itPS = m_ParticleSystemsInstances.begin();
        itPS != m_ParticleSystemsInstances.end(); ++itPS)
    {
        delete (*itPS);
    }

    return true;
}
```

These stubs need to be connected as usual to the Start(), Run(), and Shutdown() functions in the cGameEngine class. After loading, if you want to instance a particle system, all you have to do is call this:

```
cParticleSystemManager::SpawnSystemInstance(systemName, D3DXVECTOR3 location);
```

Pretty cool, huh?

The Results in Action

Check out these particle systems I put together in about 5 minutes. I'll show you the feature files and then the screenshot.

Glowing Clouds

```
ColorInitialLow        = 1.0, 1.0, 1.0, 0.2
ColorInitialHigh       = 1.0, 1.0, 1.0, 0.2
ColorFinalLow          = 1.0, 1.0, 1.0, 0.0
ColorFinalHigh         = 1.0, 1.0, 1.0, 0.0

SystemName         = clouds
SizeInitialLow       = 8.0
SizeInitialHigh      = 8.0
SizeFinalLow       = 12.0
SizeFinalHigh      = 12.0

StartRadius = 6.0, 2.0, 6.0

NumParticles = 30

VelocityInitialLow  = -0.0, 0.0,  -0.0
VelocityInitialHigh=  0.0, 0.0,   0.0

m_LifeInitialLow  = 100000
m_LifeInitialHigh = 200000

PositionInitial = -10,20,0

MassInitialLow = 0.0
MassInitialHigh = 0.0


SystemLife = 10000

AccelerationInitialLow  = 0.0,0,0.0
AccelerationInitialHigh = 0.0,0,0.0
```

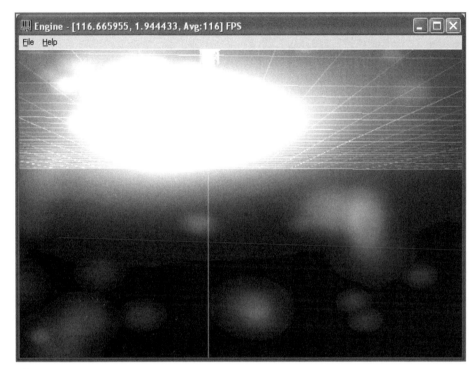

Figure 5.4
Glowing clouds.

Water Stream

```
ColorInitialLow      = 0.0, 0.3, 0.5, 0.6
ColorInitialHigh     = 0.0, 0.5, 0.7, 0.8
ColorFinalLow     = 0.0, 1.0, 1.0, 0.0
ColorFinalHigh    = 0.0, 1.0, 1.0, 0.0

SystemName          = waterfall
SizeInitialLow         = 0.8
SizeInitialHigh        = 0.9
SizeFinalLow        = 1.0
SizeFinalHigh       = 1.2

StartRadius = 0.0, 0.5, 2.0

NumParticles = 800

VelocityInitialLow = 0.4, 0.0,  0.0
```

```
VelocityInitialHigh= 0.5, 0.0,  0.0

m_LifeInitialLow  = 1000
m_LifeInitialHigh = 2000

PositionInitial = -10,10,10

EmitRate = 500


SystemLife = 10000

MassInitialLow  = 0.1
MassInitialHigh = 0.2


AccelerationInitialLow  = 0.0,0,0.0
AccelerationInitialHigh = 0.0,0,0.0
```

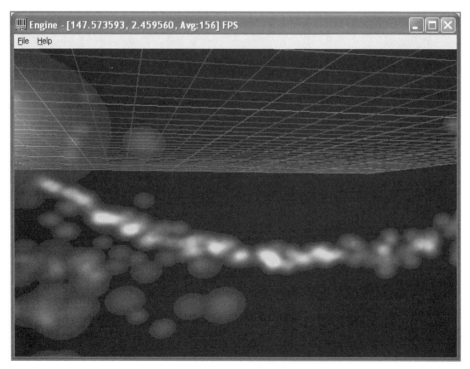

Figure 5.5
A water stream.

Fire

```
ColorInitialLow        = 1.0, 0.3, 0.0, 0.2
ColorInitialHigh       = 1.0, 0.3, 0.0, 0.2
ColorFinalLow          = 1.0, 1.0, 0.0, 0.0
ColorFinalHigh         = 1.0, 1.0, 0.0, 0.0

SystemName             = fire
SizeInitialLow         = 1.0
SizeInitialHigh        = 1.0
SizeFinalLow           = 1.0
SizeFinalHigh          = 1.0

StartRadius = 0.5, 0.0, 0.5

NumParticles = 1000

VelocityInitialLow = -0.0, 0.1,  -0.0
VelocityInitialHigh=  0.0, 0.2,   0.0

m_LifeInitialLow  = 1000
m_LifeInitialHigh = 1500

PositionInitial = 40,0,-20

MassInitialLow  = 0.0
MassInitialHigh = 0.0

EmitRate = 1000

SystemLife = 10000

AccelerationInitialLow  = 0.0,0,0.0
AccelerationInitialHigh = 0.0,0,0.0
```

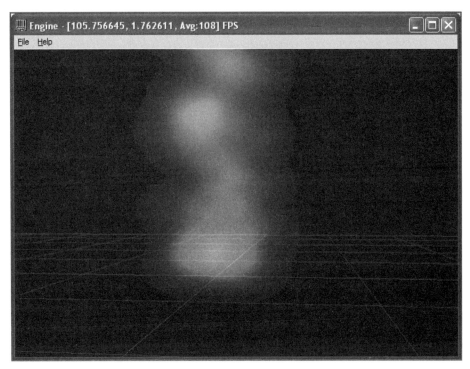

Figure 5.6
A fire system.

Conclusion

In this chapter, you learned an incredible amount about particle systems. The particle system in this chapter is infinitely expandable and is only limited by your creativity. I strongly encourage you to push yourself to see what you can achieve with your own effects. If you come up with anything cool, send me an e-mail with a (small!) .jpg screen shot. You can find my e-mail address in the book's Introduction. In this chapter, we covered the following:

- The physics of particles
- Emitters
- Controlling the emission rate of particles
- What to do at the end of a particle's life

- Grouping particles into a system
- Grouping particle systems under a manager
- Instantiating multiple systems from a particle system library

In the next chapter, we are going to cover some cool stuff to show how to render real-time videos into your game engine. What are you waiting for? Turn the page!

CHAPTER 6

Alias Maya API Model Exporters

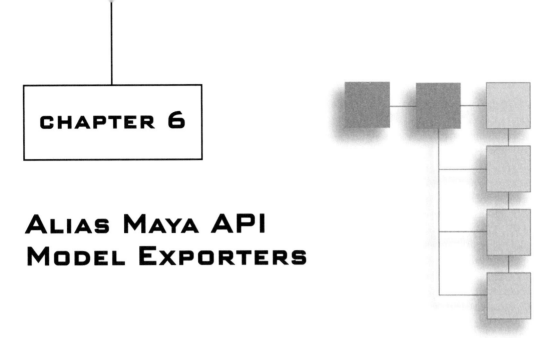

In this chapter, we're going to take a little break from the game engine so that I can show you some pretty cool exporters for Alias Maya. The other main 3D editing package is 3ds max from Discreet. These two programs are split evenly in terms of their usage, and as you are no doubt aware, they are very powerful. Game development today would not be possible without them. This chapter will only focus on Maya, because there is a huge amount of 3ds max information already available, and Maya is really lacking in this area.

However, the problem with these packages is that they generally support only a limited number of file formats, and these formats are usually not ideal for computer games. As a result, a small army of tools developers around the world are tirelessly searching for ways to export data from these packages into custom formats for their games.

Unfortunately, for Maya in particular, there is extremely little documentation and information available on how to program exporters. In fact, until recently there was virtually no information on the subject. That is where this chapter comes in. I'll be teaching you about the following:

- What a Directed Acyclic Graph is
- What a Dependency Graph is, and how to harness its power
- How to use the Maya plug-in wizard
- What function sets are

- When to use nodes, plugs, plug arrays, shaders, iterators, paths, and much more
- How to extract vertex and polygon information
- How to extract indexed vertex data
- How to convert Maya data to Direct3D data
- How to save X files

As of the April 2005 release, Direct3D includes an extremely advanced Maya exporter that is useful if you are exporting to X files. The problem is that the exporter is so advanced that it's hard to follow what it's doing. Therefore, this chapter will show you everything you need to get started with a fairly simple exporter that you can expand if you need to at a later date. I chose to export to the X file format because most people already understand it, and the intricacies of a new file format won't get in the way of learning. You should be able to replace most of the calls with custom code should you need to convert this to a custom file format later on. With that in mind, let's get started.

The Maya Plug-In Wizard

If you're lucky enough to still own Visual Studio 6.0, good for you. If you install Maya 4.0 (with the SDK), it handily adds a new wizard to your New Project dialog box, as in Figure 6.1.

Unfortunately, wizard support after this period is a little flaky, and it doesn't work at all on Visual Studio .NET. What's that? Yes, I know Visual C++ 6.0 was released like seven years ago, but that's okay because I've converted an empty Maya wizard project for you and included it with the source code for this book. Phew! No worries there. If you're unable to follow this section of the chapter, just skim over it so you know how it works and then use the finished product that's preconverted for you.

Let's see how it all works. First, fire up VC 6.0 and bring up the New Project dialog box, as in Figure 6.1. If the icon for Maya Plug-In Wizard is not visible, you probably need to reinstall Maya or the Maya SDK, type in a project name and location as usual, and click OK. For this chapter, I've given our Maya plug-in the exciting name of Custom Exporter.

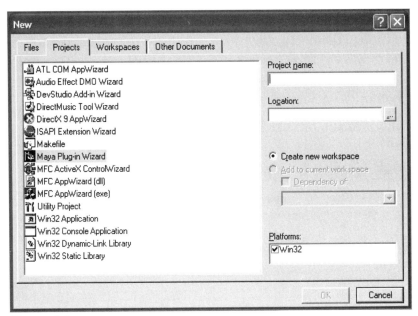

Figure 6.1
The Maya SDK Wizard in VC++ 6.0.

Next, up pops the Maya Wizard, which looks like Figure 6.2.

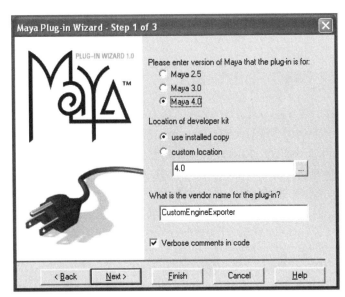

Figure 6.2
The Maya Wizard, part one of three.

We want to select Maya 4.0 and leave the rest of the settings in their default states, unless you need to change them. For those of you who are using later versions of Maya, the API is extremely similar, so you should have few problems running this code on later versions of the application. I'd recommend keeping the verbose comments turned on until you are more familiar with how it all works.

The next page of the wizard looks like Figure 6.3.

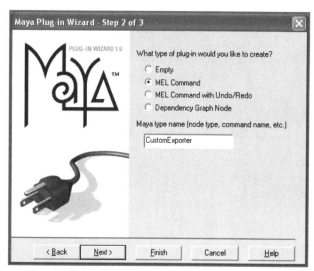

Figure 6.3
The Maya Wizard, part two of three.

There are a few options to choose from here, generally increasing complex from the top to bottom order. Empty just creates an empty project for you with the library files that you need to build your project. MEL Command is what we will be using. I'll explain more about MEL in a moment. A MEL Command with Undo/Redo is kind of like what we are doing, but there is a ton of complexity involving keeping track of states to allow the undo/redo functionality to work. Because we are just writing an exporter, which doesn't change any of Maya's data, there is no reason to care about undoing actions. Next up is a Dependency Graph Node. It's one big momma of a subject that I'll explain in just a moment.

I'll explain these subjects in much more detail later in this chapter, but I'd better give some things a cursory overview so we don't get confused. First up is MEL. There are two ways to program Maya; the first is through its scripting language called MEL, and the second is called the Maya API, which is programmed in

C++. MEL is infinitely slower than the API due to its interpreted nature. One of my first jobs as a game programmer years ago was to rewrite all the exporters that were previously in MEL in C++ using the API because it was killing the company's export pipeline. The speedup was enormous. Using the MEL implementation, an entire asset re-export (that is, thousands of models) would take more than a day. Using the API implementation, it would only take a few hours.

However, MEL *is* useful. A lot of Maya's interface and tools are written in MEL, and it is extremely powerful and easy to use. MEL is not very fast at executing, so you'll have to make the decision if you are working with Maya over whether you need speed of execution (as in batch exporting) or speed of development (as in something to help the lazy artists).

Next up a quick explanation of the Dependency Graph Node. Maya is capable of rendering an incredible range of objects. However, there will always be someone who wants to add some crazy new tool to the program, such as a quantum flux renderer or an 11-dimensional space time wormhole visualizer that Maya just isn't quite up to rendering. Each object that Maya knows about is called a *node*. If you want to add a new type of object to Maya, you need to add a new graph node and explain to Maya how to use and render it. That is the purpose of the final option in Step 2 of the wizard. Now on with the show.

Step 3 of the wizard looks like Figure 6.4.

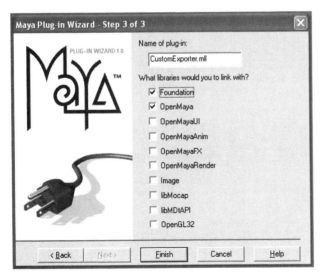

Figure 6.4
The Maya Wizard, part three of three.

This gives you a chance to tell Maya what you want your plug-in to be called. As you might know, all Maya plug-ins have the .mll file extension. We'll stick with the default for this chapter. The wizard gives us an easy way to select which libraries we will be working with. We are not doing anything too fancy, so we can just select the top two, which is usually the minimal you'll ever want to link to. Click Finish to complete the wizard. An MFC style confirmation window comes up telling you about everything you selected (see Figure 6.5).

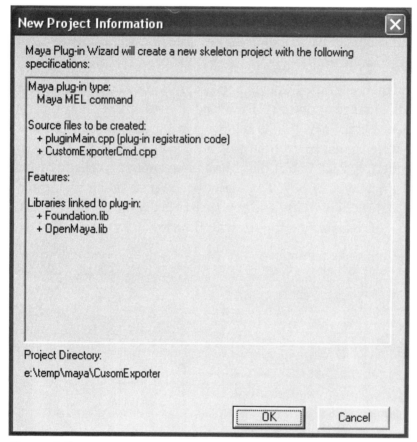

Figure 6.5
The Maya Wizard confirmation page.

Click OK. The wizard creates a new project file for you with a single file called CustomExporterCommand.cpp.

The Maya Plug-In Wizard 187

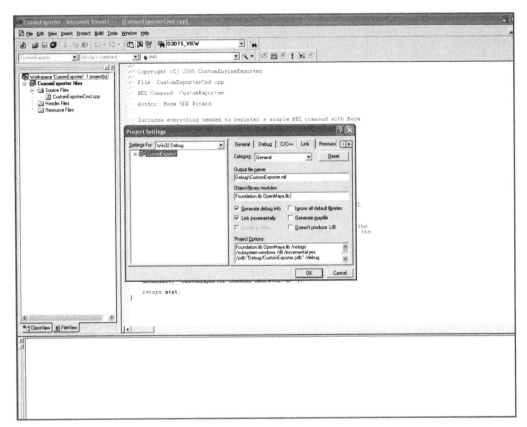

Figure 6.6
The completed wizard.

The wizard added some library files to your project automatically. At this point, we're ready to dump the Visual C++ 6.0 antique and return to Visual C++ .NET to continue development. If you are a poor soul and are stuck with 6.0, don't worry. All the code in this chapter also runs in that version; however, screen shots and instructions are for .NET. The two programs are not vastly different, so you should be able to carry on. Feel free to shut down Visual C++ 6.0 now and reopen the project in .NET.

Check out the source file the wizard generated for you:

```
//
// Copyright (C) 2005 CustomEngineExporter
//
// File: CustomExporterCmd.cpp
//
```

```
// MEL Command: CustomExporter
//
// Author: Maya SDK Wizard
//

// Includes everything needed to register a simple MEL command with Maya.
//
#include <maya/MSimple.h>

// Use helper macro to register a command with Maya. It creates and
// registers a command that does not support undo or redo. The
// created class derives off of MPxCommand.
//
DeclareSimpleCommand( CustomExporter, "CustomEngineExporter", "4.0" );

MStatus CustomExporter::doIt( const MArgList& args )
//
//      Description:
//              implements the MEL CustomExporter command.
//
//      Arguments:
//              args - the argument list that was passed to the command from MEL
//
//      Return Value:
//              MS::kSuccess - command succeeded
//              MS::kFailure - command failed (returning this value will cause the
//                             MEL script that is being run to terminate unless the
//                             error is caught using a "catch" statement.
//
{
    MStatus stat = MS::kSuccess;

    // Because this class is derived off of MPxCommand, you can use the
    // inherited methods to return values and set error messages
    //
    setResult( "CustomExporter command executed!\n" );

    return stat;
}
```

This is where all our code will be added to export Maya data to an X file. More on this stuff soon.

Reconfiguring the Plug-In Location

After you load your project, Visual C++ by default creates your plug-in in the `\debug` or `\release` subdirectories of your project. However, Maya likes its plug-ins to be in the `\AW\Maya4.0\bin\plug-ins` directory. Rather than copying the file manually every time you build it, it is far easier to change the build path to be the Maya plug-in directory. That way you can be happy in the knowledge that every time you complete a successful build, the .mll plug-in will automatically be copied for you. To change the build location settings, bring up the Project Settings dialog box and go to the Linker, General tab. Change the `Output File` setting to be this:

`Maya drive:\AW\Maya4.0\bin\plug-ins\CustomExporter.mll`

Obviously, replace `Maya drive` with the drive you want Maya installed on.

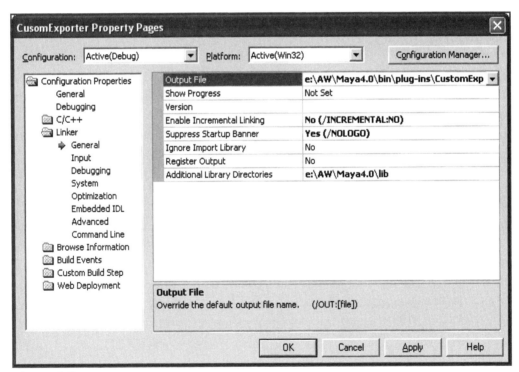

Figure 6.7
Modifying the build path.

The Directed Acyclic Graph and Other Interestingly Named Objects

I have to warn you in advance that the Maya API is possibly the most abstracted piece of code you will come across in your life. After you understand it, it makes a little sense, but it is a steep learning curve due to the unorthodox naming conventions and wide array of tongue-twisting names. Let's start climbing this mountain right now.

The DAG

First up is the DAG. You will learn to hate this beast. As the section title indicates, it stands for Directed Acyclic Graph, which roughly translated means a tree. More specifically, it is a tree in which all the child objects of the graph will never point to any of their ancestors, which would create a cycle. Because this is acyclic, there can be no pesky cycles. So whenever you see DAG, just think tree—the standard kind that all programmers know and love in which objects in the tree are known as nodes, and so on. This tree can be searched in a variety of ways, including depth first or breadth first, and you constrain the searches to nodes of a particular type. But we'll get to all that fun in a moment. The good thing about an acyclic graph is that you can never get into infinite loops while browsing through it. Everything from meshes to polygons to vertices and much more is stored in the DAG, and it is where you will get most of your data.

The DG

Similarly named, but orders of magnitude more complicated, is the Dependency Graph, or DG for short. The DG is like an evil version of the DAG because it is not constrained by any rules to do with cycles. So perusing the DG can be an interesting experience. Things like materials, textures, and shaders are stored in the DG, so if you are writing an exporter, you can't avoid it. Don't despair, though. I'll show you everything you need to know.

Dependency Nodes and Function Sets

This is where the jargon starts to get annoying. A *dependency node* represents a handle to a node in the DAG or DG. So when you see dependency node, just think of a standard handle if that makes it clearer. As you can imagine, there are an incredible number of node types in the DAG, and there are just as many dependency nodes to represent them.

A *function set* is, without wanting this to sound like a tautology, a set of functions used to interface with a dependency node. A function set is usually contained with a C++ class. So if you think about it this way, say that there is a node in the graph for a tiger's mesh. You create a dependency node to act as a handle to the mesh. You then create a function set, using the handle, to modify and access the mesh node. Make sense? Cool.

The problem is that generally any function set can be created to represent any node, whether or not that set is capable of representing that node, with interesting results, so you have to be careful not to associate the wrong type of function set with the wrong type of node.

The Maya API Naming and Coding Conventions

You would hope that the naming convention of an API would be fairly straightforward because by design an API is meant to be used by a wide variety of developers in a wide variety of roles—hence, the success of naming conventions that are similar to Hungarian notation. Maya, however, really goes out on a limb with its style, and I'm pretty sure you won't see anything like it again.

Naming Conventions

Most, if not all, of Maya's variables, functions, and classes start with a capital *M* for Maya. The *M* could stand for multifarious, meandering, muddled, mystical, manifold, or even mosaic, which all describe the API nicely, but I'll bet it's Maya. Then the type follows with a capital letter, like this:

- `MPlug`
- `MPointArray`
- `MStatus`

Multiple words in a name have the first letter of each new word as a capital letter, with the rest in lowercase. Function sets, which are usually C++ classes, have the `MFn` prefix such as `MFnMesh` and `MFnDagNode`.

Function names are in the Java style; that is, they start with a lowercase letter, and each subsequent word in the name starts with a capital letter, such as `isIntermediateObject()` or `cartestianSize()`.

The annoying thing about the *M* prefixes is that they don't make it immediately obvious what type of C++ construct they represent. There is no common *C* prefix for classes, for example. Don't worry. You'll get used to the naming conventions the more you work with Maya.

Coding Conventions

Most functions return an MStatus as an argument. This is a fairly simple enumeration that can be any of the following values:

```
enum MStatusCode
{
    /// The operation was successful
    kSuccess = 0,
    /// The operation failed
    kFailure,
    /// The operation failed due to insufficient memory
    kInsufficientMemory,
    /// An invalid parameter was provided
    kInvalidParameter,
    /// Application is not licensed for the attempted operation
    kLicenseFailure,
    /// Returned by MPxNode::compute for unrecognized plugs
    kUnknownParameter,
    /// Not currently used
    kNotImplemented,
    /// Not currently used
    kNotFound,
    /// Not currently used
    kEndOfFile
};
```

However, it's unlikely you'll come across anything other than the kSuccess and kFailure variants.

At the top of your wizard-created source file will be a line of code that looks like this:

```
DeclareSimpleCommand(CustomEngineExport, "CustomEngineExporter", "4.0");
```

This gives Maya a way to invoke your exporter from the Maya command line or from MEL scripts. In effect, you are compiling your exporter to be a natively compiled MEL command. In this case, you will be able to type

```
CustomEngineExport
```

into the Maya command line, and it will automatically call your plug-in, starting execution at the `MStatus CustomEngineExport::doIt(const MArgList& args)` entry point. Check out Figure 6.8 to see the command prompt.

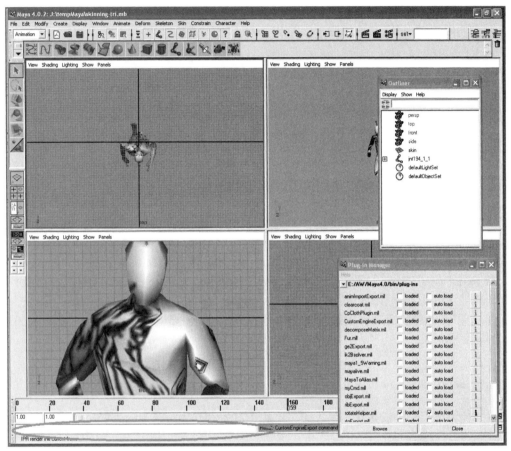

Figure 6.8
The MEL command prompt.

The Maya command line is located in the bottom-left portion of the Maya window. Simply type a command into it, such as the name of our exporter, press Enter, and the command is executed. You can also pass arguments to our exporter from the command line. For instance, say you wanted to call the exporter with a location for where the exported file would be saved. You could type the following:

```
CustomEngineExport c:\exportedfile.x
```

This would call our `CustomEngineExport::doIt(const MArgList& args)` function with the `args` parameter set to the parameter we passed. To access the parameter, you could use the following code:

```
// Path to the exported file
char exportFile[MAX_PATH] = {0};

// Copy the export path from the argument list to the local variable.
if(args.asString(0).asChar())
    strcpy(exportFile, args.asString(0).asChar());
```

Getting a Direct3D Device

You might be wondering why we need a Direct3D device when we are not doing rendering. Well, what we will be doing is saving a Direct3D X file to disk. And that requires using the D3DX libraries, which requires a Direct3D device to work. This is one aspect of D3DX that I really don't like. D3DX is a set of utility functions, many of which are going to be used in exporters and command-line tools, which have no use for rendering. So why require a DirectX device as a parameter to so many functions? Who knows? Maybe Microsoft will read this and change it for DirectX 10. You do need certain things to set up Direct3D. First, you need a couple of global pointers to an `IDirect3D9` interface, and an IDirect3DDevice9 interface, like this:

```
LPDIRECT3D9 g_pD3D = 0;
LPDIRECT3DDEVICE9 g_pDevice = 0;
```

Next, you need a function to do all the initialization work, like this:

```
bool InitializeDirect3D()
{
    if(NULL == (g_pD3D = Direct3DCreate9(D3D_SDK_VERSION)))
    {
        MessageBox(0, "Failed to create Direct3D",
            "Custom Exporter Error", MB_OK | MB_ICONERROR);
        return false;
    }

    D3DPRESENT_PARAMETERS presentParams;

    presentParams.BackBufferWidth = 320;
    presentParams.BackBufferHeight = 200;
```

Getting a Direct3D Device

```
    presentParams.BackBufferFormat = D3DFMT_UNKNOWN;
    presentParams.BackBufferCount = 0;
    presentParams.MultiSampleType = D3DMULTISAMPLE_NONE;
    presentParams.MultiSampleQuality = 0;
    presentParams.SwapEffect = D3DSWAPEFFECT_DISCARD;
    presentParams.hDeviceWindow = GetDesktopWindow();
    presentParams.Windowed = TRUE;
    presentParams.EnableAutoDepthStencil = 0;
    presentParams.AutoDepthStencilFormat = D3DFMT_UNKNOWN;
    presentParams.Flags = 0;
    presentParams.FullScreen_RefreshRateInHz = 0;
    presentParams.PresentationInterval = D3DPRESENT_INTERVAL_IMMEDIATE;

    HRESULT hr = g_pD3D->CreateDevice(
        D3DADAPTER_DEFAULT, D3DDEVTYPE_HAL, GetDesktopWindow(),
        D3DCREATE_SOFTWARE_VERTEXPROCESSING,
        &presentParams, &g_pDevice);

    if(FAILED(hr))
    {
        MessageBox(0, "Failed to create Direct3D device",
            "Custom Exporter Error", MB_OK | MB_ICONERROR);
        return false;
    }

    return true;
}
```

Fairly straightforward? I've bolded a few lines to keep in mind. First up is the size of the buffers. Sometimes device creation fails if you don't specify a valid back buffer size, so I just set it to the smallest one possible, which is usually 320×200. The D3DFMT_UNKNOWN flag just tells Direct3D to use the same surface format as is currently used. The next item to note is presentParams.hDeviceWindow. This little puppy takes a handle to the window that we are rendering into. But hang on a minute—we are not rendering anything! Try telling Direct3D this, and it will chuck a big fat E_FAIL right back at you. That's right—you can't create a device without a rendering window. Because we don't have a rendering window, we have to make one up. GetDesktopWindow() does the job nicely. It returns the handle to the window that Explorer uses for the desktop. That's a nice cheat. Then it's just a case of creating the device and making sure it succeeds.

There is also the required shutdown function:

```
bool ShutdownDirect3D()
{
    SAFE_RELEASE(g_pDevice);
    SAFE_RELEASE(g_pD3D);

    return true;
}
```

These two functions should be roughly the first and last functions called, respectively, from the doIt() function.

The Maya Plug-In Manager

To use a plug-in with Maya, you need to ensure that Maya knows where your plug-in is and have it loaded into memory. Just having it built into the correct folder is not enough. To tell Maya about the plug-in, select Window, Settings/Preferences, Plug-In Manager from the menu.

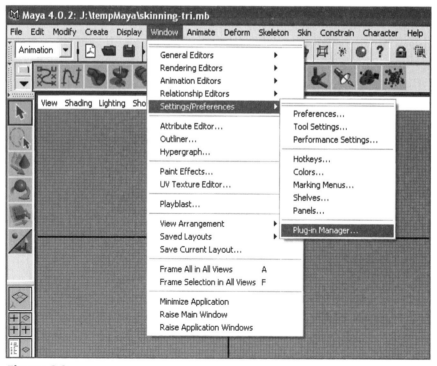

Figure 6.9
The Plug-In Manager from the Maya menu.

This brings up the Plug-In Manager, which lets you control the status of all the plug-ins that Maya uses. Check out Figure 6.10.

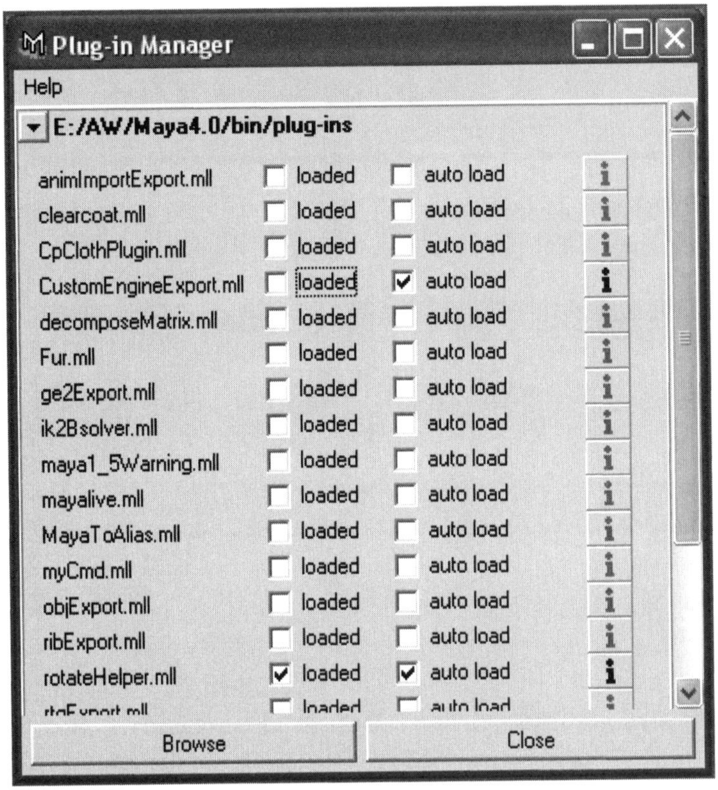

Figure 6.10
The Plug-In Manager.

There are two check boxes for every plug-in. The Auto Load check box tells Maya to automatically load your plug-in at startup and have it enabled. The Loaded check box indicates whether your plug-in is currently loaded into memory. This is important for the following reasons:

- You can't use your plug-in when it's not loaded. If you try to call it, Maya gives you an error saying it can't find the plug-in (see Figure 6.11).
- You can't rebuild your plug-in while it's loaded because it causes a sharing violation. If you try to, Visual Studio complains bitterly, as in Figure 6.12.

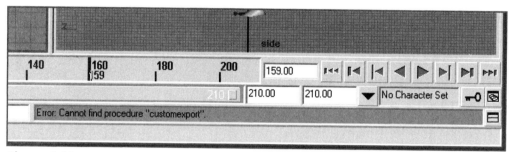

Figure 6.11
Errors when trying to use a plug-in while it's unloaded.

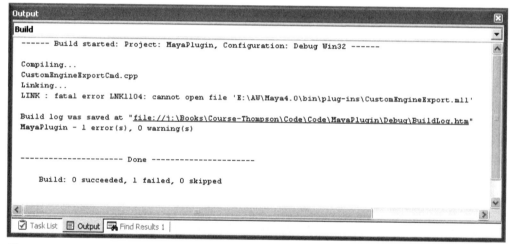

Figure 6.12
Errors while trying to build a plug-in while it's loaded.

Remember to load your plug-in into Maya when you want to use it with Maya, and unload it when you want to rebuild it with Visual Studio.

Export Formats

Maya is a massive beast of a program, and it can handle data in so many forms that it could make you ill to think about it. It supports a variety of surface formats from Non-Uniform Rational B-Splines (NURBS) to multi-vertex polygons, to quads, and even the humble triangle. However, none of this is of any concern to us apart from the triangle format. Therefore, it is vital that the data we export from Maya is in the correct format for us to export. What this means is that we need to get the artists, or whoever will be using our exporter, to *triangulate* their models before export. This means that all the insane surface formats are removed and you are left with just a nice simple model made of triangles—the kind that your GPU loves.

It is easy to triangulate a model. Check out the model in Figure 6.13, which is composed of quads and other multi-vertex polygons.

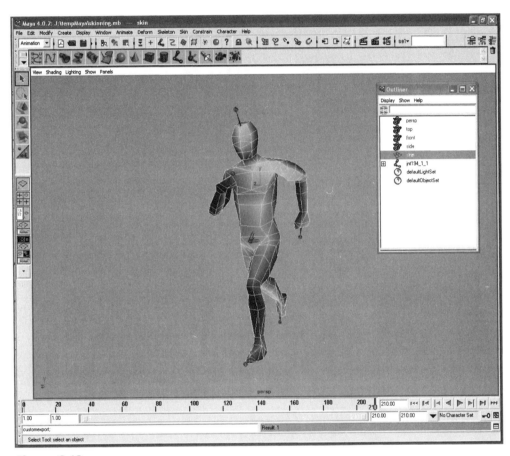

Figure 6.13
A model made of polygons and quads.

Our exporter would choke on this, and it's not worth us programming a ton of triangulation code when Maya already does this for us. Simply select the mesh you want to triangulate from the outliner, and then bring up the Maya menu (see Figure 6.14) by holding down the spacebar.

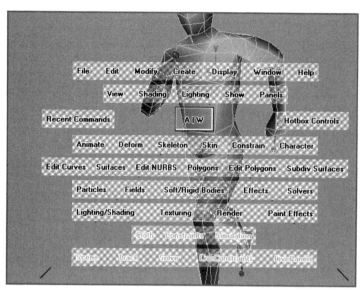

Figure 6.14
The Maya hot menu.

Select from the menu Polygons, Triangulate. Lo and behold, all the weird shapes are gone, and all that is left are lovely triangles! Check out the before and after in Figure 6.15.

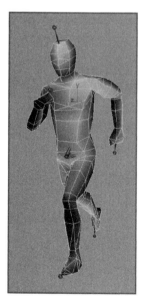 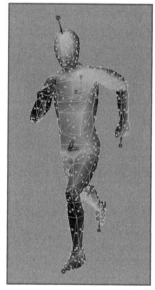

Figure 6.15
The results—notice the quads turned into triangles.

Don't worry. I've added a little message box that pops up if the exporter detects any vertices in the wrong format. Now on with show…

Writing the Exporter

Okay, cool. We have enough of the prerequisites out of the way to write the actual exporter. It's going to get a little complicated now, but I'll go through it step by step so everything's clear. First things first, we need to decide what format we're going to store our data in for DirectX. This requires us to declare an FVF vertex as is usually done in the game engine:

```
typedef struct MESH_VERTEX
{
    D3DXVECTOR3 position;
    D3DCOLOR color;
    float tx, ty;
}MESH_VERTEX;

const DWORD MESH_VERTEXFORMAT = D3DFVF_XYZ | D3DFVF_DIFFUSE | D3DFVF_TEX1;
```

This declares that our exported vertices will have a position, a color, and two-dimensional texture coordinates. It's nothing you haven't seen before. Now we need to siphon out the export file name that the user wants to use.

```
MStatus CustomEngineExport::doIt(const MArgList& args)
//
//    Description:
//        implements the MEL CustomEngineExport command.
//
//    Arguments:
//        args - the argument list that was passes to the command from MEL
//
//    Return Value:
//        MS::kSuccess - command succeeded
//        MS::kFailure - command failed (returning this value will cause the
//                       MEL script that is being run to terminate unless the
//                       error is caught using a "catch" statement.
//
{
    MStatus returnStatus = MS::kSuccess;
```

```cpp
// Path to the exported file
char exportFile[MAX_PATH] = {0};

// Copy the export path from the argument list to the local variable
if(args.asString(0).asChar())
    strcpy(exportFile, args.asString(0).asChar());

if(!exportFile[0])
{
    // Use default export name if none was specified
    strcpy(exportFile, "c:\\export.x");
    MessageBox(0, "No output file specified, defaulting to c:\\export.x",
        "Custom Exporter Error", MB_OK | MB_ICONERROR);
}
```

The code starts by declaring a status handler. This will be used as the return value to let Maya know if the plug-in succeeded. Then I declare a local character array to hold the file name to export to. The code attempts to get a parameter out of the arguments passed into the plug-in in the formal parameter. If one is available, it is copied to the local variable. Otherwise, a default export name is used, along with an error to let the user know he exported incorrectly. Next we need to initialize Direct3D so it can be used with D3DX for saving X files:

```cpp
// Initialize Direct3D
if(!InitializeDirect3D())
{
    // Have to quit... can't continue without DirectX
    MessageBox(0, "Fatal Error: Failed to create Direct3D objects",
        "Custom Exporter Error", MB_OK | MB_ICONERROR);
    return MS::kFailure;
}
```

Now it gets interesting:

```cpp
// Create the DAG iterator
MItDag itDAG(MItDag::kBreadthFirst, MFn::kInvalid, &returnStatus);

// Loop over all the DAG objects
for (;!itDAG.isDone(); itDAG.next())
{
```

`MItDag` is an iterator that recurses over the entire acyclic graph, which contains all the meshes. Iterators in Maya assume the position of the current object they represent. So you access the iterator kind of like it's the object you are after. When you want the next object, just call `next()` on the iterator, and it will move on and behave as if it's the next object. It's quite intuitive after you get used to it:

```
MDagPath DAGPath;
// Get the current path
returnStatus = itDAG.getPath(DAGPath);

if (returnStatus)
{
```

Next, we need to get a path into the graph for the current node represented by the iterator. A *path* is basically a map that tells Maya how to get from one place to another. Typically a graph is in text format and looks like this node name separated by the pipe symbol like this:

someNode | anotherNode | anotherNode

And so on. Now you know why the Maya logo looks like Alias|Maya. It's a path from Alias to Maya. Anyway, the return status is checked to make sure we were able to get a valid path. All being well, we can start to mess around with this node. Remember earlier in the chapter I said that a function set controls the nodes. Well, check out this code:

```
// Get the node that the path points to
MFnDagNode dagNode(DAGPath, &returnStatus);
if(!returnStatus)
    continue;

// Continue if the object is an intermediate object
if (dagNode.isIntermediateObject())
{
    continue;
}

// Continue if the object is not a mesh
if (!DAGPath.hasFn(MFn::kMesh))
{
    continue;
}
```

```
// Continue if the object is a transform
if (DAGPath.hasFn(MFn::kTransform))
{
    continue;
}
```

First we see if we can get a general `MFnDagNode` function set to represent the node. This should be capable of representing nearly every conceivable node, so if it doesn't work, we can't deal with it, and we can continue past it for the next iteration of the loop. Then we perform three checks on the node. First, is it an intermediate object like a shape modifier? If it is, there's nothing we can do with it; we should move on. Second, does it contain a mesh? If it doesn't, we need to skip it. Third, is it just a transform node? Because we can't export those either. At the end of these three checks, we should be able to be fairly sure we are dealing with a node that represents a mesh. So we can apply an `MFnMesh` function set to the node to get more detailed control over it:

```
MFnMesh currentMesh(DAGPath);
```

Next, we need to extract some information from the mesh about how many faces and vertices it contains. We can achieve this with `MPointArray` and `MItMeshPolygon`. Check out the code, which is fairly self-explanatory:

```
// Get an array of all vertices in this mesh
MPointArray vertexList;
currentMesh.getPoints(vertexList, MSpace::kWorld);

// Calculate the number of faces and vertices in this mesh
MItMeshPolygon polygonIterator(DAGPath);
int numPolygons = polygonIterator.count();
int numVertices = vertexList.length();
```

Using this information, we can create a D3DXMesh:

```
// Create a mesh to hold the export data
LPD3DXMESH pD3DXMesh = 0;
D3DXCreateMeshFVF(numPolygons, numVertices,
    D3DXMESH_MANAGED,
    MESH_VERTEXFORMAT, g_pDevice, &pD3DXMesh);

// Return if there was an error creating the mesh
if(!pD3DXMesh)
{
```

```
            MessageBox(0, "Failed to create d3dx mesh",
                "Custom Exporter Error", MB_OK | MB_ICONERROR);
            return MS::kFailure;
    }
```

Now that we have a D3DX mesh to store the export data, we can start to iterate through the mesh data. This is done by material. So we find all the materials in the mesh. Then we iterate through each material and export the vertices with that particular material attached. Finally, when all the vertices are exported, we can export the indices for those vertices into the mesh's index buffer. To start this process, we ask Maya to return all the objects in the dependency graph that are connected to our mesh:

```
        unsigned DAGInst = DAGPath.instanceNumber();
        MObjectArray meshSets;
        MObjectArray meshComponents;
        currentMesh.getConnectedSetsAndMembers(
                    DAGInst, meshSets, meshComponents, true);

        for (UINT meshSetCount = 0;
                meshSetCount < meshSets.length(); meshSetCount++)
         {
```

Now we need to narrow this down to only connected objects that are materials:

```
            // Get the current mesh set and component
            MObject currentMeshSet = meshSets[meshSetCount];
            MObject currentMeshComponent = meshComponents[meshSetCount];

            // Create function sets to handle the mesh set and component
            MFnSet setFN(currentMeshSet);
            MFnDependencyNode setDN(currentMeshSet);

            // Create an attribute to help search for shaders
            MObject surfaceShaderAttribute =
                        setDN.attribute(MString("surfaceShader"));

            // Connect a plug to the current mesh's surface shader
            MPlug surfaceShaderPlug(currentMeshSet, surfaceShaderAttribute);

            // Get an array of all the surface shaders
            MPlugArray surfaceShaderPlugArray;
            surfaceShaderPlug.connectedTo(surfaceShaderPlugArray, true, false);
```

```
// Check that surface shaders actually exist
if (surfaceShaderPlugArray.length() == 0)
    continue;
```

We do all this by checking whether each object contains an attribute called surfaceShader, which in English means *material*. If the node does not contain this attribute, we can skip it. Otherwise, we can connect an MPlug and MPlugArray to the object and see if it contains shaders. If it does, we can extract the material information; otherwise, we can set it to the default color of white:

```
// Get the current surface shader node
MObject surfaceShaderNode = surfaceShaderPlugArray[0].node();

// The default color if the color cannot be extracted
MColor diffuseColor(1,1,1,1);

// Check whether the surface shader is a lambert shader
if (surfaceShaderNode.hasFn(MFn::kLambert))
{
    MFnLambertShader lambertShader(surfaceShaderNode);
    diffuseColor = lambertShader.color();
}
else
{
    MessageBox(0,
        "ERROR: Found unknown material - add required handler",
        "Custom Exporter Error", MB_OK | MB_ICONERROR);
            continue;
}
```

Now we can lock the D3DX mesh's vertex buffer and start copying across vertices:

```
// Create a pointer to currentVertex to the vertex data
MESH_VERTEX* pVertexData = 0;

// Lock the vertex buffer of the mesh we created earlier
pD3DXMesh->LockVertexBuffer(D3DLOCK_DISCARD,
                    reinterpret_cast<void**>(&pVertexData));
if(!pVertexData)
{
    // Can't lock the buffer
    MessageBox(0, "Fatal Error: Failed to lock d3dx mesh
vertex buffer",
```

```cpp
                "Custom Exporter Error", MB_OK | MB_ICONERROR);
            return MS::kFailure;
        }

        // Get a vertex iterator for all the vertices
        // in the mesh with the current material
        MItMeshVertex vertexIterator(DAGPath, currentMeshComponent);

        // Loop over all vertices with the current material
        for (; !vertexIterator.isDone(); vertexIterator.next())
        {
            // Get the position of the vertex
            MPoint currentVertex = vertexIterator.position();

            // Transfer the position into the vertex buffer
            pVertexData->position.x = static_cast<float>(currentVertex.x);
            pVertexData->position.y = static_cast<float>(currentVertex.y);
            pVertexData->position.z = static_cast<float>(currentVertex.z);

            // Copy the color information into the vertex buffer
            pVertexData->color =
                D3DXCOLOR(diffuseColor.r, diffuseColor.g,
                diffuseColor.b, diffuseColor.a);

            // Set the texture coordinates
            pVertexData->tx = 0.0f;
            pVertexData->ty = 0.0f;
            pVertexData++;
        }
    }

    // Unlock the vertex buffer now that it is filled with vertex data
    pD3DXMesh->UnlockVertexBuffer();
```

Now that half the battle is over, we just need to copy the indices to the index buffer:

```cpp
    // Create an index buffer to index the vertices
    LPDIRECT3DINDEXBUFFER9 pMeshIB = 0;

    // Get the index buffer for the mesh
    pD3DXMesh->GetIndexBuffer(&pMeshIB);
    if(!pMeshIB)
```

```cpp
        {
            MessageBox(0, "Failed to get index buffer pointer",
                "Custom Exporter Error", MB_OK | MB_ICONERROR);
            return MS::kFailure;
        }

        D3DINDEXBUFFER_DESC ibDesc;
        // Verify that the indices are kept in 16-bit integers
        pMeshIB->GetDesc(&ibDesc);

        if(ibDesc.Format == D3DFMT_INDEX16) // 16 bit indices
        {
            // Create a pointer to the index data
            short* pIndexData = 0;

            // Lock the index buffer
            pD3DXMesh->LockIndexBuffer(D3DLOCK_DISCARD,
reinterpret_cast<void**>(&pIndexData));
            if(!pIndexData)
            {
                MessageBox(0, "Failed to lock index buffer - 16 bit",
                    "Custom Exporter Error", MB_OK | MB_ICONERROR);
                return MS::kFailure;
            }

            // Loop over all the polygons
            for (; !polygonIterator.isDone(); polygonIterator.next())
            {
                // Array to hold the indexes for this
                MIntArray vertexIndices;
                polygonIterator.getVertices(vertexIndices);

                UINT length = vertexIndices.length();

                if(length != 3)
                {
                    MessageBox(0,
                    "This mesh is not triangulated! Select \Hotbox -> 
Polygons -> Triangulate before \ export",
                    "Custom Exporter Error",  MB_OK | MB_ICONERROR);
                    return MS::kFailure;
                }
```

```
                // Copy the indices into the index buffer
                *pIndexData = vertexIndices[0];
                pIndexData++;
                *pIndexData = vertexIndices[1];
                pIndexData++;
                *pIndexData = vertexIndices[2];
                pIndexData++;
            }
        }
        else if(ibDesc.Format == D3DFMT_INDEX32)      // 32-bit indices
        {
            MessageBox(0, "Error: Unsupported 32bit indices in mesh",
                "Custom Exporter Error", MB_OK | MB_ICONERROR);
            return MS::kFailure;
        }

        // Unlock the index buffer
        pD3DXMesh->UnlockIndexBuffer();
```

Finally, we need to create a dummy D3DXMATERIAL because some programs, like older versions of Direct3D's meshview utility, don't like X files without materials:

```
        // Create a default material
        D3DXMATERIAL material;
        material.pTextureFilename = 0;
        material.MatD3D.Diffuse = D3DXCOLOR(1,1,1,1);
        material.MatD3D.Ambient = D3DXCOLOR(1,1,1,1);
        material.MatD3D.Specular = D3DXCOLOR(1,1,1,1);
        material.MatD3D.Emissive = D3DXCOLOR(1,1,1,1);
        material.MatD3D.Power = 1.0f;

        // Save out the X file
        HRESULT hr = D3DXSaveMeshToX(exportFile, pD3DXMesh, 0, 0, 0, 0,
            D3DXF_FILEFORMAT_TEXT);
        if(FAILED(hr))
        {
            MessageBox(0, "Failed to save d3dx mesh",
                "Custom Exporter Error", MB_OK | MB_ICONERROR);
            return MS::kFailure;
        }

        SAFE_RELEASE(pMeshIB);
        SAFE_RELEASE(pD3DXMesh);
    }
}
```

210 Chapter 6 ■ Alias Maya API Model Exporters

After a little cleanup code, we are finished:

```
// Because this class is derived off of MPxCommand, you can use the
// inherited methods to return values and currentMeshSet error messages
//
setResult("CustomEngineExport command executed!\n");

// Release all the Direct3D resources
ShutdownDirect3D();

return returnStatus;
}
```

That wasn't so bad, was it? We now have a pretty cool exporter that will export a model and its material. It doesn't do anything fancy like textures yet, but it should be a good start to base your future work on. Don't let all the crazy Maya coding practices freak you. Just try to focus on the good stuff!

Check out the results. Figure 6.16 shows the model in Maya.

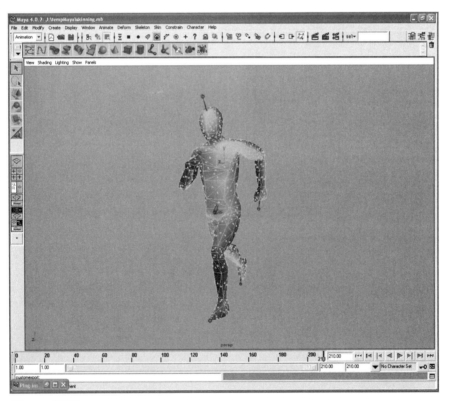

Figure 6.16
The model in Maya prior to export.

Figure 6.17 shows the fruits of your labor with the model in game.

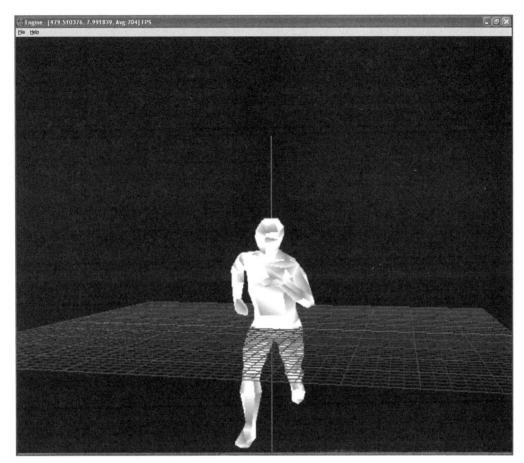

Figure 6.17
The same model in the game after export.

The lighting is slightly different, but other than that, it's good as new. You'll probably need to work some sort of scaling system to make sure everything exported from Maya ends up being the same size in your game. This is a minor issue that you can implement in the game if required.

Conclusion

You've learned an awful lot in this chapter—a whole new style of coding in a new environment. Don't worry if you're a little confused. It takes most people a while to get into the swing of working with Maya. In this chapter, I covered

- What a Directed Acyclic Graph is
- What a Dependency Graph is, and how to harness its power
- How to use the Maya plug-in wizard
- What function sets are
- When to use nodes, plugs, plug arrays, shaders, iterators, paths, and much more
- How to extract vertex and polygon information
- How to extract indexed vertex data
- How to convert Maya data to Direct3D data
- How to save X files

CHAPTER 7

APPLIED HLSL—WATER

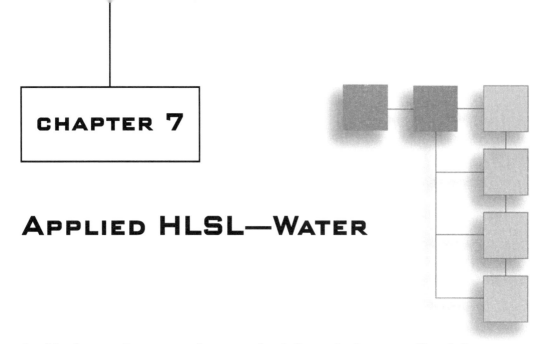

In this chapter, I want to take a step back from the heavy stuff and show you a more advanced shader built with HLSL to give you a better understanding of what goes into more advanced shaders. You'll learn how to create a really cool water effect that uses the following techniques:

- Using the passage of time within shaders
- Using multiple textures in a shader
- Modifying texture coordinates
- Cubic environment mapping
- Dynamic color modification

I chose water because it is prevalent in games, and it is also hard to get right. In this chapter, I'm not aiming to get photorealistic water—just an effect that would make people look once and say, "Wow." Let's get started.

Water has the following features in a 3D game:

- Vertices that move in subtle wave motion
- Swirling textures
- Reflections in the water of the surrounding environment
- Changing color and transparency

We'll implement all of this in our shader in this chapter.

Generating the Media

To work with water, we need a model to apply it. Nothing fancy is required—just a square plane made of triangles. Now that we have a Maya exporter, we can create all our geometry easily and export it for use in the game. In Maya, I started by creating a Non-Uniform Rational B-Splines (NURBS) plane and then triangulating it into about 800 triangles. Check out Figure 7.1.

If you are following along, make sure you apply a texture before exporting it to generate default texture coordinates. Then export the plane into an X file so that we can use it in the game.

Tracking Time

Usually any large collection of water has subtle waves that change over time. This means we are going to need a way to track time in the vertex shader, because that is where the actual waves will be generated. To implement this, I added a little extra functionality to our cGameEngine class, as in the following new variable:

```
UINT            m_EngineStartTime;
```

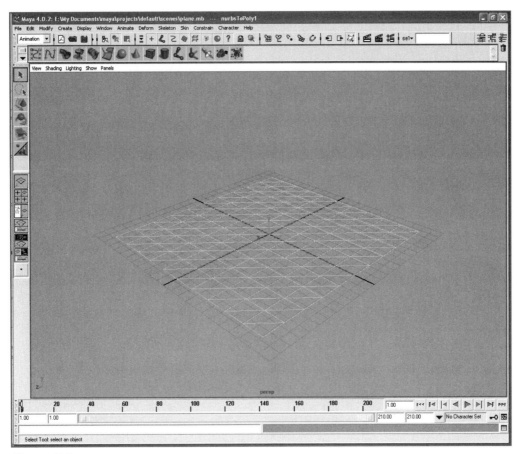

Figure 7.1
Using Maya to create media for the game engine.

This private member contains the time that the engine was started in milliseconds, returned from the windows function timeGetTime(), called from the constructor:

```
cGameEngine::cGameEngine()
{
    .
    .  // Other code
    .
    m_EngineStartTime = timeGetTime();
    .
    .  // Other code
    .
}
```

I also added a new function called GetEngineRunTime(), which returns the time since the engine was started in milliseconds:

```
UINT GetEngineRunTime()
{
    // Time game has run in milliseconds
    UINT time = timeGetTime();
    return time - m_EngineStartTime;
}
```

Now you can call this any time you want to find out how long the game has been executing. This is handy in the cEffect:Dispatch() method for passing through to the shader:

```
indBool cEffect::Dispatch()
{
    UINT runTime = GAMEENGINE->GetEngineRunTime();
    float secondsElapsed = (float)(runTime) / 1000.0f;
    m_pD3DEffect->SetFloat("time", secondsElapsed);

    m_pD3DEffect->SetMatrix("World", &m_matWorld);
    m_pD3DEffect->SetMatrix("View", &m_matView);
    m_pD3DEffect->SetMatrix("Projection", &m_matProj);

    return true;
}
```

Here I get the elapsed engine time, convert it to a floating point representation in seconds, and pass it to the shader every frame. Then all you have to do in your effect file is declare a global variable called time, which will automatically contain the current elapsed time of the engine. For this chapter, I created a new effect file called water.fx. Check it out in this chapter's code if you want to see it in full. At the top is this line:

```
float time : TIME;
```

Notice that it is bound to the TIME semantic. This is so that you can use the same shader in EffectEdit.exe for testing. EffectEdit automatically updates the TIME semantic with the elapsed time every frame. By declaring the variable called time and binding it to TIME, you enable the shader to work correctly, either in EffectEdit or in the game. This is really useful during development when you don't want to have to reload the game every time you make a change to the effect file.

For a full list of the semantics that EffectEdit supports, load it and select Help, Help Topics and read through the text.

Overriding Textures

When we first wrote the cVisualResource class a few chapters ago, it was done with X files in mind, which usually contain their own textures and materials. However, for our water example, we want to be able to override the texture used with our own water texture. This is quite easy functionality to add. First, you need a couple of extra member variables: one to hold the pointer to the overridden texture, and one flag to figure out if we want to use the overridden texture:

```
LPDIRECT3DTEXTURE9       m_pOverrideTexture;
indBool                  m_bOverrideTexture;
```

There is a new function to set the overridden texture that is pretty self-explanatory. It takes a path to a new texture to load. It loads it and does a little housekeeping code, too:

```
indBool cVisualResource::OverrideTexture(indChar* newTexturePath)
{
    HRESULT hr = S_OK;

    if(newTexturePath == 0)
    {
        m_bOverrideTexture = false;
        SAFE_RELEASE(m_pOverrideTexture);
    }
    else
    {
        if(m_pOverrideTexture)
        {
            SAFE_RELEASE(m_pOverrideTexture);
        }

        hr = D3DXCreateTextureFromFileEx(GAMEENGINE->GetDevice(), newTexturePath,
            D3DX_DEFAULT, D3DX_DEFAULT,
            D3DX_DEFAULT, 0, D3DFMT_FROM_FILE,
            D3DPOOL_MANAGED, D3DX_FILTER_TRIANGLE,
            D3DX_FILTER_TRIANGLE, 0, 0, 0, &m_pOverrideTexture);

        if(FAILED(hr))
```

```
            {
                OutputDebugString("Failed to load override texture\n");
                assert(0);
                m_bOverrideTexture = false;
                m_pOverrideTexture = 0;
            }

            m_bOverrideTexture = true;
    }

    return true;
}
```

In the render function, we check to see if the override is required and then set it as texture in the shader instead:

```
indBool cVisualResource::Render()
{
    VisualEffects::cEffect* pCurrentEffect = EFFECTMANAGER->GetEffect(m_EffectID);

    pCurrentEffect->SetTransforms(
        m_matWorld, CAMERA->GetViewMatrix(), CAMERA->GetProjectionMatrix());
    pCurrentEffect->Dispatch();

    indUInt numPasses = 0;
    pCurrentEffect->Begin(numPasses);

    GAMEENGINE->GetDevice()->SetFVF(m_pMesh->GetFVF());

    for(indUInt passCount = 0 ; passCount < numPasses ; passCount++)
    {
        pCurrentEffect->BeginPass(passCount);

        if(!m_bOverrideTexture)
        {
            for(indUInt i = 0 ; i < m_NumMeshMaterials ; i++)
            {
                if(m_pMeshTextures[i])
                    GAMEENGINE->GetDevice()->SetTexture(0, m_pMeshTextures[i]);
                GAMEENGINE->GetDevice()->SetMaterial(&m_pMeshMaterials[i]);
                m_pMesh->DrawSubset(i);
            }
```

```
        }
        else
        {
            if(m_pOverrideTexture)
                GAMEENGINE->GetDevice()->SetTexture(0, m_pOverrideTexture);

            for(indUInt i = 0 ; i < m_NumMeshMaterials ; i++)
                m_pMesh->DrawSubset(i);
        }
        pCurrentEffect->EndPass();
    }

    pCurrentEffect->End();

    GAMEENGINE->GetDevice()->SetTexture(0, 0);

    return true;
}
```

We'll be using overridden textures to force the water texture shown in Figure 7.2 onto our water.

Figure 7.2
The water texture.

Cubic Environment Mapping

As you know, water is reflective. You can generally see the surrounding environment reflected off the surface of the water. Think of a lake in the mountains. When viewed from a distance, you can see the upside-down reflected mountains across the surface of the lake. To implement this in our engine, we can use cubic environment maps.

Cubic environment maps are basically six textures in one, with one picture to represent every side of a cube. There is a texture for front and back (+Z,–Z), left and right (+X,–X), and of course up and down (+Y,–Y). Using reflection vectors, which you will see computed later in the shader, you can index into these six textures to create a seamless texture that creates a realistic 3D reflection. Check out the environment map in Figure 7.3, which I'll be using for this chapter's environment mapping.

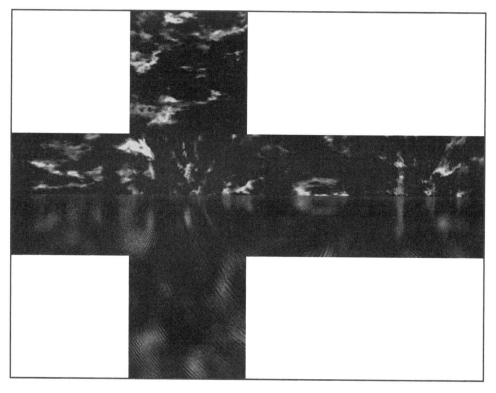

Figure 7.3
A cubic environment map for water reflection.

To implement this, we again need to add a holder for the environment map to the cVisualResource class:

```
LPDIRECT3DCUBETEXTURE9        m_pEnvironmentMap;
```

And we need to add another function to load it:

```
indBool cVisualResource::SetEnvironmentMap(char* envMapName)
{
    if(m_pEnvironmentMap)
        SAFE_RELEASE(m_pEnvironmentMap);

    D3DXCreateCubeTextureFromFile(GAMEENGINE->GetDevice(),
                                  envMapName, &m_pEnvironmentMap);
    if(!m_pEnvironmentMap)
    {
        assert(0);
        OutputDebugString("Failed to create environment map");
        return false;
    }

    return true;
}
```

Due to the way environment maps work and the fact that you might want to use them for something else, I've added some code to the cEffect class to look after environment maps. This is similar to the code in cVisualResource. First up is the pointer to hold the environment map:

```
LPDIRECT3DCUBETEXTURE9 m_pEnvironmentMap;
```

And here's the code to set it:

```
indBool SetEnvMap(LPDIRECT3DCUBETEXTURE9 envMap)
{
    SAFE_RELEASE(m_pEnvironmentMap);

    if(envMap)
    {
        envMap->AddRef();
        m_pEnvironmentMap = envMap;
    }
    else
        return false;

    return true;
}
```

Notice the `AddRef()` call. This is so the map doesn't get released accidentally outside this class. It is released every time the function is called, and in the destructor. That way there are no memory leaks.

The environment map is sent to the shader from the `cEffect::Dispatch()` function:

```
indBool cEffect::Dispatch()
{
    UINT runTime = GAMEENGINE->GetEngineRunTime();
    float secondsElapsed = (float)(runTime) / 1000.0f;
    m_pD3DEffect->SetFloat("time", secondsElapsed);

    m_pD3DEffect->SetMatrix("World", &m_matWorld);
    m_pD3DEffect->SetMatrix("View", &m_matView);
    m_pD3DEffect->SetMatrix("Projection", &m_matProj);

    if(m_pEnvironmentMap)
        m_pD3DEffect->SetTexture("envTex", m_pEnvironmentMap);

    return true;
}
```

Now we have just about everything we need to put all this together, apart from the effect file, of course. Check out the new `cGameEngine::LoadAssets()` function:

```
indBool cGameEngine::LoadAssets()
{
    Resources::cVisualResource* pNewResource =
        new Resources::cVisualResource("bigplane.x",
        RESOURCEMANAGER->GenerateUniqueID());

    pNewResource->ChangeEffect("water.fx");
    pNewResource->OverrideTexture("media\\water.bmp");
    pNewResource->SetEnvironmentMap("media\\skybox02.dds");

    RESOURCEMANAGER->AddVisualResource(pNewResource);

    return true;
}
```

Now let's look at the effect file to see how it all works.

The Water Shader Step by Step

I highly suggest that you work with this file in EffectEdit during development instead of constantly restarting the game. That's how I wrote the effect for this chapter. Look at Figure 7.4, which shows EffectEdit in action displaying the shader from this chapter.

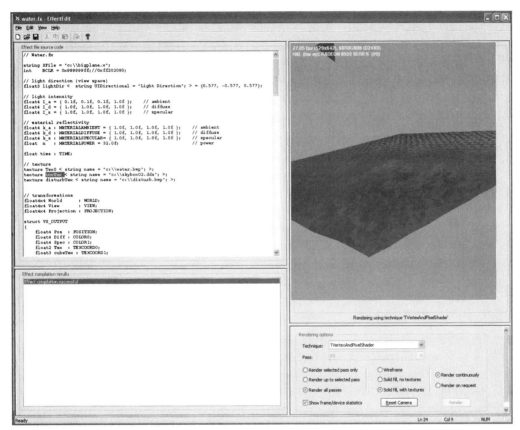

Figure 7.4
Using EffectEdit for writing effect files.

I'll take you line by line through the important code and then show you the full shader all at once. First up are the semantics for the time, water texture, and environment map, which are set using the cEffect::Dispatch() method:

```
float time : TIME;

// texture
texture Tex0 < string name = "water.bmp"; >;
texture envTex < string name = "skybox02.dds"; >;
```

The file names after the textures just affect the edit to load the textures. They do not affect the shader in the actual game. Next, we have the vertex shader, which starts out by getting the light direction and calculating the world view matrix:

```
VS_OUTPUT VS(
    float3 Pos  : POSITION,
    float3 Norm : NORMAL,
    float2 Tex  : TEXCOORD0)
{
    VS_OUTPUT Out = (VS_OUTPUT)0;

    float3 L = -lightDir;
    float4x4 WorldView = mul(World, View);
```

After that, we convert the vertex position and normal from local to world, and then to view space:

```
float3 P = mul(float4(Pos, 1), (float4x3)WorldView);  // position (view space)
float3 N = normalize(mul(Norm, (float3x3)WorldView)); // normal (view space)
```

Next we need to define an initial color for the water, which will be a mid-blue color:

```
float4 diff = float4(0.0, 0.0, 0.6, 0.65f);
```

I'll modify this color later on in the shader. Check out the next two lines, which are the real meat and potatoes of the function:

```
float sinWaveDelta= (sin(time * (abs(Pos.x)) / 5)) * 0.07;
float cosWaveDelta= (cos(time * (abs(Pos.z)) / 5))  * sinWaveDelta;
```

This code calculates two waves using the sin and cos functions. Note that it's actually a really bad idea to do trigonometry inside a shader because it is slow. Usually you precompute the values outside the shader and pass them through from the cEffect::Dispatch() function. However, that is one optimization that makes it unclear what the code is doing, so I left it out. The code is taking the position of the vertex, multiplying it by time, and then getting the sin and cos of this value to compute a subtle wave pattern. We can apply this to the vertices of the plane easily:

```
P.y += sinWaveDelta;
P.y += cosWaveDelta;
```

See Figure 7.5, which shows the resulting wave in the vertices.

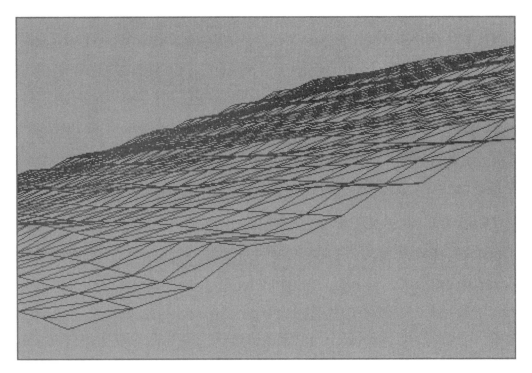

Figure 7.5
Wave action applied to the vertices.

You have to look at the water effect in real time to fully appreciate the fluidity of the movement. Next up, the code does some work to calculate the reflection vector to look up in the cube map:

```
float3 eye = normalize(-P) + (cosWaveDelta * 0.30);
float3 reflect = 2 * dot(eye, N)  * N - eye;
```

As you can see, the formula is a little different from a normal reflection vector calculation because the wave is multiplied into the calculation. Why? It's so that the environment map reflection is perturbed by the action of the waves. This gives the waves a much more realistic, glossy look. Next, the code modifies the alpha value of the waves:

```
diff.a -= cosWaveDelta * 5;
```

As you know, the rolling of waves affects your ability to see through the water. This fact modifies the transparency of the water with the wave so that its translucency changes with the waves:

```
Tex.y += (sinWaveDelta * abs(Out.Tex.x)) / 3;
    Tex.x += (cosWaveDelta * (Out.Tex.y)) / 3;
```

This code modifies the texture coordinates of the vertex, so that the water texture appears to swirl with the movement of the wave. Finally, we need to output all these calculated values to the pixel shader:

```
Out.cubeTex = reflect;
    Out.Pos  = mul(float4(P, 1), Projection);
    Out.Diff = diff * 2;
    Out.Tex  = Tex;

    return Out;
}
```

The pixel shader is pretty straightforward. It combines all the values into a single color and sends the color off to be rasterized:

```
float4 PS(
    float4 Diff : COLOR0,
    float4 Spec : COLOR1,
    float2 Tex  : TEXCOORD0,
    float3 cubeTex : TEXCOORD1) : COLOR
{
```

```
        float4 color = tex2D(Sampler, Tex) * Diff ;
        color += pow(texCUBE(EnvSampler, cubeTex ),4) * 0.25;

        return color;
}
```

The code samples the water texture with the swirled texture coordinates and multiplies it with the diffuse color. Then the environment map is sampled and added to the color, and the color is returned for rasterization.

The Water Shader in Full

Check out the full effect file that follows to see how everything fits together:

```
// Water.fx

string XFile = "c:\\bigplane.x";
int    BCLR = 0x999999ff;//0xff202080;

// light direction (view space)
float3 lightDir < string UIDirectional = "Light Direction"; > = {0.577, -0.577, 0.577};

// light intensity
float4 I_a = { 0.1f, 0.1f, 0.1f, 1.0f };    // ambient
float4 I_d = { 1.0f, 1.0f, 1.0f, 1.0f };    // diffuse
float4 I_s = { 1.0f, 1.0f, 1.0f, 1.0f };    // specular

// material reflectivity
float4 k_a : MATERIALAMBIENT = { 1.0f, 1.0f, 1.0f, 1.0f };    // ambient
float4 k_d : MATERIALDIFFUSE = { 1.0f, 1.0f, 1.0f, 1.0f };    // diffuse
float4 k_s : MATERIALSPECULAR= { 1.0f, 1.0f, 1.0f, 1.0f };    // specular
float  n   : MATERIALPOWER = 32.0f;                           // power

float time : TIME;

// texture
texture Tex0 < string name = "water.bmp"; >;
texture envTex < string name = "skybox02.dds"; >;
```

```hlsl
// transformations
float4x4 World      : WORLD;
float4x4 View       : VIEW;
float4x4 Projection : PROJECTION;

struct VS_OUTPUT
{
    float4 Pos  : POSITION;
    float4 Diff : COLOR0;
    float4 Spec : COLOR1;
    float2 Tex  : TEXCOORD0;
    float3 cubeTex : TEXCOORD1;
};

VS_OUTPUT VS(
    float3 Pos  : POSITION,
    float3 Norm : NORMAL,
    float2 Tex  : TEXCOORD0)
{
    VS_OUTPUT Out = (VS_OUTPUT)0;

    float3 L = -lightDir;
    float4x4 WorldView = mul(World, View);

    float3 P = mul(float4(Pos, 1), (float4x3)WorldView);  // position (view space)
    float3 N = normalize(mul(Norm, (float3x3)WorldView)); // normal (view space)

    float4 diff = float4(0.0, 0.0, 0.6, 0.65f);

    float sinWaveDelta= (sin(time * (abs(Pos.x)) / 5)) * 0.07;
    float cosWaveDelta= (cos(time * (abs(Pos.z)) / 5))  * sinWaveDelta;

    P.y += sinWaveDelta;
    P.y += cosWaveDelta;

    float3 eye = normalize(-P) + (cosWaveDelta * 0.30);
    float3 reflect = 2 * dot(eye, N)  * N - eye;

    diff.a -= cosWaveDelta * 5;
    Tex.y += (sinWaveDelta * abs(Out.Tex.x)) / 3;
    Tex.x += (cosWaveDelta * (Out.Tex.y)) / 3;
```

```
    Out.cubeTex = reflect;
    Out.Pos  = mul(float4(P, 1), Projection);
    Out.Diff = diff * 2;
    Out.Tex  = Tex;

    return Out;
}

sampler Sampler = sampler_state
{
    Texture   = (Tex0);
    MipFilter = LINEAR;
    MinFilter = LINEAR;
    MagFilter = LINEAR;
};

sampler EnvSampler = sampler_state
{
    Texture   = (envTex);
    MipFilter = LINEAR;
    MinFilter = LINEAR;
    MagFilter = LINEAR;
};

float4 PS(
    float4 Diff : COLOR0,
    float4 Spec : COLOR1,
    float2 Tex  : TEXCOORD0,
    float3 cubeTex : TEXCOORD1) : COLOR
{
        float4 color = tex2D(Sampler, Tex) * Diff ;
        color += pow(texCUBE(EnvSampler, cubeTex ),4) * 0.25;

        return color;
}



technique TVertexAndPixelShader
{
    pass P0
    {
        alphablendenable = true;
```

```
                srcblend = srcalpha;
                destblend = invsrcalpha;
                VertexShader = compile vs_1_1 VS();
                PixelShader  = compile ps_1_1 PS();
            }

        }

        technique TVertexShaderOnly
        {
            pass P0
            {
                // lighting
                Lighting       = FALSE;
                SpecularEnable = TRUE;

                // samplers
                Sampler[0] = (Sampler);

                // texture stages
                ColorOp[0]   = MODULATE;
                ColorArg1[0] = TEXTURE;
                ColorArg2[0] = DIFFUSE;
                AlphaOp[0]   = MODULATE;
                AlphaArg1[0] = TEXTURE;
                AlphaArg2[0] = DIFFUSE;

                ColorOp[1]   = DISABLE;
                AlphaOp[1]   = DISABLE;

                // shaders
                VertexShader = compile vs_1_1 VS();
                PixelShader  = NULL;
            }
        }

        technique TNoShader
        {
            pass P0
            {
                // transforms
                WorldTransform[0] = (World);
                ViewTransform     = (View);
```

```
            ProjectionTransform = (Projection);

            // material
            MaterialAmbient  = (k_a);
            MaterialDiffuse  = (k_d);
            MaterialSpecular = (k_s);
            MaterialPower    = (n);

            // lighting
            LightType[0]      = DIRECTIONAL;
            LightAmbient[0]   = (I_a);
            LightDiffuse[0]   = (I_d);
            LightSpecular[0]  = (I_s);
            LightDirection[0] = (lightDir);
            LightRange[0]     = 100000.0f;

            LightEnable[0] = TRUE;
            Lighting       = TRUE;
            SpecularEnable = TRUE;

            // samplers
            Sampler[0] = (Sampler);

            // texture stages
            ColorOp[0]   = MODULATE;
            ColorArg1[0] = TEXTURE;
            ColorArg2[0] = DIFFUSE;
            AlphaOp[0]   = MODULATE;
            AlphaArg1[0] = TEXTURE;
            AlphaArg2[0] = DIFFUSE;

            ColorOp[1]   = DISABLE;
            AlphaOp[1]   = DISABLE;

            // shaders
            VertexShader = NULL;
            PixelShader  = NULL;
        }
    }
```

Try changing some values to see how everything fits together. Then check out the result from the game, as shown in Figure 7.6.

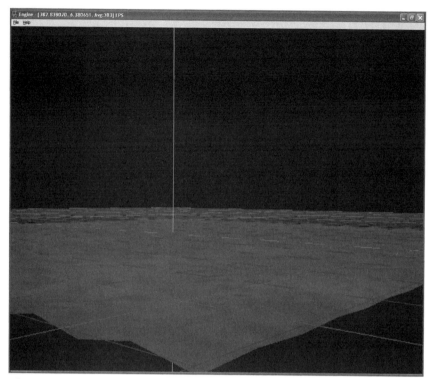

Figure 7.6
The water effect running in the game.

Conclusion

In this chapter, you learned about taking effect files and shaders to the next level to create a much more advanced water effect than anything you have seen before in this book. You learned about the following:

- Using the passage of time within shaders
- Using multiple textures in a shader
- Modifying texture coordinates
- Cubic environment mapping
- Dynamic color modification

In the next chapter, it's back to the heavy stuff as we explore advanced skinned animation with DirectX. Hold on to your hats!

CHAPTER 8

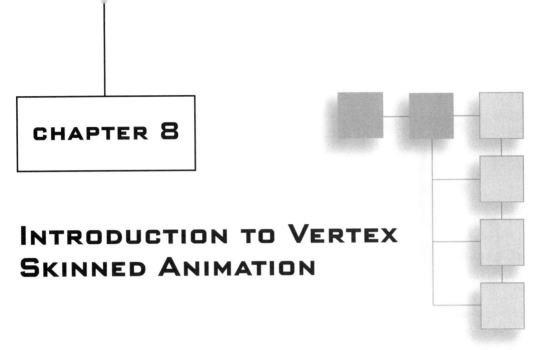

INTRODUCTION TO VERTEX SKINNED ANIMATION

Vertex Skinned Animation. It has a lovely ring to it, doesn't it? Not. It makes me think of an abattoir. Nonetheless, this is what some kind soul decided to name one of the coolest animation techniques out there. Because this is the only type of animation I'm going to be showing in this book, I'll simply refer to it as *animation*. If I'm talking about other methods, I'll use their full names to make it clear. In this chapter, I'm going to cover the following:

- Introduction to vertex skinning, including all the weird terms that go along with it
- Introduction to frames, bones, mesh containers, and allocation hierarchies
- Joint hierarchies
- Animation sets
- Bone combination buffers
- And a whole lot more

Let's get started!

It's All About Skin and Bones!

Before I tell you about this amazing form of animation, let me take a minute to show you older animation techniques and the problems they suffered. Originally, animation was simply changing textures really quickly so that it mimicked animation. For instance, in the killer game *Duke Nukem 3D*, the water was just a load of textures that were played in a loop (see Figure 8.1). Each frame of the animation had a slightly different version of the water so that when played fast, it looked like water rippling. This kind of 2D animation was the main form of animation in the mid 1990s. It originated in the old sprite animation used in games like the original *Prince of Persia*.

Figure 8.1
2D sprite animation in *Duke Nukem 3D*.

The next step up in animation was similar to the 2D method except that it was 3D. The 3D model to be animated was captured throughout its animation sequence and output as a separate mesh. These meshes were then shown in sequence quickly to create the effect of an animated character. This is the form of animation that was used in the original *Quake*, released way back in May 1996 (see Figure 8.2).

Figure 8.2
Basic 3D animation in the original *Quake*.

With the release of *Tomb Raider* in October 1996, the world was shown full 3D animation for the first time, and they loved it. It was a major leap forward. The difference with *Tomb Raider* was that each body part was animated in real time, which led to an incredible range of realistic motion. However, looking back, the deficiencies are clear. Look closely at Lara's legs (woo hoo!) around the knee joint, and you can see the geometry clashing between her upper and lower legs (see Figure 8.3). Although they're well hidden, it's impossible to hide the geometry collision points as they move. This is because each part of Lara's body was made of a separate model. There was a model for her upper and lower arms, upper and lower legs, torso, head, and so on. Each of these is moved independently to create the impression of a moving female.

Figure 8.3
Full 3D animation in *Tomb Raider* before vertex skinning.

The solution to the problem is vertex skinning. Rather than dividing a body into little models that represent each moving part, there is a single model representing the entire body. This model is usually shaped into what is called a *base pose*. A base pose for a human usually means that the person is standing straight up with legs together and with both arms sticking straight out to the left and right. It doesn't really matter too much what form the base pose is, but this is usually it.

Attached to the base pose is a skeleton made of bones. Yes, I know this is sounding a bit grim! The skeleton, just like in a human body, specifies how all the bones connect to each other. The bones in turn are set to modify specific vertices that make up the polygon model representing the person. Hence the term *skin*—the bones move the skin of the model in effect.

Just What Is a Bone?

Before I go any further, I'm going to let you in on a little secret that other authors don't usually let on for a long time when teaching about skinned animation: A bone is just a standard transformation matrix. In fact, the term *bone* is really misleading; it should be a *joint*, because it describes transformation about a specific point, not along a line. So when you hear *bone*, think *simple little matrix*. And I mean simple—there is nothing more to a matrix used for vertex skinned animation than there is to a matrix used to transform a normal model. The real magic of vertex skinning comes from putting the matrices into a hierarchy and vertex weighting.

Let's talk about the hierarchy, because it's quite cool. You know that you can combine matrices to combine transforms. So if you have one matrix that moves a point up the y axis and another that rotates it 90 degrees, you can combine these into a single matrix that does both of these actions. Fantastic! That means you can create dependencies of matrices. This is how skeletal hierarchies work. Usually the root bone is at the base of the back for a humanoid. Coming down from that are two hip bones, two upper leg bones, two lower leg bones, and finally foot bones. Up from the root bone are bones sprouting off for the arms and up for the head. Look at Figure 8.4; it shows a skeleton hierarchy in Maya.

If you want to move the entire character, you apply a transformation to the root bone. This will then be multiplied down to all the other bones also included in this transformation, and the entire character will move. All the vertices in the mesh are set (more on this soon) to be affected by a particular bone, so when the bones move, so does the mesh. But what if you just want the character to wave? In that case, apply a rotation transformation to the shoulder bone. This will flow down through the rest of the arm bones and create a wave effect. If you apply both transformations, the character will move *and* wave.

What does it mean to "apply a transformation to the root bone?" Well, I'll tell you. Remember that the bone is just a matrix. A transformation is another matrix. So if you want to move the character 5 units down the z axis, create a translation matrix with (0,0,5) and multiply it by the root bone matrix. Job done. See, it's not too hard. Other people just make it seem that way!

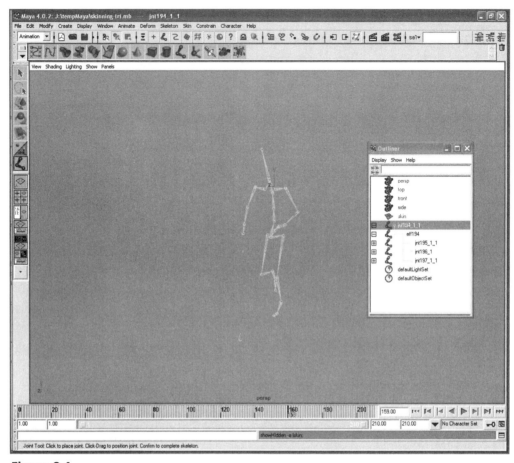

Figure 8.4
A skeleton rendered in Maya.

More About Skeletons

So now you know a little about how bones work. But how do they create complex movement? A transformation matrix is multiplied down the hierarchy but never back up again. So the root affects the shoulders affects the elbow affects the hand. But the hand never affects the elbow, and the elbow never affects the shoulder. Get it? Otherwise, you might have a tail wagging the dog effect!

Complex animations are not created by some poor programmer in a back room writing code like, "Apply this rotation, now that, now this, now translate, rotate again, and back again." That would take forever. The key is sophisticated modeling software like 3ds Max or Maya, or motion capture data. Motion capture data is usually video or a series of photographs of someone performing an act, like falling over, for instance. On their bodies are bright circles that the computer can pick out and turn into a transformation to apply to bones in your model. Creating and applying motion capture data is so far out of the scope of this book that I can barely see it in the distance. However, with a bit of studying, you should be able to pick up how to do it in max or Maya. Alternatively, there is a wide selection of free animations you can play around with while learning.

Luckily for us, DirectX ships with a few models that are great for showing off the skinned animation code. Check out our hero Tiny in Figure 8.5. Tiny ships with DirectX and is the model I'll be using to demonstrate the code in this chapter. You can find Tiny in the media subdirectory of your DirectX install path.

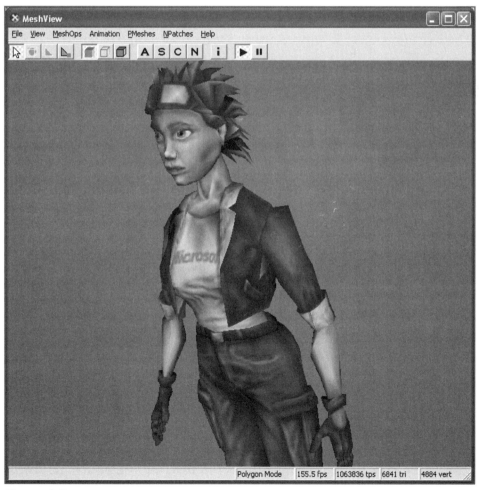

Figure 8.5
The tiny.x model rendered in the mesh viewer application.

Weights and Indices

This is the other half of the magic that makes skinned animation possible. Each vertex in a skinned mesh has additional data that states which bones affect it and by how much. The indices tell which bones affect the vertex, and the weight tells by how much. The index is just a number that indexes into an array of bones. The weight is a floating point number that ranges from 0.0 for no effect to 1.0 for full effect.

What is the reason for weights? Well, look at your arm from your elbow joint to your wrist. Now rotate your wrist. See how the skin moves a lot near your wrist but not so much near your elbow? If this were a game, for the vertices of the model near your wrist, you would index the wrist joints with a high weight. For vertices near your elbow, you would index both your wrist joint *and* your elbow joint. The wrist joint has a low influence and the elbow joint has a high one. This setup creates the same effect you see in real life on your 3D model.

Adding skinning information is really a pain in the skeleton. It's best left to artists if you work in a games company, because they like that sort of thing. Alternatively, there are automation tools that can help you with the task. The best automation tool, though, is your nearest artist in the art department. I can't tell you how tedious it is to manually add skinning information to a model. Hey, we have to stare at text all day. Skinning is the least the artists can do!

Bringing It All Together

Now you know the main ingredients that go into making killer animations. The first ingredient is a set of matrices that act as joints that are organized into a hierarchy to form a skeleton. The second is a skinned mesh, which is just a regular mesh but with extra information added to each vertex to hold information about which bone affects it and by how much. And that's it, right? Heck no! Those things alone aren't going to animate a model. You need animation data!

Just like in the old days, animated models have to have something that tells them what to do to animate. Years ago, it was a series of images that showed an animated character in a slightly different pose that when shown quickly became like fluid movement.

The same is true of skinned animation, except in this case you need a number of keyed poses. So for your character walking, you might have 10 frames of keyed data containing the walk sequence. But just what is this data? It's the skeleton, of course. Each frame of an animation sequence is a snapshot of all the transformation matrices that make up the skeleton. Then during playback, these various key frames are interpolated together to show a perfectly smooth animated character no matter what speed the animation is played back.

Again, think back to basics, and don't let all this terminology get in the way of how easy this is. A skeleton is made of bones, which are just a hierarchy of matrices. So each frame of animation is really just a list of matrices. Load up the matrices and apply them at the correct time to the model, and lo and behold the model moves in a fluid manner.

This saves an incredible amount of space compared to the old animation methods used in *Quake*, and it looks a lot better. Think about it this way. If you wanted to store 10 seconds of *Quake* animation for a 25KB model, you would need at least 10 frames per second, which is 10 animated models per second. So 25KB×10 models per second×10 seconds = 2.5MB! Conversely, for skinned animation, you can get away with 5 samples per second or less because the samples can be interpolated. And we're only storing 16 matrices per sample, so that's a 25KB model + (16-byte matrix * 16 matrices * 5 samples per second * 10 seconds) = 37.8KB! That's a savings of 2.46 megabytes!

And the coolest part? Imagine that you have three actions that your character can do, which are walking, standing still, and waving. In old animation methods, you would have to have your art team develop not just the three animation sequences, but a sequence to smoothly transform from standing to waving and from standing to walking. If your character is waving, you can't just start walking. First you have to play the sequence back to standing idle and then play the stand to walk sequence, and finally play the walk animation. The only way around this is to create more and more intermediate sequences. As the number of sequences increases, the number of intermediate sequences increases exponentially until it quickly becomes impractical. That's why early games had limited 3D animation sequences.

But none of this applies to skinned animation. Why? Because the animations are really just a set of matrices. So you have a sequence of matrices for walking, a sequence for standing, and another for waving. Because they are matrices, they can easily be blended together and interpolated, which means you can quickly and seamlessly move from one animation sequence to another without a skip, and without intermediate sequences. If the character is waving and suddenly you want him to run, set up a blend of 250 milliseconds to blend out the wave and blend in the run. From the outside, it looks like the character quickly puts his hand down and starts to run, which is exactly what you would expect in real life, and why skinned animation is so powerful.

Okay, before we drown in theory, it's time to check out some code and see this baby in action. Check out Figure 8.6.

Figure 8.6
A skinned mesh viewed from Maya.

Skinned Animation with Direct3D

Now, I have to say that I've come across some nasty code in my life. I've seen some abstractions that took longer to learn than the technology they were designed to hide. I've programmed Xbox 360 alpha kits while they were still being bottle fed, with broken hardware, incomplete middleware, and broken engines. I've...gulp...written execute buffers in Direct3D 3.0. But never in my life have I come across anything like the animation system in Direct3D. Without saying more, I'll leave you to make up your own mind about it.

So here in all its pure glory is how you write a skinned animation engine using DirectX. The main problem with it is not looking at it once it's written, but the fact that you have to write, oh, about 450 lines of code before you can even begin to start testing your code. So bear with me while I get this introductory code out of the way before I can show you the magic.

First, you need to learn about Direct3D's terminology. For some reason, Microsoft decided to use the word *frame* in place of *bone*. I mean, it's not like the word *frame* is used anywhere else, like in these cases:

- Frames per second
- Frame of animation
- Frame buffer
- Key frame
- Network frame

So just keep in mind that *frame* also means *bone*. It's all part of Microsoft's doublethink campaign. Eventually everything will be called a frame. To clear this up, I've derived my own classes where necessary and used the term *bone* in its place, just like everyone else outside of Redmond.

In the Beginning...

All animations start somewhere, usually in the mind of a mad artist, but for us coders, animation begins with D3DXLoadMeshHierarchyFromX(). Check out the prototype:

```
HRESULT WINAPI D3DXLoadMeshHierarchyFromX(
    LPCSTR Filename,
    DWORD MeshOptions,
    LPDIRECT3DDEVICE9 pDevice,
    LPD3DXALLOCATEHIERARCHY pAlloc,
    LPD3DXLOADUSERDATA pUserDataLoader,
    LPD3DXFRAME* ppFrameHierarchy,
    LPD3DXANIMATIONCONTROLLER* ppAnimController
);
```

I say everything begins here because it really does; everything in this chapter begins with this simple function. If you follow those seven parameters through several hundred pages of poor documentation, you will eventually end up with a simple 400-line skinned animation system. I'll not go into this in too much detail just yet, because there is a lot of introductory material to cover first. Just keep in mind that this function needs all these components:

- **Filename.** The file name of animation to load
- **MeshOptions.** Various options flags similar to the D3DXLoadMeshFromX() function
- **pDevice.** A standard D3D device
- **pAlloc.** An allocation hierarchy, which I'll discuss in a moment and you'll learn to hate
- **ppFrameHierarchy.** A pointer to a skeleton hierarchy of bones
- **ppAnimController.** An animation controller that is responsible for playing back and mixing animations

Now back to the hard work...

Frames and Mesh Containers

Frames and mesh containers are the two cornerstones of DirectX's animation implementation. Frames are, of course, bones. They are joined into a hierarchy to comprise the skeleton that transforms your mesh. Direct3D uses this structure to represent a bone:

```
typedef struct _D3DXFRAME {
    LPSTR Name;
    D3DXMATRIX TransformationMatrix;
    LPD3DXMESHCONTAINER pMeshContainer;
    struct _D3DXFRAME *pFrameSibling;
    struct _D3DXFRAME *pFrameFirstChild;
} D3DXFRAME, *LPD3DXFRAME;
```

This structure has a few interesting members. Name holds the name of the bone, which is incredibly useful for debugging because most 3D packages force you to names bones. You can quickly find bones that are acting funny if you ensure that this member is filled out correctly and not just with *bone*. Notice that this variable is simply a pointer, and it is up to you to allocate and deallocate the memory for this string. I'll show you why shortly. The next member is TransformationMatrix, which is the meat and potatoes of this structure. It holds the matrix that is the bone. pMeshContainer holds a pointer to the D3DXMESHCONTAINER structure that this bone affects. More of this anon. pFrameSibling and pFrameFirstChild allow the creation of the skeleton hierarchy. For instance, if this "frame" were the right hip bone, its sibling would be the left hip joint, and its child would be the right knee joint. To clean up and rename this messy structure, I've derived my own class from it:

```
// Represents a single bone matrix in the skeleton
class cBone : public D3DXFRAME
{
public:
    cBone()
    {
        D3DXMatrixIdentity(&TransformationMatrix);
        D3DXMatrixIdentity(&m_CombinedTransformationMatrix);
        pMeshContainer = NULL;
        pFrameSibling = NULL;
        pFrameFirstChild = NULL;
    }

    ~cBone()
    {
        SAFE_DELETE_ARRAY(Name);
    }

    D3DXMATRIXA16       m_CombinedTransformationMatrix;
};
```

This code renames the structure to cBone to stick with a standard naming convention, and it adds a new member m_CombinedTransformationMatrix. This is a little optimization I picked up from one of Phil Taylor's (a DirectX program manager) animation examples. As matrices are combined down the hierarchy, it's useful to store the combination at each level so that you don't have to recompute the entire hierarchy every time a matrix changes.

Next up is the mesh container, which looks after your mesh that is being animated. This structure looks like this:

```
typedef struct _D3DXMESHCONTAINER {
    LPSTR Name;
    D3DXMESHDATA MeshData;
    LPD3DXMATERIAL pMaterials;
    LPD3DXEFFECTINSTANCE pEffects;
    DWORD NumMaterials;
    DWORD *pAdjacency;
    LPD3DXSKININFO pSkinInfo;
    struct _D3DXMESHCONTAINER *pNextMeshContainer;
} D3DXMESHCONTAINER, *LPD3DXMESHCONTAINER;
```

This structure looks after everything to do with meshes. Often, skinned animations are composed of more than one source mesh, which doesn't really have many benefits but does add to the complexity. The code in this book covers singly animated meshes. Only a small number of modifications are required to support multiple meshes. Let's look a little closer at this structure. `Name` again holds the name of the model, which is useful during development for debugging. Again, like `D3DXFRAME`, look out for the fact that this memory must be allocated manually for the string. `MeshData` is a small structure that holds a pointer to the actual mesh that's being modified:

```
typedef struct D3DXMESHDATA {
    D3DXMESHDATATYPE Type;
    union
    {
        LPD3DXMESH       pMesh;
        LPD3DXPMESH      pPMesh;
        LPD3DXPATCHMESH pPatchMesh;
    }
} D3DXMESHDATA, *LPD3DXMESHDATA;
```

As you can see, this structure comprises various unionized pointers and a type variable. We are only dealing with standard meshes, so this structure will always contain an `LPD3DXMESH` pointer and `Type` set to `D3DXMESHTYPE_MESH`. Next up in the original `D3DXMESHCONTAINER` structure is `pMaterials`, which is a pointer to all the materials that the mesh uses. `pEffects` is rarely used; it is a pointer effect that renders the animation, which is usually `NULL`. `NumMaterials` obviously contains the number of materials in the `pMaterials` array. `pAdjacency` is a pointer to adjacency in the mesh, which is not always required. You can always get ID3DXMesh to generate it for you automatically if you need to. pSkinInfo is yet another monster embedded object (don't you love when API designers do that?) that contains all the mesh skinning information, including all the weights and indices. Last and least is the pNextMeshContainer structure, which contains a link to the next mesh if one is available.

It's important that you know at least peripherally about that structure because it is the basis of the D3DX animation system. As I said before, this stuff ain't pretty. Like D3DXFRAME, I have derived a class from this structure to clean up initialization and shutdown and to add a few extra members to help us on the way. Check out the class definition:

```
class cAnimatedMeshContainer : public D3DXMESHCONTAINER
{
public:
    cAnimatedMeshContainer()
    {
        m_ppTextures = 0;
        m_pOriginalMesh = 0;
        m_pAttributeTable = 0;
        m_NumAttributeGroups = 0;
        m_NumBoneInfluencesPerVertex = 0;
        m_pBoneCombinationBuffer = 0;
        m_ppBoneMatrixPtrs = 0;
        m_pBoneOffsetMatrices = 0;
        m_NumPaletteEntries = 0;
        m_bUseSoftwareVP = false;
        m_AttributeSW = 0;

        // Base members
        Name = 0;
        ZeroMemory(&MeshData, sizeof(MeshData));
        pMaterials = 0;
        pEffects = 0;
        NumMaterials = 0;
        pAdjacency = 0;
        pSkinInfo = 0;

    }
```

```cpp
~cAnimatedMeshContainer()
{
    SAFE_DELETE_ARRAY(Name);
    SAFE_DELETE_ARRAY(pAdjacency);
    SAFE_DELETE_ARRAY(pMaterials);
    SAFE_DELETE_ARRAY(m_pBoneOffsetMatrices);

    UINT materialCount = 0;
    if(m_ppTextures != NULL)
    {
        for(materialCount = 0; materialCount < NumMaterials; materialCount++)
        {
            SAFE_RELEASE(m_ppTextures[materialCount]);
        }
    }

    SAFE_DELETE_ARRAY(m_ppTextures);
    SAFE_DELETE_ARRAY(m_ppBoneMatrixPtrs);
    SAFE_RELEASE(m_pBoneCombinationBuffer);
    SAFE_RELEASE(MeshData.pMesh);
    SAFE_RELEASE(pSkinInfo);
    SAFE_RELEASE(m_pOriginalMesh);
}

LPDIRECT3DTEXTURE9*  m_ppTextures;
LPD3DXMESH           m_pOriginalMesh;
LPD3DXATTRIBUTERANGE m_pAttributeTable;
DWORD                m_NumAttributeGroups;
DWORD                m_NumBoneInfluencesPerVertex;
LPD3DXBUFFER         m_pBoneCombinationBuffer;
D3DXMATRIX**         m_ppBoneMatrixPtrs;
D3DXMATRIX*          m_pBoneOffsetMatrices;
DWORD                m_NumPaletteEntries;
};
```

There are a few extra members in there. m_ppTextures holds an array of texture pointers that the animated mesh uses. m_pOriginalMesh holds a backup pointer to the mesh when it was loaded. This pointer is modified just before rendering. m_pAttributeTable holds an array of all the attributes, which basically is a list of vertices and faces that used a particular material. Here is the structure so that you are aware of it:

```
typedef struct _D3DXATTRIBUTERANGE {
    DWORD AttribId;
    DWORD FaceStart;
    DWORD FaceCount;
    DWORD VertexStart;
    DWORD VertexCount;
} D3DXATTRIBUTERANGE;
```

m_NumAttributeGroups contains the number of attributes in the table. The next new member is m_NumBoneInfluencesPerVertex, which contains the number of bones that can affect a vertex. This is usually four or less. To say it slightly differently, each vertex can be influenced by up to four different bones, which in programming means that each vertex can be affected by up to four matrices. m_pBoneCombinationBuffer is a simple ID3DXBUFFER that is basically scratch memory space that D3DX uses when calculating the bone interpolations. m_ppBoneMatrixPtrs is a pointer to an array of the bones extracted as from the cBone class (that is, D3DXFRAME). m_pBoneOffsetMatrices is kind of interesting. It contains the translations that are necessary to change from local model space to bone space so that rotations work out correctly. m_NumPaletteEntries contains the number of matrices in the matrix arrays. Okay, that's most of the annoying Direct3D stuff out of the way. Now we just need to see how to put it to work…

Working with DirectX

As I've hinted at before, DirectX is not always pretty or easy to work with, and the same is more than true for animation. Due to the complex nature of animation, Direct3D makes a lot of its structures and interfaces overridable so that you can add your own implementation. Personally, I think this is ridiculous because it adds so much complexity to the system, and in a real project you are never going to override parts of the Direct3D animation system—you're either going to work with it or without it, but not both.

Let's get started. Direct3D has an interface specification called ID3DXAllocateHierarchy. This interface is nothing but a definition—you must provide the implementation yourself and fill in all the necessary code. The purpose of this interface is to create all the structures that Direct3D needs to animate your mesh, such as the evil D3DXFRAME and D3DXMESHCONTAINER structure I was telling you about before.

Look at the interface definition for starters, because it's truly a thing of beauty:

```
DECLARE_INTERFACE(ID3DXAllocateHierarchy)
{
    STDMETHOD(CreateFrame)(THIS_ LPCSTR Name,
                               LPD3DXFRAME *ppNewFrame) PURE;

    STDMETHOD(CreateMeshContainer)(THIS_
        LPCSTR Name,
        CONST D3DXMESHDATA *pMeshData,
        CONST D3DXMATERIAL *pMaterials,
        CONST D3DXEFFECTINSTANCE *pEffectInstances,
        DWORD NumMaterials,
        CONST DWORD *pAdjacency,
        LPD3DXSKININFO pSkinInfo,
        LPD3DXMESHCONTAINER *ppNewMeshContainer) PURE;

    STDMETHOD(DestroyFrame)(THIS_ LPD3DXFRAME pFrameToFree) PURE;
    STDMETHOD(DestroyMeshContainer)(THIS_ LPD3DXMESHCONTAINER pMeshContainerToFree)
PURE;
};
```

Cutting through all the COM stuff, there are four functions that need to be overridden. You can accomplish this by deriving your own class from ID3DXAllocateHierarchy, like this:

```
class cSkinnedAnimationMesh :
    public cAnimatedMeshContainer,
    public ID3DXAllocateHierarchy
{
public:
    cSkinnedAnimationMesh(void);
    ~cSkinnedAnimationMesh(void);

    //
    // Other code
    //

private:
    // ID3DXAllocateHierarchy callback implementation for loading
    STDMETHOD(CreateFrame)(const char* name, LPD3DXFRAME *ppNewBone);
    STDMETHOD(CreateMeshContainer)(const char* name,
```

```
        const D3DXMESHDATA* pMeshData,
        const  D3DXMATERIAL* pMaterials,
        const D3DXEFFECTINSTANCE* pEffectInstances,
        DWORD numMaterials,
        const  DWORD* pAdjacency,
        LPD3DXSKININFO pSkinInfo,
        LPD3DXMESHCONTAINER* ppNewMeshContainer);

    STDMETHOD(DestroyFrame)(LPD3DXFRAME pBone);
    STDMETHOD(DestroyMeshContainer)(LPD3DXMESHCONTAINER pMeshContainer);
};
```

This class will be the basis for each animated mesh in our game. Notice how it is also derived from cAnimatedMeshContainer, which is a wrapping class for D3DXMESHCONTAINER. This neatly packs all the various bits needed for animation under one class. Now let's look at implementing these functions, starting with the creation and destruction of frames.

Creating and Destroying Frames

The first two functions to implement are CreateFrame() and DestroyFrame(). During loading, CreateFrame() is called for every bone in the skeleton. This function is where you allocate all the memory and anything else you might need in a bone. Check out the code:

```
HRESULT cSkinnedAnimationMesh::CreateFrame(const char* name, LPD3DXFRAME *ppNewBone)
{
    if(!ppNewBone)
        return E_FAIL;

    *ppNewBone = NULL;
    cBone* pTempBone = new cBone;

    if(!pTempBone)
    {
        OutputDebugString("ERROR: Memory Exhausted creating a new animation\n");
        assert(0);
        return E_OUTOFMEMORY;
    }

    if(name)
```

```
    {
        pTempBone->Name = new char[strlen(name)+1];
        strcpy(pTempBone->Name, name);
    }
    else
    {
        char* tempName = "UnnamedFrame";
        pTempBone->Name = new char[strlen(tempName)+1];
        if(pTempBone->Name)
        {
            strcpy(pTempBone->Name, tempName);
        }
        else
        {
            pTempBone->Name = 0;
            OutputDebugString("ERROR: Memory Exhausted creating a new animation\n");
            assert(0);
            return E_OUTOFMEMORY;
        }
    }

    *ppNewBone = pTempBone;
    return S_OK;
}
```

There is a lot of error checking here, but basically the code creates a new D3DXFRAME, allocates more memory for the string name, and then copies the string into the frame. Finally, if all goes well, the source pointer is updated to point at the newly created frame. Notice how the string memory is created with the new operator and not just set to a string. It is important to know that all memory in animation is under your control. You need to release it during destruction, or you'll end up with a lot of memory leaks. That's where this function comes in:

```
HRESULT cSkinnedAnimationMesh::DestroyFrame(LPD3DXFRAME pBone)
{
    SAFE_DELETE_ARRAY(pBone->Name);
    SAFE_DELETE(pBone);
    return S_OK;
}
```

Creating and Destroying Mesh Containers

This part is much trickier, so keep yourself alert lest you fall into the pit of endless confusion, despair, and doom (no, not the White House). Before I explain what the heck is going on, here is the entire function. This code is loosely based on Phil Taylor's sample animation stuff in the SDK, if you want to see a different approach to using this material:

```
HRESULT cSkinnedAnimationMesh::CreateMeshContainer(const char* name,
        const D3DXMESHDATA* pMeshDataIn,
        const D3DXMATERIAL* pMaterialsIn,
        const D3DXEFFECTINSTANCE* pEffectInstancesIn,
        DWORD numMaterialsIn,
        const DWORD* pAdjacencyIn,
        LPD3DXSKININFO pSkinInfoIn,
        LPD3DXMESHCONTAINER* ppNewMeshContainerOut)
{

    UINT numFaces;
    UINT materialIndex;
    UINT numBones, boneIndex;
    LPD3DXMESH pMesh = NULL;
    HRESULT hr = 0;

    *ppNewMeshContainerOut = NULL;

    if(!pMeshDataIn)
    {
        assert(0);
        return E_FAIL;
    }

    if(pMeshDataIn->Type != D3DXMESHTYPE_MESH)
    {
        OutputDebugString("Invalid mesh type passed to CreateMeshContainer\n");
        assert(0);
        return E_FAIL;
    }

    pMesh = pMeshDataIn->pMesh;

    if(pMesh->GetFVF() == 0)
    {
```

```
            OutputDebugString("Mesh has invalid FVF in CreateMeshContainer\n");
            assert(0);
            return E_FAIL;
        }


        if(name)
        {
            SAFE_DELETE(Name);
            Name = new char[strlen(name)+1];
            strcpy(Name, name);
        }
        else
        {
            char* tempName = "Unnamed mesh container";
            Name = new char[strlen(tempName)+1];
            strcpy(Name, tempName);
        }

        numFaces = pMesh->GetNumFaces();

        // Add normals to mesh if not there already
        if(!(pMesh->GetFVF() & D3DFVF_NORMAL))
        {
            MeshData.Type = D3DXMESHTYPE_MESH;

            if(FAILED(pMesh->CloneMeshFVF(pMesh->GetOptions(),
                                                pMesh->GetFVF() | D3DFVF_NORMAL,
                GAMEENGINE->GetDevice(), &MeshData.pMesh)))
            {
                OutputDebugString(
                    "Failed when attempting to add normal info to a mesh\n");
                assert(0);
                return E_FAIL;
            }

            D3DXComputeNormals(pMesh, NULL);

        }
        else
        {
            MeshData.pMesh = pMesh;
```

```
        MeshData.Type = D3DXMESHTYPE_MESH;
        pMesh->AddRef();
    }

    SAFE_DELETE(pMaterials);
    SAFE_DELETE(pAdjacency);
    SAFE_DELETE(m_ppTextures);

    NumMaterials = max(1, numMaterialsIn);
    pMaterials = new D3DXMATERIAL[NumMaterials];
    pAdjacency = new DWORD[numFaces*3];

    m_ppTextures = new LPDIRECT3DTEXTURE9[NumMaterials];

    if(!pMaterials ||
        !m_ppTextures ||
        !m_ppTextures)
    {
        OutputDebugString("Memory exhausted in CreateMeshContainer\n");
        assert(0);
        return E_OUTOFMEMORY;
    }

    memcpy((void*)pAdjacency, pAdjacencyIn, sizeof(DWORD) * numFaces*3);
    memset(m_ppTextures, 0, sizeof(LPDIRECT3DTEXTURE9) * NumMaterials);

    if(numMaterialsIn > 0)
    {
        memcpy((void*)pMaterials, pMaterialsIn, sizeof(D3DXMATERIAL) * NumMaterials);

        for(materialIndex = 0; materialIndex < NumMaterials ; materialIndex++)
        {
            if(pMaterials[materialIndex].pTextureFilename != NULL)
            {
                char texturePath[MAX_PATH];
                strcpy(texturePath, "media\\");
                strcat(texturePath, pMaterials[materialIndex].pTextureFilename);

                if(FAILED(D3DXCreateTextureFromFile(
                    GAMEENGINE->GetDevice(),
                    texturePath,
                    &m_ppTextures[materialIndex])))
```

```cpp
                {
                    OutputDebugString("FAILED to load animated mesh texture:\n");
                    OutputDebugString(pMaterialsIn[materialIndex].pTextureFilename);
                    m_ppTextures[materialIndex] = NULL;
                    assert(0);
                }
            }
        }
    }
    else // use default material
    {
        pMaterials[0].pTextureFilename = NULL;

        memset((void*)&pMaterials[0].MatD3D, 0, sizeof(D3DMATERIAL9));
        pMaterials[0].MatD3D.Diffuse.r = 1.0f;
        pMaterials[0].MatD3D.Diffuse.g = 0.5f;
        pMaterials[0].MatD3D.Diffuse.b = 0.5f;
        pMaterials[0].MatD3D.Specular = pMaterials[0].MatD3D.Diffuse;
    }

    if(pSkinInfoIn != NULL)
    {
        pSkinInfo = pSkinInfoIn;
        pSkinInfo->AddRef();

        m_pOriginalMesh = pMesh;
        pMesh->AddRef();

        // Array of offset matrices
        numBones = pSkinInfo->GetNumBones();
        m_pBoneOffsetMatrices = new D3DXMATRIX[numBones];
        if(m_pBoneOffsetMatrices == NULL)
        {
            OutputDebugString("Memory exhausted in CreateMeshContainer\n");
            assert(0);
            return E_OUTOFMEMORY;
        }

        for(boneIndex = 0; boneIndex < numBones; boneIndex++)
        {
            m_pBoneOffsetMatrices[boneIndex] = *(pSkinInfo->GetBoneOffsetMatrix(boneIndex));
        }
```

```
hr = m_pOriginalMesh->
    CloneMeshFVF(D3DXMESH_MANAGED, m_pOriginalMesh->GetFVF(),
                 GAMEENGINE->GetDevice(), &MeshData.pMesh);
if (FAILED(hr))
{
    OutputDebugString("Failed to CloneMeshFVF\n");
    assert(0);
    return E_FAIL;
}

hr = MeshData.pMesh->
    GetAttributeTable(NULL, &m_NumAttributeGroups);
if (FAILED(hr))
{
    OutputDebugString("Failed to GetAttributeTable\n");
    assert(0);
    return E_FAIL;
}

if(m_pAttributeTable)
    SAFE_DELETE(m_pAttributeTable);

m_pAttributeTable = new D3DXATTRIBUTERANGE[m_NumAttributeGroups];
if (m_pAttributeTable == NULL)
{
    OutputDebugString("Memory exhausted trying to allocate attribute range\n");
        assert(0);
        return E_OUTOFMEMORY;
}

hr = MeshData.pMesh->GetAttributeTable(m_pAttributeTable, NULL);
if (FAILED(hr))
{
    OutputDebugString("Failed to GetAttributeTable\n");
    assert(0);
    return E_FAIL;
}

// allocate a buffer for bone matrices
m_NumBoneMatricesMax = pSkinInfo->GetNumBones();
```

```
        // Allocate space for blend matrices
        m_pBoneMatrices  = ::new D3DXMATRIXA16[m_NumBoneMatricesMax];
        if(m_pBoneMatrices == NULL)
        {
            OutputDebugString("Memory exhausted trying to allocate bone matrices\n");
            assert(0);
            return E_OUTOFMEMORY;
        }
    }

    *ppNewMeshContainerOut = this;
    return S_OK;
}
```

Okay, the first part of the function is self-explanatory error checking to make sure we are not being passed dodgy data. Then, as with CreateFrame(), I allocate memory to the string name of the mesh container:

```
if(name)
{
    SAFE_DELETE(Name);
    Name = new char[strlen(name)+1];
    strcpy(Name, name);
}
else
{
    char* tempName = "Unnamed mesh container";
    Name = new char[strlen(tempName)+1];
    strcpy(Name, tempName);
}
```

It's been fairly simple so far. By the way, I've made this function re-entrant so that if it is accidentally called more than once, it deletes all its resources before creating them again to prevent memory leaks. Next up, we need to make sure the mesh has normals so that FVFs match up with what we're expecting:

Note

FVF stands for *Flexible Vertex Format*. As you saw earlier in this book, the FVF allows you to define only the minimum data necessary for the vertices that you are working with. However, it is important that if you are working with two models, they both have the same FVF type when copying memory.

```
if(!(pMesh->GetFVF() & D3DFVF_NORMAL))
{
    MeshData.Type = D3DXMESHTYPE_MESH;

    if(FAILED(pMesh->CloneMeshFVF(pMesh->GetOptions(), pMesh->GetFVF() |
D3DFVF_NORMAL,
        GAMEENGINE->GetDevice(), &MeshData.pMesh)))
    {
        OutputDebugString("Failed when attempting to add normal info to a mesh\n");
        assert(0);
        return E_FAIL;
    }

    D3DXComputeNormals(pMesh, NULL);
}
else
{
    MeshData.pMesh = pMesh;
    MeshData.Type = D3DXMESHTYPE_MESH;
    pMesh->AddRef();
}
```

This function checks the FVF of the mesh. If it does not have normals, the mesh is cloned (or copied, in English) into MeshData.pMesh; The CloneMeshFVF() function is useful for automatically changing the vertex format of a mesh. Finally, D3DXComputeNormals() is called to automatically create the normals for the mesh. On the other hand, if the mesh does have normals already, it is just manually copied into MeshData.pMesh.

Next up, we need to allocate memory for all the materials and textures used by the mesh and actually load the textures. This code looks after the memory allocation:

```
NumMaterials = max(1, numMaterialsIn);
pMaterials = new D3DXMATERIAL[NumMaterials];
pAdjacency = new DWORD[numFaces*3];

m_ppTextures = new LPDIRECT3DTEXTURE9[NumMaterials];

if(!pMaterials ||
    !m_ppTextures ||
    !m_ppTextures)
```

```
{
    OutputDebugString("Memory exhausted in CreateMeshContainer\n");
    assert(0);
    return E_OUTOFMEMORY;
}

memcpy((void*)pAdjacency, pAdjacencyIn, sizeof(DWORD) * numFaces*3);
memset(m_ppTextures, 0, sizeof(LPDIRECT3DTEXTURE9) * NumMaterials);
```

This code creates arrays to hold the materials and textures. Then we need to copy the material data across and load the textures into the allocated arrays. This task requires us to loop through all the materials and copy the data over, and then load the textures from disk. If there are no materials or textures, we can assign a default one:

```
if(numMaterialsIn > 0)
{
    memcpy((void*)pMaterials, pMaterialsIn, sizeof(D3DXMATERIAL) * NumMaterials);

    for(materialIndex = 0; materialIndex < NumMaterials ; materialIndex++)
    {
        if(pMaterials[materialIndex].pTextureFilename != NULL)
        {
            char texturePath[MAX_PATH];
            strcpy(texturePath, "media\\");
            strcat(texturePath, pMaterials[materialIndex].pTextureFilename);

            if(FAILED(D3DXCreateTextureFromFile(GAMEENGINE->GetDevice(),
                texturePath,
                &m_ppTextures[materialIndex])))
            {
                OutputDebugString("FAILED to load animated mesh texture:\n");
                OutputDebugString(pMaterialsIn[materialIndex].pTextureFilename);
                m_ppTextures[materialIndex] = NULL;
                assert(0);
            }
        }
    }
}
else // use default material
{
    pMaterials[0].pTextureFilename = NULL;
```

```
    memset((void*)&pMaterials[0].MatD3D, 0, sizeof(D3DMATERIAL9));
    pMaterials[0].MatD3D.Diffuse.r = 1.0f;
    pMaterials[0].MatD3D.Diffuse.g = 0.5f;
    pMaterials[0].MatD3D.Diffuse.b = 0.5f;
    pMaterials[0].MatD3D.Specular = pMaterials[0].MatD3D.Diffuse;
}
```

We are nearly there now; all that is left is to allocate memory to hold skin and bone information. First up, we need to allocate and copy the bone offset matrices like this:

```
numBones = pSkinInfo->GetNumBones();
m_pBoneOffsetMatrices = new D3DXMATRIX[numBones];
if(m_pBoneOffsetMatrices == NULL)
{
    OutputDebugString("Memory exhausted in CreateMeshContainer\n");
    assert(0);
    return E_OUTOFMEMORY;
}

for(boneIndex = 0; boneIndex < numBones; boneIndex++)
{
    m_pBoneOffsetMatrices[boneIndex] = *(pSkinInfo->GetBoneOffsetMatrix(boneIndex));
}
```

Then we need to allocate and copy over the attribute information for the model, which is basically just information about which faces and vertices use which materials:

```
if(m_pAttributeTable)
    SAFE_DELETE(m_pAttributeTable);

m_pAttributeTable = new D3DXATTRIBUTERANGE[m_NumAttributeGroups];
if (m_pAttributeTable == NULL)
{
    OutputDebugString("Memory exhausted trying to allocate attribute range\n");
    assert(0);
    return E_OUTOFMEMORY;
}

hr = MeshData.pMesh->GetAttributeTable(m_pAttributeTable, NULL);
if (FAILED(hr))
{
```

```
        OutputDebugString("Failed to GetAttributeTable\n");
        assert(0);
        return E_FAIL;
}
```

Last and definitely not least, we can copy the bone matrices to our structures:

```
m_NumBoneMatricesMax = pSkinInfo->GetNumBones();

m_pBoneMatrices  = ::new D3DXMATRIXA16[m_NumBoneMatricesMax];
if(m_pBoneMatrices == NULL)
{
    OutputDebugString("Memory exhausted trying to allocate bone matrices\n");
    assert(0);
    return E_OUTOFMEMORY;
}
```

As you can see, the function is long and looks nasty. But it's really not doing much except allocating memory, copying data, and checking that everything went okay. The only thing left to do is to fully destroy the mesh container when it is no longer needed. You'll be happy to hear that that's a lot easier than creating a mesh container:

```
HRESULT cSkinnedAnimationMesh::DestroyMeshContainer(LPD3DXMESHCONTAINER
pMeshContainer)
{
    // This class must be destroyed manually using Delete because the container and
    // alloc hierarchy are both the same class.

    if(m_pBoneMatrices)
    {
        // Aligned matrices have own memory operators
        ::delete[] m_pBoneMatrices;
        m_pBoneMatrices = 0;
    }

    SAFE_RELEASE(m_pOriginalMesh);
    SAFE_DELETE(m_pAttributeTable);
    SAFE_DELETE_ARRAY(m_pBoneOffsetMatrices);
    SAFE_DELETE_ARRAY(m_ppBoneMatrixPtrs);
    SAFE_DELETE_ARRAY(m_ppTextures);
    SAFE_DELETE_ARRAY(pAdjacency);
    SAFE_DELETE_ARRAY(pMaterials);
```

```
        SAFE_DELETE_ARRAY(Name);

        return S_OK;
}
```

Well, ain't that the nastiest code you've ever seen? Now that everything's out of the way, we can get on with the fun stuff.

Loading an Animation

We need to look at loading an animation with all our shiny new code. The new Start() function added to the cSkinnedAnimationMesh class takes care of this for us. Check out the code:

```
bool cSkinnedAnimationMesh::Start(char* filename)
{
    if(!filename)
    {
        OutputDebugString("Invalid filename passed to cSkinnedAnimationMesh\n");
        assert(0);
    }

    strcpy(m_Filename, filename);

    if(FAILED(D3DXLoadMeshHierarchyFromX(m_Filename,
            D3DXMESH_MANAGED, GAMEENGINE->GetDevice(),
        this, NULL, (LPD3DXFRAME*)
            &m_pBoneHierarchy, &m_pAnimationController)))
    {
        OutputDebugString("Failed to load skinned anim mesh\n");
        assert(0);
        return false;
    }

    m_EffectID = EFFECTMANAGER->FindEffect("default.fx");
    SetupBoneMatrixPointers(m_pBoneHierarchy);
}
```

Do you spot the D3DXLoadMeshHierarchyFromX() call that I introduced earlier in this chapter? This function loads an animated X file from disk. It takes the file name to load, which is passed through in the Start() function formal parameter. The second parameter, D3DXMESH_MANAGED, tells Direct3D to make sure a copy is always in memory even if the video memory is wiped at some stage. The third parameter is just the standard device. The fourth parameter takes a pointer to an `ID3DXAllocateHierarchy` interface to handle allocating and storing animation data. This is what the previous section of this chapter discussed implementing. As we derive from the interface, we can pass through the `this` pointer. The next parameter is `NULL` because we don't have private data to load. The penultimate parameter takes a pointer to the place where you want to store your bone hierarchy. The final parameter takes a pointer to an animation controller, which you will learn about in a moment when I show you how to render.

If all goes according to plan, the allocation hierarchy puts all the memory together, and the animation is ready to use. If the plan is disrupted, the animation file has something wrong with it. To debug animated X files, try to load one in the DirectX SDK Mesh Viewer program, called `mview.exe`. Look at Figure 8.7 to see mesh view in action. If that can't load it, there is definitely something wrong with your animated mesh. If your mesh *can* load it, the problem lies with your code, unfortunately. However, if you are working in a games company on a deadline, it's useful to blame the artists to buy you some time. Artists are great for so many things, aren't they?

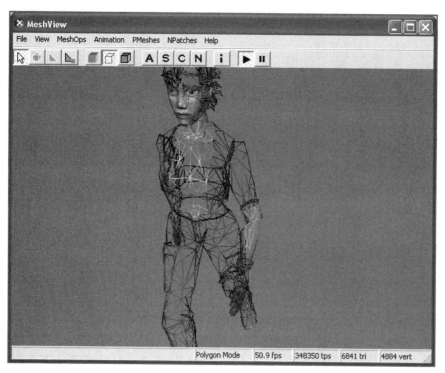

Figure 8.7
An animated mesh rendered in the mesh viewer.

Finally, the effect manager loads the default effect used for rendering. This can be overridden with any effect you like. In fact, just for fun I typed water.fx from the previous chapter, and it rendered an animated character with a water effect; very freaky indeed. Then the function calls SetupBoneMatrixPointers(). This is a recursive function with sets up the skeleton hierarchy. Check out the code:

```
HRESULT cSkinnedAnimationMesh::SetupBoneMatrixPointers(cBone* pBone)
{
    HRESULT hr = S_OK;

    if (pBone->pMeshContainer != NULL)
    {
        hr = SetupBoneMatrixPointersOnMesh();
        if (FAILED(hr))
        {
            OutputDebugString("Failed to SetupBoneMatrixPointersOnMesh\n");
            assert(0);
            return hr;
        }
    }

    if (pBone->pFrameSibling != NULL)
    {
        hr = SetupBoneMatrixPointers((cBone*)pBone->pFrameSibling);
        if (FAILED(hr))
        {
            OutputDebugString("Failed to SetupBoneMatrixPointers\n");
            assert(0);
            return hr;
        }
    }

    if (pBone->pFrameFirstChild != NULL)
    {
        hr = SetupBoneMatrixPointers((cBone*)pBone->pFrameFirstChild);
        if (FAILED(hr))
        {
            OutputDebugString("Failed to SetupBoneMatrixPointers\n");
            assert(0);
            return hr;
        }
```

```
    }

    return S_OK;
}
```

This function calls itself, repeatedly going through the tree of child and sibling bones and setting up the bone matrix pointers for each mesh it finds. The function that does the hard work is SetupBoneMatrixPointersOnMesh():

```
HRESULT cSkinnedAnimationMesh::SetupBoneMatrixPointersOnMesh()
{
    UINT numBones = 0;
    cBone* pBone = 0;

    if(pSkinInfo != NULL)
    {
        numBones = pSkinInfo->GetNumBones();

        if(m_ppBoneMatrixPtrs)
        {
            delete[] m_ppBoneMatrixPtrs;
            m_ppBoneMatrixPtrs = 0;
        }

        m_ppBoneMatrixPtrs = new D3DXMATRIX*[numBones];
        if (m_ppBoneMatrixPtrs == NULL)
        {
            OutputDebugString(
                        "Memory Exhausted in
                SetupBoneMatrixPointersOnMesh\n");
            assert(0);
            return E_OUTOFMEMORY;
        }

        for (UINT boneIndex = 0; boneIndex < numBones; boneIndex++)
        {
            pBone = (cBone*)D3DXFrameFind(
                        m_pBoneHierarchy, pSkinInfo->GetBoneName(boneIndex));
            if (pBone == NULL)
            {
                OutputDebugString("Failed to find a bone matching index");
                assert(0);
```

```
                return E_FAIL;
            }

            m_ppBoneMatrixPtrs[boneIndex] = &pBone->m_CombinedTransformationMatrix;
        }
    }

    return S_OK;
}
```

This code allocates memory for matrices and then constructs the hierarchy by searching through the skin info frames and looking for a match with the bone's name. If the code finds a match, the bone's matrix is copied for fast access later on.

Updating the Mesh

Every frame, before the animated mesh is rendered, needs to be updated, and the time needs to be advanced. The new Run() function added to the cSkinnedAnimationMesh class contains the code for updating the animation. This function is relatively simple. It starts by finding out how much time has passed since the last call; then it tells the animation controller to advance the time by that amount. This way, no matter how fast your game is actually executing, your animations play at the correct speed:

```
bool cSkinnedAnimationMesh::Run()
{
    D3DXMATRIX matWorld;
    D3DXMatrixIdentity(&matWorld);
    D3DXMatrixTranslation(&matWorld, m_Position.x, m_Position.y, m_Position.z);

    if(m_LastUpdateTime == 0)
    {
        m_LastUpdateTime = timeGetTime();
    }

    DWORD currentTime = timeGetTime();
    DWORD duration = currentTime - m_LastUpdateTime;

    float secondsPassed = (float)duration / 1000.0f;

    if( m_pAnimationController != NULL )
```

```
            m_pAnimationController->AdvanceTime(secondsPassed, NULL);
        else
            assert(0);

        UpdateBoneMatrices(m_pBoneHierarchy, &matWorld);

    m_LastUpdateTime = currentTime;

    return true;
}
```

Notice the last call to the recursive function UpdateBoneMatrices(). This is really important because it is where all the bone matrices in the skeleton are multiplied together to compute the current state of the animated mesh:

```
void cSkinnedAnimationMesh::UpdateBoneMatrices(cBone* pBoneBase, LPD3DXMATRIX
pParentMatrix)
{
    if(!pBoneBase || !pParentMatrix)
    {
        assert(0); // Invalid data
        return;
    }
    cBone* pBone = pBoneBase;

    if (pParentMatrix != NULL)
        D3DXMatrixMultiply(&pBone->m_CombinedTransformationMatrix,
            &pBone->TransformationMatrix, pParentMatrix);
    else
        pBone->m_CombinedTransformationMatrix = pBone->TransformationMatrix;

    if (pBone->pFrameSibling != NULL)
    {
        UpdateBoneMatrices((cBone*)pBone->pFrameSibling, pParentMatrix);
    }

    if (pBone->pFrameFirstChild != NULL)
    {
        UpdateBoneMatrices(
                    (cBone*)pBone->pFrameFirstChild,
                    &pBone->m_CombinedTransformationMatrix);
    }
}
```

This function goes through all the bones in the tree, multiplies them with their parents, and stores the results in the m_CombinedTransformationMatrix. If the bone is the root bone, it is set to be its own transform matrix because there is nothing else to multiply the bone with. And that's all there is to updating the mesh. Now it's time to render!

Rendering an Animated Mesh

There are only a few steps to rendering the animated mesh, but the code looks pretty involved, so I'll give you a summary first:

1. Get the current matrix for every bone by multiplying together the bone offset matrices with the actual bone matrices.

2. Send all the usual stuff to the vertex shader, like the world, view, and projection matrices.

3. Lock the mesh's vertex buffer.

4. Multiply all the vertices by their associated bones to animate the mesh.

5. Unlock the vertex buffer.

6. Render the mesh as usual!

Check out the code:

```
bool cSkinnedAnimationMesh::Render()
{
    HRESULT hr = S_OK;
    UINT numBlend = 0;
    DWORD attributeIndexPrev = 0;
    LPD3DXBONECOMBINATION pBoneCombination = 0;
    UINT matrixIndex = 0;
    D3DXMATRIXA16 matTemp;

    static int numRenderCalls = 0;
    DWORD       numBones  = pSkinInfo->GetNumBones();
    BYTE*       pbVerticesSrc;
    BYTE*       pbVerticesDest;

    // set up bone transforms
    for (UINT boneCount = 0; boneCount < numBones; boneCount++)
```

```
    {
        D3DXMatrixMultiply(&m_pBoneMatrices[boneCount],
            &m_pBoneOffsetMatrices[boneCount],
            m_ppBoneMatrixPtrs[boneCount]
        );
    }

    D3DXMATRIX   rotMat, worldMatrix;
    D3DXMatrixIdentity(&worldMatrix);
    D3DXMatrixRotationX(&rotMat, -D3DX_PI / 2.0f);

    D3DXMatrixScaling(&worldMatrix, 0.025f, 0.025f, 0.025f);
    worldMatrix *= rotMat;

    D3DXMatrixRotationY(&rotMat, D3DX_PI);
    worldMatrix *= rotMat;

    EFFECTMANAGER->GetEffect(m_EffectID)->SetTransforms(
        worldMatrix, CAMERA->GetViewMatrix(), CAMERA->GetProjectionMatrix());
    EFFECTMANAGER->GetEffect(m_EffectID)->Dispatch();

    //GAMEENGINE->GetDevice()->SetTransform(D3DTS_WORLD, &identityMatrix);
    GAMEENGINE->GetDevice()->SetFVF(MeshData.pMesh->GetFVF());

    m_pOriginalMesh->LockVertexBuffer(D3DLOCK_READONLY, (LPVOID*)&pbVerticesSrc);
    MeshData.pMesh->LockVertexBuffer(0, (LPVOID*)&pbVerticesDest);

    // generate skinned mesh
    pSkinInfo->UpdateSkinnedMesh(m_pBoneMatrices, NULL, pbVerticesSrc,
pbVerticesDest);

    m_pOriginalMesh->UnlockVertexBuffer();
    MeshData.pMesh->UnlockVertexBuffer();

    UINT numPasses = 0;
    EFFECTMANAGER->GetEffect(m_EffectID)->Begin(numPasses);

    for(UINT passCount = 0 ; passCount < numPasses ; passCount++)
    {
        EFFECTMANAGER->GetEffect(m_EffectID)->BeginPass(passCount);
```

```
        for (UINT attribIndex = 0; attribIndex < m_NumAttributeGroups;
attribIndex++)
        {
            GAMEENGINE->GetDevice()->SetMaterial(&(pMaterials
                    [m_pAttributeTable[attribIndex].AttribId].MatD3D));

            GAMEENGINE->GetDevice()->SetTexture(0, m_ppTextures
                    [m_pAttributeTable[attribIndex].AttribId]);

            MeshData.pMesh->DrawSubset(m_pAttributeTable[attribIndex].AttribId);
        }

        EFFECTMANAGER->GetEffect(m_EffectID)->EndPass();
    }

    EFFECTMANAGER->GetEffect(m_EffectID)->End();

    numRenderCalls++;
    return true;
}
```

Make sense? I guess the only function to look out for there that I haven't shown you so far is `ID3DXSkinInfo::UpdateSkinnedMesh()`. This is a black box function that runs through all the vertices and multiplies them by their influencing joints. Out of sight, out of mind! Well, in case you're interested, it works like this for a vertex influenced by two bones:

1. Get the next vertex to be animated.

2. Get the index and weight of the first influencing bone.

3. Get the same for the second influencing bone.

4. Multiply the respective weights by the matrices. That is, if both weights were 0.5, then each matrix multiplied by that now only has 50 percent effect on the vertex.

5. Multiply each matrix with the vertex position to transform it.

6. Move to the next vertex.

Simple? Cool. And that, ladies and gentlemen, is all there is to rendering an animated skinned mesh. Other than that, only housekeeping is left, like releasing everything when you are ready to destroy it, like this:

```
bool cSkinnedAnimationMesh::Shutdown()
{
    for(UINT i = 0 ; i < 4 ; ++i)
    {
        SAFE_DELETE(m_VecSequences[i]);
    }

    D3DXFrameDestroy(m_pBoneHierarchy, this);
    m_pBoneHierarchy = 0;
    SAFE_RELEASE(m_pAnimationController);
    SAFE_DELETE_ARRAY(m_pBoneMatrices);

    return true;
}
```

You now have everything you need to render animated meshes. It's a little simplistic at the moment, but it's not bad. Check out Figure 8.8 to see the rendered mesh animating in-game. What we really need is some advanced features like the ability to play multiple animation sequences, spawn multiple animation sequences, and render with hardware acceleration. Not to worry—all that's covered in the next chapter!

Conclusion

This chapter has been a whirlwind of how to load, render, and update vertex skinned animated meshes with Direct3D. Here's what we covered:

- Introduction to vertex skinning, including all the weird terms that go along with it
- Introduction to frames, bones, mesh containers, and allocation hierarchies
- Joint hierarchies
- Animation sets
- All about bone combination buffers

Now check out the next chapter, where you'll learn how to make this stuff really impress.

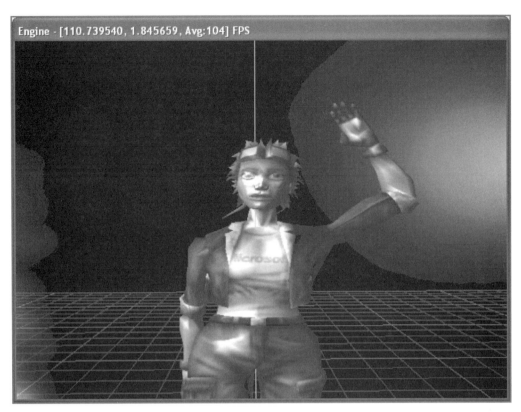

Figure 8.8
The finished product—skinned animated mesh rendering in our engine.

CHAPTER 9

ADVANCED ANIMATION TECHNIQUES

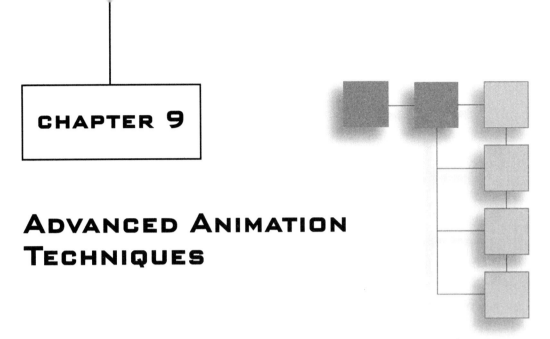

In this chapter, I'm going to show you how to take what you learned in the previous chapter and turn it into something you can use in a professional game engine. In particular, you'll learn the following:

- How to spawn multiple instances of an animation
- How to blend seamlessly between different animation sequences
- How to create an animation manager
- And much more

Let's begin by looking at multiple animation sequences.

Animation Sequences

An *animation sequence* is just another name for a particular animation that's applied to a mesh. For instance, you could have animation sets for walking, running, waving, falling, and so on. As the character goes through specific motions, you play the appropriate animation sequence and the character reacts correctly, which leads to a cool gaming experience. Of course, you can't just instantly play the required sequence you want, or there would be a visible break in the animation. For instance, if the character is walking and then falls, if you were to play the fall animation immediately, there would be a visible pop. The solution, as I mentioned briefly in the previous chapter, is to smoothly interpolate between the animations quickly, which leads to a clean perceptive experience. I'll show you how to do smooth interpolation shortly. Look at Figures 9.1, 9.2, and 9.3, which show the Tiny model animating with different animation sequences.

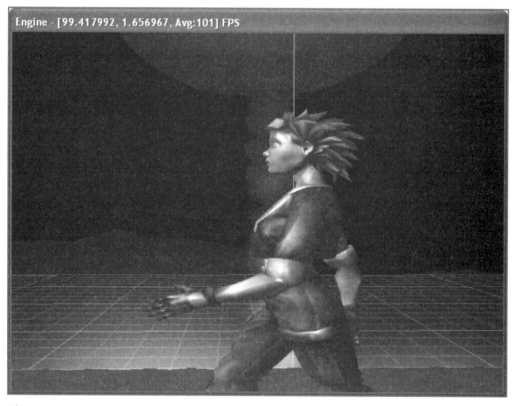

Figure 9.1
An animation sequence of the Tiny model walking.

As always, you have to deal with DirectX's insane terminology, so here is the translation. An *animation sequence*, in Direct3D, is an *animation set*. In Direct3D, an animation set is made up of multiple *animations*, which are just strings of matrices for specific bones. You'll never really need to deal with *Direct3D animations* because they are hidden away behind the API (mostly). However, you will have to deal with animation sets, because they are animation sequences like walking and running.

Figure 9.2
An animation sequence of the Tiny model running.

The next bit of annoyingness is how Direct3D plays animations with its animation controller. You saw this a few times in Chapter 8. The animation controller, as you saw before, is responsible for updating the time, playing animations sequences, and other such things. Now the animation controller is based around a track system, kind of like your old 1970's 8-track, but in this case it's a two-track. You make it work by applying an animation sequence to an animation track. If you're not connected to a track, you can't play an animation.

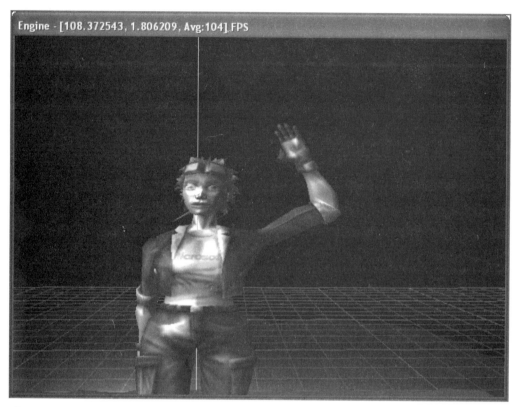

Figure 9.3
An animation sequence showing the Tiny model waving.

You might be wondering why there are two tracks. Well, this is the secret to blending between two different animation sequences. You could connect the current walk animation on Track 0 and then connect the new run animation on Track 1. As it comes time to change animations, you can tell the animation controller to quickly blend out the current animation at the same time the new animation is blending in. The end result is a seamless blend from the old animation to the new, with no popping. But before we get to that, let's check out how multiple sequences work.

Animation sequences are easily encapsulated because they are just a bunch of matrices under the hood, and you are likely to have many animation sequences for your mesh. To that end, I've created a class to wrap up an animation sequence. An animation sequence doesn't need much to work except a pointer to an animation controller, an index to the track it's playing on, and the time it takes to blend in the sequence if another sequence is playing. Check out the class definition:

```
typedef unsigned int HANIMSEQUENCE;

class cSkinnedAnimationSequence
{
public:
    cSkinnedAnimationSequence(LPD3DXANIMATIONCONTROLLER pAnimationController,
HANIMSEQUENCE sequenceHandle);
    ~cSkinnedAnimationSequence(void);

    // Data
public:


private:
    HANIMSEQUENCE m_SequenceHandle;
    LPD3DXANIMATIONCONTROLLER m_pAnimationController;
    LPD3DXANIMATIONSET m_pAnimationSet;

    LPCTSTR m_AnimationName;

    float m_BlendTime;

    static UINT m_CurrentPlayingTrack; // 0 or 1

    // Methods
public:
    bool Start();
    bool Run();
    bool Shutdown();

    void BlendIn();

private:
};
```

280 Chapter 9 ■ Advanced Animation Techniques

Notice how the class includes a pointer to a D3DXANIMATIONSET. This is the actual interface that Direct3D uses to represent an animation sequence. The process to turn this class into an object occurs when the X file is loaded. The number of sequences is determined, and a new cSkinnedAnimationSequence is created for each one. This code added to cSkinnedAnimationMesh::Start() is the code that detects and creates the sequences:

```
UINT numAnims = m_pAnimationController->GetNumAnimationSets();
for(UINT i = 0 ; i < numAnims ; ++i)
{
    cSkinnedAnimationSequence* pNewSequence =
        new cSkinnedAnimationSequence(m_pAnimationController, i);
    if(!pNewSequence)
    {
        OutputDebugString("Memory exhausted while creating animation sequence\n");
        assert(0);
        break;
    }

    if(!pNewSequence->Start())
    {
        OutputDebugString("Failed to start animation sequence\n");
        assert(0);
        SAFE_DELETE(pNewSequence);
        continue;
    }

    m_VecSequences.push_back(pNewSequence);
}
```

The code starts by getting the number of animation sequences from the animation controller and then looping through for each sequence. A new cSkinnedAnimationSequence object is created to represent each sequence. As you can see, the constructor takes a pointer to the animation controller and the index of the sequence. You'll see why this is important in a moment. Following successful creation, the new sequence is initialized and then added to a new member vector of sequences. Let's look more closely at the actual creation of the sequence. Here's the constructor:

```
cSkinnedAnimationSequence::cSkinnedAnimationSequence(
LPD3DXANIMATIONCONTROLLER pAnimationController, HANIMSEQUENCE sequenceHandle)
{
```

```
    m_pAnimationController = pAnimationController;
    m_pAnimationController->AddRef();
    m_SequenceHandle = sequenceHandle;
    m_pAnimationSet = 0;
    m_AnimationName = 0;

    m_BlendTime = 0.3f;
}
```

The constructor starts by getting a copy of the animation controller and a copy of the index of the animation set that this sequence object will represent. This is used later on in the initialization function:

```
bool cSkinnedAnimationSequence::Start()
{
    HRESULT hr = S_OK;

    hr = m_pAnimationController->GetAnimationSet(m_SequenceHandle, &m_pAnimationSet);
    if(FAILED(hr))
    {
        OutputDebugString("Failed to create animation set\n");
        assert(0);
        Shutdown();
        return false;
    }

    m_AnimationName = m_pAnimationSet->GetName();

    return true;
}
```

Initialization is simple. The code uses the index to get a copy of the animation set and get a copy of the name. Direct3D can access animations by index or name, so it's useful to keep a copy of both. After that, all that is left is to shut down the code when we are finished with the sequence:

```
bool cSkinnedAnimationSequence::Shutdown()
{
    SAFE_RELEASE(m_pAnimationController);
    SAFE_RELEASE(m_pAnimationSet);
    return true;
}
```

There's nothing too difficult about that. Now let's look at how to play the animation sequence. This is the edited version that instantly pops between animations. I'll show you smooth blending in a moment. This is all it takes to play the animation:

```
void cSkinnedAnimationSequence::BlendIn()
{
        m_pAnimationController->SetTrackAnimationSet(0, m_pAnimationSet);
}
```

That's it. If you were to put the following code in bool cSkinnedAnimationMesh::Run(), the animation would play each animation sequence for three seconds before moving on to the next one:

```
// Timing code to set up duration not shown for simplicity. Assumes an animation
with 4 sequences.
if(duration > 3000)
{
    static UINT index = 0;
    index++;

    m_VecSequences[index]->BlendIn();
    lastTime = timeGetTime();

    if(index == 3)
        index = 0;
}
```

Seamless Blending Between Sequences

Multiple sequences are great, but only if you can change them without that annoying popping effect. You might think this blending stuff is going to be complicated, but it's not. Luckily, Direct3D handles all the interpolation for us, so there are only about 20 lines of code to implement. Check out the new BlendIn() function, and then I'll run through what is happening:

```
void cSkinnedAnimationSequence::BlendIn()
{
    m_BlendTime = 0.25f;

    double globalTime = m_pAnimationController->GetTime();
    double transitionTime = globalTime + m_BlendTime;
```

```
    m_pAnimationController->SetTrackAnimationSet(!m_CurrentPlayingTrack,
m_pAnimationSet);

    m_pAnimationController->UnkeyAllTrackEvents(m_CurrentPlayingTrack);
        m_pAnimationController->UnkeyAllTrackEvents(!m_CurrentPlayingTrack);

    m_pAnimationController->KeyTrackEnable(
        m_CurrentPlayingTrack, FALSE, globalTime + m_BlendTime );
        m_pAnimationController->KeyTrackSpeed(
        m_CurrentPlayingTrack, 0.0f, globalTime, m_BlendTime, D3DXTRANSITION_LINEAR );
        m_pAnimationController->KeyTrackWeight(
        m_CurrentPlayingTrack, 0.0f, globalTime, m_BlendTime, D3DXTRANSITION_LINEAR );

        m_pAnimationController->SetTrackEnable(
        !m_CurrentPlayingTrack, TRUE );
        m_pAnimationController->KeyTrackSpeed(
        !m_CurrentPlayingTrack, 1.0f, globalTime, m_BlendTime, D3DXTRANSITION_LINEAR );
        m_pAnimationController->KeyTrackWeight(
        !m_CurrentPlayingTrack, 1.0f, globalTime, m_BlendTime, D3DXTRANSITION_LINEAR );

    m_CurrentPlayingTrack = !m_CurrentPlayingTrack;
}
```

Blending relies on making things happen at specific times. In this case, one animation might be currently playing, so we want to blend it out quickly, but not instantly; otherwise, there would be a noticeable pop. So the first line of code sets the transition time to be 0.25 of a second, or 250 milliseconds. This time is used later in the code.

The code then calls

```
    double globalTime = m_pAnimationController->GetTime();
    double transitionTime = globalTime + m_BlendTime;
```

The global time is the *real* time in the animation controller. Each animation set has its own local time as it plays through, but the global time is the main time that all other times are based off of. From that, we can calculate that we want this transition to be completed at global time *plus* blend time, or 250 milliseconds from when the transition is initially requested. Next up is this line:

```
    m_pAnimationController->SetTrackAnimationSet(!m_CurrentPlayingTrack,
m_pAnimationSet);
```

This sets the new sequence to play onto the track that is *not* currently playing anything. If we set it onto the currently playing track, it would pop, which is not what we want:

```
m_pAnimationController->UnkeyAllTrackEvents(m_CurrentPlayingTrack);
m_pAnimationController->UnkeyAllTrackEvents(!m_CurrentPlayingTrack);
```

These two lines sound complicated, but they're not. Basically the tracks are being swapped around so that any events that were set up on them previously are now totally invalid. They need to be unkeyed (removed) before the tracks are swapped. Now we come to the first part of code that actually does some work:

```
m_pAnimationController->KeyTrackEnable(
    m_CurrentPlayingTrack, FALSE, globalTime + m_BlendTime );
m_pAnimationController->KeyTrackSpeed(
    m_CurrentPlayingTrack, 0.0f, globalTime, m_BlendTime,
D3DXTRANSITION_LINEAR );
m_pAnimationController->KeyTrackWeight(
    m_CurrentPlayingTrack, 0.0f, globalTime, m_BlendTime,
D3DXTRANSITION_LINEAR );
```

The first line tells the animation controller that the currently playing track should not be enabled in 250 milliseconds, or whatever blend time is set to. The parameters are the track to enable or disable, a Boolean variable setting its enable status, and finally the time the event should happen. In English: Turn off the currently playing track in 250 milliseconds.

The second line sets the track speed. It takes as parameters an index of the track to change (that is, 0 or 1), the new speed, the time at which the new speed will take effect, and the way in which the current time should be transitioned to the new time. The play speed is 0.0 for fully stopped or 1.0 for normal speed. In English again: Blend the current play speed down to 0.0 linearly over 250 milliseconds.

The final line changes the track weight, or in other words its influence over the mesh. It takes the same parameters as the previous function except the second parameter is now the weight rather than play speed. A weight of 1.0 means that the playing sequence has full effect over the mesh. Conversely, 0.0 has no effect. English translation: Linearly change the influence of the currently playing track to nothing over 250 milliseconds.

Make sense? Cool. Now that you've seen how to blend out the currently playing sequence, you can see how to blend in the new one, which is the same code but in reverse:

```
m_pAnimationController->SetTrackEnable(
    !m_CurrentPlayingTrack, TRUE );
m_pAnimationController->KeyTrackSpeed(
    !m_CurrentPlayingTrack, 1.0f, globalTime, m_BlendTime,
D3DXTRANSITION_LINEAR );
m_pAnimationController->KeyTrackWeight(
    !m_CurrentPlayingTrack, 1.0f, globalTime, m_BlendTime,
D3DXTRANSITION_LINEAR );
```

These lines of code enable the new track, linearly increase its playing speed, and linearly increase its influence over the mesh, all over 250 milliseconds. The final line of code reverses the currently playing track monitor. Because the code lines can be set to only 0 or 1, a simple Boolean switch is made:

```
m_CurrentPlayingTrack = !m_CurrentPlayingTrack;
```

So, over a quarter of a second, the old track is being slowed down and made weaker, while the new track is being enabled, made faster, and made stronger. The end result is a seamless transition from one animation sequence to the other, which is cool. You should load up the code for this chapter and see it in action.

An Animated Mesh Manager

Most games tend to have more than one animation in them, so it's pretty important to have a manager to look after all the different animations in your game. The cSkinnedAnimationManager is built for this purpose. It is a lightweight manager class that can be extended to suit your needs. At the moment, it can create and remove animated meshes and store them in a vector. You can access any particular animation by its name or index to set its parameters. Check out the class definition:

```
namespace Animation
{
    class cSkinnedAnimationManager
    {
    public:
            virtual ~cSkinnedAnimationManager();
    private:
                cSkinnedAnimationManager();
```

```cpp
    public:
        static DestroySingleton()
        {
            if(ms_pAnimMeshManager)
            {
                delete ms_pAnimMeshManager;
                ms_pAnimMeshManager = 0;
            }
        }

        static cSkinnedAnimationManager* cSkinnedAnimationManager::getInstance();
        int AddAnimatedMesh(char* filename);

        DWORD GetNumAnimatedMeshes()
        {
            return m_vAnimatedMeshes.size();
        }

        cSkinnedAnimationMesh* GetAnimatedMesh(int index)
        {
            assert(index >= 0);
            assert(index < (int)m_vAnimatedMeshes.size());
            return m_vAnimatedMeshes[index];
        }

        bool Start();
        bool Run();
        bool Render();
        bool Shutdown();


    private:
        static cSkinnedAnimationManager *ms_pAnimMeshManager;
        static bool    ms_InstanceFlag;

        typedef std::vector<cSkinnedAnimationMesh*> vANIMMESH;
        vANIMMESH    m_vAnimatedMeshes;
};
}
```

As you can see, this manager, like all the other major components of the engine, is a singleton. That means there can only be one of them. The heart of the class is the m_vAnimatedMeshes vector, which stores all the active animated meshes. The class needs almost no initialization:

```
bool cSkinnedAnimationManager::Start()
{
    m_vAnimatedMeshes.reserve(10);
    return true;
}
```

It reserves space for the first 10 meshes. Running and rendering the meshes is simple. The manager just runs through the vector and calls the appropriate function within each animated mesh:

```
bool cSkinnedAnimationManager::Run()
{
    for(UINT i = 0 ; i < m_vAnimatedMeshes.size() ; ++i)
    {
        m_vAnimatedMeshes[i]->Run();
    }

    return true;
}

bool cSkinnedAnimationManager::Render()
{
    for(UINT i = 0 ; i < m_vAnimatedMeshes.size() ; ++i)
    {
        m_vAnimatedMeshes[i]->Render();
    }

    return true;
}
```

The shutdown code is also simple. However, pay attention to the chain of events that must happen to delete each animated mesh in the vector:

```
bool cSkinnedAnimationManager::Shutdown()
{
    for(UINT i = 0 ; i < m_vAnimatedMeshes.size() ; ++i)
    {
        cSkinnedAnimationMesh* pCurAnimMesh = m_vAnimatedMeshes[i];
```

```
        pCurAnimMesh->Shutdown();
        delete pCurAnimMesh;
    }
    m_vAnimatedMeshes.clear();

    return true;
}
```

First, the current mesh is shut down and deleted. Then the entire vector is clear()ed. If you miss out on any of these steps, there will be a memory leak, because the animated meshes are allocated dynamically, and they allocate their own memory internally and dynamically.

Now that all the housekeeping is out of the way, let's check out how to add a new animated mesh to the manager:

```
int cSkinnedAnimationManager::AddAnimatedMesh(char* filename)
{
    if(!filename)
        return false;

    cSkinnedAnimationMesh* pNewAnimMesh = new cSkinnedAnimationMesh;
    if(!pNewAnimMesh)
    {
        OutputDebugString("Memory exhausted while creating new animated mesh\n");
        assert(0);
        return -1;
    }

    bool bSuccess = pNewAnimMesh->Start(filename);
    if(!bSuccess)
    {
        delete pNewAnimMesh;
        OutputDebugString("Failed to create animated mesh ");
        OutputDebugString(filename);
        OutputDebugString("\n");
        assert(0);
        return -1;
    }

    m_vAnimatedMeshes.push_back(pNewAnimMesh);
    return m_vAnimatedMeshes.size()-1; // return its id in the vector
}
```

First, a new animated mesh is dynamically created. If all goes well, this mesh is initialized with the file name of the new animation to load. If the file is loaded successfully, it is added to the back of the vector. Notice that the return value is the index of the new mesh in the vector. That way, it can be accessed quickly the next time. Now let's look at an example of actually using the mesh manager to spawn multiple animated meshes.

Multiple Managed Animated Meshes

Wow! This section heading is a bit of a mouthful. Still, check out how easy it is to add animations to our engine. I added the following code to the initialization of the game engine in `cGameEngine::Start()`:

```
ANIMATIONMANAGER->Start();
```

The code gets put into `cGameEngine::Render()`:

```
ANIMATIONMANAGER->Render();
```

And, of course, we need to update the animated meshes, so check this out in `cGameEngine::Run()`:

```
ANIMATIONMANAGER->Run();
```

To shut down the animation stuff when we exit in `cGameEngine::Shutdown()`, use this:

```
ANIMATIONMANAGER->Shutdown();
ANIMATIONMANAGER->DestroySingleton();
```

Okay, it's all connected. Now let's load up some animations in `cGameEngine::LoadAssets()`:

```
ANIMATIONMANAGER->AddAnimatedMesh("media\\tiny_4anim.x");
ANIMATIONMANAGER->AddAnimatedMesh("media\\tiny_4anim.x");
ANIMATIONMANAGER->AddAnimatedMesh("media\\tiny_4anim.x");
ANIMATIONMANAGER->GetAnimatedMesh(0)->SetCurrentAnimationByIndex(2);
ANIMATIONMANAGER->GetAnimatedMesh(1)->SetCurrentAnimationByIndex(1);
ANIMATIONMANAGER->GetAnimatedMesh(2)->SetCurrentAnimationByIndex(0);
ANIMATIONMANAGER->GetAnimatedMesh(0)->SetPosition(D3DXVECTOR3(-100,0,0));
ANIMATIONMANAGER->GetAnimatedMesh(1)->SetPosition(D3DXVECTOR3(100,0,0));
```

This code loads all three animated meshes and sets their respective animations to be run, walk, and wave. All it needs now is a little bit of code to make the animated meshes run around the scene, like this code in `cGameEngine::Run()`:

```
UINT runTime = GetEngineRunTime();

float value = (float)runTime / 1000;
float x1 = sin(value) * 500;
float y1 = cos(value) * 500;
float x2 = sin(-value) * 1000;
float y2 = cos(-value) * 1000;

ANIMATIONMANAGER->GetAnimatedMesh(0)->SetRotation(0, 0, -(value - 1.57f));
ANIMATIONMANAGER->GetAnimatedMesh(1)->SetRotation(0, 0, (value - 1.57f));
ANIMATIONMANAGER->GetAnimatedMesh(0)->SetPosition(D3DXVECTOR3(x1,y1,0));
ANIMATIONMANAGER->GetAnimatedMesh(1)->SetPosition(D3DXVECTOR3(x2,y2,0));
```

This creates a really cool sample program that you should load and check out. There is one animated mesh standing at the origin waving, a second walking around in circles, and a third running in a circle in the opposite direction. Check out Figure 9.4.

Figure 9.4
Multiple instances of animations, all playing various animation sequences.

Conclusion

This chapter has brought a lot of life to the animation system so that it is now slick, advanced, and capable of handling a range of advanced effects. In particular, in this chapter you learned the following:

- How to spawn multiple instances of an animation
- How to blend seamlessly between different animation sequences
- How to create an animation manager
- And much more

In the next chapter, we are going to take a slight step back from graphics and look at another important feature of any game engine: how to implement your own scripting language into the engine, which can eventually be used to control the animation system we just created. Let's get moving…

Chapter 10

Implementing Scripting

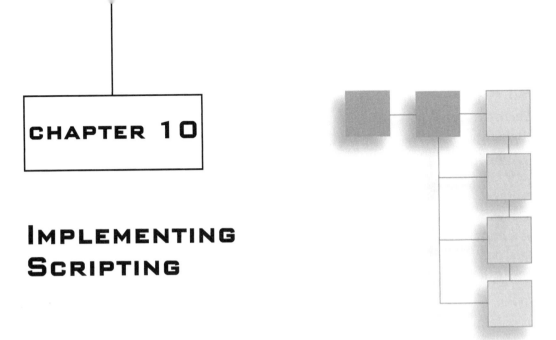

This is a really exciting and useful chapter because this topic is not covered in enough detail anywhere. Scripting is one of those topics that you are just expected to know when you are in the game industry, but there is virtually no other documentation available. As a result, every programmer goes through the same trial and error process implementing a script and gains experience that way. If you are not yet in the game industry professionally, you probably don't know about scripting because you haven't felt it necessary to implement scripting into your demo work. This chapter is all about removing these barriers to tell you everything you need to know about scripting. In particular, I'll show you the following:

- Importance of using scripting languages
- Different scripting languages that are available for games
- Introduction to the LUA language and why it's great
- Development of a scripting management interface
- Glue code to allow your code to talk to scripts and scripts to talk to your code
- Way to expose functionality to scripts
- Method for implementing object orientation into a non-object-orientated language
- And much more

Let's begin with an introduction about what exactly scripting is and why we need it.

All About Scripting

There are some good reasons to implement scripting in a professional game engine and some reasons not to. At the top of the list of reasons to have scripting is compile time. On best-selling titles—and even just large projects—compile time takes a while. In fact, on the latest Xbox 360 game that I'm working on at the moment, a single configuration takes almost an hour to fully compile. I typically deal with four configurations at any one time, and all it takes is a single key press in a heavily nested header file to make the recompile happen. Recompilation is a total pain. The more you can do to reduce it, the happier you, your team, and your boss will be. Luckily, scripts do not need recompilation.

Artists and designers usually like to think visually, which means they *hate* programming languages, just as programmers usually do not enjoy making thousands of textures tileable. In fact, if you give designers a script that is almost like C++, they will happily learn it as long as it is called a *script*. But as soon as they hear the words C++ *code*, they start running. Designers are happy to work with scripts because they don't have to recompile them, and they don't need to write C++ code.

Development of games usually involves a lot of tinkering. And large games take a long time to start, typically up to three minutes while debugging. So every time you have to restart your build, even if it didn't need a recompile, you waste three minutes. It only takes about 10 code changes to take up an hour of your time. The less time you change your code and re-execute, the more productive you are. Luckily, you can change scripts on the fly, and you don't need to restart the game to see the results. Do you have your health bar located at (10,10) and want to move it to (10,15)? Fire the script into Notepad, change the coordinates, click Save, and bang your screen updates immediately by noticing that the file timestamp has changed. Cool? Yes, very cool.

As you can see, as soon as you are working on a project of any size, you are committing coder suicide by not implementing scripts. Your boss and team will hate you, you'll be fired, you'll lose your house and your wife, and your kids will never speak to you again. Save your life and use scripts!

Scripts in Games

Scripts are usually just text files with code in them that varies depending on the type of language you decide to use. Some of you might be thinking, "Hang on…

text files that don't need to be compiled? Is that another word for an interpreted language? Yuck." Yes, it's true that scripts are interpreted, which means they usually aren't compiled down into a binary code that the CPU can directly execute. Instead, they are semicompiled into an intermediate language that is converted to real CPU instructions on the fly, which means they are not nearly as fast as if you had written the same functionality in straight C++ code. But many people have gone down that route and have discovered that, like all major game development companies in existence, you must use a scripting language to allow development of a large project to be completed in a sane amount of time.

And, unless you are rather challenged, you would never use scripts for anything that is processor intensive. Usually people who are not normally programmers use scripts to define the user interface, AI, high-level physics, load configurations, and other such mundane things that change a lot. The biggest use of scripting is AI control, but we'll get to that shortly.

In the old days, developers would spend an inordinate amount of time developing their custom scripting languages, which is an incredibly difficult and time-consuming process. It has disadvantages, such as the amount of time wasted developing, debugging, and maintaining the language over the life of the project. Also, all the designers have to relearn a brand new language when the language is finished. And it's not good if you decide to rerelease your game next year with a new engine, because you have to rewrite all of it again.

These days, most companies choose a script that has already been written and is well, tried, tested, and deployed. The only exceptions are large companies that mainly make engines to sell to other people, such as the makers of *Quake* and *Unreal.* For everyone else, writing your own language is not a good thing. The number of languages used has, like the game industry, become more centralized recently, and one particular language has come out on top. That language is Lua.

Lua

Lua (see Figure 10.1) has been used in more games than any other scripting language and is now the language of choice for developers. Why is it so popular? Well, the most important reason is that it is completely free. It's free for noncommercial use, for commercial use, for anything at all. You don't have to pay the makers a penny. All they ask is that they are credited in a read-me file if possible.

Figure 10.1
The scripting language of choice for modern games, large or small.

The second reason for Lua's popularity is that it is shipped with its source publicly available and it is totally ANSI C compatible, which means you can recompile it to run on any environment. I've personally implemented or worked with Lua on the PC, PlayStation 2, Xbox, GameCube, and Xbox 360 on a variety of best-selling games made by the likes of EA, Microsoft, and others. So the next time you're playing a modern console game, you can bet your bottom dollar that the scripting was almost certainly implemented with Lua.

What is Lua, and where did it come from? *Lua* is actually Portuguese for *moon*, which is a small hint to its origins in Brazil, around 1993. Amazingly, Lua started out as a limited scripting language developed by a Brazilian oil company to help engineers enter numbers for gaskets and other items used in simulations. It then moved on to become a report generator for lithologists (people who like rocks). As the language grew and was put to wider uses, it was named *Sol*, which, of course, means *sun*. The language grew and was merged with another language and renamed *Lua*, which eventually grew into the language we are about to work with.

Because Lua originated on slow machines and was put to an incredibly wide range of uses, its performance was always high on the agenda. The result of years of development is that it is now arguably the cleanest and fastest scripting language available. According to the makers of Lua, as soon as it was let loose on the general public in 1996 and written about in the popular Dr. Dobbs journal, game developers from LucasArts jumped at Lua and started replacing their in-house scripting language with it. The rest is history. Lua is used by game developers, NASA, research companies, and various other companies around the world. And the best part is that as a developer or designer, as you move from company to company, the language always stays the same.

After you learn how great this little language is, make sure to send a thank you e-mail to the developers at http://www.lua.org, because they love to hear about where Lua is being used. Okay, that's enough marketing for Lua. Let's get on with the code.

Glue Code Introduction

The worst part about scripting is writing the so-called *glue code*. C++ is obviously one programming language. Lua is effectively another language, albeit interpreted like VB used to be. Glue code is the code that allows different languages to talk to each other. Languages sometimes don't like each other very much. If you have ever done COM development, you will understand glue code, because much of COM is about making languages work together. Recent developments like .NET rewrote the core of all languages to be the same, so there was no need for glue code. However, that is a whole other can of worms. Neither C++ nor Lua is .NET compatible, so we still need to write glue code.

So what kinds of things does glue code need to handle? Well, first of all and most important is the calling of functions. Your code needs to be able to call functions in Lua if it is going to be of any use. And, of course, Lua is going to need to be able to call your C++ functions from within the script. Also, you need a way to pass data from C++, which is in one format, to Lua, which has somewhat different data types. Next, you need to be able to monitor code so that you can tell when errors occur and report debugging information to the user when things go wrong.

In other words, you need some glue that will perform these tasks:

- Expose C++ functions to Lua so they can be called from scripts
- Expose Lua functions to C++ so they can be called from code
- Allow C++ data to be passed to Lua and back again
- Monitor execution

Finally, you need to get some sort of object orientation to work with Lua, because it is written in C, so there is no object orientation support on that side. And Lua is not an object-orientated language, so there is no support there either. However, I can show you a few little tricks to get around that little issue.

Before I show you glue code, I'll show you a little bit of the language so that it all makes sense.

Writing Lua Code

Luckily, Lua is similar enough to C that it should be an easy learning curve for you, and it's different enough from C that designers will be able to use it without too much nagging. I'm not going to provide a huge amount of information on how to program with Lua. Why? First, it's simple, and you'll pick it up quickly after you start using it. Second, there is a wealth of information on the Internet, and it would detract from the point of the chapter. Don't worry, though; I'll cover everything that's important.

Lua has four weirdness factors, from a C/C++ programmer's perspective, that will make sense after you look at the code. These are, in order of weirdness:

1. Lua functions can return more than one value at a time. Yes, you read that correctly. I'll explain it shortly.

2. Semicolons are not required at the end of lines. You can put them there if you are from a C/C++ background or omit them if you are a VB wuss. Either way, the Lua compiler is happy.

3. Comments are not made with // or /* */. Instead, you use a double minus for comments, like this: --.

4. Variables have no particular type, because all of them are variants. This means you can declare any variable and set it to be a number, string, or anything else, and it will work.

That wasn't too bad now, was it? The only point that needs further explanation is the first item. Lua is based on a stack system, which means that more than one value can be returned from a script function at a time. So it's totally reasonable to write the following:

```
-- Assume x, y, and z are valid variables

// other code
return x, y, z
```

Yes, I know… very strange. But you'll get used to it. It's actually really helpful for cutting down the number of script calls you have to make.

Declaring variables is simple. You just write the variable's name, and it instantly becomes a new variable, which can be assigned to be anything, like this:

```
firstNumber = 5;
secondNumber = 6;
thirdNumber = firstNumber + secondNumber;
string = "Hello World";
```

Functions are also easy. You just write `function`, followed by its name and parameters, as in C++:

```
function SomeLuaFunction()

end
```

Here's another example with parameters. (Remember that they have no set type, so nothing needs to be written about their type.)

```
function AnotherLuaFunction(someNumber, anotherString, anotherNumber)
    -- This is a comment
end
```

Notice the lack of opening and closing parentheses; instead, there is just the `end` statement, which is also used to end loops and other things. Speaking of loops, they are straightforward also. The main type of loop is the `for` loop, which looks like this:

```
for i=1, 25 do
-- do work
end
```

Or there's the `do..while` loop, shown here:

```
i = 10
while i do
    i = i -1;
end
```

And, of course, there are if/then/else statements, which are similar to normal code:

```
if somestatement then
    -- do something
else if someOtherStatement
    -- do something else
else
    -- ring your mother; it's been weeks
```

The only other pertinent point is nil, which is kind of like C's NULL. All variables are initialized to nil on creation, until you set them to something. nil is interpreted as false in if statements.

The rest will become clear as you see it used. Check out http://www.lua.org/manual/5.0/ for the full manual, which will tell you everything you need to know if you get stuck along the way.

Add Lua to Your Project

First things first: You are going to need to add Lua to your project before you can start using it. To do that, you need to go to http://www.lua.org/download.html and get the latest version, which is 5.0.2 at the time of this writing. This allows you to download the Lua source code. However, it also needs to be compiled into binaries, which is a pain unless you are a Linux freak. So, the next thing to do is to download the binaries, which are available all over the Internet, including here: http://lua-users.org/wiki/LuaBinaries. You should place the downloaded Lua files as a subfolder of your project called—you guessed it—Lua. Then create a new subfolder in your new folder and call it lib. That's where you should place the downloaded binaries.

Now you need to add Lua to your project. To do this, in Visual Studio 2003, go to Project, Properties, C/C++, General. Add a new directory to Additional Include Directories, which is LUA/include, assuming you have put the downloaded files where I said; otherwise, feel free to change this to your specified location. Next, you need to add to the library file's path. To change this, while still in the dialog box, go the Linker, General page. Add a new directory in the Additional Library Directories section called LUA/lib, again assuming you put the downloaded binaries where I said in the previous paragraph. Otherwise, set the path to your own location. The final step is to add the necessary library files, so change to the Linker, Input page. Add lua.lib and lualib.lib to the Additional Dependencies item. Click OK, and you are ready to rock and roll or get down and boogie, depending on your music preferences.

Then, to any file you are using Lua with, you have to add these `include` files:

```
extern "C"
{
#include <lua.h>
#include <lualib.h>
#include <lauxlib.h>
}
```

Notice the extra notation wrapping the `include` files to ensure that they are compiled as normal C code with the C calling convention. Omitting that gives you a load of pretty link errors.

Programming Glue Code

We want the glue code to be as simple as possible for the end user. Sometimes glue code can be messy. The glue code I'm going to show you is elegant. It consists of only two classes: a simple manager that looks after the *lua state*, and another class that you can inherit from to add script functionality to any other class. Wham bam, thank you, ma'am! With a few function calls, any class is instantly script enabled. First up, let's check out the Manager class, which is really just a singleton that does nothing at the moment except hold the Lua state, which I'll tell you more about in a moment:

```
class cScriptManager
{
public:
    virtual ~cScriptManager();
private:
    cScriptManager();

public:
    static cScriptManager* cScriptManager::getInstance();
    static DestroySingleton()
    {
        if(ms_pScriptManager)
        {
            delete ms_pScriptManager;
            ms_pScriptManager = 0;
```

```
        }
    }
private:
    lua_State* m_pLuaState;

    static cScriptManager *ms_pScriptManager;
    static indBool     ms_InstanceFlag;

public:
    indBool Start();
    indBool Run();
    indBool Shutdown();

    lua_State* GetLuaState()
    {
        assert(m_pLuaState);
        return m_pLuaState;
    }
};
```

As you can see, the Manager class doesn't do anything, but you can extend it into a rather useful debugger at a later stage if you want. For the moment, let's just leave it empty. The source code is just your usual housekeeping stuff, apart from the Start() function:

```
cScriptManager::cScriptManager(void)
{
    m_pLuaState = 0;
}

cScriptManager::~cScriptManager(void)
{
}

cScriptManager* cScriptManager::getInstance()
{
    if(!ms_InstanceFlag)
    {
        ms_pScriptManager = new cScriptManager();
        ms_InstanceFlag = true;
        return ms_pScriptManager;
    }
    else
```

```
        {
            return ms_pScriptManager;
        }
    }

    indBool cScriptManager::Start()
    {
        m_pLuaState = lua_open();

        luaopen_io(m_pLuaState);
        luaopen_base(m_pLuaState);
        luaopen_table(m_pLuaState);
        luaopen_string(m_pLuaState);
        luaopen_math(m_pLuaState);
        luaopen_loadlib(m_pLuaState);
        lua_baselibopen(m_pLuaState);
        luaopen_debug(m_pLuaState);

        return true;
    }

    indBool cScriptManager::Run()
    {
        return true;
    }

    indBool cScriptManager::Shutdown()
    {
        lua_close(m_pLuaState);
        m_pLuaState = 0;

        return true;
    }
```

Just like your #include files in C/C++, this opens the standard functionality for Lua to use. But what is that Lua State all about? Well, because Lua was written in C, it needs to maintain a structure with all its data in it. The Lua state is a pointer to the current instance of Lua, and it needs to be passed as the first argument to every Lua call you make. If you've ever done work programming DirectX in straight C, you'll know about always passing the this pointer as the first argument; it is similar with Lua.

An Inheritable Scripting Class

The next class I'm going to show you, `cScriptableObject`, is cool, and it contains all the code to make the magic happen. However, it is also quite complex, so keep an eye out on what's going on along the way. Basically, this class is designed to be a simple class from which you can inherit any other class that you want to use scripting with. After you've written it, you can treat it like a black box. Writing it, however, requires a bit of work.

The logic behind this class is that every scriptable class will have its own script file, and there will be only one script file per class. So you could have a class representing all Non-Player Characters (NPCs) in your game. Each descendent of the class, such as enemies, bosses, or vehicles, can inherit from `cScriptableObject` and have its own script to run. Make sense? Cool. Check out the class definition so that you can keep it in mind as we go through this mental code:

```
class cScriptableObject
{
public:
    // Constructor loads the script
    cScriptableObject(indString scriptName, indString objectName);
    ~cScriptableObject();

    // Get/Set functions for passing and retrieving data to/from Lua functions
    indBool SetLuaMethodParameter(indReal32 parameter);
    void GetLuaMethodParameter(indReal32& parameter);
    indBool SetLuaMethodParameter(indString parameter);
    void GetLuaMethodParameter(indChar& parameterm);
    indBool SetLuaMethodParameter(indInt parameter);
    void GetLuaMethodParameter(indInt& parameter);

    // Selects the next Lua function to call
    indBool ActivateLuaMethod(indString methodName);
    // Calls the active Lua function
    indBool ExecuteActiveLuaMethod(indInt numberOfExpectedReturns);

    // Function pointer definition for exposed functions
    typedef indInt (cScriptableObject::*LUA_FUNCTION)() const;
    // Exposes a class method to Lua
    indBool ExposeMethodToScript(LUA_FUNCTION pNewFunction, indString methodName);
    // Takes a Lua function call and actually calls the function
    static indInt LuaLocalMethodHandler(lua_State *pLuaState);
```

```
    // Translates a Lua function call and looks up the function
    indInt LuaTranslateLocalMethodRequest(indInt methodIndex);

private:
    // The registry reference key to the name of this class
    indInt m_RegistryReferenceKey;

    // Number of exposed methods in this class
    indInt m_NumLuaCallableMethods;
    // Number of arguments pushed on the Lua stack for
    // the next called script function
    indInt m_NumPushedArguments;

    // The name of the descendent class that inherits from this class
    indChar m_ScriptObjectName[MAX_PATH];

    // Vector of exposed functions
    typedef std::vector<LUA_FUNCTION> VECLOCAL_FUNCTIONS;
    VECLOCAL_FUNCTIONS m_vLocalFunctions;
};
```

All will be explained in the coming sections.

Therefore, on construction, you pass the name of a script as a parameter to the constructor of cScriptableObject, which gets the ball rolling. Okay, now check out the constructor, and don't scream. I'll explain it all:

```
cScriptableObject::cScriptableObject(indString scriptName, indString objectName)
{
    if(!scriptName || !objectName)
    {
        OutputDebugString("Invalid values passed to new scriptable object\n");
        assert(0);
        return;
    }

    strcpy(&m_ScriptObjectName[0], objectName);

    m_NumLuaCallableMethods = 0;
    m_NumPushedArguments = 0;

    m_vLocalFunctions.clear();
    m_vLocalFunctions.reserve(10);
```

```
lua_newtable (SCRIPTMANAGER->GetLuaState());
m_RegistryReferenceKey =
            luaL_ref (SCRIPTMANAGER->GetLuaState(), LUA_REGISTRYINDEX);

LUA_STACK_RECORD;

lua_rawgeti(
    SCRIPTMANAGER->GetLuaState(), LUA_REGISTRYINDEX, m_RegistryReferenceKey);
lua_pushlightuserdata(
    SCRIPTMANAGER->GetLuaState(), static_cast<void*>(this));
lua_rawseti(SCRIPTMANAGER->GetLuaState(), -2, 0);

LUA_STACK_RESTORE;

lua_getglobal(SCRIPTMANAGER->GetLuaState(), objectName);
indInt previousIndex = luaL_ref(SCRIPTMANAGER->GetLuaState(), LUA_REGISTRYINDEX);

lua_rawgeti(SCRIPTMANAGER->GetLuaState(),
            LUA_REGISTRYINDEX, m_RegistryReferenceKey);
lua_setglobal(SCRIPTMANAGER->GetLuaState(), objectName);

indInt result = luaL_loadfile(SCRIPTMANAGER->GetLuaState(), scriptName);
if(result != 0)
{
    OutputDebugString("Failed to load lua script: ");
    OutputDebugString(scriptName);
    OutputDebugString("\n");
    assert(0);
}

if (lua_pcall (SCRIPTMANAGER->GetLuaState(), 0, LUA_MULTRET, 0) != 0)
{
    assert(0);
}

if(previousIndex > 0 )
{
    lua_rawgeti(SCRIPTMANAGER->GetLuaState(), LUA_REGISTRYINDEX, previousIndex);
    lua_setglobal(SCRIPTMANAGER->GetLuaState(), objectName);
    luaL_unref(SCRIPTMANAGER->GetLuaState(), LUA_REGISTRYINDEX, previousIndex);
}
```

```
    OutputDebugString("SCRIPT: Loaded lua script: ");
    OutputDebugString(scriptName);
    OutputDebugString("\n");
}
```

I said not to scream. First, look at the parameters. First is the name of the script to load, as I mentioned before. Second is the name of the object that inherits from this class, so that the script functions can sneakily act as member functions to this object. As long as both parameters are there, we can continue creating the object. Then a few member variables are initialized:

```
strcpy(&m_ScriptObjectName[0], objectName);

m_NumLuaCallableMethods = 0;
m_NumPushedArguments = 0;

m_vLocalFunctions.clear();
m_vLocalFunctions.reserve(10);
```

The object name is copied into a member variable. You'll see how these work later on, but for now just know that functions that the descendent class exposes to Lua are held in that little vector you see, and the number of them is tracked in m_NumLuaCallableMethods. The m_NumPushedArguments member holds the number of arguments that are about to be passed to a Lua function. So if you were about to pass two integers to a Lua function that was going to add them, then m_NumPushedArguments would be equal to 2. Next up is this code:

```
lua_newtable (SCRIPTMANAGER->GetLuaState());
m_RegistryReferenceKey = luaL_ref (SCRIPTMANAGER->GetLuaState(), LUA_REGISTRYINDEX);
```

lua_newtable tells Lua to create a new table for us. A table is Lua's version of a really fancy array/structure. Because Lua is based around a stack system, this creates a new table (read array) and puts it at the top of the stack. Next, we populate that table with Lua's registry index. But first we need to get a reference to Lua's registry with the luaL_ref() function. Using that index, we can call a this a little later on:

```
lua_rawgeti(SCRIPTMANAGER->GetLuaState(), LUA_REGISTRYINDEX, m_RegistryReferenceKey);
```

This uses the registry index that we just got to fill in the newly created table. What is all this registry table business for? Well, Lua uses the double as its default number type, which isn't very good for storing integers, or in this case pointers.

Because we want our scripts to work with object orientation, we need to store a pointer to our object somehow in Lua. We can achieve this sneakily with registry reference. By hiding the `this` pointer inside it, we can later on fetch it back out again when handling Lua's C calls, effectively translating them into C++ calls. We hide the pointer like this:

```
lua_rawgeti(SCRIPTMANAGER->GetLuaState(), LUA_REGISTRYINDEX, m_RegistryReferenceKey);
lua_pushlightuserdata(SCRIPTMANAGER->GetLuaState(), static_cast<void*>(this));
lua_rawseti(SCRIPTMANAGER->GetLuaState(), -2, 0);
```

This is pretty ugly code. `lua_rawgeti()` is used to directly index into an array. The first parameter, as always, is the state. The second says we'll be messing with the registry array, and the third is the key from before, which says where in the registry we'll be changing. The next line does the actual dirty work, pushing the `this` pointer onto the stack. Finally, the third line pushes the top of the stack into the value somewhere else in the stack, which in this case is –2. Lua uses negative numbers to index the stack. We pushed the registry first to make it –1. Then we pushed the `this` pointer to make it –1 and the registry reference –2. We want to push –1 into the destination held in –2 effectively with the third line. The end result is that the `this` pointer is now nicely held away in the registry for us.

You might be wondering about the stack restoration functions that bound those three function lines. They are actually macros that restore the stack after we are finished messing with it. Check it out:

```
#define LUA_STACK_RECORD indInt stackindex = lua_gettop(SCRIPTMANAGER->GetLuaState())
#define LUA_STACK_RESTORE lua_settop(SCRIPTMANAGER->GetLuaState(), stackindex)
```

The first macro gets the top of the stack, which you place before code that modifies the stack. The second sets the stack back to its original value, which is called when you are finished. It's a handy way to restore the stack. The next two lines look like this:

```
lua_getglobal(SCRIPTMANAGER->GetLuaState(), objectName);
indInt previousIndex = luaL_ref(SCRIPTMANAGER->GetLuaState(), LUA_REGISTRYINDEX);
```

I know this is nasty stuff. The first function is `lua_getglobal()`, which returns a global variable and puts it at the top of the stack. However, if the global does not exist, it is created and pushed to the top of the stack. In this case, we are calling the variable the name of the object that was passed to the constructor. Effectively, this line creates a new global string variable and sets it to the name of the creating object. Why, you might ask? So that we can associate the this pointer we just stored with the name of object that the pointer relates to. It's all very sneaky. Then the second line gets the previous index of the registry. Next up is this:

```
lua_rawgeti(SCRIPTMANAGER->GetLuaState(), LUA_REGISTRYINDEX, m_RegistryReferenceKey);
lua_setglobal(SCRIPTMANAGER->GetLuaState(), objectName);
```

Now we bring back the registry reference location to the top of the stack and set it equal to the name of the class. What these lines have done is pushed the this pointer back into the registry and then pushed the name of the class back, allowing us to convert a class name into a class pointer! You vastly underestimate my sneakiness. Actually, this technique is extremely common and is used by anyone writing Lua scripts with C++.

Now that we have all our nasty object-orientated glue written, we can load the script with this call:

```
indInt result = luaL_loadfile(SCRIPTMANAGER->GetLuaState(), scriptName);
if(result != 0)
{
    OutputDebugString("Failed to load lua script: ");
    OutputDebugString(scriptName);
    OutputDebugString("\n");
    assert(0);
}
```

A simple function, it only takes the omnipresent Lua state pointer and a file name to load. It couldn't be easier. If it fails, it pops up an assert so that you know it's all gone pear shaped. Assuming that all went well, we need to make Lua run through the file once by asking it to call an empty function. This allows Lua to interpret the file and make itself ready for future function calls. This is the code:

```
if (lua_pcall (SCRIPTMANAGER->GetLuaState(), 0, LUA_MULTRET, 0) != 0)
{
    OutputDebugString("Failed to make initial call into Lua script");
    assert(0);
}
```

This function takes as parameters the Lua state, the number of arguments being passed, and the number of return values you are expecting. (Remember that you can return multiple values from the script.) In this case, we're not expecting it to do anything other than associate the top of the stack, which is our object name, with script function names. Finally, if all goes according to plan, we reset the registry index by bringing it to the stack, pushing our new value, and then releasing the reference:

```
if(previousIndex > 0 )
{
    lua_rawgeti(SCRIPTMANAGER->GetLuaState(), LUA_REGISTRYINDEX, previousIndex);
    lua_setglobal(SCRIPTMANAGER->GetLuaState(), objectName);
    luaL_unref(SCRIPTMANAGER->GetLuaState(), LUA_REGISTRYINDEX, previousIndex);
}

OutputDebugString("SCRIPT: Loaded lua script: ");
OutputDebugString(scriptName);
OutputDebugString("\n");
```

The code finishes by spitting out some debug information to let you know all went according to plan. The hardest part of the glue functionality is over now; the rest is far more straightforward.

If you are having trouble with this section, read through the rest of this chapter to get a better idea of how it all fits together. Then come back and reread this initial section, and it will make much more sense.

Exposing Class Functions to Lua

Lua isn't going to be very useful if it can't call functions in your class. Often, you'll want to implement the actual hardcore code in C++ for speed, but let the script decide when it is called. It works like this: During your inherited class's construction, you register all functions you want to expose to Lua. When they are exposed, the base class keeps a pointer to the function in a simple vector and associates the function with an index and string in Lua. When Lua calls your function, the index is retrieved, which is magically converted to an index in the vector of functions. This allows you to call the function originally registered automatically. You'll also see the reverse of the process started in the constructor, which extracts the `this` pointer to transfer the call to the correct class.

Let's start by looking at the actual function that exposes the method:

```
indBool cScriptableObject::ExposeMethodToScript(LUA_FUNCTION pNewFunction,
indString methodName)
{
    LUA_STACK_RECORD;
```

```
    m_NumLuaCallableMethods += 1;
    lua_rawgeti(
        SCRIPTMANAGER->GetLuaState(), LUA_REGISTRYINDEX, m_RegistryReferenceKey);
    lua_pushstring(
        SCRIPTMANAGER->GetLuaState(), methodName);
    lua_pushnumber(
            SCRIPTMANAGER->GetLuaState(), static_cast<lua_Number>(m_NumLua-
            CallableMethods));
    lua_pushcclosure(
        SCRIPTMANAGER->GetLuaState(), cScriptableObject::LuaLocalMethodHandler, 1);
    lua_settable(
        SCRIPTMANAGER->GetLuaState(), -3);

    m_vLocalFunctions.push_back(pNewFunction);

    LUA_STACK_RESTORE;

    return true;
}
```

This function takes two parameters: a pointer to the function to be exposed, and a string, which is how you want the function to be called from Lua. You always want this to be the same as the actual function name. Function pointers are the bane of everyone's life in C/C++, especially pointers to member functions. But to refresh your memory, here is the syntax for creating a function pointer to a member function that takes no parameters and returns an integer:

```
typedef indInt (cScriptableObject::*LUA_FUNCTION)() const;
```

This is the format that all exposed functions must take, unless you change this definition to suit your needs. Using that `typedef`, you can then pass function pointers as formal parameters in functions, as I did for this function:

```
indBool cScriptableObject::ExposeMethodToScript(
        LUA_FUNCTION pNewFunction, indString methodName)
{
    .
    .
    .
```

You can also use function pointers to define a vector of pointers to functions, like this:

```
typedef std::vector<LUA_FUNCTION> VECLOCAL_FUNCTIONS;
VECLOCAL_FUNCTIONS m_vLocalFunctions;
```

This code in the class definition defines a vector that will hold pointers to all the functions that derived classes expose to the script. Let's look at the code to see how it works. First up, we record the stack so that it can be restored at the end of the function, and we increment the counter that looks after the number of exposed functions. Then the function moves on to retrieve the registry reference key that we stored during construction. This allows us to push data onto the stack about our function, including its name in string form, and an index value. The index value is used to index into the vector when the function is called from Lua. Finally, the function `lua_pushcclosure()` is called, which is kind of interesting. `lua_pushcclosure()` pushes a function that will be called whenever the script comes across this function identifier. In this case, it is set to the static member function `cScriptableObject::LuaLocalMethodHandler()`. Why static? Because Lua has no concept of classes or objects. This static function is called instead, which extracts the `this` pointer and function index and automagically calls the correct class and member function. Yes, I know... very cool.

Later, the new function pointer is pushed back onto the vector of exposed functions. Then the stack is restored, and you have one exposed function. Now all the derived class has to do is something like this in its constructor:

```
cMyDerivedClass::cMyDerivedClass()
{
    LUA_FUNCTION pExposeFunction = (LUA_FUNCTION)MyFunctionToExpose;
    ExposeMethodToScript(pExposeFunction, " MyFunctionToExpose ");
}
```

Repeat ad nauseum until you have all your functions exposed to the script. Now let's look at the actual decoding process when Lua calls your function.

Translating Lua Calls to C++ Calls

Now let's look at the process that happens when a Lua script decides it wants to call one of your exposed functions. First it notices the name and checks its list of registered functions that we set up earlier. Remember before that when we exposed functions, we registered with Lua a static function for Lua to call? Well, the function we told Lua about was this one:

```cpp
indInt cScriptableObject::LuaLocalMethodHandler(lua_State *pLuaState)
{
    if(!lua_istable(pLuaState, 1))
    {
        OutputDebugString("Error trying to call class function from Lua. Invalid Bind Table\n");
        assert(0);
        return 0;
    }

    lua_rawgeti(pLuaState, 1, 0);

    if(!lua_islightuserdata(pLuaState, -1))
    {
        OutputDebugString("Error trying to call class function from Lua\n");
        assert(0);
        return 0;
    }

    cScriptableObject* pScriptObject =
        static_cast<cScriptableObject*>(lua_touserdata(pLuaState, -1));
    if(!pScriptObject)
    {
        OutputDebugString("Error trying to call class function from Lua. Invalid object pointer\n");
        assert(0);
        return 0;
    }

    indInt callableMethodStackLocation = lua_upvalueindex(1);
    indInt callableMethodIndex =
        static_cast<indInt>(lua_tonumber(pLuaState, callableMethodStackLocation));

    UINT numReturns = pScriptObject->LuaTranslateLocalMethodRequest(callableMethodIndex);

    lua_remove(pLuaState, 1);
    lua_remove(pLuaState, -1);

    return numReturns;
}
```

Keep in mind that this is a static method of the class, and that is how Lua is able to call it. Lua has no concept of what classes are. So when this is called, the table we set up when registering the function should be at the top of the stack; otherwise, there is something very wrong. After checking for a valid table, the code goes on to extract the `this` pointer from the stack with this code:

```
lua_rawgeti(pLuaState, 1, 0);
if(!lua_islightuserdata(pLuaState, -1))
{
    OutputDebugString("Error trying to call class function from Lua \n");
    assert(0);
    return 0;
}
```

This code brings the pointer to the top of the stack, ready to remove it and cast it back to its original pointer type like this:

```
cScriptableObject* pScriptObject =
static_cast<cScriptableObject*>(lua_touserdata(pLuaState, -1));
if(!pScriptObject)
{
    OutputDebugString("Error trying to call class function from Lua. Invalid object pointer\n");
    assert(0);
    return 0;
}
```

Now that we know the object that the call is intended for, we just need to find out the actual function. To do this, we get from Lua the index of the function that we set when it was originally registered:

```
indInt callableMethodStackLocation = lua_upvalueindex(1);
indInt callableMethodIndex = static_cast<indInt>(lua_tonumber(pLuaState,
callableMethodStackLocation));
```

At this point, we have the object pointer and method index. We just need to call the function. We do this in the next line, which calls the correct member function of the object:

```
UINT numReturns = pScriptObject->LuaTranslateLocalMethodRequest(callableMethodIndex);

lua_remove(pLuaState, 1);
lua_remove(pLuaState, -1);
```

The last two lines remove the object pointer and the table from the stack and reset them to their correct state. Now let's check out the cScriptableObject::LuaTranslateLocalMethodRequest() function in a little more detail. This is the function that takes the index and translates it into an actual function call. It just takes a single parameter, which is the index of the function we want to call:

```
indInt cScriptableObject::LuaTranslateLocalMethodRequest(indInt methodIndex)
{
    methodIndex--;
    assert(methodIndex >= 0);
    assert(methodIndex < (indInt)m_vLocalFunctions.size());

    LUA_FUNCTION pFunction = m_vLocalFunctions[methodIndex];
    if(pFunction)
        return (this->*pFunction)();
    else
    {
        OutputDebugString("Unable to find local function\n");
        assert(0);
        return 0;
    }
}
```

First up, the index is decremented to make it zero based, and a couple of debug checks are run to make sure the number is within limits. The rest is really easy. The index is actually the index of the vector of pointers, so all we have to do is find the function pointer in the vector at the location of the index and then call it. Simple? Cool. That's how a script call is translated into an object-orientated function call. Now let's look at this process in reverse: calling Lua functions.

Calling Lua Script Functions

This is a lot easier than the code we have just been looking at. To call a Lua function, you need to follow three steps. First you select the function you want to call. By this I mean that you tell Lua which function you want to call by pushing its name onto the stack. Then you set the parameters of the function you want to call, which again means pushing them onto the stack. Finally, you call the actual script function.

Let's look at these steps in a little more detail. The first step is selecting the function you want to call, which you do with the cScriptableObject::ActiveLuaMethod() function. This function takes a single parameter, which is the name of the function you want to call:

```
indBool cScriptableObject::ActivateLuaMethod(indString methodName)
{
    lua_rawgeti(SCRIPTMANAGER->GetLuaState(),
            LUA_REGISTRYINDEX, m_RegistryReferenceKey);
    lua_pushstring (SCRIPTMANAGER->GetLuaState(), methodName);
    lua_rawget(SCRIPTMANAGER->GetLuaState(), -2);
    lua_remove(SCRIPTMANAGER->GetLuaState(), -2);

    lua_rawgeti(SCRIPTMANAGER->GetLuaState(),
            LUA_REGISTRYINDEX, m_RegistryReferenceKey);

    if(!lua_isfunction (SCRIPTMANAGER->GetLuaState(), -2))
    {
        // Error
        assert(0);
        lua_pop(SCRIPTMANAGER->GetLuaState(), 2);
    }

    m_NumPushedArguments = 0;
    return true;
}
```

What's happening here? What this function is doing is basically getting the name of our class onto the stack in an awkward way and then pushing our function name to call onto the stack with it. Then it's running a test with lua_isfunction() to make sure the method actually exists in the script before calling it. Finally, the function is resetting the number of arguments that are currently pushed back to 0, because this is a newly selected function. After activating a function, you can set parameters and then call the function.

Let's look at how to set parameters. The main types in Lua are numbers and strings, so it makes sense to program three functions: one to pass an integer parameter, one to pass a floating point parameter, and one to pass a string parameter. We also need the reverse of these functions to retrieve return values after the method has been called. Here is the function to pass an integer:

```
indBool cScriptableObject::SetLuaMethodParameter(indInt parameter)
{
    m_NumPushedArguments += 1;
    lua_pushnumber(    SCRIPTMANAGER->GetLuaState(), (lua_Number)(parameter));
    return true;
}
```

That's pretty simple, right? The member counter that records how many arguments have been pushed is incremented, and the new parameter is pushed onto the stack. Notice how the integer is cast to be a lua_Number. This is because Lua really only supports doubles, so the integers need to be cast before they're sent onto the stack. It's a similar process for other types of values:

```
indBool cScriptableObject::SetLuaMethodParameter(indReal32 parameter)
{
    m_NumPushedArguments += 1;
    lua_pushnumber(SCRIPTMANAGER->GetLuaState(), static_cast<lua_Number>(parameter));
    return true;
}
indBool cScriptableObject::SetLuaMethodParameter(indString parameter)
{
    m_NumPushedArguments += 1;
    lua_pushstring(SCRIPTMANAGER->GetLuaState(), parameter);
    return true;
}
```

Retrieving return values off the stack is just as easy. Following is code to retrieve an integer return value after a function has been called:

```
void cScriptableObject::GetLuaMethodParameter(indInt& parameter)
{
        parameter = (indInt)lua_tonumber(SCRIPTMANAGER->GetLuaState(), -1);
    lua_pop(SCRIPTMANAGER->GetLuaState(), 1);
}
```

It's as painless as converting the top of the stack to an integer and then popping the value off the stack. The same applies to other data types:

```
void cScriptableObject::GetLuaMethodParameter(indReal32& parameter)
{
        parameter = (indReal32)lua_tonumber(SCRIPTMANAGER->GetLuaState(), -1);
    lua_pop(SCRIPTMANAGER->GetLuaState(), 1);
}
```

Chapter 10 ■ Implementing Scripting

```
void cScriptableObject::GetLuaMethodParameter(indChar& parameter)
{
    const indString string = lua_tostring(SCRIPTMANAGER->GetLuaState(), -1);
    if(string)
        strcpy((indString)&parameter, string);
    else
    {
        OutputDebugString("Error trying to retrieve string");
        assert(0);
    }
    lua_pop(SCRIPTMANAGER->GetLuaState(), 1);
}
```

There is a little more error checking put into the string version of the function, but the main code is the same. It's easy to crash a system with broken strings, so there is no harm in beefing it up a little. Now that we've activated a function and set its parameters, we can execute the function like this:

```
indBool cScriptableObject::ExecuteLuaMethod(indInt numberOfExpectedReturns)
{
    if (lua_isfunction (SCRIPTMANAGER->GetLuaState(), -tempArgs))
    {
        indInt tempArgs = m_NumPushedArguments+1;
        indInt result = lua_pcall(
            SCRIPTMANAGER->GetLuaState(),
            tempArgs,
            numberOfExpectedReturns, 0);

        if (result != 0)
        {
            OutputDebugString("LUA SCRIPT ERROR: ");
            OutputDebugString(lua_tostring (SCRIPTMANAGER->GetLuaState(), -1));
            OutputDebugString("\n");
            assert(0);
        }
    }

    m_NumPushedArguments = 0;

    return true;
}
```

Again, we do a little sanity check with lua_isfunction() to make sure there is actually a valid function set up and ready to call. Then we call the actual function with lua_pcall(), which takes as parameters the Lua state, the number of arguments passed, the number of expected returns, and an optional function pointer to call if there is an error. If all goes according to plan, we reset the number of pushed arguments and continue on. After executing a method, we can retrieve its return values with the methods discussed a moment ago.

Implementing a Scriptable Object

Implementing a scripted object is a breeze now that the glue code is written. Here's all we have to do:

```
class cScriptTestObject : public cScriptableObject
{
public:
    cScriptTestObject(indString scriptName)
        :cScriptableObject(scriptName, CODE_TO_STRING(cScriptTestObject))
    {
        LUA_FUNCTION pFun = (LUA_FUNCTION)LuaPrintString;
        ExposeMethodToScript(pFun, CODE_TO_STRING(LuaPrintString));
    }

    ~cScriptTestObject()
    {

    }

    const indInt LuaPrintString(void)
    {
        OutputDebugString("Hello World from cpp\n");
        return 0;
    }

    void Run()
    {
        indReal32 floatParam = 100.1234f;
        indInt intParam = 200;
        char stringParam[] = "Hello World";
```

```
        char returnedString[256] = {0};
        indReal32 returnedFloat;
        indInt returnedInt;

        ActivateLuaMethod("callme");
        SetLuaMethodParameter(intParam);
        SetLuaMethodParameter(floatParam);
        SetLuaMethodParameter(&stringParam[0]);

        ExecuteActiveLuaMethod(0);

        GetLuaMethodParameter(returnedString[0]);
        GetLuaMethodParameter(returnedFloat);
        GetLuaMethodParameter(returnedInt);

        indInt x = 0;

    }

private:

};
---------- Lua script code in EngineTest.Lua
function cScriptTestObject.callme(this, intParam, floatParam)
    cScriptTestObject:LuaPrintString()

    x = intParam * 2
    y = floatParam * 2
    z = "Hello hello"

    return x, y, z
end
```

This simple class exposes a single function that prints a message when called to the debug window. Is that easy or what? You can now expose all your classes to scripting and wave goodbye to all that recompiling. And the great thing is that after you've written that awful glue code, you never have to look at it again. It's just a black box that works!

Conclusion

Well, I bet this chapter has been an eye opener for you if you haven't dealt with scripts before. You've learned a whole ton of stuff that is incredibly useful when developing large-scale games. In particular, you learned about the following:

- Importance of using scripting languages
- Different scripting languages available for games
- Introduction to the Lua language and why it's great
- Development of a scripting management interface
- Glue code to allow your code to talk to scripts and scripts to talk to your code
- Way to expose functionality to scripts
- Method of implementing object orientation into a non-object-orientated language

In the next chapter, I'll return to graphics to show you how to implement incredibly vivid and realistic volumetric shadows.

CHAPTER 11

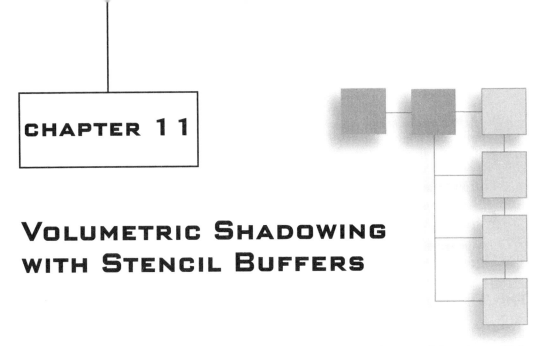

VOLUMETRIC SHADOWING WITH STENCIL BUFFERS

Without a shadow of a doubt (get it?), this chapter is going to add an incredible amount of realism to your game engine. Shadows are incredibly important to the human visual system when working out perspective. For example, think about a sphere hovering over a plane. Is a large sphere hovering above the plane, or is the sphere small and close to the camera? If the sphere casts a shadow over the plane, there is immediate additional reference data that your brain can use to work out the relative sizes of the two objects. In addition, shadows add a great sense of immersion to a game. Rather than just having a character appear onscreen, you could have him sneak up on the player from behind with the shadow appearing first.

If you have done any investigation into shadows, you will find that they are incredibly difficult to implement. Actually, they're really not. It's just that there are so many people who don't understand shadowing properly and then go and write about it. Luckily, I have years of experience with volumetric shadows and have personally implemented them on two completed best-selling games, so I'm a pretty good source of information on this subject. In this chapter, I'm going to show you the following:

- The theory of shadowing
- Ways to tell if a model's vertices are shadowed
- Extruding a shadow volume

- Rendering to the stencil buffer
- Restrictive rendering with the stencil buffer
- Self-shadowing
- Eliminating popping artifacts
- Creating degenerate quads to replace face edges

Let's get the ball rolling!

The Theory of Volumetric Shadowing

Hold your hand up to a light source if you can and check out the shadow that your hand is casting. If you look closely for a moment, you'll see that roughly half of your hand is being lit by the light source and the other half is hidden from the light source and is darker, or shadowed. That's simple enough so far. The word for this is that your hand is an *occluder*.

Look at the shadow that your hand casts. If you think about it, the shape of the shadow is really just the shape of the part of your hand that is in shadow, but extended away from the light and made bigger. This is the short and sweet of how volumetric shadows work. Now let's move into the game world a little bit more, and imagine that your hand is a standard mesh.

Roughly half of your hand's vertices are lit by the light source, and the other half is occluded. Let's say that we group all the vertices that are occluded and extend them away from the light source until they hit a surface. If you are having trouble imagining this, think of a flat square casting a shadow. Now extrude its vertices away from the light so that it forms an elongated cube. Get it? It's the same with your occluding hand.

So you now have this volume. If you think about it, anything that enters that volume is going to be shadowed. As another example, think of a large square office block. Two sides are lit by the sun, and two are occluded. If you extend an imaginary volume away from the building in the direction of the sunlight, anything that enters that volume will be shadowed.

Okay, so now you have this volume where everything is shadowed in. You might think that you could just render this volume as a dark alpha'd object, but this won't work, because it would darken objects *behind* the volume even though they are now within the volume. What we really need is a way to render the darkened volume only if it *intersects* with other geometry. So how the heck do you check whether objects are intersecting with a volume that could be incredibly complicated if cast from a complex object? That's where the magic of stencil buffers come in, which I'll tell you about next.

The worst part about volumetric shadowing is that there are a lot of little steps to go through, and it is easy to make a minor error and break the whole system. You then spend hours trying to fix the problem by tinkering with lots of render states. To make it a little easier, I'll show you the results of the most common errors so that if they happen to you, you'll know exactly what the solution is.

The Wonderful World of Stencil Buffers

The term *stencil buffer* generally causes most programmers to bolt in various directions screaming, "Stop the pain! Please, stop the pain!" This is because of the incredibly poor documentation and examples that shipped with DirectX when stencil buffers were first released. I shudder just thinking about it. These days the documentation has improved to such a point that… Actually, they haven't improved at all, and I'm secretly hoping that Boeing doesn't employ the guy who wrote the docs to write aircraft maintenance manuals.

So I'll do Microsoft's job and tell you all about stencil buffers. I'm guessing you have a fairly good understanding of the z-buffer because it's virtually impossible to write a game without one working in the background. For a quick refresher, z-buffers hold the depth of every pixel rendered to the screen. That way, when it comes time to render another object, the graphics card can instantly tell if the new object is in front of or behind objects that are already rendered. Because it is per-pixel accurate, it usually does a pretty good job. The exception is when objects are extremely close together, in which case you get lots of z-fighting and flickering. Z-buffers usually take up 16 to 24 bits. This means there is usually a minimum of 8 bits wasted in the z-buffer. Luckily, someone came up with a novel idea for these wasted bits as a place to hold a stencil buffer.

So what is a stencil buffer? Well, you can never actually see a stencil buffer, which kind of adds to its complexity. However, put simply, a stencil buffer holds the outcome of a test. For instance, you could test to see if one rendered object was in front of another, and render the results of the test to the stencil buffer. For our shadow example, you could test whether two objects *intersected* and write the results to the stencil buffer. Then later on, you could restrict rendering only to places where the intersection happened. Wham bam, thank you, ma'am! You're on your way to shadows!

Remember that the main problem was our need to restrict the rendering to areas where the shadow volume intersected with other geometry. Well, the stencil buffer allows us to test and record intersections and then limit rendering to areas where the intersections occurred. Is that cool or what? I'm sure you're a little confused, but hang in there, and it will all make sense when you get to see the code.

Now that you know the sketchy theory of how shadow volumes work, let's recap about what needs to happen to render shadows:

1. Find out which vertices are occluders, and group these together.

2. Extrude these occluder vertices away from the light source to form a shadow volume.

3. Set up the stencil buffer to record the intersections between the shadow volume and other geometry in the scene.

4. Use the stencil buffer to control rendering of dark shadows only to locations where intersections occurred.

And that's all there is to it! Let's look at these steps in more detail and construct a really cool and versatile shadowing system.

Building a Versatile Shadowing System

Now I'm going to go through how to add a shadow system to the game engine. This is really independent of any particular engine, so it should be easy to adapt this stuff to your own engine. Let's start with the most obvious part of shadowing: the light source.

Adding a Global Light Source

Obviously, to have shadows, you need to have a light source to cast shadows from. To this end, I've added some code to the game engine to create and control a global light. A *global light* is the main light in your scene, such as the sun, moon, and stadium lights. Volumetric shadowing uses little CPU time, but it absolutely murders your fill rate. That's why you should limit the number of lights you shadow from to a bare minimum. There is rarely a reason to use more lights than this. Two exceptions are if your game is entirely indoors, or if you are writing a sports game and there are many stadium lights. If you are indoors, you can get around this problem by only shadowing from the light nearest to the player. As the player moves around, you can interpolate between lights to get the average of two lights. If you are writing a sports game, the light direction is normally fixed, so you don't even need to work out shadowing. You can just attach prerendered shadows to the player.

So over in the engine, I added a vector to hold the light's position. That's all you need really, because there are no falloff factors or anything like that—just its position:

```
private:
    D3DXVECTOR3     m_GlobalLightPosition;
```

Then I added a few helper functions to the class definition:

```
void GetGlobalLightPosition(D3DXVECTOR3& lightPos)
{
    lightPos = m_GlobalLightPosition;
}

void GetLightDirectionToPosition(D3DXVECTOR3 position, D3DXVECTOR3& lightDir)
{
    lightDir = position - m_GlobalLightPosition;
    D3DXVec3Normalize(&lightDir, &lightDir);
}

void GetLightDirection(D3DXVECTOR3& lightDir)
{
    // Get light direction to origin
    lightDir = -m_GlobalLightPosition;
    D3DXVec3Normalize(&lightDir, &lightDir);
}
```

The first function just returns the position of the light. The second returns a normalized direction vector from the light to any other point in the world. Finally, the last function returns the light direction to the origin, which is what I'll generally use to work out the shadow directions. By default, the light is positioned at (20, 100, 20), or high above the origin at a slight angle. I also put in a function that is called every frame to update the light's position, because shadows look cool with a moving light source. This code gives the light a slow rotation:

```
void cGameEngine::UpdateGlobalLight()
{
    float secondsElapsed = (float)GetEngineRunTime() / 1000.0f;
    m_GlobalLightPosition.x = sin(secondsElapsed) * 100;
    m_GlobalLightPosition.z = cos(secondsElapsed) * 100;
}
```

You could hook this up to a script or other code if you added more advance time-of-day code.

Find Occluded Vertices

Finding occluded vertices might sound difficult, but it's actually easy. How do you tell if a vertex is in shadow? Well, first you get a vector from the light source to the vertex in question. If you think about it, you can tell the way the vertex is facing from its normal. So if you know the vector from the light to the vertex and the way the vertex is pointing, you can tell if it's facing the light. If the angle between the vertex and the light vector is less than 90 degrees, the vertex must be lit by the light. All you have to do is test each vertex to see if the angle between it and the light is greater than 90 degrees, and if so extrude it out to form the shadow volume. This is a perfect job for a vertex shader because the operation needs to be done every frame for every vertex, and vertex shaders are designed to do that.

How do you determine the angle between the light and its normal? I'm sure you remember that the dot product returns a number less than 0.0f if an angle between two vectors is greater than 90 degrees. Therefore, all we need to test whether a vertex is occluded is this:

```
if(dot(normalize(Normal), LightToVertexVector) < 0.0f )
{
    // Extrude the vertex
}
```

Simple, huh? I'll show you the full shader shortly, but first we need to go through a little more theory.

Extruding an Occluded Vertex

To form the shadow volume, as I said before, you move the shadowed vertex away from the light source. This sounds harder than it actually is. If you think about it, you already have the vector from the light source to the vertex. This *is* the light direction. So just move the vertex along this vector by as far as you want the shadow to cast. That's it! This code does it:

```
P.xyz += LightVector * 100.0f;
```

You can't get any easier than that! Now let's look at the full shader:

```
VS_OUTPUT_EXTRUDE VS(
    float3 Pos    : POSITION,
    float3 Norm   : NORMAL)
{


    VS_OUTPUT_EXTRUDE Out;

    float4x4 WorldView     = mul(World, View);
    float4x4 WorldViewProj = mul(WorldView, Projection);

    float3 N = mul(Norm, (float3x3)World);
    float3 L = normalize(lightDirection);


    if( dot(normalize(N), L) < 0.0f )
    {
        float4 P = mul(float4(Pos,1), WorldView);

        P.xyz += L * 100.0f;
         Out.Pos   = mul(P, Projection);
        Out.color = float4(1,0,0,0.5);
    }
    else
    {
        float3 P = mul(float4(Pos, 1), (float4x3)WorldView);
        Out.Pos   = mul(float4(P, 1), Projection);
        Out.color = float4(1,1,0,0.5);
    }
    return Out;
}
```

Let's go through that slowly and see what's going on. The shader takes the vertex position and its normal as input. The first thing it does is multiply a couple of matrices that will be used later:

```
float4x4 WorldView = mul(World, View);
float4x4 WorldViewProj = mul(WorldView, Projection);
```

Next we put the vertex normal into world space and normalize the light direction so that it has a length of 1.0f:

```
float3 N = mul(Norm, (float3x3)World);
float3 L = normalize(lightDirection);
```

Now we do our test to see if the vertex is shadowed:

```
if( dot(normalize(N), L) < 0.0f )
{
```

If the vertex passes the test and is shadowed, we need to extrude it. First we work out where the vertex is in camera space:

```
float4 P = mul(float4(Pos,1), WorldView);
```

Then we extend the vertex away from the light source along the light vector to create the shadow volume:

```
P.xyz += L * 100.0f;
```

This extends the vertex 100 units along the light direction vector to create the shadow volume. Remember that only the shadowed vertices are being extruded; the lit vertices stay at their normal locations. The result is that roughly half the model is where it should be, and the other half is stretched 100 units away in the direction the light is traveling. Next we just have to transform the vertex into projection space prior to rendering:

```
Out.Pos   = mul(P, Projection);
Out.color = float4(1,0,0,0.5);
```

I also set the color to transparent red. The nonextruded vertices are set to yellow. Although these colors are never actually rendered to the screen, it is useful during development to see the actual extruded vertices so that you can ensure everything is working okay. The nonextruded vertices are set to yellow, so it's easy to tell along the yellow to red gradient which way the vertices are being extruded. More on this shortly. The other half of the if statement looks like this:

```
else
{
    float3 P  = mul(float4(Pos, 1), (float4x3)WorldView);
    Out.Pos   = mul(float4(P, 1), Projection);
    Out.color = float4(1,1,0,0.5);
}
```

As you can see, nothing really happens to these vertices. They are just transformed to world, view, and finally projection space. The color is set as I mentioned a moment ago.

The pixel shader that goes with this vertex shader could not be easier:

```
float4 PS(float4 Diff : COLOR0) : COLOR
{
    return Diff;
}
```

The pixel shader just spits out the color set in the vertex shader. This pixel shader never actually renders anything to screen. As you'll see shortly, the results of these shaders end up in the stencil buffer, which is not visible directly. To see what the extrusion looks like before rendering, look at Figure 11.1.

Figure 11.1
The extruded shadow volume.

The Stencil Buffer Rendering Process

Now we get to a slightly more technical part of the process. Let's look at how this shadowy stencily stuff fits together. As I said in the beginning of this chapter, the stencil buffer can record the results of tests. For shadowing, we need to do a couple of intersection tests. The process goes like this.

Render all the faces of the extruded volume that are facing the camera. Record in the stencil buffer everywhere they hit another piece of geometry. Then render all the faces of the extruded volume that are *not* facing the camera. In this stage, you perform the same test again, except you also unmark all the sections of stencil buffer that failed this test but passed the first test. The shape you are left with is the correct shadow volume. So, as you can see, this is a two-pass process.

All of this is completed through the use of render states from the technique in the shader. Let's look at the code, and then I'll explain it all in more detail. Don't scream.

```
technique TVertexAndPixelShader
{

pass P0
    {
        ZWRITEENABLE = FALSE;
        ZENABLE = TRUE;
        ZFUNC = LESS;

        STENCILENABLE = TRUE;
        STENCILFUNC = ALWAYS;
        STENCILPASS = KEEP;
        STENCILFAIL = KEEP;
        STENCILZFAIL = DECR;
        STENCILREF = 0x1;

        alphatestenable = false;
        alphablendenable = false;
        colorwriteenable = 0;
        cullmode = ccw;

        StencilMask = 0xFFFFFFFF;
        StencilWriteMask = 0xFFFFFFFF;
```

```
        VertexShader = compile vs_1_1 VS();
        PixelShader  = compile ps_1_1 PS();
    }
    pass P1
    {

        ZWRITEENABLE = FALSE;
        ZENABLE = TRUE;
        ZFUNC = LESS;

        STENCILENABLE = TRUE;
        STENCILFUNC = ALWAYS;
        STENCILPASS = keep;
        STENCILFAIL = KEEP;
        STENCILZFAIL = INCR;
        STENCILREF = 0x1;

        alphatestenable = false;
        alphablendenable = false;
        colorwriteenable = 0;
        cullmode = cw;

        StencilMask = 0xFFFFFFFF;
        StencilWriteMask = 0xFFFFFFFF;

        VertexShader = compile vs_1_1 VS();
        PixelShader  = compile ps_1_1 PS();
    }
}
```

You gotta stop screaming! It's not so bad! Let's look at the first pass and check out the states it's changing. In English, the first pass is doing the following in order:

1. Z-writing is disabled. The volume will never be rendered to screen, so we don't want it messing up the depth buffer.

2. Z-testing is enabled. This should already be on, but we need to be sure. Basically we want the volume to render to the stencil buffer only if it passes the z-test. That is, it's only visible if it's not blocked by other objects that are already rendered.

3. The z-test function is set to be Less. This means it will pass the z-test only if it's closer to the camera than other objects. This is usually set to LessEqual.

4. The stencil buffer is turned on. Obviously, we can't render to the buffer if it's off.

5. The stencil test function is set to always pass the stencil test. Basically, we aren't using stencil testing here. We're using z testing to see if there is an intersection, and we're using the result of that to change the stencil buffer.

6. The stencil test is set to keep, which means the stencil buffer won't be changed. Again, we are not using stencil testing, so this effectively disables it.

7. For completeness, the stencil fail is set to keep, although this should never happen because we set the stencil test to always pass the test.

8. This is the real meat and potatoes of the function. If the z-test fails, another object might be intersecting with the shadow volume, so we decrement the value in the buffer.

9. The next line sets the stencil reference value to 1. This is what the stencil uses as a comparison value when doing testing.

10. The next line turns off alpha blending and alpha testing. Because these shaders write to the stencil buffer and not the frame buffer, there is no point in turning on alpha testing or blending.

11. Next that the colorwriteenable flag is set to 0, which disables rendering to the frame buffer.

12. The cull mode is set to counterclockwise, which renders all the faces in the extruded volume that are not facing the camera. This is really important, because it is what changes in the second pass and allows the shadow shape to be isolated.

13. Next, the stencil mask and stencil write mask are set to permit writing to the stencil buffer.

And that's how you render your first pass of shadows to the stencil buffer. In a nutshell, these states disable rendering to screen and modify the stencil buffer wherever the volume intersects the geometry. However, the stencil buffer is full of errors at the moment because large parts of it are set incorrectly. The second pass isolates the shadow to the correct region. Looking at the previous code again, the second pass is the same except for these two lines:

```
STENCILZFAIL = INCR;
cullmode = cw;
```

This reverses the cull mode to render only the faces of the shadow volume that *do* face the camera. The Z fail test is changed to increment the stencil buffer if there is an intersection with other geometry. The result of these two passes is that the stencil buffer now has a set of pixels set to the value of 1 that indicate where the shadow should lie. Now we just need to render the shadow.

Rendering the Shadows to the Frame Buffer

Most of the hard work is over. Now we just need to render the actual shadows, which is kind of interesting. Keep in mind that the previous step rendered only the shadows to the stencil buffer, which isn't visible. The stencil buffer now contains the regions that are in shadow, so we need to render only to those regions.

The solution is to set the stencil buffer to allow rendering to the frame buffer only if the stencil buffer contains a region marked as shadowed. What we can do is render a giant quad that is the same size as the screen in the color that we want the shadows to be. Because the stencil buffer is restricting the rendering, the quad will be rendered only where the shadow should be. The result is correctly rendered shadows. So the first thing to do is learn how to render a full-screen quad. That's easy. You just define a standard vertex structure like this and declare it:

```
typedef struct tSHADOW_VERT
{
    D3DXVECTOR3 position;
    D3DCOLOR color;
}SHADOW_VERT;
#define SHADOW_FVF D3DFVF_XYZ | D3DFVF_DIFFUSE
.
.
.
SHADOW_VERT    m_ShadowQuadVerts[6];
```

Notice how the vertex structure has a color component. This is how we set the shadow color. Also note the six vertices for the full-screen quad. The quad is composed of two triangles, of three vertices each. These can be filled in like this:

```
m_ShadowColor = D3DXCOLOR(0,0,0.2f,0.5f);

m_ShadowQuadVerts[0].color = (D3DCOLOR)m_ShadowColor;
m_ShadowQuadVerts[1].color = (D3DCOLOR)m_ShadowColor;
m_ShadowQuadVerts[2].color = (D3DCOLOR)m_ShadowColor;
m_ShadowQuadVerts[3].color = (D3DCOLOR)m_ShadowColor;
m_ShadowQuadVerts[4].color = (D3DCOLOR)m_ShadowColor;
m_ShadowQuadVerts[5].color = (D3DCOLOR)m_ShadowColor;

m_ShadowQuadVerts[0].position = D3DXVECTOR3(-1.0f,-1.0f, 0.0f);
m_ShadowQuadVerts[1].position = D3DXVECTOR3( 1.0f,-1.0f, 0.0f);
m_ShadowQuadVerts[2].position = D3DXVECTOR3( 1.0f, 1.0f, 0.0f);

m_ShadowQuadVerts[3] = m_ShadowQuadVerts[2];
m_ShadowQuadVerts[4].position = D3DXVECTOR3(-1.0f, 1.0f, 0.0f);
m_ShadowQuadVerts[5] = m_ShadowQuadVerts[0];
```

See how the coordinates are all in the range −1.0 to 1.0f? That's because we're drawing them straight to screen without world, view, or projection transformations. The coordinates need to be in screen space ready for the viewport transformation. I wrote a simple custom shader to render these in screen space. Check out the code:

```
VS_OUTPUT_EXTRUDE VS(
    float3 Pos    : POSITION,
    float4 shadCol : COLOR0)
{

    VS_OUTPUT_EXTRUDE Out;

    Out.Pos = float4(Pos,1);
    Out.color = shadCol;

    return Out;
}

float4 PS(float4 Diff : COLOR0) : COLOR
{
    return Diff;
}
```

It doesn't get much easier than that. There is no transformation or anything else to do except for the vertex shader to pass the data, untouched, to the pixel shader. The pixel shader has nothing to do except spit out the shadow color to the screen.

Figure 11.2
Early rendered shadows.

There is some interesting code in the technique that tells Direct3D to restrict rendering to the correct stencil buffer regions:

```
technique TVertexAndPixelShader
{
    pass P0
    {
        STENCILFUNC= LESSEQUAL;
        STENCILPASS= KEEP;
        STENCILZFAIL = keep;
        STENCILFAIL = KEEP;
```

```
            STENCILREF= 0x1;
            ZENABLE = true;
            ZFUNC = LESSEQUAL;
            ZWRITEENABLE = FALSE;
            SRCBLEND = SRCALPHA;
            DESTBLEND = INVSRCALPHA;

            cullmode = none;

            STENCILENABLE = TRUE;
            ALPHABLENDENABLE = TRUE;

            VertexShader = compile vs_1_1 VS();
            PixelShader  = compile ps_1_1 PS();
        }

    }
```

The render states here are doing the following, in order:

1. Setting the stencil function to LessEqual. This means that rendering is allowed only if the stencil pixel is less than or equal to the stencil reference value, which is set with the STENCILREF command. The previous steps have filled the stencil buffer with the correct values.

2. Setting all the stencil tests to keep, which leaves the stencil buffer untouched. We don't want the stencil buffer to change; we want to control rendering to the frame buffer.

3. Setting the stencil ref to 0x1, which is what the LessEqual command from step 1 will work with.

4. Turning on Z testing so that we don't render the shadows on top of objects that are in front of the shadow.

5. Resetting the Z function to its default LessEqual.

6. Turning off Z writing. Because this is a quad drawn in front of everything else, if we wrote to the Z buffer, nothing else would render!

7. Setting up the source and destination alpha blending rules so that the shadow will be partially transparent.

8. Turning off culling. Because it's just a quad, culling doesn't matter.

9. Making sure the stencil buffer is still enabled.

10. Turning on alpha blending.

Rendering with these render states and the shaders is the final step toward making the shadows appear onscreen.

Bringing It All Together

Now that you've seen what's required to render shadows, let's look at what you would do to render an object with shadows. First up, you need to make sure that at the start of every frame the stencil buffer is cleared, along with the depth and frame buffers. This code takes care of that and should be the line called at the start of every frame:

```
m_pDevice->Clear(0, NULL, D3DCLEAR_TARGET | D3DCLEAR_ZBUFFER |
                 D3DCLEAR_STENCIL, D3DCOLOR_RGBA(0,0,150,0), 1.0f, 0 );
```

I also put together a little class to hold all the shadow stuff in one place. This is the class definition:

```
namespace VisualEffects
{
    typedef struct tSHADOW_VERT
    {
        D3DXVECTOR3 position;
        D3DCOLOR color;
    }SHADOW_VERT;
    #define SHADOW_FVF D3DFVF_XYZ | D3DFVF_DIFFUSE

class cVolumetricShadow
    {
    public:
        cVolumetricShadow();
        ~cVolumetricShadow(void);

    public:
        indInt StartShadowPass();
        void EndShadowPass();
        void RenderShadows();
```

```
            void SetShadowColor(D3DXCOLOR& shadowColor)
            {
                m_ShadowColor = shadowColor;
            }
        private:
            indUInt m_EffectID;
            SHADOW_VERT   m_ShadowQuadVerts[6];
            D3DXCOLOR m_ShadowColor;
        };

    }
```

And this is the corresponding code for the class that I've been talking about throughout this chapter:

```
        cVolumetricShadow::cVolumetricShadow()
    {
        m_EffectID = EFFECTMANAGER->FindEffect("volumeshadow1.fx");


        m_ShadowQuadVerts[0].position = D3DXVECTOR3(-1.0f,-1.0f, 0.0f);
        m_ShadowQuadVerts[1].position = D3DXVECTOR3( 1.0f,-1.0f, 0.0f);
        m_ShadowQuadVerts[2].position = D3DXVECTOR3( 1.0f, 1.0f, 0.0f);

        m_ShadowQuadVerts[3] = m_ShadowQuadVerts[2];
        m_ShadowQuadVerts[4].position = D3DXVECTOR3(-1.0f, 1.0f, 0.0f);
        m_ShadowQuadVerts[5] = m_ShadowQuadVerts[0];

        m_ShadowColor = D3DXCOLOR(0,0,0.2f,0.5f);
    }

    cVolumetricShadow::~cVolumetricShadow(void)
    {
    }


    indInt cVolumetricShadow::StartShadowPass()
    {
        m_ShadowQuadVerts[0].color = (D3DCOLOR)m_ShadowColor;
        m_ShadowQuadVerts[1].color = (D3DCOLOR)m_ShadowColor;
        m_ShadowQuadVerts[2].color = (D3DCOLOR)m_ShadowColor;
        m_ShadowQuadVerts[3].color = (D3DCOLOR)m_ShadowColor;
        m_ShadowQuadVerts[4].color = (D3DCOLOR)m_ShadowColor;
```

```cpp
        m_ShadowQuadVerts[5].color = (D3DCOLOR)m_ShadowColor;
        return m_EffectID;
    }

    void cVolumetricShadow::EndShadowPass()
    {
        GAMEENGINE->GetDevice()->SetRenderState(D3DRS_STENCILENABLE, FALSE);
        GAMEENGINE->GetDevice()->SetRenderState(D3DRS_ALPHABLENDENABLE, FALSE);
        GAMEENGINE->GetDevice()->SetRenderState(D3DRS_CULLMODE, D3DCULL_NONE);
        GAMEENGINE->GetDevice()->SetRenderState(D3DRS_ZWRITEENABLE, TRUE);
        GAMEENGINE->GetDevice()->SetRenderState(D3DRS_ZENABLE, TRUE);
        GAMEENGINE->GetDevice()->SetRenderState(D3DRS_COLORWRITEENABLE,
            D3DCOLORWRITEENABLE_RED|
            D3DCOLORWRITEENABLE_GREEN|
            D3DCOLORWRITEENABLE_BLUE|
            D3DCOLORWRITEENABLE_ALPHA);
    }

    void cVolumetricShadow::RenderShadows()
    {
        D3DXMATRIX matWorld;
        D3DXMatrixIdentity(&matWorld);
        indUInt shadowEffectID = EFFECTMANAGER->FindEffect("volumeshadow3.fx");

        VisualEffects::cEffect* pCurrentEffect =
EFFECTMANAGER->GetEffect(shadowEffectID);
        GAMEENGINE->GetDevice()->SetFVF(SHADOW_FVF);
        pCurrentEffect->SetTransforms(
            matWorld, CAMERA->GetViewMatrix(), CAMERA->GetProjectionMatrix());
        pCurrentEffect->Dispatch();
        indUInt numPasses = 0;
        pCurrentEffect->Begin(numPasses);

        for(indUInt passCount = 0 ; passCount < numPasses ; passCount++)
        {
            pCurrentEffect->BeginPass(passCount);

            GAMEENGINE->GetDevice()->DrawPrimitiveUP(
                D3DPT_TRIANGLELIST, 2,
                  (const void*)&m_ShadowQuadVerts[0], sizeof(SHADOW_VERT));

            pCurrentEffect->EndPass();
        }
```

Chapter 11 ■ Volumetric Shadowing with Stencil Buffers

```
        pCurrentEffect->End();

        GAMEENGINE->GetDevice()->SetRenderState(D3DRS_STENCILENABLE, FALSE);
        GAMEENGINE->GetDevice()->SetRenderState(
                            D3DRS_ALPHABLENDENABLE, FALSE);
        GAMEENGINE->GetDevice()->SetRenderState(D3DRS_CULLMODE, D3DCULL_NONE);
        GAMEENGINE->GetDevice()->SetRenderState(D3DRS_ZWRITEENABLE, TRUE);
        GAMEENGINE->GetDevice()->SetRenderState(D3DRS_ZENABLE, TRUE);

        GAMEENGINE->GetDevice()->Clear(0, NULL, D3DCLEAR_STENCIL, 0, 1.0f, 0);
    }
```

Let's look at this code in action. The first step is to add a new member to our cVisualResource class (that we created at the start of this book) to render standard meshes. Simply declare the new variable like this with a Boolean for shadowing:

```
VisualEffects::cVolumetricShadow    m_ShadowRenderer;
indBool     m_bShadowed;
```

Then we modify the rendering slightly. Originally, there was only one render function, and it looked like this:

```
indBool cVisualResource::Render ()
{
    VisualEffects::cEffect* pCurrentEffect = EFFECTMANAGER->GetEffect(m_EffectID);
    pCurrentEffect->SetEnvMap(m_pEnvironmentMap);

    D3DXMatrixIdentity(&m_matWorld);
    D3DXMatrixTranslation(&m_matWorld, m_Position.x, m_Position.y, m_Position.z);
    pCurrentEffect->SetTransforms(
        m_matWorld, CAMERA->GetViewMatrix(), CAMERA->GetProjectionMatrix());
    pCurrentEffect->Dispatch();

    indUInt numPasses = 0;
    pCurrentEffect->Begin(numPasses);

    GAMEENGINE->GetDevice()->SetFVF(m_pMesh->GetFVF());

    for(indUInt passCount = 0 ; passCount < numPasses ; passCount++)
    {

        pCurrentEffect->BeginPass(passCount);
```

```
        if(!m_bOverrideTexture)
        {
            for(indUInt i = 0 ; i < m_NumMeshMaterials ; i++)
            {
                if(m_pMeshTextures[i])
                    GAMEENGINE->GetDevice()->SetTexture(0, m_pMeshTextures[i]);

                GAMEENGINE->GetDevice()->SetMaterial(&m_pMeshMaterials[i]);
                m_pMesh->DrawSubset(i);
            }
        }
        else
        {
            if(m_pOverrideTexture)
                GAMEENGINE->GetDevice()->SetTexture(0, m_pOverrideTexture);

            for(indUInt i = 0 ; i < m_NumMeshMaterials ; i++)
                m_pMesh->DrawSubset(i);
        }
        pCurrentEffect->EndPass();

    }

    pCurrentEffect->End();

    GAMEENGINE->GetDevice()->SetTexture(0, 0);

    return true;
}
```

We need to change this because we now have the option to render with or without shadows. So we rename this old render function to RenderResource() and make it private. We replace it with this function, which figures out how to render the model:

```
indBool cVisualResource::Render()
{
    if(m_bShadowed)
        return RenderShadowed();
    else
        return RenderResource();
}
```

Pretty simple so far. If the variable m_bShadowed is false, the code just renders normally as before; however, if the variable is true, it calls the new rendering routine first:

```
indBool cVisualResource::RenderShadowed()
{
    UINT oldEffectID = m_EffectID;

    m_EffectID = m_ShadowRenderer.StartShadowPass();
    RenderResource();

    m_EffectID = oldEffectID;
    m_ShadowRenderer.EndShadowPass();
    m_ShadowRenderer.RenderShadows();

    RenderResource();

    return true;
}
```

This shadow rendering function starts by overriding the effect used to render this object with the effect ID given by the cVolumetricShadow class. It then calls the RenderResource() function as before. Its behavior will be different, though, because we secretly changed the effect it will use to render, which is, of course, the two-pass rendering stencil rendering shader I showed you at the start of the chapter. Then the function calls the cVolumetricShadow cleanup functions and renders the object again, but this time with its normal rendering effect. Therefore, the normal object is rendered on top of its shadow. Without this step, you would have a shadow but no object.

Self-Shadowing

One of the coolest features of volumetric shadowing is that objects can shadow themselves. So, for instance, a character's arm will cast a shadow over the character's body. It looks realistic. However, you don't always want to self-shadow because some models, particularly low poly models, do not self-shadow very well. It's good to have an option to change it.

Enabling self-shadowing is easy. You just have to render the model *before* its shadow, and the shadow will render on top of the model. Due to the work of the stencil buffer, the shadow will only render on the model where the shadow should be located. Areas out of shadow will not be changed. If you don't want self-shadowing, change the rendering order to render the shadow *after* the shadow.

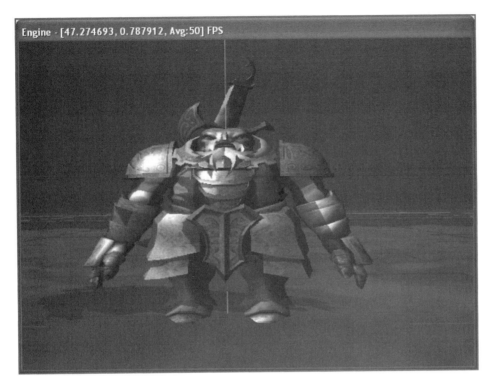

Figure 11.3
Self-shadowing in action.

These simple changes to the render function implement this functionality:

```
indBool cVisualResource::RenderShadowed()
{
    UINT oldEffectID = m_EffectID;
    if(m_bSelfShadow)
        RenderResource();

    m_EffectID = m_ShadowRenderer.StartShadowPass();
    RenderResource();

    m_EffectID = oldEffectID;

    m_ShadowRenderer.EndShadowPass();
    m_ShadowRenderer.RenderShadows();
```

```
if(!m_bSelfShadow)
    RenderResource();

return true;
}
```

Some things aren't meant to be so easy. Fire up the sample application and check out the shadows for yourself.

Volume Shadow Restrictions

There is an itsy little elephant-in-the-refrigerator problem when it comes to volumetric shadows: Any model you want to shadow must be *closed*. This is a complex subject, but the best way to describe it is to imagine your model in real life and filled with water. No matter which way you orientate the model, there is no way for the water to leak out. It's kind of like the way *Quake* levels have to be closed, but it's even more restrictive.

An example of a hole is the window in a car. To fix the model, you create an interior of the car that seamlessly connects to the outside body of the car. This is really an art issue, and most artists understand how to create closed geometry in 3ds max or Maya. Single objects like characters are usually fine, but anything with an interior, such as a building with windows, is probably going to cause you problems. The result of a leaky model with holes is that your shadowing will be totally wrecked and there will be weird lines everywhere because the stencil buffer won't be able to properly isolate where the intersections are occurring.

You might think that holes won't affect you, but they already have. You see, the problem occurs a lot with the extrusion process even with properly closed models. The vertices are extruded based on the angle of the vertex normal with the light, so what happens to a face that is half in the light and half in shadow? It all goes wrong, that's what. Basically, the result is that the extruded models are full of holes, and you will notice lots of popping and other visual artifacts if you look closely at the rendered shadow. It's not the kind of thing you expect to see in a shipping game. So how do you fix this problem?

Well, you're probably not going to like my answer, but it has to be done. You have to go through every face in the model and replace every edge with a new quad so that when it is stretched, it will never cause a hole. This is extremely tedious and complicated code to write, and it's beyond the scope of this book, but there is

Volume Shadow Restrictions 347

Figure 11.4
Typical serious rendering errors caused by having an unclosed model.

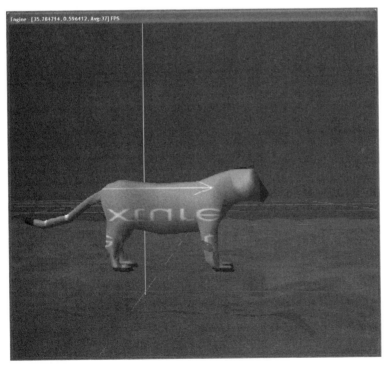

Figure 11.5
Other artifacts caused by unclosed models.

happiness at the end of the tunnel. Microsoft kindly wrote a function to do this for us; however, it is hidden away in one of the sample programs. Luckily for us, it does exactly what we need.

Simply pass their function a mesh, and it will happily convert it for you and throw back to you a brand spanking new mesh that is a fair bit larger (in memory) than your old mesh but is perfect for shadowing. The function looks like this, which I'm not going to explain in detail because it is very low level:

```
HRESULT GenerateShadowMesh(
 IDirect3DDevice9 *pd3dDevice,
 ID3DXMesh *pMesh, ID3DXMesh **ppOutMesh )
{
 HRESULT hr = S_OK;
 ID3DXMesh *pInputMesh;

 if( !ppOutMesh )
  return E_INVALIDARG;
 *ppOutMesh = NULL;

 // Convert the input mesh to a format same as the output mesh using
 // 32-bit index.
 hr = pMesh->CloneMesh( D3DXMESH_32BIT,
  MSSHADOWVERT_CONVERSION::Decl, pd3dDevice, &pInputMesh );
 if( FAILED( hr ) )
  return hr;

 //  DXUTTRACE( L"Input mesh has %u vertices, %u faces\n", pInputMesh->
 //  GetNumVertices(), pInputMesh->GetNumFaces() );

 // Generate adjacency information
 DWORD *pdwAdj = new DWORD[3 * pInputMesh->GetNumFaces()];
 DWORD *pdwPtRep = new DWORD[pInputMesh->GetNumVertices()];
 if( !pdwAdj || !pdwPtRep )
 {
  delete[] pdwAdj; delete[] pdwPtRep;
  pInputMesh->Release();
  return E_OUTOFMEMORY;
 }
```

Volume Shadow Restrictions

```cpp
hr = pInputMesh->GenerateAdjacency( 0.0001f, pdwAdj );
if( FAILED( hr ) )
{
 delete[] pdwAdj; delete[] pdwPtRep;
 pInputMesh->Release();
 return hr;
}

pInputMesh->ConvertAdjacencyToPointReps( pdwAdj, pdwPtRep );
delete[] pdwAdj;

MSSHADOWVERT_CONVERSION *pVBData = NULL;
DWORD *pdwIBData = NULL;

pInputMesh->LockVertexBuffer( 0, (LPVOID*)&pVBData );
pInputMesh->LockIndexBuffer( 0, (LPVOID*)&pdwIBData );

if( pVBData && pdwIBData )
{
 // Maximum number of unique edges = Number of faces * 3
 DWORD dwNumEdges = pInputMesh->GetNumFaces() * 3;
 CEdgeMapping *pMapping = new CEdgeMapping[dwNumEdges];
 if( pMapping )
 {
  int nNumMaps = 0;  // Number of entries that exist in pMapping

  // Create a new mesh
  ID3DXMesh *pNewMesh;
  hr = D3DXCreateMesh( pInputMesh->GetNumFaces() +
      dwNumEdges * 2,
      pInputMesh->GetNumFaces() * 3,
      D3DXMESH_32BIT,
      MSSHADOWVERT_CONVERSION::Decl,
      pd3dDevice,
      &pNewMesh );
  if( SUCCEEDED( hr ) )
  {
   MSSHADOWVERT_CONVERSION *pNewVBData = NULL;
   DWORD *pdwNewIBData = NULL;
```

```
pNewMesh->LockVertexBuffer( 0, (LPVOID*)&pNewVBData );
pNewMesh->LockIndexBuffer( 0, (LPVOID*)&pdwNewIBData );

// nNextIndex is the array index in IB that the next vertex index value
// will be store at.
int nNextIndex = 0;

if( pNewVBData && pdwNewIBData )
{
 ZeroMemory( pNewVBData, pNewMesh->GetNumVertices() *
   pNewMesh->GetNumBytesPerVertex() );
 ZeroMemory( pdwNewIBData, sizeof(DWORD) *
   pNewMesh->GetNumFaces() * 3 );

 // pNextOutVertex is the location to write the next
 // vertex to.
 MSSHADOWVERT_CONVERSION *pNextOutVertex =
         pNewVBData;

 // Iterate through the faces.  For each face, output new
 // vertices and face in the new mesh, and write its edges
 // to the mapping table.

 for( UINT f = 0; f < pInputMesh->GetNumFaces(); ++f )
 {
  // Copy the vertex data for all 3 vertices
  CopyMemory( pNextOutVertex, pVBData + pdwIBData[f * 3],
        sizeof(MSSHADOWVERT_CONVERSION) );
  CopyMemory( pNextOutVertex + 1, pVBData + pdwIBData
        [f * 3 + 1], sizeof(MSSHADOWVERT_CONVERSION) );
  CopyMemory( pNextOutVertex + 2, pVBData + pdwIBData
        [f * 3 + 2], sizeof(MSSHADOWVERT_CONVERSION) );

  // Write out the face
  pdwNewIBData[nNextIndex++] = f * 3;
  pdwNewIBData[nNextIndex++] = f * 3 + 1;
  pdwNewIBData[nNextIndex++] = f * 3 + 2;

  // Compute the face normal and assign it to
  // the normals of the vertices.
  D3DXVECTOR3 v1, v2;
```

```cpp
// v1 and v2 are the edge vectors of the face
D3DXVECTOR3 vNormal;
v1 = *(D3DXVECTOR3*)(pNextOutVertex + 1) -
    *(D3DXVECTOR3*)pNextOutVertex;
v2 = *(D3DXVECTOR3*)(pNextOutVertex + 2) -
    *(D3DXVECTOR3*)(pNextOutVertex + 1);
D3DXVec3Cross( &vNormal, &v1, &v2 );
D3DXVec3Normalize( &vNormal, &vNormal );

pNextOutVertex->Normal = vNormal;
(pNextOutVertex + 1)->Normal = vNormal;
(pNextOutVertex + 2)->Normal = vNormal;

pNextOutVertex += 3;

// Add the face's edges to the edge mapping table

// Edge 1
int nIndex;
int nVertIndex[3] = { pdwPtRep[pdwIBData[f * 3]],
    pdwPtRep[pdwIBData[f * 3 + 1]],
    pdwPtRep[pdwIBData[f * 3 + 2]] };
nIndex = FindEdgeInMappingTable(
     nVertIndex[0], nVertIndex[1], pMapping, dwNumEdges );

// If error, we are not able to proceed, so abort.
if( -1 == nIndex )
{
 hr = E_INVALIDARG;
 goto cleanup;
}

if( pMapping[nIndex].m_anOldEdge[0] == -1 &&
        pMapping[nIndex].m_anOldEdge[1] == -1 )
{
 // No entry for this edge yet.  Initialize one.
 pMapping[nIndex].m_anOldEdge[0] = nVertIndex[0];
 pMapping[nIndex].m_anOldEdge[1] = nVertIndex[1];
 pMapping[nIndex].m_aanNewEdge[0][0] = f * 3;
 pMapping[nIndex].m_aanNewEdge[0][1] = f * 3 + 1;
```

```
      ++nNumMaps;
  } else
  {
  // An entry is found for this edge.  Create
  // a quad and output it.
  assert( nNumMaps > 0 );

  pMapping[nIndex].m_aanNewEdge[1][0] = f * 3;        // For clarity
  pMapping[nIndex].m_aanNewEdge[1][1] = f * 3 + 1;

  // First triangle
  pdwNewIBData[nNextIndex++] =
      pMapping[nIndex].m_aanNewEdge[0][1];
  pdwNewIBData[nNextIndex++] =
      pMapping[nIndex].m_aanNewEdge[0][0];
  pdwNewIBData[nNextIndex++] =
      pMapping[nIndex].m_aanNewEdge[1][0];

  // Second triangle
  pdwNewIBData[nNextIndex++] =
       pMapping[nIndex].m_aanNewEdge[1][1];
  pdwNewIBData[nNextIndex++] =
      pMapping[nIndex].m_aanNewEdge[1][0];
  pdwNewIBData[nNextIndex++] =
      pMapping[nIndex].m_aanNewEdge[0][0];

  // pMapping[nIndex] is no longer needed. Copy the last map entry
  // over and decrement the map count.

  pMapping[nIndex] = pMapping[nNumMaps-1];
  FillMemory( &pMapping[nNumMaps-1],
   sizeof( pMapping[nNumMaps-1] ), 0xFF );
  --nNumMaps;
  }

  // Edge 2
  nIndex = FindEdgeInMappingTable( nVertIndex[1],
       nVertIndex[2], pMapping, dwNumEdges );
```

```
// If error, we are not able to proceed, so abort.
if( -1 == nIndex )
{
 hr = E_INVALIDARG;
 goto cleanup;
}

if( pMapping[nIndex].m_anOldEdge[0] == -1 &&
 pMapping[nIndex].m_anOldEdge[1] == -1 )
{
 pMapping[nIndex].m_anOldEdge[0] = nVertIndex[1];
 pMapping[nIndex].m_anOldEdge[1] = nVertIndex[2];
 pMapping[nIndex].m_aanNewEdge[0][0] = f * 3 + 1;
 pMapping[nIndex].m_aanNewEdge[0][1] = f * 3 + 2;

 ++nNumMaps;
} else
{
 // An entry is found for this edge.  Create
 // a quad and output it.
 assert( nNumMaps > 0 );

 pMapping[nIndex].m_aanNewEdge[1][0] = f * 3 + 1;
 pMapping[nIndex].m_aanNewEdge[1][1] = f * 3 + 2;

 // First triangle
 pdwNewIBData[nNextIndex++] =
     pMapping[nIndex].m_aanNewEdge[0][1];
 pdwNewIBData[nNextIndex++] =
     pMapping[nIndex].m_aanNewEdge[0][0];
 pdwNewIBData[nNextIndex++] =
    pMapping[nIndex].m_aanNewEdge[1][0];

 // Second triangle
 pdwNewIBData[nNextIndex++] =
   pMapping[nIndex].m_aanNewEdge[1][1];
 pdwNewIBData[nNextIndex++] =
     pMapping[nIndex].m_aanNewEdge[1][0];
 pdwNewIBData[nNextIndex++] =
     pMapping[nIndex].m_aanNewEdge[0][0];
```

```cpp
        // pMapping[nIndex] is no longer needed.  Copy the last map entry
        // over and decrement the map count.

        pMapping[nIndex] = pMapping[nNumMaps-1];
        FillMemory( &pMapping[nNumMaps-1],
            sizeof( pMapping[nNumMaps-1] ), 0xFF );
        --nNumMaps;
    }

    // Edge 3
    nIndex = FindEdgeInMappingTable( nVertIndex[2],
                    nVertIndex[0], pMapping, dwNumEdges );

    // If error, we are not able to proceed, so abort.
    if( -1 == nIndex )
    {
     hr = E_INVALIDARG;
     goto cleanup;
    }

    if( pMapping[nIndex].m_anOldEdge[0] == -1 &&
        pMapping[nIndex].m_anOldEdge[1] == -1 )
    {
     pMapping[nIndex].m_anOldEdge[0] = nVertIndex[2];
     pMapping[nIndex].m_anOldEdge[1] = nVertIndex[0];
     pMapping[nIndex].m_aanNewEdge[0][0] = f * 3 + 2;
     pMapping[nIndex].m_aanNewEdge[0][1] = f * 3;

     ++nNumMaps;
    } else
    {
     // An entry is found for this edge.  Create
     // a quad and output it.
     assert( nNumMaps > 0 );

     pMapping[nIndex].m_aanNewEdge[1][0] = f * 3 + 2;
     pMapping[nIndex].m_aanNewEdge[1][1] = f * 3;

     // First triangle
     pdwNewIBData[nNextIndex++] =
```

```
            pMapping[nIndex].m_aanNewEdge[0][1];
        pdwNewIBData[nNextIndex++] =
            pMapping[nIndex].m_aanNewEdge[0][0];
        pdwNewIBData[nNextIndex++] =
            pMapping[nIndex].m_aanNewEdge[1][0];

        // Second triangle
        pdwNewIBData[nNextIndex++] =
            pMapping[nIndex].m_aanNewEdge[1][1];
        pdwNewIBData[nNextIndex++] =
            pMapping[nIndex].m_aanNewEdge[1][0];
        pdwNewIBData[nNextIndex++] =
            pMapping[nIndex].m_aanNewEdge[0][0];

        // pMapping[nIndex] is no longer needed. Copy the last map entry
        // over and decrement the map count.

        pMapping[nIndex] = pMapping[nNumMaps-1];
        FillMemory( &pMapping[nNumMaps-1],
            sizeof( pMapping[nNumMaps-1] ), 0xFF );
        --nNumMaps;
    }
}

// Now the entries in the edge mapping table represent
// non-shared edges.  What that means is that the original
// mesh has openings (holes), so we attempt to patch them.
// First we need to re-create our mesh with a larger vertex
// and index buffers so the patching geometry can fit.

//      DXUTTRACE( L"Faces to patch: %d\n", nNumMaps );

// Create a mesh with large enough vertex and
// index buffers.

MSSHADOWVERT_CONVERSION *pPatchVBData = NULL;
DWORD *pdwPatchIBData = NULL;

ID3DXMesh *pPatchMesh = NULL;
// Make enough room in IB for the face and up to 3
// quads for each patching face
```

```
hr = D3DXCreateMesh( nNextIndex / 3 + nNumMaps * 7,
    ( pInputMesh->GetNumFaces() + nNumMaps ) * 3,
    D3DXMESH_32BIT,
    MSSHADOWVERT_CONVERSION::Decl,
    pd3dDevice,
    &pPatchMesh );

if( FAILED( hr ) )
 goto cleanup;

hr = pPatchMesh->LockVertexBuffer(
        0, (LPVOID*)&pPatchVBData );
if( SUCCEEDED( hr ) )
 hr = pPatchMesh->LockIndexBuffer(
        0, (LPVOID*)&pdwPatchIBData );

if( pPatchVBData && pdwPatchIBData )
{
 ZeroMemory( pPatchVBData,
    sizeof(MSSHADOWVERT_CONVERSION) *
    ( pInputMesh->GetNumFaces() + nNumMaps ) * 3 );
 ZeroMemory( pdwPatchIBData, sizeof(DWORD) *
    ( nNextIndex + 3 * nNumMaps * 7 ) );

 // Copy the data from one mesh to the other

 CopyMemory( pPatchVBData, pNewVBData,
    sizeof(MSSHADOWVERT_CONVERSION) *
    pInputMesh->GetNumFaces() * 3 );
 CopyMemory( pdwPatchIBData,
    pdwNewIBData, sizeof(DWORD) * nNextIndex );
} else
{
 // Some serious error is preventing us from locking.
 // Abort and return error.

 pPatchMesh->Release();
 goto cleanup;
}
```

```cpp
// Replace pNewMesh with the updated one.  Then the code
// can continue working with the pNewMesh pointer.

pNewMesh->UnlockVertexBuffer();
pNewMesh->UnlockIndexBuffer();
pNewVBData = pPatchVBData;
pdwNewIBData = pdwPatchIBData;
pNewMesh->Release();
pNewMesh = pPatchMesh;

// Now, we iterate through the edge mapping table and
// for each shared edge, we generate a quad.
// For each non-shared edge, we patch the opening
// with new faces.

// nNextVertex is the index of the next vertex.
int nNextVertex = pInputMesh->GetNumFaces() * 3;

for( int i = 0; i < nNumMaps; ++i )
{
 if( pMapping[i].m_anOldEdge[0] != -1 &&
  pMapping[i].m_anOldEdge[1] != -1 )
 {
  // If the 2nd new edge index is -1,
  // this edge is a non-shared one.
  // We patch the opening by creating new
  // faces.
  if( pMapping[i].m_aanNewEdge[1][0] == -1 ||

     // must have only one new edge
    pMapping[i].m_aanNewEdge[1][1] == -1 )
  {
   // Find another non-shared edge that
   // shares a vertex with the current edge.
   for( int i2 = i + 1; i2 < nNumMaps; ++i2 )
   {
    if( pMapping[i2].m_anOldEdge[0] != -1 &&

     // must have a valid old edge
      pMapping[i2].m_anOldEdge[1] != -1 &&
      ( pMapping[i2].m_aanNewEdge[1][0] == -1 ||
```

```
                        // must have only one new edge
                      pMapping[i2].m_aanNewEdge[1][1] == -1 ) )
                  {
                    int nVertShared = 0;
                    if( pMapping[i2].m_anOldEdge[0] ==
                        pMapping[i].m_anOldEdge[1] )
                      ++nVertShared;
                    if( pMapping[i2].m_anOldEdge[1] ==
                          pMapping[i].m_anOldEdge[0] )
                      ++nVertShared;

                    if( 2 == nVertShared )
                    {
                      // These are the last two edges of this particular
                      // opening. Mark this edge as shared so that a degenerate
                      // quad can be created for it.

                      pMapping[i2].m_aanNewEdge[1][0] =
                        pMapping[i].m_aanNewEdge[0][0];
                      pMapping[i2].m_aanNewEdge[1][1] =
                        pMapping[i].m_aanNewEdge[0][1];
                      break;
                    }
                    else
                    if( 1 == nVertShared )
                    {
                      // nBefore and nAfter tell us which edge comes before the other.
                      int nBefore, nAfter;
                      if( pMapping[i2].m_anOldEdge[0] ==
                          pMapping[i].m_anOldEdge[1] )
                      {
                        nBefore = i;
                        nAfter = i2;
                      } else
                      {
                        nBefore = i2;
                        nAfter = i;
                      }
```

```
// Found such an edge. Now create a face along with two
// degenerate quads from these two edges.

pNewVBData[nNextVertex] =
  pNewVBData[pMapping[nAfter].m_aanNewEdge[0][1]];
pNewVBData[nNextVertex+1] =
  pNewVBData[pMapping[nBefore].m_aanNewEdge[0][1]];
pNewVBData[nNextVertex+2] =
  pNewVBData[pMapping[nBefore].m_aanNewEdge[0][0]];
// Recompute the normal
D3DXVECTOR3 v1 = pNewVBData[nNextVertex+1].Position -
  pNewVBData[nNextVertex].Position;
D3DXVECTOR3 v2 = pNewVBData[nNextVertex+2].Position -
  pNewVBData[nNextVertex+1].Position;

D3DXVec3Normalize( &v1, &v1 );
D3DXVec3Normalize( &v2, &v2 );
D3DXVec3Cross(
  &pNewVBData[nNextVertex].Normal, &v1, &v2 );
pNewVBData[nNextVertex+1].Normal =
    pNewVBData[nNextVertex+2].Normal =
    pNewVBData[nNextVertex].Normal;

pdwNewIBData[nNextIndex] = nNextVertex;
pdwNewIBData[nNextIndex+1] = nNextVertex + 1;
pdwNewIBData[nNextIndex+2] = nNextVertex + 2;

// 1st quad

pdwNewIBData[nNextIndex+3] =
  pMapping[nBefore].m_aanNewEdge[0][1];
pdwNewIBData[nNextIndex+4] =
  pMapping[nBefore].m_aanNewEdge[0][0];
pdwNewIBData[nNextIndex+5] = nNextVertex + 1;

pdwNewIBData[nNextIndex+6] = nNextVertex + 2;
pdwNewIBData[nNextIndex+7] = nNextVertex + 1;
pdwNewIBData[nNextIndex+8] =
  pMapping[nBefore].m_aanNewEdge[0][0];
```

```
            // 2nd quad

            pdwNewIBData[nNextIndex+9] =
               pMapping[nAfter].m_aanNewEdge[0][1];
            pdwNewIBData[nNextIndex+10] =
              pMapping[nAfter].m_aanNewEdge[0][0];
            pdwNewIBData[nNextIndex+11] = nNextVertex;

            pdwNewIBData[nNextIndex+12] = nNextVertex + 1;
            pdwNewIBData[nNextIndex+13] = nNextVertex;
            pdwNewIBData[nNextIndex+14] =
              pMapping[nAfter].m_aanNewEdge[0][0];

            // Modify mapping entry i2 to reflect the third edge
            // of the newly added face.

            if( pMapping[i2].m_anOldEdge[0] ==
               pMapping[i].m_anOldEdge[1] )
            {
             pMapping[i2].m_anOldEdge[0] = pMapping[i].m_anOldEdge[0];
            } else
            {
             pMapping[i2].m_anOldEdge[1] = pMapping[i].m_anOldEdge[1];
            }
            pMapping[i2].m_aanNewEdge[0][0] = nNextVertex + 2;
            pMapping[i2].m_aanNewEdge[0][1] = nNextVertex;

            // Update next vertex/index positions

            nNextVertex += 3;
            nNextIndex += 15;

            break;
          }
         }
        }
      } else
      {
        // This is a shared edge.  Create the degenerate quad.
```

```cpp
            // First triangle
            pdwNewIBData[nNextIndex++] =
                pMapping[i].m_aanNewEdge[0][1];
            pdwNewIBData[nNextIndex++] =
                pMapping[i].m_aanNewEdge[0][0];
            pdwNewIBData[nNextIndex++] =
                pMapping[i].m_aanNewEdge[1][0];

            // Second triangle
            pdwNewIBData[nNextIndex++] =
                pMapping[i].m_aanNewEdge[1][1];
            pdwNewIBData[nNextIndex++] =
                pMapping[i].m_aanNewEdge[1][0];
            pdwNewIBData[nNextIndex++] =
                pMapping[i].m_aanNewEdge[0][0];
          }
        }
      }
    }

cleanup:;
    if( pNewVBData )
    {
     pNewMesh->UnlockVertexBuffer();
     pNewVBData = NULL;
    }
    if( pdwNewIBData )
    {
     pNewMesh->UnlockIndexBuffer();
     pdwNewIBData = NULL;
    }

    if( SUCCEEDED( hr ) )
    {
     // At this time, the output mesh may have an index buffer
     // bigger than what is actually needed, so we create yet
     // another mesh with the exact IB size that we need and
     // output it.  This mesh also uses 16-bit index if
     // 32-bit is not necessary.
```

```
//      DXUTTRACE( L"Shadow volume has %u vertices, %u faces.\n",
( pInputMesh->GetNumFaces() + nNumMaps ) * 3, nNextIndex / 3 );

    bool bNeed32Bit =
( pInputMesh->GetNumFaces() + nNumMaps ) * 3 > 65535;
    ID3DXMesh *pFinalMesh;
    hr = D3DXCreateMesh( nNextIndex / 3,  // Exact number of faces
        ( pInputMesh->GetNumFaces() + nNumMaps ) * 3,
        D3DXMESH_WRITEONLY |
        ( bNeed32Bit ? D3DXMESH_32BIT : 0 ),
        MSSHADOWVERT_CONVERSION::Decl,
        pd3dDevice,
        &pFinalMesh );
    if( SUCCEEDED( hr ) )
    {
     pNewMesh->LockVertexBuffer( 0, (LPVOID*)&pNewVBData );
     pNewMesh->LockIndexBuffer( 0, (LPVOID*)&pdwNewIBData );

     MSSHADOWVERT_CONVERSION *pFinalVBData = NULL;
     WORD *pwFinalIBData = NULL;

     pFinalMesh->LockVertexBuffer( 0, (LPVOID*)&pFinalVBData );
     pFinalMesh->LockIndexBuffer( 0, (LPVOID*)&pwFinalIBData );

     if( pNewVBData && pdwNewIBData &&
         pFinalVBData && pwFinalIBData )
     {
      CopyMemory( pFinalVBData, pNewVBData,
        sizeof(MSSHADOWVERT_CONVERSION) *
         ( pInputMesh- >GetNumFaces() + nNumMaps ) * 3 );

      if( bNeed32Bit )
       CopyMemory( pwFinalIBData, pdwNewIBData,
               sizeof(DWORD) * nNextIndex );
      else
      {
       for( int i = 0; i < nNextIndex; ++i )
        pwFinalIBData[i] = (WORD)pdwNewIBData[i];
      }
     }
```

```
        if( pNewVBData )
         pNewMesh->UnlockVertexBuffer();
        if( pdwNewIBData )
         pNewMesh->UnlockIndexBuffer();
        if( pFinalVBData )
         pFinalMesh->UnlockVertexBuffer();
        if( pwFinalIBData )
         pFinalMesh->UnlockIndexBuffer();

        // Release the old
        pNewMesh->Release();
        pNewMesh = pFinalMesh;
       }

       *ppOutMesh = pNewMesh;
      }
      else
       pNewMesh->Release();
    }
    delete[] pMapping;
  } else
    hr = E_OUTOFMEMORY;
 } else
  hr = E_FAIL;

 if( pVBData )
  pInputMesh->UnlockVertexBuffer();

 if( pdwIBData )
  pInputMesh->UnlockIndexBuffer();

 delete[] pdwPtRep;
 pInputMesh->Release();

 return hr;
}
int FindEdgeInMappingTable( int nV1, int nV2,
    CEdgeMapping *pMapping, int nCount )
{
```

```
  for( int i = 0; i < nCount; ++i )
  {
    // If both vertex indexes of the old edge in mapping entry are -1, then
    // we have searched every valid entry without finding a match.  Return
    // this index as a newly created entry.
    if( ( pMapping[i].m_anOldEdge[0] == -1 &&
      pMapping[i].m_anOldEdge[1] == -1 ) ||

      // Or if we find a match, return the index.
      ( pMapping[i].m_anOldEdge[1] == nV1 &&
        pMapping[i].m_anOldEdge[0] == nV2 ) )
    {
      return i;
    }
  }

  return -1;   // We should never reach this line
}
```

Like I said, the function is low level and repetitive, but you should treat it like a black box. It goes through your mesh and replaces all the edges with quads so that the extrusion will work. It's one of the only nasty parts to volumetric shadowing. There are a couple of changes you need to make because this function really wrecks all the normal and texture coordinate data in a mesh. Normals that are good for shadowing are generally poor for lighting and texturing, so most people keep two copies of the mesh around: one for rendering shadows, and one for actually rendering to the screen.

All that is required is a second mesh pointer added to cVisualResource like this:

indBool	m_bShadowed;	
bool	m_bShadowModelCreated;	
LPD3DXMESH	m_pMesh;	// normal mesh
LPD3DXMESH	**m_pShadowMesh;**	**// shadow mesh**

Then you can generate the mesh like this the first time shadowing is enabled:

```
void SetShadowed(bool bShadowed)
{
    m_bShadowed = bShadowed;
```

```
    if(m_bShadowModelCreated)
        return;

    LPD3DXMESH pTempMesh = 0;

    if(SUCCEEDED(VisualEffects::GenerateShadowMesh(
        GAMEENGINE->GetDevice(), m_pMesh, &m_pShadowMesh)))
        m_bShadowModelCreated = true;
}
```

Some slight changes to the rendering code mean the new mesh is used for rendering in place of the normal one:

```
indBool cVisualResource::RenderShadowed()
{
    UINT oldEffectID = m_EffectID;
    if(m_bSelfShadow)
        RenderResource();

    m_EffectID = m_ShadowRenderer.StartShadowPass();
    LPD3DXMESH pTempMesh = m_pMesh;
    m_pMesh = m_pShadowMesh;
    RenderResource();
    m_pMesh = pTempMesh;
    m_EffectID = oldEffectID;

    m_ShadowRenderer.EndShadowPass();
    m_ShadowRenderer.RenderShadows();

    if(!m_bSelfShadow)
        RenderResource();

    return true;
}
```

As you can see, we now override the effect *and* the mesh for the shadowing pass. And that, ladies and gentleman, is how you implement a cool shadow rendering system. The quality improvement after calling Microsoft's function is incredible. Check out the results for yourself.

Figure 11.6
Volumetric shadows in all their glory!

Conclusion

This has been one of the most advanced chapters so far. You've seen how to use shaders to really take rendering to the next level. In particular, you've learned about the following:

- The theory of shadowing
- Ways to tell if a model's vertices are shadowed
- Extruding a shadow volume
- Rendering to the stencil buffer
- Restrictive rendering with the stencil buffer
- Self-shadowing
- Eliminating popping artifacts
- Creating degenerate quads to replace face edges

In the next chapter, I'm going to show you how to take shaders to the next level with advanced bump mapping techniques.

CHAPTER 12

ENVIRONMENT GENERATION

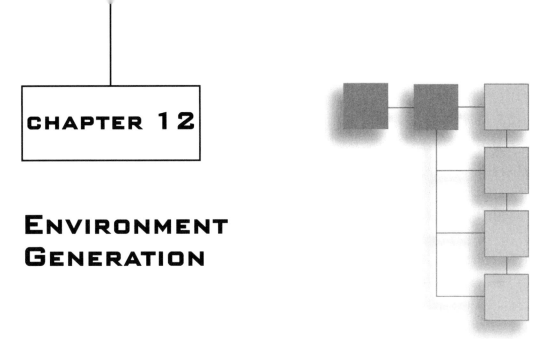

Environment generation is one of the most important topics in computer games because it covers the creation of the environment that your game will exist in. It is an enormous topic with many areas, but this chapter concentrates on two of the most important topics: pixel blended terrain generation and spherical sky box techniques. Both of these use advanced vertex and pixel shader techniques to create a realistic world for your game. In particular, this chapter focuses on the following:

- The mechanics of terrains
- Heightmaps
- Reading pixel values directly from textures
- Using multiple texture samplers
- Blending multiple textures in the pixel shader
- The difference between `DrawPrimitive` and `DrawPrimitiveUP`
- Fog with pixel shaders
- Sky boxes
- Generating a sky box
- Spherical texture coordinates
- Cubic environment mapping

And, of course, there is much more along the way. Let's start with generating terrains.

Terrain

There are many advanced techniques for generating terrain, but they are all suited to a specific type of game. My aim with this chapter is not to show you the most advanced terrain generation and optimization techniques, but to show you a fairly general technique to highlight how you can use the vertex and pixel shaders to blend textures. After you have written one terrain generator, you'll rapidly see ways to optimize it for your own particular use.

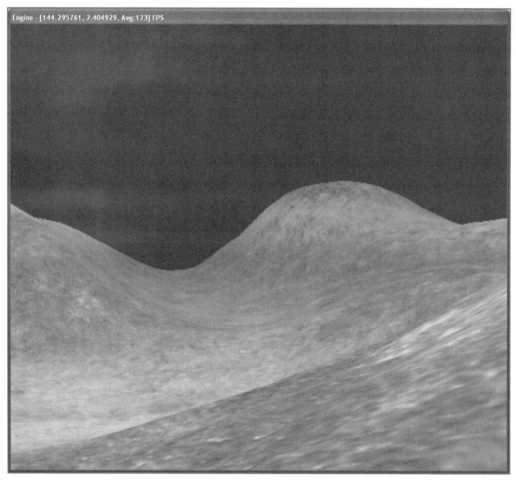

Figure 12.1
Terrain created from the code in this chapter.

So what exactly is terrain? Well, *terrain* is generally used to describe large areas of a game environment that mimic outdoor landscapes with features such as rolling hills, mountains, and changing textures based on height. The most common way to create terrain is to generate a plane of triangles first. The height of each triangle is modified by some input source to create the illusion of an outdoor environment. Typically, the input data is a texture.

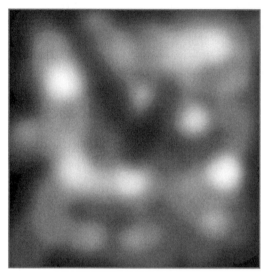

Figure 12.2
A typical heightmap texture created in Photoshop.

A texture used for this purpose is known as a *heightmap*. A heightmap is just a standard texture with one of the texture channels that contains height information. In this case, I am using the red channel, but you can use any channel you like. How do you fill the heightmap with height data? It's incredibly easy. You just have to paint onto the texture with any image editing program such as Adobe Photoshop. Dark colors indicate low-lying land, and lighter areas indicate higher land. By carefully drawing your heightmap, you can create realistic terrain.

Figure 12.3
Typical textures used to generate terrain.

Loading Assets

To encapsulate the terrain generator, I created the `cTerrainGenerator` class. All the interesting stuff happens in its `Start()` function. Let's look at it in stages to see what's going on:

```
HRESULT hr = D3DXCreateTextureFromFileEx(
    GAMEENGINE->GetDevice(), "media\\heightmap.bmp",
    D3DX_DEFAULT, D3DX_DEFAULT,
    D3DX_DEFAULT, 0, D3DFMT_FROM_FILE, D3DPOOL_SYSTEMMEM, D3DTEXF_LINEAR,
    D3DTEXF_LINEAR, 0, 0, 0, &m_pHeightMapTexture);
if(FAILED(hr))
{
    OutputDebugString("Failed to load terrain heightmap\n");
    assert(0);
    return false;
}
```

First, we need to load the actual heightmap data, which is stored in a standard bitmap. This isn't anything you haven't seen before. Next, there is a call to `LoadTerrainTextures()` which, as the name implies, loads all the textures that will be used to texture the terrain.

Next, we need to create a vertex buffer to hold all the vertices that will make up the terrain:

```
UINT vbSize = m_NumVerticesWidth * m_NumVerticesLength * sizeof(TERRAIN_VERTEX);
hr = GAMEENGINE->GetDevice()->CreateVertexBuffer(
```

```
          vbSize, D3DUSAGE_WRITEONLY, TERRAIN_FVF, D3DPOOL_MANAGED, &m_pTerrainVB, 0);
if(FAILED(hr))
{
    OutputDebugString("Failed to create terrain Vertex Buffer\n");
    assert(0);
    return false;
}
```

The size is just the width multiplied by the length multiplied by the size of your FVF (Flexible Vertex Format) vertex structure. By default, the width and length are 4,096 units in each direction. The vertex buffer is stored in the member variable m_pTerrainVB. Assuming that all went well, our vertex buffer is now created, which means we can lock it to start filling it with data:

```
TERRAIN_VERTEX* pTerrainVBData = 0;
m_pTerrainVB->Lock(0, 0, (void**)&pTerrainVBData, 0);
if(!pTerrainVBData)
{
    OutputDebugString("Failed to lock terrain Vertex Buffer\n");
    assert(0);
    return false;
}
```

That is just a standard vertex buffer lock call that returns a pointer to the vertex buffer data. It's unusual for this call to fail, because the vertex buffer was created as managed. That means Direct3D keeps a copy of it in system memory in case the graphics cards memory gets wiped. It's best to check anyway to stay on the safe side. The vertex format I'm using here looks like this:

```
typedef struct tTERRAIN_VERTEX
{
    D3DXVECTOR3 position;
    D3DXVECTOR3 normal;
    D3DCOLOR diffuse;
    D3DXVECTOR2 tex;
    D3DXVECTOR3 tex2;

}TERRAIN_VERTEX;
#define TERRAIN_FVF (D3DFVF_XYZ | D3DFVF_NORMAL |      \
D3DFVF_DIFFUSE | D3DFVF_TEXCOORDSIZE2(0) |   \
D3DFVF_TEX2 | D3DFVF_TEXCOORDSIZE3(1))
```

This is one of the heaviest vertex structures used so far in this book. It includes data for the position, normal, color, and two texture coordinates, which you'll learn more about later. Notice that one of the texture coordinates is three dimensional.

The next line in the function sets up our effect file. The terrain needs custom texture blending, so it has its own effect file:

```
m_EffectID = EFFECTMANAGER->FindEffect("terrain.fx");
```

Creating the Terrain

The next four lines are where the action starts:

```
float segmentWidth = m_TerrainWidth / (float)m_NumVerticesWidth;
float segmentLength = m_TerrainLength / (float)m_NumVerticesLength;

float startX = m_TerrainWidth / 2.0f - m_TerrainWidth;
float startZ = m_TerrainLength / 2.0f - m_TerrainLength;
```

The `segmentWidth` variable holds the width of one segment of the terrain mesh. The mesh is just a big rectangular plane of triangles. The width and height of each segment control the size of the triangles that make up the mesh. As you can see, the width and height are calculated by dividing the entire terrain width by the number of terrain vertices. By default, the number of vertices is 128 for width and height, which leads to a total of 16,384 vertices. You generally want to keep your vertex count below 65,536, because most graphics cards do not like to render meshes larger than this in a single call. The solution if you want more is to split your terrain across multiple vertex buffers and render them one after the other. The 128 vertices for the width and height mean that each segment of the mesh will be 32.0×32.0.

After that, the `startX` and `startZ` variables are calculated. This is because you usually don't want your terrain to start as extending out into positive x and z. If you did this and located your player at 0,0, then 75 percent of the area around the player would contain nothing. To fix it, we translate the terrain so that it's centered about the origin.

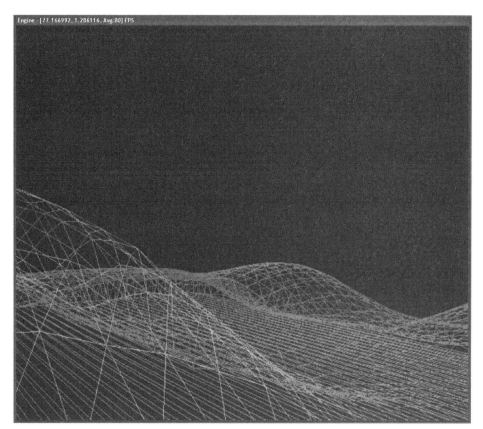

Figure 12.4
Terrain strips rendered in wireframe.

Now that we have our initial data calculated, we can lock the heightmap texture to read data from it:

```
D3DLOCKED_RECT lockedRect;
hr = m_pHeightMapTexture->LockRect(0, &lockedRect, 0, D3DLOCK_READONLY);
if(FAILED(hr))
{
    OutputDebugString("Failed to lock heightmap to create terrain\n");
    assert(0);
    return false;
}

DWORD pitchDWORD = lockedRect.Pitch / 4;
D3DCOLOR* pColorData = (D3DCOLOR*)lockedRect.pBits;
```

Direct3D locks a texture with the aptly named LockRect() function. The first parameter is the level of the texture to lock. If you had a mipmap texture, it would have multiple levels. However, this texture has only one level, so we just pass in 0. The next parameter is a pointer to a D3DLOCKED_RECT structure. This gets filled with a pointer to the actual image data and information about the texture stride, which I'll talk about in a moment. It's called LockRect() because you can use it to lock a small portion of the entire texture. We are locking the entire texture, so for the third parameter we can pass NULL. The final parameter tells Direct3D that we will be reading only from the texture, which saves a little time if we're locking compressed textures. This texture is not compressed, so it doesn't help, but if you ever use a compressed texture, this flag will make the execution slightly faster.

If you've ever done work with older versions of DirectDraw, you will remember the fun of pitches. Basically, in the good old days of software engines, your texture took up exactly the amount of room that its size required. However, these days, with hardware acceleration, graphics cards can get a little picky and require textures to be aligned to certain boundaries, which in some (actually most) cases means there is extra unused data hanging off the end of your texture. So when you're reading from the texture bits directly, you need to be sure to take the pitch into account, or all your coordinates will be off.

The pitch returned from lock is the number of bytes in a single line of your texture. For example, if you had a 256×256 texture, there would be 1024 bytes in one row of the texture. This is because each pixel would be a 32-bit integer. Thirty-two bits = 4 bytes, and 4 bytes * 256 pixels = 1024 bytes. However, your pitch might be 1280 bytes. The extra 256 bytes are unused and are just there to keep the hardware happy. Because you are dealing with 32-bit pixels, it makes sense to convert the pitch into 32 bits also to make your calculations simpler. That is what this line of code does:

```
DWORD pitchDWORD = lockedRect.Pitch / 4;
```

The next line converts the void pointer to a D3DCOLOR (that is, a DWORD) pointer. These two variables will become important later for indexing into the texture. So how do you actually index into a texture to get a height location at specific coordinates? Well, it's quite easy, and most old-school programmers will be able to tell you this without blinking. Here is the code:

```
inline D3DCOLOR GetColorAtLocation(UINT x, UINT y, DWORD pitchDWORD, D3DCOLOR* pData)
{
    return pData[y*pitchDWORD + x];
}
```

As you can see, the function takes the coordinates to return the color for, a pointer to the data, and the pitch of the texture, in DWORD format. This is important, because if you pass the data through as its original byte format, either the wrong value will be read or it will cause an access violation. The index of the location is simply the y coordinate multiplied by the pitch and added to the x coordinate. The value at this location in the array is the color of the pixel. So this is returned. This function is inlined for speed.

Next, we need to declare a few variables used while generating the mesh:

```
D3DSURFACE_DESC surfaceDesc;
m_pHeightMapTexture->GetLevelDesc(0, &surfaceDesc);

float xCoord = 0.0f;
float zCoord = 0.0f;
float height = 0.0f;
UINT texLocationX, texLocationY;

float numTextureTiles = 15.0f;
UINT currentVertex = 0;
```

First, we get the description of the heightmap texture so that we know how big it is. As we move across rendering the terrain, we need to move in equal steps in the texture so that the samples are taken from the correct location. Taking the size of the texture here allows us to support any size of heightmap texture automatically.

The next five variables hold temporary values for the current x,y,z location of the terrain vertices and texture coordinates. The numTextureTiles variable is kind of interesting. It holds a value that determines the density of the textures rendered across the terrain. A value of 1.0, for instance, implies that only one texture will be rendered across the entire terrain, which would be kind of blocky. So the default value is 15, which means the selected texture will be repeated 15 times across the surface to create a smoother look. If you have too low a value, the result is blocky, whereas two high a value makes the repeating nature of the texture too noticeable. Depending on the textures you use, you might want to modify this value. Finally, the last variable holds the current vertex in the vertex buffer that we are creating. Now let's look at creating the actual terrain.

The terrain is created in a series of strips that are each as wide as the terrain. As I mentioned earlier, by default this terrain will have 128 strips, with each strip being 128 segments across. It is generated like this:

```
for(UINT lengthCount = 0 ; lengthCount < m_NumVerticesLength ; lengthCount++)
{
    for(UINT widthCount = 0 ; widthCount < m_NumVerticesWidth ; widthCount+=2)
    {
```

First, we loop for each strip, and then we create all the segments for the current strip. The triangle strip is created two vertices at a time, which is why the inner loop has a double increment. Next, we need to figure out the current location for the first vertex and how far into the current strip we are:

```
xCoord = widthCount * segmentWidth;
zCoord = lengthCount * segmentLength;

float widthPercent = xCoord / m_TerrainWidth;
float lengthPercent = zCoord / m_TerrainLength;
```

The current vertex location is easily calculated from the number of segments completed multiplied by the size of each segment. The percentage completed of the segment is just the current coordinates divided by the entire size of the terrain. These values are used to re-ratio the coordinates from terrain size to texture size, so the correct values are read from the texture later on. This is done next:

```
if(xCoord > 0.0f && zCoord > 0.0f)
{
    texLocationX = (UINT)((widthPercent * (float)surfaceDesc.Width));
    texLocationY = (UINT)((lengthPercent * (float)surfaceDesc.Height));
}
else
{
    texLocationX = texLocationY = 0;
}
```

The `if` statement ensures that there are no divide by zero errors, which return NANs (Not a Numbers) and make the mesh display kind of ugly. Now that we know how far across the terrain we are, we just multiply that value by the size of the texture. Hey, presto! We are now magically located at the correct place in the texture and in 3D space. And that means we can read the heightmap value for this location:

```
D3DCOLOR heightMapColor =
    GetColorAtLocation(texLocationX, texLocationY, pitchDWORD, pColorData);
D3DXCOLOR heightColorBottom(heightMapColor);
float heightMapSample = heightColorBottom.r;
height = heightMapSample * m_TerrainHeight;
```

Pretty simply, huh? You just pass in the location in the texture just calculated, and out pops the color at that location. Notice that the color is initially read into a D3DCOLOR. As you probably know, this is the structure that Direct3D uses to hold four packed color values, ranging from 0 to 255, in a single DWORD. D3DXCOLOR has a handy constructor for converting these into normal unpacked RGBA values ranging from 0.0 to 1.0f.

The height value is then sampled from the red channel into the float heightMapSample. Finally, this value is scaled by the height we want our map to be, which by default is 50.0 units. This scaled value will be the location of the vertex for the terrain. The unscaled value is used to work out which texture to apply to the vertex in the pixel shader, which I'll discuss later in this chapter. However, for now, you can see that there are three textures, and the degree to which they are rendered is based on how closely they match the current height of the vertex. The second texture coordinate holds modulation factors, which are multiplied in the pixel shader to correctly blend the correct texture:

```
if(heightMapSample <= 0.33)
{
    heightMapSample *= 3.0f;
    pTerrainVBData[currentVertex].tex2.x = heightMapSample;
    pTerrainVBData[currentVertex].tex2.y = 1.0f - heightMapSample;
    pTerrainVBData[currentVertex].tex2.z = 0.0f;
}
else if(heightMapSample <= 0.66)
{
    heightMapSample -= 0.33f;
    heightMapSample *= 3.0f;

    if(heightMapSample > 0.5f)
    {
        pTerrainVBData[currentVertex].tex2.x = 0.0f;
        pTerrainVBData[currentVertex].tex2.y = heightMapSample;
        pTerrainVBData[currentVertex].tex2.z = 1.0f - heightMapSample;
    }
```

```
        else
        {

            pTerrainVBData[currentVertex].tex2.x = 1.0f - heightMapSample;
            pTerrainVBData[currentVertex].tex2.y = heightMapSample;
            pTerrainVBData[currentVertex].tex2.z = 0.0f;
        }

}
else
{
    heightMapSample -= 0.66f;
    heightMapSample *= 3.0f;

    pTerrainVBData[currentVertex].tex2.x = 0.0f;
    pTerrainVBData[currentVertex].tex2.y = 1.0f - heightMapSample;
    pTerrainVBData[currentVertex].tex2.z = heightMapSample;
}
```

Next, we can fill in the actual vertex data for the current vertex. Here is the code:

```
pTerrainVBData[currentVertex].position.x = startX + xCoord;
pTerrainVBData[currentVertex].position.y = height;
pTerrainVBData[currentVertex].position.z = startZ + zCoord;
pTerrainVBData[currentVertex].diffuse = D3DCOLOR_RGBA(255,255,255,255);
pTerrainVBData[currentVertex].normal = D3DXVECTOR3(0,1,0);
pTerrainVBData[currentVertex].tex.x = numTextureTiles * widthPercent;
pTerrainVBData[currentVertex].tex.y = numTextureTiles * lengthPercent;

currentVertex++;
```

So that's the first vertex created. There is one more to go, except this time its z coordinate is added to be one segment length longer. Then the code runs through like it did for the first vertex:

```
zCoord += segmentLength;
lengthPercent = zCoord / m_TerrainLength;
if(xCoord > 0.0f && zCoord > 0.0f)
{
    texLocationX = (UINT)((widthPercent * (float)surfaceDesc.Width));
    texLocationY = (UINT)((lengthPercent * (float)surfaceDesc.Height));
}
```

```
else
{
    texLocationX = texLocationY = 0;
}

heightMapColor =
    GetColorAtLocation(texLocationX, texLocationY, pitchDWORD, pColorData);
D3DXCOLOR heightColorTop(heightMapColor);
heightMapSample = heightColorTop.r;
height = heightMapSample * m_TerrainHeight;

if(heightMapSample <= 0.33)
{
    heightMapSample *= 3.0f;
    pTerrainVBData[currentVertex].tex2.x = heightMapSample;
    pTerrainVBData[currentVertex].tex2.y = 1.0f - heightMapSample;
    pTerrainVBData[currentVertex].tex2.z = 0.0f;
}
else if(heightMapSample <= 0.66)
{
    heightMapSample -= 0.33f;
    heightMapSample *= 3.0f;

    if(heightMapSample > 0.5f)
    {
        pTerrainVBData[currentVertex].tex2.x = 0.0f;
        pTerrainVBData[currentVertex].tex2.y = heightMapSample;
        pTerrainVBData[currentVertex].tex2.z = 1.0f - heightMapSample;
    }
    else
    {

        pTerrainVBData[currentVertex].tex2.x = 1.0f - heightMapSample;
        pTerrainVBData[currentVertex].tex2.y = heightMapSample;
        pTerrainVBData[currentVertex].tex2.z = 0.0f;
    }

}
else
{
```

```
            heightMapSample -= 0.66f;
            heightMapSample *= 3.0f;

            pTerrainVBData[currentVertex].tex2.x = 0.0f;
            pTerrainVBData[currentVertex].tex2.y = 1.0f - heightMapSample;
            pTerrainVBData[currentVertex].tex2.z = heightMapSample;
        }


        pTerrainVBData[currentVertex].position.x = startX + xCoord;
        pTerrainVBData[currentVertex].position.y = height;
        pTerrainVBData[currentVertex].position.z = startZ + zCoord;
        pTerrainVBData[currentVertex].diffuse = D3DCOLOR_RGBA(255,255,255,255);
        pTerrainVBData[currentVertex].normal = D3DXVECTOR3(0,1,0);
        pTerrainVBData[currentVertex].tex.x = numTextureTiles * widthPercent;
        pTerrainVBData[currentVertex].tex.y = numTextureTiles * lengthPercent;

    currentVertex++;

    m_NumVertices+=2;
    }
```

The last thing we need to do is a little tidying up by unlocking the vertex buffer and unlocking the texture:

```
        m_pTerrainVB->Unlock();
    m_pHeightMapTexture->UnlockRect(0);

        return true;
}
```

And that is how you generate a simple terrain mesh. If the concept is confusing, you should load the sample code and change around the different values and see how it all works. There is nothing fancy in there, like the level of detail changing based on the view distance, but it wouldn't be a huge task for you to add that kind of functionality.

Rendering the Terrain

Now let's look at rendering the terrain. This type of rendering is actually very simple, and it's almost identical to rendering any other mesh. Here is the code. I've bolded the parts that are not the same as when you render other meshes:

Rendering the Terrain

```
indBool cTerrainGenerator::Render()
{
    D3DXMATRIX matWorld;
    D3DXMatrixIdentity(&matWorld);

    VisualEffects::cEffect* pCurrentEffect = EFFECTMANAGER->GetEffect(m_EffectID);
    GAMEENGINE->GetDevice()->SetFVF(TERRAIN_FVF);
    pCurrentEffect->SetTransforms(
        matWorld, CAMERA->GetViewMatrix(), CAMERA->GetProjectionMatrix());
    pCurrentEffect->Dispatch();
    indUInt numPasses = 0;
    pCurrentEffect->Begin(numPasses);

    UINT numVerts = min(m_NumVertices-2, 30000);

    pCurrentEffect->GetD3DEffect()->SetTexture("Tex0", m_pTerrainTextures[0]);
    pCurrentEffect->GetD3DEffect()->SetTexture("Tex1", m_pTerrainTextures[1]);
    pCurrentEffect->GetD3DEffect()->SetTexture("Tex2", m_pTerrainTextures[2]);
    pCurrentEffect->GetD3DEffect()->SetTexture("Tex3", m_pTerrainTextures[3]);

    GAMEENGINE->GetDevice()->SetStreamSource(
                    0, m_pTerrainVB, 0, sizeof(TERRAIN_VERTEX));
    GAMEENGINE->GetDevice()->SetFVF(TERRAIN_FVF);
    for(indUInt passCount = 0 ; passCount < numPasses ; passCount++)
    {
        pCurrentEffect->BeginPass(passCount);

        GAMEENGINE->GetDevice()->DrawPrimitive(D3DPT_TRIANGLESTRIP, 0, numVerts);

        pCurrentEffect->EndPass();
    }

    pCurrentEffect->End();
    return true;
}
```

The only real difference is that we pass four textures to the shader instead of the usual of just one.

DrawPrimitive and DrawPrimitiveUP

In the first iteration of this code, I didn't create a vertex buffer. Instead, I used the vertex definition to dynamically allocate space with new and then filled it up with terrain data. The way to draw this data is with a function called DrawPrimitiveUP(). The UP stands for *user pointer*. The function works in the same way as DrawPrimitive() except that it takes a pointer to vertex data in memory, instead of a pointer to a vertex buffer.

So why not always use DrawPrimitiveUP()? Why go through the hassle of setting up a vertex buffer every time you want to render something? Because DrawPrimitiveUP() is *incredibly* slow. That's because if your data is in a vertex buffer, Direct3D has control over it and, most importantly, can shift it to video memory for rendering. The difference in speed is phenomenal. Every time you render with DrawPrimtiveUP(), Direct3D has to transfer the data over the AGP or PCI bus to the graphics card, which takes an incredible amount of time. However, with DrawPrimitive(), the vertex buffer has to be transferred only once and can then be rendered over and over from video memory very quickly. Also, it doesn't have to be moved again until it is relocked. Here's a real-world example of this: Just changing a few lines in the terrain generation code to use a vertex buffer instead of a memory pointer gave a 250 percent speedup. So try never to draw with DrawPrimitiveUP().

However, on saying that, there are situations in which you want to use the UP version instead, like when you are doing a lot of vertex changing every frame on large vertex buffers. For instance, if you had some custom wave generation code that was modifying the vertex buffer every frame, then every time the vertex buffer was locked and modified, it would have to be recopied to video memory before it could be used. And that would place a large burden on the bus. This is a rare situation now that vertex shaders have arrived. Unless you are heavily modifying vertex buffers, use the standard DrawPrimitive() call.

Figure 12.5
Close-up of pixel-perfect texture blending.

The Terrain Shaders

Let's examine the shader in more detail now. The vertex shader looks like this:

```
VS_OUTPUT VS(
    float3 Pos   : POSITION,
    float3 Norm  : NORMAL,
    float3 Tex   : TEXCOORD0,
    float3 Tex2  : TEXCOORD1,
    float4 color : COLOR0)
{
```

```
    VS_OUTPUT Out = (VS_OUTPUT)0;

    float3 L = normalize(-lightDirection);

    float4x4 WorldView = mul(World, View);

    float3 P = mul(float4(Pos, 1), (float4x3)WorldView);   // position (view space)
    float3 N = normalize(mul(Norm, (float3x3)WorldView));  // normal (view space)

    float  fogDist = P.z;
    Out.Pos  = mul(float4(P, 1), Projection);              // position (projected)
    Out.Diff = I_a * k_a + I_d * k_d * max(0, dot(N, L));  // diffuse + ambient


    Out.Tex1 = Tex;
    Out.Tex2 = Tex2;
    Out.Tex3 = Tex / 5.0f;

    Out.Tex4 = Tex * 10.0f;

    Out.Fog  = 1.0f / exp(fogDist * g_FogDensity);

    return Out;
}
```

The only major difference is the number of texture coordinates. Notice the number of texture coordinates that the shader outputs. The first set is passed through unchanged. This set is the actual coordinates that the main textures will use. The second set is also passed through unchanged, because it contains the modulation values to blend the textures in the pixel shader. The third set of coordinates is the same as the first set except that it's five times larger (because it's a decimal division). The reason we do the division here rather than the pixel shader is because on all PS1.X pixel shaders, pixel shader values are clamped from 0.0 to 1.0. This makes it impossible to divide by 5.0f. Why divide by 5.0? Because terrains are susceptible to looking rubbish because the textures repeat so many times. However, by changing the texture coordinates of some textures to be larger than others, you reduce the ability of your brain to see the repetition substantially. The same is true of the fourth set of coordinates, which is made very small (10 times smaller than the normal textures). This is so that the texture that is close to the viewpoint looks detailed. The end result is that you get the best of both worlds: Most of the terrain looks good with general textures. Far-away areas look great with the larger texture coordinates providing macro data for your brain, and the tiny coordinates provide lots of detail up close. It's just like real life, in fact! Also note the fog values, which I'll explain a little later. Now let's check out the pixel shader:

```
float4 PS(
    float4 Diff : COLOR0,
    float2 TexCoord1  : TEXCOORD0,
    float3 TexCoord2  : TEXCOORD1,
    float2 TexCoord3  : TEXCOORD2,
    float2 TexCoord4  : TEXCOORD3) : COLOR
{

    float4 sample0 = tex2D(Sampler0, TexCoord1);
    float4 sample1 = tex2D(Sampler1, TexCoord1);
    float4 sample2 = tex2D(Sampler2, TexCoord1);
    float4 sample3 = tex2D(Sampler2, TexCoord3);

    float4 sample4 = tex2D(Sampler3, TexCoord4);

    sample0 *= TexCoord2.x;
    sample1 *= TexCoord2.y;
    sample2 *= TexCoord2.z;

    float4 result = ((sample0 + sample1) + ((sample2 * sample3)*2));

    return result + ((sample3/4));
}
```

This pixel shader takes four separate samples from the textures we sent in earlier from the generation code. These are then combined in a variety of ways that create some stunning visuals. Keep in mind when dealing with pixel shaders that adding texture samples generally brightens the result, while multiplying them usually darkens. So you'll want to test a combination of methods to get your terrain shader looking just right. You might notice some constants there that are not in the range of 0.0 to 1.0. Although I said this applied to pixel shaders, there is one exception, which is the number 2.0. Under the hood, the compiler can do some nifty tricks to allow any value that is a direct multiple of 2.0 to be used. So 2, 4, and 8 are valid, but 5, 7, and 9 are not. Also, 0.5 and 0.25 are valid. The technique for the terrain shader uses the following render states:

```
technique TVertexAndPixelShader
{
    pass P0
    {
        //fillmode = wireframe;
        //cullmode = none;
        STENCILFUNC = 0;
        zEnable = true;
        zwriteenable = true;
        AlphaBlendEnable = true;
        stencilenable = false;
        srcblend = srcalpha;
        destblend = invsrcalpha;
        FOGENABLE       = TRUE;
        FOGCOLOR        = (g_FogColor);
        VertexShader = compile vs_1_1 VS();
        PixelShader  = compile ps_1_4 PS();
    }

}
```

You can uncomment the top two render states during debugging if you want to render the terrain without culling in wireframe. It also just looks cool.

This shader supports the blending of only four textures onto your terrain, which is usually not enough in more advanced games. I limited it to four so that the example would work with PS1.4 shaders, which support a maximum of six samplers but generally lack the instructions necessary to combine six textures in a pixel shader. There are a few solutions to this. First, you can write for higher-pixel shader versions, like 2.0 or even 3.0. Most cards now support them, and they allow far more samplers to be used. Another solution is to pack multiple textures into a single texture and use the pixel shader to modify the texture coordinates to extract the correct texture. So you could have a single 1024×1024 texture that contains 16 256×256 textures. Yet another solution is to render your terrain in multiple passes, with each pass rendering the three blended textures. Finally, you could have a team of artists manually blend and apply textures to the terrain. That's what most large companies do.

Terrain Fog

As a little aside, I added fog support to the terrain because most terrain generators use it to mask off in the distance where they are being culled. This terrain is not large enough to cull, but I thought I'd show you in case you need it. First, you need a fog color, which usually looks silly if it is not the same color as your sky. The sky is in effect what you clear the back buffer to before rendering. So we want the sky and fog color to be the same. To achieve this, I added the following variable to cGameEngine:

```
D3DXCOLOR            m_SkyColor;
void SetSkyColor(D3DXCOLOR& newColor)
{
    m_SkyColor = newColor;
}
D3DXCOLOR& GetSkyColor()
{
    return m_SkyColor;
}
```

By default, this is set to dark blue:

```
m_SkyColor = D3DXCOLOR(0.1f, 0.1f, 0.4f, 1.0f);
```

Now, to implement this, we need to do three things:

1. Set up the clear function to clear to the correct color

2. Pass the sky color to the shaders

3. Enable fogging in the shaders

First let's look at modifying the clear function, which is easy:

```
m_pDevice->Clear(0, NULL, D3DCLEAR_TARGET | D3DCLEAR_ZBUFFER | D3DCLEAR_STENCIL,
        (D3DCOLOR)m_SkyColor, 1.0f, 0 );
```

Simple? Cool. Notice how D3DXCOLOR automatically converts itself to a D3DCOLOR if you cast it like the previous code, which is quite handy. Now let's look at the second step, which requires a change to the effect dispatch function:

```
D3DXCOLOR skyColor = GAMEENGINE->GetSkyColor();
m_pD3DEffect->SetVector("g_FogColor",
        &D3DXVECTOR4(skyColor.r, skyColor.g, skyColor.b, skyColor.a));
```

This copies the sky color to the shader to the global variable g_FogColor if it is available. Over in the shader, we add these variables:

```
float  g_FogDensity = 0.00025f;
float4 g_FogColor   = { 1.0f, 1.0f, 1.0f, 1.0f };
```

This defaults the fog color to pure white if it is not set, which should make it pretty obvious if something has gone wrong. Then, as you saw a moment ago, you need to enable the fog render states in the technique:

```
FOGENABLE          = TRUE;
FOGCOLOR           = (g_FogColor);
```

We're almost there now. Fog multiplies the fog color with the pixel color based on its distance from the camera. Therefore, we need to make sure we return the distance from the camera from the vertex shader. There is a semantic set up specially to deal with fog. To use it, you just need to add a new float value to your vertex shader output shader. In the case of the terrain shader, it looks like this:

```
struct VS_OUTPUT
{
    float4 Pos  : POSITION;
    float4 Diff : COLOR0;
    float2 Tex1 : TEXCOORD0;
    float3 Tex2 : TEXCOORD1;
    float3 Tex4 : TEXCOORD3;
    float3 Tex3 : TEXCOORD2;
    float Fog : FOG;
};
```

The distance from the camera is easy to work out. It is just the vertice's z value after the view matrix has been applied. However, to provide more realistic exponential falloff, a little extra code is used. So the following code in the vertex shader is all that is needed:

```
float3 P = mul(float4(Pos, 1), (float4x3)WorldView);
float  fogDist = P.z;
Out.Fog  = 1.0f / exp(fogDist * g_FogDensity);
```

And that's how you can add fog to any shader.

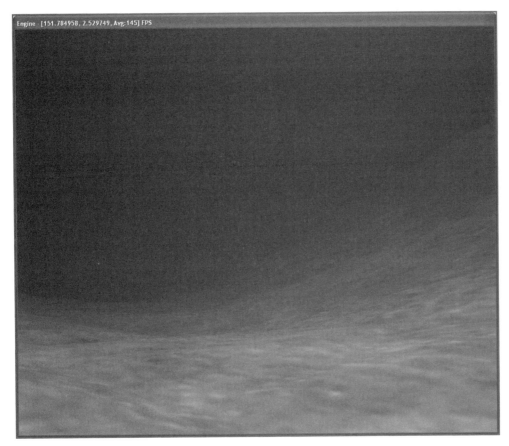

Figure 12.6
Vertex shader fog applied to the terrain.

Sky Box Techniques

The sky box I'm going to show you in this article is not really a box, but a sphere. However, the term *sky box* has come to cover all kinds of shapes that are used to mimic our sky. To start with, a sky box is any shape that is placed around the player environment to mimic a large open area, such as the sky, underwater, outer space, and so on. In the past, sky boxes were actually boxes. They had few polygons and could be rendered quickly. However, they also suffered from a number of problems due to their strange shape.

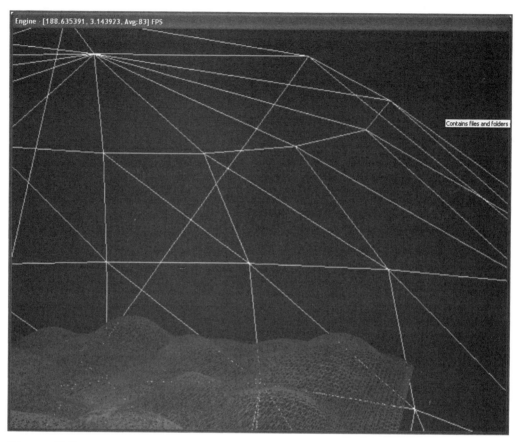

Figure 12.7
A close-up of the sky box sphere.

These days, the hardware is powerful enough to easily draw a sphere around the game world. That gives us much more flexibility because it more accurately represents most of the world around us. It also lets us do easy texture mapping, as you will see later on. So what do sky boxes usually do? Well, they normally have the following properties:

- They are large enough to cover the entire visible section of the world.

- They generally move with the camera so that you never reach them.

- They do not need to do any z-writing or z-testing as they are usually the first thing rendered.

To create and encapsulate the sky box, I created the `cSkyBox` class, which has this prototype:

```
class cSkyBox
{
public:
    cSkyBox(void);
    ~cSkyBox(void);

    // Data
public:



private:
    LPDIRECT3DCUBETEXTURE9 m_pCubeTexture;
    LPDIRECT3DVERTEXBUFFER9 m_pVertices;
    UINT m_EffectID;

    UINT m_NumVertices;

    float m_SkyBoxRadius;

    static const int m_NumLongitudeStrips = 30;
    static const int m_NumLatitudeStrips = 30;

    float m_HeightModifier;
    float m_TextureDensityX;
    float m_TextureDensityY;

    // Functions
public:
    indBool Start();
    indBool Run();
    indBool Render();
    indBool Shutdown();

private:
};
```

I've highlighted the important bits of the class. First up is a new kind of texture that you might not have seen before. This is a cubic texture, which means that it contains six subtextures, each representing one side of a cube. By doing some fancy addressing, you can create realistic environment map effects using cubic maps.

The next variable of interest is the `m_pVertices` vertex buffer, which holds all the vertices for the sky box. The vertex definition for this vertex buffer is simple:

```
typedef struct tSKYBOX_VERTEX
{
    D3DXVECTOR3 position;
}SKYBOX_VERTEX;
#define SKYBOX_FVF (D3DFVF_XYZ)
```

As you can see, the vertex structure just contains a position. It couldn't be simpler than that. You might be wondering how we pass through cubic texture coordinates to the vertex and pixel shader because there are no texture coordinate entries in this vertex definition. Well, I have a little trick up my sleeve. Because the sky box is a sphere, the texture coordinates automatically translate to be the normalized position of the vertices. So with a sphere, you don't need to calculate the texture coordinates at all. You'll learn more about this shortly.

The next variable is `m_NumVertices`, which contains the number of vertices that will be in the vertex buffer. The variable `m_SkyboxRadius` contains the actual radius of the sphere that will make up the sky box. This should be large enough to encompass your visible world, although depending on how you decide to do your z-testing, you can set it smaller than this. `m_HeightModifier` modifies the location of the sphere. Sometimes you want the horizon to be slightly above or below the actual 0.0 Y coordinate, so you can set this to place where the sky box starts vertically. Finally, there are two texture density variables that control the number of times the texture is repeated if you use standard 2D texture mapping, which is similar to the terrain generator.

Generating the Sky Box

Now let's look at the code to generate the sky box. The sky box is generated as usual in the class's `Start()` function. Here's the code, line by line:

```
indBool cSkyBox::Start()
{
    m_EffectID = EFFECTMANAGER->FindEffect("skybox.fx");
```

The code starts as usual by setting up the effect to render with. Because the sky box does custom work with texture coordinates, it has its effect file. Next, we set up a load of values to be used while generating the sphere:

```
const float rad90 = D3DX_PI / 2.0f;
const float rads = D3DX_PI / 180.0f;
int numLatDegrees = 180;
int numLongDegrees = 360;
int finalLat = numLatDegrees - m_NumLatitudeStrips;
int finalLong = numLongDegrees - m_NumLongitudeStrips;
int currentVertex = 0;
```

You'll see how these are used shortly. Because we are generating a sphere, we need to generate it in strips, in a similar way to the terrain earlier in the chapter. In this case, the strips range from 0 to 180 degrees for the latitude of the sphere and 0 to 360 degrees for the longitude. We can calculate the number of vertices like this:

```
m_NumVertices = (UINT)((numLongDegrees / (float)m_NumLongitudeStrips) *
        (numLatDegrees / (float)m_NumLatitudeStrips) * 4.0f);
```

Then we can use this value to create a vertex buffer like this:

```
HRESULT hr = GAMEENGINE->GetDevice()->CreateVertexBuffer(
        m_NumVertices * sizeof(SKYBOX_VERTEX),
        D3DUSAGE_WRITEONLY,
        SKYBOX_FVF,
        D3DPOOL_MANAGED,
        &m_pVertices,
        NULL);
    if(FAILED(hr))
    {
        OutputDebugString("Failed to create sky box vertex buffer\n");
        assert(0);
        return false;
    }
```

The vertex buffer is created as managed because it's not going to be modified after it's created. Now that the vertex buffer is created, the cubic texture can be loaded:

```
hr = D3DXCreateCubeTextureFromFile(GAMEENGINE->GetDevice(),
        "media\\environmentmap.dds", &m_pCubeTexture);

    if(FAILED(hr))
```

```
        {
            OutputDebugString("Failed to load skybox environment texture");
            OutputDebugString("media\\ environmentmap.dds");
            OutputDebugString("\n");
            assert(0);
            return false;
        }
```

The call takes the same parameters as the normal texture-loading functions. However, this time the texture is in DDS format, which is Direct3D's own format that supports advanced features like mipmapping, cubic textures, and weird texture formats. This is the texture that is passed to the shader for rendering. Next, we need to lock the vertex buffer so that we can add our sky box vertices to it:

```
SKYBOX_VERTEX* pVBData = 0;
        hr = m_pVertices->Lock(0, 0, (void**)&pVBData, 0);
        if(FAILED(hr))
        {
            OutputDebugString("Failed to lock skybox vertex buffer\n");
            assert(0);
            return false;
        }
```

If all goes according to plan, we can start creating the actual sky box. Creating the sky box involves sphere generation code that uses some trigonometry based on the current latitude and longitude of the sphere loop to work out the coordinates. You'll probably recognize what's going on from high school math. Keep in mind that the loop is working in degrees. Trig functions obviously take radians, so there is much multiplying by rads (0.017453) to convert degrees to radians. Also look out for the last test in the loop, which adds a quad (two triangles) instead of a single triangle if we are not at the poles of the sphere:

```
for(int latCount = 0 ;
    latCount <= finalLat ;
    latCount += m_NumLatitudeStrips)
{
    for(int longCount = 0 ;
        longCount <= finalLong ;
        longCount += m_NumLongitudeStrips)
    {
        pVBData[currentVertex].position = D3DXVECTOR3(
```

```
                m_SkyBoxRadius * sin((float)latCount * rads) *
cos((float)longCount*rads),
                m_SkyBoxRadius * cos((float)latCount * rads) + m_HeightModifier,
                m_SkyBoxRadius * sin((float)latCount * rads) *
sin((float)longCount*rads));

        currentVertex++;

        pVBData[currentVertex].position = D3DXVECTOR3(
            m_SkyBoxRadius * sin((float)(latCount+m_NumLatitudeStrips) * rads) *
cos((float)longCount*rads),
            m_SkyBoxRadius * cos((float)(latCount+m_NumLatitudeStrips) * rads) +
m_HeightModifier,
            m_SkyBoxRadius * sin((float)(latCount+m_NumLatitudeStrips) * rads) *
sin((float)longCount*rads));

        currentVertex++;

        pVBData[currentVertex].position = D3DXVECTOR3(
            m_SkyBoxRadius * sin((float)latCount * rads) *
                cos((float)(longCount+m_NumLongitudeStrips)*rads),
            m_SkyBoxRadius * cos((float)latCount * rads) + m_HeightModifier,
            m_SkyBoxRadius * sin((float)latCount * rads) *
                sin((float)(longCount+m_NumLongitudeStrips)*rads));

        currentVertex++;

        if(latCount > -90 && latCount < 90)
        {
            pVBData[currentVertex].position = D3DXVECTOR3(
            m_SkyBoxRadius * sin((float)(latCount+m_NumLatitudeStrips) * rads) *
                cos((float)(longCount+m_NumLongitudeStrips)*rads),
            m_SkyBoxRadius * cos((float)(latCount+m_NumLatitudeStrips) * rads) +
m_HeightModifier,
            m_SkyBoxRadius * sin((float)(latCount+m_NumLatitudeStrips) * rads) *
                sin((float)(longCount+m_NumLongitudeStrips)*rads));

            currentVertex++;
        }
    }
}
```

And that's how you create a sphere. It's pretty easy if you are not scared of a little math. Next, we just need to unlock the vertex buffer:

```
    m_pVertices->Unlock();
    return true;
}
```

Rendering the Sky Box

Rendering on the C++ side is again very general and follows the same steps as rendering any other object. The interesting stuff happens in the shader. Here's the code:

```
indBool cSkyBox::Render()
{
    D3DXMATRIX matWorld;
    D3DXMatrixIdentity(&matWorld);

    D3DXVECTOR3 camPos = CAMERA->GetPosition();
    D3DXMatrixTranslation(&matWorld, camPos.x, camPos.y, camPos.z);

    VisualEffects::cEffect* pCurrentEffect = EFFECTMANAGER->GetEffect(m_EffectID);
    pCurrentEffect->SetTransforms(
        matWorld, CAMERA->GetViewMatrix(), CAMERA->GetProjectionMatrix());
    pCurrentEffect->Dispatch();
    indUInt numPasses = 0;
    pCurrentEffect->Begin(numPasses);

    pCurrentEffect->GetD3DEffect()->SetTexture("TexCubic", m_pCubeTexture);

    GAMEENGINE->GetDevice()->SetStreamSource(0, m_pVertices, 0, sizeof(SKYBOX_VERTEX));
    GAMEENGINE->GetDevice()->SetFVF(SKYBOX_FVF);
    for(indUInt passCount = 0 ; passCount < numPasses ; passCount++)
    {
        pCurrentEffect->BeginPass(passCount);

        GAMEENGINE->GetDevice()->DrawPrimitive(D3DPT_TRIANGLESTRIP, 0, m_NumVertices-2);

        pCurrentEffect->EndPass();
    }

    pCurrentEffect->End();
    return true;
}
```

I've highlighted the important sections of the code. The first part moves the sky box with the camera. This is as simple as getting the camera's location and then using that to create a translation world matrix for the sky box. Therefore, every time the camera moves, the sky box moves with it in step. Without this, the sky box would approach the camera too quickly, ruining the intended effect, and eventually you could pop out the other side of the sky box. If during testing you want to look outside the sky box, just comment out those lines.

Figure 12.8
The sky box completely rendered with the cubemap texture.

Also, note how the cubic texture is passed through to the shader. It's nothing complex; in fact, it's the same process as if you were passing through a normal texture. Now let's look at the shader in more detail.

The Sky Box Shader

These are the render states that are used:

```
technique TVertexAndPixelShader
{
    pass P0
    {
        fogenable = false;
        cullmode = ccw;
        STENCILFUNC = 0;
        zEnable = false;
        zwriteenable = false;
        AlphaBlendEnable = false;
        stencilenable = false;
        VertexShader = compile vs_1_1 VS();
        PixelShader  = compile ps_1_1 PS();
    }
}
```

Basically it's just your usual render states except for the states relating to the Z buffer. There's no need to turn on the Z buffer testing because the sky box will always be the first object rendered every frame. This gives us a minor speed increase. All the other states are disabled or set to their default values. Now let's look at the vertex shader, which is really simple:

```
struct VS_OUTPUT
{
    float4 Pos  : POSITION;
    float3 Tex  : TEXCOORD0;
};
VS_OUTPUT VS(
    float3 Pos  : POSITION)
{
    VS_OUTPUT Out = (VS_OUTPUT)0;

    float3 TexPos = Pos;
    Out.Tex = normalize(TexPos);

    float4x4 WorldView = mul(World, View);
    float3 P = mul(float4(Pos, 1), WorldView );
    Out.Pos  = mul(float4(P, 1), Projection);

    return Out;
}
```

Notice that the vertex shader outputs three-dimensional texture coordinates. These will be used in the pixel shader to index into the cubic texture. See how they are set up? They are just the normalized position of the sphere vertex. You can't get much more efficient than that. Here is the pixel shader:

```
texture TexCubic;
sampler Sampler = sampler_state
{
    Texture   = (TexCubic);
    MipFilter = LINEAR;
    MinFilter = LINEAR;
    MagFilter = LINEAR;
};
float4 PS(float3 Tex  : TEXCOORD0) : COLOR
{
    return texCUBE(Sampler, Tex);
}
```

How simple is that? The pixel shader uses a new texture sampling function that you might not have seen before. It takes a cubic texture and a 3D texture coordinate as input and automatically samples the correct pixel, which gives a realistic effect when rendered.

Conclusion

This chapter has introduced some new ways of using vertex and pixel shaders to bring new life to traditional terrain generation and sky box techniques. Hopefully you'll be able to take these ideas and apply them to more extensive implementations that you create yourself. In this chapter, you learned about the following:

- The mechanics of terrains
- Heightmaps
- Reading pixel values directly from textures
- Using multiple texture samplers
- Blending multiple textures in the pixel shader
- The difference between `DrawPrimitive` and `DrawPrimitiveUP`

- Fog with pixel shaders
- Sky boxes
- Generating a sky box
- Spherical texture coordinates
- Cubic environment mapping

CHAPTER 13

ADVANCED SPLINE AND ROUTE SYSTEMS

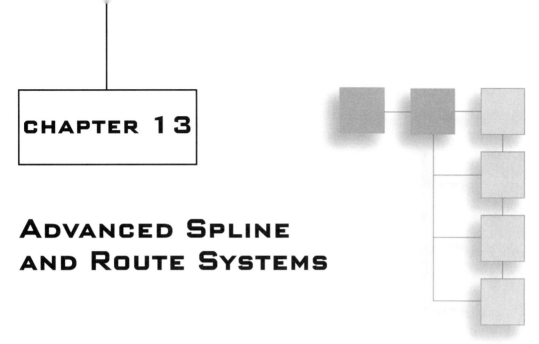

An advanced spline and route system is one of the coolest systems you can add to any game engine. It's the ability to load routes to control the movement of anything from the camera to a particle system to a mesh object—anything visual, in fact. In this chapter, I'm going to show you how to define your own simple route file format to define a series of points that create a route. You can use routes for any purpose, including defining the path of an eagle flying through the mountains, using a helicam effect around a race course prior to a race, or even controlling the movement of AI characters. The list of uses is endless. In this chapter, you will learn about the following:

- Defining a route point
- Creating a route class
- Linear interpolation of points
- Advanced Catmull-Rom interpolation
- Smoothly interpolating across a large array of points
- Creating a Look At vector that smoothly follows the route
- Attaching the route system to cameras and particle systems
- Creating a route file format to store your routes
- Creating a route manager to manage your routes

Let's roll!

Introduction to Routes

So what exactly is a route? A *route* is basically just a series of points that define a movement path over an area. Routes are versatile; if you program them properly, you can apply them to numerous situations. Each point in a route is really just a position. However, you can add all sorts of advanced features to each point, such as modifying the speed between points, launching an AI script at a particular point, or even triggering a sound effect. For this example, I've created a simple class to encapsulate a route point. At the moment, it just holds a position, but you can extend it to hold whatever information you need. Here's the code:

```
class cRoutePoint
{
public:
    cRoutePoint()
    {
        m_Position = D3DXVECTOR3(0,0,0);
    }
    ~cRoutePoint()
    {
    }

    // Data
public:

private:
    D3DXVECTOR3 m_Position;

    // Functions:
public:
    void SetPosition(D3DXVECTOR3& newPosition)
    {
        m_Position = newPosition;
    }
    D3DXVECTOR3 GetPosition()
    {
        return m_Position;
    }
private:

};
```

This little class will form the basis for our route system.

Moving Between Points on a Route

Obviously, if we are going to have a route system, we are going to need a surefire way to move smoothly between points on the route. There are a number of ways to do this, but the easiest is called *linear interpolation*. In this case, only two points are considered at a time on the route: the current point, and the point we are heading toward next. When we reach the next point, it becomes the current point, and the one after that becomes the target point. This means that between any two points, the interpolation is good. However, at the time of switchover, there is a noticeable popping effect as the two points being considered are swapped. This pop can be a mild jump to a neck-breaking jerk depending on how different the angles are between the segments. Linear interpolation can be pretty poor at simulating lots of things, but it has its uses.

The other way to evaluate a route is with some fancy-sounding spline functions. Numerous spline functions are available, but most have major issues like not being able to guarantee that your route will pass exactly through all the points you specify. And that's not good for computer games. If you are defining a tight camera curve route through city blocks, you *need* to be sure that the camera isn't going to wander off through the geometry while rendering. Luckily, there is a nice spline function created by a couple of gods of the computer graphics industry, Edwin Catmull and Rafael Rom. They developed what is now known as the Catmull-Rom spline calculation algorithm. This algorithm is nice because it smoothly interpolates between curves *and* guarantees that the route will always pass exactly through the specified points. It's also fast and easy to use. The only downside is that you need at least four points to calculate a Catmull-Rom curve. This allows the algorithm to smoothly go around bends and never violently jerk no matter what angles are used between segments of a curve.

Creating a Route Class

A route is basically just made up of points, as I mentioned before. However, it also has to do the nasty business of interpolating between the points on a route and controlling objects that it is attached to. Here is the class definition for cSplineRoute:

```
class cSplineRoute
{
public:
    cSplineRoute(void);
```

Chapter 13 ■ Advanced Spline and Route Systems

```cpp
        ~cSplineRoute(void);

        enum eInterpolationMode
        {
            eInterpolation_Linear = 0,
            eInterpolation_CatmullRom
        };
        //Data
public:

private:

        static const int MAX_ROUTE_POINTS = 1000;
        D3DXVECTOR3 m_ComputePoints[4];

        cRoutePoint* m_pRoutePoints;

        float m_CurrentTime;
        float m_Speed;
        D3DXVECTOR3 m_CurrentPosition;
        D3DXVECTOR3 m_LookVector;
        UINT m_NumPoints;

        ROUTE_VERTEX* m_pRouteVertsRender;
        UINT m_DebugRenderEffectID;
        eInterpolationMode m_InterpolationMode;

        bool m_bAttachedToCamera;
        ParticleSystem::cParticleSystem* m_pControlledParticleSystem;

        char m_FileName[MAX_PATH];
        char m_RouteName[MAX_PATH];

        // Functions
public:

        D3DXVECTOR3 GetCurrentSplinePosition()
        {
            return m_CurrentPosition;
        }
        D3DXVECTOR3 GetCurrentLookVector()
        {
```

```
        return m_LookVector;
    }

    void SetCameraAttach(bool bAttach)
    {
        m_bAttachedToCamera = bAttach;
    }

    const char* GetRouteName()
    {
        return (const char*)&m_RouteName[0];
    }
    void AttachToParticleSystem(ParticleSystem::cParticleSystem* pSystem)
    {
        assert(pSystem);
        m_pControlledParticleSystem = pSystem;
    }

    indBool Start(char* routeFile);
    indBool Run();
    indBool Render();
    indBool Shutdown();

private:

    indBool ExecuteLinearInterpolation();
    indBool ExecuteCatmullRomInterpolation();
};
```

Let's look at a few of the important members here. First up is MAX_ROUTE_POINTS, which limits the number of nodes that will be in the route. If you need any more than this, feel free to change the value. You might notice that the constant is initialized directly in the class definition. Some developers are not aware of this, but it is perfectly valid to initialize variables in the class definition as long as they are *constant*, *static*, and *integers*. It's a handy way of encapsulating constant values into classes. You can access the value as usual from outside the class using the scope resolution operator(::).

Next up is the array of D3DXVECTOR3s called m_ComputePoints. This array contains the current four points being calculated for interpolation. If linear interpolation is used, only the first two values of the array are utilized. However, if Catmull-Rom interpolation is used, all four values are utilized, because this algorithm requires at least four points to work. Remember: The minimum number of points that you can have in a route is four if you are using the advanced Catmull-Rom interpolation. As we work through the route, we transfer the current two (or four) valid points to the m_ComputePoints array.

The next item of interest is the cRoutePoint pointer m_pRoutePoints. This holds the actual array of points that make up the route. There can be any number of them as long as the number is greater than two (or four) and less than MAX_ROUTE_POINTS. You'll see this being filled later on in the Start() function.

Next up are these values:

```
float m_CurrentTime;
float m_Speed;
D3DXVECTOR3 m_CurrentPosition;
D3DXVECTOR3 m_LookVector;
UINT m_NumPoints;
```

m_CurrentTime ranges from 0.0f to 1.0f and monitors how far through the entire route we are, with 0.0 being the start, and 1.0 being the end. m_Speed is the speed at which we go through the route. It is added to m_CurrentTime every frame. You can modify this easily to be frame rate independent if you need it. m_CurrentPosition holds the current position on the route. Your position on the route is determined by how much time has passed, and the route is evaluated for a particular time. Evaluating the route produces a position that is stored here. m_LookVector is kind of interesting. If you are traveling along a route, you generally want the camera, or model, to face in the direction of movement. To make this easy, the Look At vector is calculated every frame so that the object being modified by the route always faces the correct direction. Finally, m_NumPoints contains the number of points held in the m_pRouteVertsRender array.

The next two values are really useful:

```
ROUTE_VERTEX* m_pRouteVertsRender;
UINT m_DebugRenderEffectID;
```

Developing routes is really cool, but something always goes wrong. And unless you can actually see the current route, you are not going to be able to tell what the problem is. So m_pRouteVertsRender is a pointer to an array of vertices that make up the route to render it. It's important to note that I *only* enable the route rendering code in debug builds (with #define _DEBUG) for testing. That is why the vertices are held in a data pointer rather than a vertex buffer. It's slower, but it's also much simpler, and speed is not important in debug builds. The effect ID holds the effect to render with. I used the same effect as is used for the grid discussed in Chapter 4.

The next value is m_InterpolationMode, which holds an enumeration describing the current interpolation mode. Currently, there are only two values this can be set to:

```
enum eInterpolationMode
{
    eInterpolation_Linear = 0,
    eInterpolation_CatmullRom
};
```

However, the code is designed to be extensible if you want to add different types of interpolation (for example, script controlled) to the project. The default interpolation mode is Catmull-Rom, because it is a lot nicer.

The next two values let the route control the camera, a particle system, or both:

```
bool m_bAttachedToCamera;
ParticleSystem::cParticleSystem* m_pControlledParticleSystem;
```

If the first value is true, the route will update the camera's position and Look At vector every frame. If the second is a valid pointer, the particle system is moved along by the route, which can make cool effects. Imagine an advanced particle system flying around your level following a complicated path. Your friends will be wondering for weeks how you did it!

Finally, two member variables hold the path to the route file and the name of the route, which is just the path name with directory data removed. You'll notice in the class definition the various Get/Set routines for a lot of these member variables.

Now that we've covered the class definition, let's look at creating routes. First up, we need a file format to hold the route. For this, I created the simplest of formats, which you can expand later to hold your own data if needed. The .route file specification is just a text file that includes a list of all the points that you want in your route. Check out this one as an example:

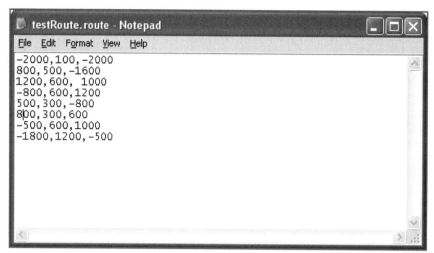

Figure 13.1
The simple route file format.

Pretty simple, huh? It's just a load of positions that make up the route. Later, you could add more data following each point, like the speed of the node or a script to call.

Loading a Route

As with all the classes I've shown you, most of the work happens in the Start() function, which looks like this:

```
indBool cSplineRoute::Start(char* routeFile)
{
    m_DebugRenderEffectID = EFFECTMANAGER->FindEffect("grid.fx");

    if(!routeFile)
    {
        OutputDebugString("Invalid file passed to cSplineRoute\n");
        assert(0);
        return false;
    }

    char tempFile[MAX_PATH];
    strcpy((char*)&tempFile, "routes\\");
    strcat((char*)&tempFile, routeFile);
        strcpy((char*)&m_FileName, tempFile);
```

```cpp
    strcpy((char*)&m_RouteName, routeFile);

    FILE* pFile = fopen(m_FileName, "r");
    if(!pFile)
    {
        OutputDebugString("Failed to load route file: ");
        OutputDebugString(routeFile);
        OutputDebugString("\n");
        assert(0);
        return false;
    }

    UINT pointCount = 0;
    D3DXVECTOR3 routePoints[MAX_ROUTE_POINTS];

    float x,y,z;
    int result = 0;
    while(1)
    {
        result = fscanf(pFile, "%f, %f, %f", &x, &y, &z);
        if(result == EOF)
            break;

        routePoints[pointCount] = D3DXVECTOR3(x,y,z);
        pointCount++;

        if(pointCount >= MAX_ROUTE_POINTS)
        {
            OutputDebugString("Warning: Maximum points in a route reached in file \n");
            OutputDebugString(routeFile);
            OutputDebugString("\n");
            assert(0);
            break;
        }
    }

    m_pRoutePoints = new cRoutePoint[pointCount];
    if(!m_pRoutePoints)
    {
        OutputDebugString("Memory exhausted loading routes\n");
        assert(0);
```

```
            return false;
    }

    m_NumPoints = pointCount;
    for(UINT i = 0 ; i < m_NumPoints ; ++i)
    {
        m_pRoutePoints[i].SetPosition(routePoints[i]);
    }

    fclose(pFile);
    return true;
}
```

This function isn't too complicated. It starts by setting up the debug effect ID so that we can render lines between the route points for testing. After checking that the passed route path is a valid string, the function copies the path name and route name into the member variables. Then it attempts to open the file with `fopen()`.

If the file opened all right, it loops through until the end of the file scanning each line into the temporary local array `routePoints`. The file is scanned first into the local array because we don't know how many points there will be until they are all loaded. Because our member variable `m_pRoutePoints` is a dynamically allocated array, we need to know how many points there are before it is allocated.

After all the points are temporarily allocated, the new array is created, and each point is initialized with its position. We are now ready to do some work with them.

Debug Rendering a Route

Before I show how the interpolation works, I'll show the function that renders the route for debugging. Here you will see in action the slower `DrawPrimtiveUp()` function that I talked about in Chapter 12:

```
indBool cSplineRoute::Render()
{
#ifdef _DEBUG

    if(!m_pRouteVertsRender)
    {
        m_pRouteVertsRender = new ROUTE_VERTEX[m_NumPoints];
        if(!m_pRouteVertsRender)
        {
            OutputDebugString("Memory Exhausted rendering routes\n");
```

```cpp
            assert(0);
            return false;
        }
    }

    bool flipflop = false;
    for(UINT i = 0 ; i < m_NumPoints ; i++)
    {
        flipflop = !flipflop;
        m_pRouteVertsRender[i].position = m_pRoutePoints[i].GetPosition();
        m_pRouteVertsRender[i].diffuse = D3DCOLOR_RGBA(255, flipflop?255:0, 0, 255);
    }

    D3DXMATRIX matWorld;
    D3DXMatrixIdentity(&matWorld);

    VisualEffects::cEffect* pCurrentEffect =
                EFFECTMANAGER->GetEffect(m_DebugRenderEffectID);
    GAMEENGINE->GetDevice()->SetFVF(ROUTE_FVF);
    pCurrentEffect->SetTransforms(
        matWorld, CAMERA->GetViewMatrix(), CAMERA->GetProjectionMatrix());
    pCurrentEffect->Dispatch();
    indUInt numPasses = 0;

    pCurrentEffect->Begin(numPasses);

    for(indUInt passCount = 0 ; passCount < numPasses ; passCount++)
    {
        pCurrentEffect->BeginPass(passCount);

        GAMEENGINE->GetDevice()->DrawPrimitiveUP(
        D3DPT_LINESTRIP, m_NumPoints-1, (void*) m_pRouteVertsRender,
sizeof(ROUTE_VERTEX));

        pCurrentEffect->EndPass();
    }

    pCurrentEffect->End();

#endif
    return true;
}
```

Again, this is just a standard rendering function. The interesting bit is where all the loaded vertices are copied to any array of ROUTE_VERTEX to be rendered. Notice the bFlipflop variable. This is toggled between true and false every iteration to change colors so that the start of every line is yellow, and the end is red. This makes it much clearer which direction the route is moving. Note the DrawPrimitiveUP() member, too. It takes as parameters the type of primitive to draw, the number of primitives, a pointer to the vertex data, and the stride of the vertex. The vertex in this case contains the position and color and is rendered in the usual way with the grid.fx file.

Figure 13.2
Rendering the routes with a series of lines to aid debugging.

Linear Interpolation

Okay, now that our points are loaded and rendering onscreen, let's see if we can make them work as a route. The interpolation is done every call from the Run() function:

```
indBool cSplineRoute::Run()
{
    m_CurrentTime += m_Speed;

    if(m_CurrentTime > 1.0f)
        m_CurrentTime = 0.0f;


    switch(m_InterpolationMode)
    {
    case eInterpolation_Linear:
        {
            ExecuteLinearInterpolation();
            break;
        }
    case eInterpolation_CatmullRom:
        {
            ExecuteCatmullRomInterpolation();
            break;
        }
    }

    if(m_bAttachedToCamera)
    {
        CAMERA->SetPosition(m_CurrentPosition);
        CAMERA->SetLookVector(m_LookVector);
    }

    if(m_pControlledParticleSystem)
    {
        m_pControlledParticleSystem->SetEmitterPosition(m_CurrentPosition);
    }

    return true;
}
```

414   Chapter 13 ■ Advanced Spline and Route Systems

This function is simple. It starts by updating the time and looping it back to 0.0 if needed. This means that as the route reaches the end, it starts back at the beginning again, going smoothly from the last point back to the first point. Remove or modify these lines if you don't want looping routes. Then the magic happens in different ways depending on the interpolation mode. After interpolation, the camera or particle system is updated with the new location points.

Let's look at linear interpolation now because it's easier than Catmull-Rom. Here's the code:

```
indBool cSplineRoute::ExecuteLinearInterpolation()
{
    float fcurrentPoint = m_CurrentTime * (float)m_NumPoints;
    UINT currentPoint = (UINT)floor(fcurrentPoint);

    float segmentLength = (1.0f / (float)m_NumPoints);
    float timeStart = (float)currentPoint * segmentLength;
    float timeFinish = timeStart + segmentLength;

    float segmentTime = (m_CurrentTime - timeStart) / segmentLength;

    UINT nextPoint = 0;
    if(currentPoint < m_NumPoints-2)
        nextPoint = currentPoint + 1;

    m_ComputePoints[0] = m_pRoutePoints[currentPoint].GetPosition();
    m_ComputePoints[1] = m_pRoutePoints[nextPoint].GetPosition();

    D3DXVec3Lerp(&m_CurrentPosition, &m_ComputePoints[0],
                         &m_ComputePoints[1], segmentTime);
    D3DXVec3Lerp(&m_LookVector, &m_ComputePoints[0],
                         &m_ComputePoints[1], segmentTime + m_Speed);

    m_LookVector = -m_CurrentPosition;// m_LookVector - m_CurrentPosition;
    D3DXVec3Normalize(&m_LookVector, &m_LookVector);

    return true;
}
```

There's a lot going on here, so let's look at it in detail. First, we find out which point we are currently traveling away from like this:

```
float fcurrentPoint = m_CurrentTime * (float)m_NumPoints;
UINT currentPoint = (UINT)floor(fcurrentPoint);
```

We can find the current point by multiplying the current time, which ranges from 0.0 to 1.0, by the number of points. We ensure that it's the previous point by calling floor() on the value and casting it to an integer. As you probably know, floor() returns the next lowest integer no matter what the decimal value is. For example, 10.3->10.0. 11.999 -> 11.0 55.1 -> 55.0. Its opposite function, if you ever need it, is ceil().

Now that we know the point we are moving away from, we need to work out how far into the current segment we are. A *segment* is the line between the two current points. So if there were 10 points, there would be 9 segments. We need to know the following three things:

- How long the segment is in time
- When it starts
- When it finishes

We can figure that out here:

```
float segmentLength = (1.0f / (float)m_NumPoints);
float timeStart = (float)currentPoint * segmentLength;
float timeFinish = timeStart + segmentLength;
```

We need these values to scale the time from the global time of the entire route to the time across the current segment. The current segment time is found like this:

```
float segmentTime = (m_CurrentTime - timeStart) / segmentLength;
```

Now we need to copy the current points from our dynamic array to the array used for calculating the current interpolation. We also need to wrap around to point 0 if we are at the end of the list:

```
UINT nextPoint = 0;
if(currentPoint < m_NumPoints-2)
    nextPoint = currentPoint + 1;

m_ComputePoints[0] = m_pRoutePoints[currentPoint].GetPosition();
m_ComputePoints[1] = m_pRoutePoints[nextPoint].GetPosition();
```

Now comes the actual interpolation, which D3DX provides useful functions for:

```
D3DXVec3Lerp(&m_CurrentPosition, &m_ComputePoints[0],
        &m_ComputePoints[1], segmentTime);
```

```
D3DXVec3Lerp(&m_LookVector,
        &m_ComputePoints[0], &m_ComputePoints[1], segmentTime + m_Speed);
```

D3DXVec3Lerp() is used to linearly interpolate two vectors or positions. It takes as parameters an output vector, two input vectors, and an interpolation factor. The two input vectors are the two current points we want to travel between, and the interpolation factor is the current segment time. Voilà! We have a new position that is correct to wherever in the segment we want to be at a particular time. When we reach the end of the segment, we automatically flip over to the next segment and continue our journey. It's handy. The only downside, as I mentioned before, is that the movement between segments can be jerky, which is where Catmull-Rom comes in.

The last thing the function does is update the member variables that hold the position and Look At vector. The Look At vector is simply the route sample slightly ahead of the current route position, subtracted from the current position, which leaves us with a vector pointing straight down the route.

Advanced Catmull-Rom Interpolation

This function is similar to the previous linear interpolation function except this time we are dealing with four points instead of two. Here is the code:

```
indBool cSplineRoute::ExecuteCatmullRomInterpolation()
{
    float fcurrentPoint = m_CurrentTime * (float)m_NumPoints;
    UINT currentPoint = (UINT)floor(fcurrentPoint);

    float segmentLength = (1.0f / (float)m_NumPoints);
    float timeStart = (float)currentPoint * segmentLength;
    float timeFinish = timeStart + segmentLength;

    float segmentTime = (m_CurrentTime - timeStart) / segmentLength;

    UINT p1, p2, p3, p4;

    if(currentPoint > 0)
        p1 = currentPoint - 1;
    else
        p1 = m_NumPoints-1;
```

```
        p2 = currentPoint;

        if(currentPoint < m_NumPoints-1)
            p3 = currentPoint + 1;
        else
            p3 = 0;

        if(currentPoint < m_NumPoints-2)
            p4 = currentPoint + 2;
        else
            p4 = 1;

        m_ComputePoints[0] = m_pRoutePoints[p1].GetPosition();
        m_ComputePoints[1] = m_pRoutePoints[p2].GetPosition();
        m_ComputePoints[2] = m_pRoutePoints[p3].GetPosition();
        m_ComputePoints[3] = m_pRoutePoints[p4].GetPosition();

        D3DXVec3CatmullRom(&m_CurrentPosition,
            &m_ComputePoints[0],
            &m_ComputePoints[1],
            &m_ComputePoints[2],
            &m_ComputePoints[3],
            segmentTime);

        // Look 1.0 speed units ahead
        D3DXVec3CatmullRom(&m_LookVector,
            &m_ComputePoints[0],
            &m_ComputePoints[1],
            &m_ComputePoints[2],
            &m_ComputePoints[3],
            segmentTime + m_Speed);

        m_LookVector = -m_CurrentPosition;m_LookVector - m_CurrentPosition;
        D3DXVec3Normalize(&m_LookVector, &m_LookVector);

        return true;
}
```

The main differences are bold. The first difference is that we are dealing with four route points instead of two, so we need to do a bit of juggling if we are near the beginning or end of a route, because the points need to wrap around the source array. Next up is the actual interpolation call with D3DXVec3CatmullRom().

This function is like the linear interpolation factor except that it takes four positions, and the time at which to evaluate the route. The resulting smooth sample is guaranteed to pass through the source points of the route. Finally, the member position and Look At vectors are updated to include the updated position and Look At vectors.

Writing a Route Manager

A route system wouldn't be complete without a manager to automatically load all the routes and take care of their resources. For the routes, I wrote another simple manager to encapsulate the entire route system. Again, it is based on a singleton that wraps a vector of routes. Here is the class definition:

```
class cRouteManager
{
public:
    cRouteManager(void);
    ~cRouteManager(void);

    // Data:
public:

private:
    std::vector <cSplineRoute*> m_vecRoutes;

    static cRouteManager *ms_pRouteManager;
    HINSTANCE              m_hInstance;
    static bool            ms_InstanceFlag;

    // Functions:
public:
    indBool Start();
    indBool Run();
    indBool Render();
    indBool Shutdown();

    static cRouteManager* getInstance();
    static DestroySingleton()
    {
        if(ms_pRouteManager)
        {
```

```
            delete ms_pRouteManager;
            ms_pRouteManager = 0;
        }
    }

    cSplineRoute* FindRoute(char* name)
    {
        UINT size = m_vecRoutes.size();
        for(UINT i = 0 ; i < size ; ++i)
        {
            if(!strcmp(m_vecRoutes[i]->GetRouteName(), name))
                return m_vecRoutes[i];
        }

        OutputDebugString("Failed to find route: ");
        OutputDebugString(name);
        OutputDebugString("\n");
        return NULL;
    }

private:

};
```

As you can see, there is not much to this class at the moment. It basically loads all the routes it can find automatically at startup, which I'll show you in a moment. It also lets you access routes by searching for them by their name. Here is the class implementation:

```
cRouteManager* cRouteManager::getInstance()
{
    if(!ms_InstanceFlag)
    {
        ms_pRouteManager = new cRouteManager();
        ms_InstanceFlag = true;
        return ms_pRouteManager;
    }
    else
    {
        return ms_pRouteManager;
    }
}
```

```cpp
cRouteManager::cRouteManager(void)
{
    m_vecRoutes.reserve(10);
}

cRouteManager::~cRouteManager(void)
{
}

indBool cRouteManager::Start()
{
    WIN32_FIND_DATA FileData;
    HANDLE hSearch;
    BOOL fFinished = FALSE;

    hSearch = FindFirstFile("routes\\*.route", &FileData);
    if (hSearch == INVALID_HANDLE_VALUE)
    {
        OutputDebugString("No .Route files found.\n");
    }

    while (!fFinished)
    {
        cSplineRoute* pNewRoute = new cSplineRoute();
        OutputDebugString("Found new Route: ");
        OutputDebugString(FileData.cFileName);
        OutputDebugString("\n");
        assert(pNewRoute);
        pNewRoute->Start(FileData.cFileName);
        m_vecRoutes.push_back(pNewRoute);

        if(!FindNextFile(hSearch, &FileData))
        {
            if (GetLastError() == ERROR_NO_MORE_FILES)
            {
                fFinished = TRUE;
            }
            else
            {
                OutputDebugString("Couldn't find next route file.\n");
                assert(0);
            }
        }
    }
```

```
    // Close the search handle.
    FindClose(hSearch);
    return true;
}

indBool cRouteManager::Run()
{
    UINT size = m_vecRoutes.size();
    for(UINT i = 0 ; i < size ; ++i)
    {
        m_vecRoutes[i]->Run();
    }
    return true;
}

indBool cRouteManager::Render()
{
    UINT size = m_vecRoutes.size();
    for(UINT i = 0 ; i < size ; ++i)
    {
        m_vecRoutes[i]->Render();
    }
    return true;
}

indBool cRouteManager::Shutdown()
{
    UINT size = m_vecRoutes.size();
    for(UINT i = 0 ; i < size ; ++i)
    {
        delete (m_vecRoutes[i]);
    }

    m_vecRoutes.clear();
    return true;
}
```

The code in start is almost identical to the code I showed you in Chapter 2 for loading effect files. It uses Win32 API calls to locate and load all .route files in a specific directory and creates a new cSplineRoute class to hold it. I won't go through it in detail because I've explained it in other parts of the book.

Putting the Routes into Action

Using the routes is easy. If you had a particle system called "fire," for instance, you could simply do the following to attach it to a route called "fireRoute":

```
ROUTEMANAGER->FindRoute("fireRoute.route")->
    AttachToParticleSystem(PARTICLEMANAGER->FindSystemInstance("fire"));
```

Pretty nifty, huh? The fire particle system then acts normal and follows the path of the route, spraying particles as it goes. Obviously, a little error checking in the preceding code would have been useful to ensure that the route and particle system actually exist before connecting them, but I left it out to show you just how easy it is to connect routes to objects.

If you wanted to attach a specific route to the camera, the following is all you need to write:

```
ROUTEMANAGER->FindRoute("camRoute.route")->SetCameraAttach(true);
```

Figure 13.3
A particle system loyally following its route.

You now have a camera that can fly around your world following routes.

Conclusion

In this chapter, you learned how to take your engine a step above everything else that is out there. The techniques shown here are used as the basis for exactly the type of professional camera animation systems you see in production titles. Learn this chapter well, and there's no limit to what you can achieve. In particular, you learned about the following:

- Defining a route point
- Creating a route class
- Linear interpolation of points
- Advanced Catmull-Rom interpolation
- Smoothly interpolating across a large array of points
- Creating a Look At vector that smoothly follows the route
- Attaching the route system to cameras and particle systems
- Creating a route file format to store your routes
- Creating a route manager to manage your routes

Now let's start at the beginning of this end and look at how to put everything in this book into a single sample application. It looks great, so keep reading!

Chapter 14

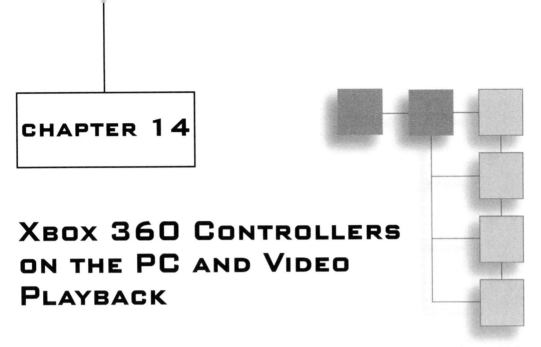

Xbox 360 Controllers on the PC and Video Playback

This chapter covers two bonus and somewhat unrelated subjects. Why include them in this book? Well, they're important for games development. The first subject, which might seem slightly obscure if you're reading this book soon after publication, is how to program Xbox 360 controllers on the PC. The second is how to play back videos from AVI files and render them in your game using DirectShow. In this chapter, I'll show you the following:

- How to get your PC to recognize an Xbox 360 controller
- How to retrieve the states of the buttons, triggers, and sticks
- How to control rumble effects on the controller
- What DirectShow and video playback can do
- How to use graphs and media controllers
- How to detect and respond to DirectShow events
- How to play a video file

I'll bet the hint of the Xbox 360 controller topic has you flipping pages with excitement. Don't worry—I'm covering that first!

The Xbox 360 Controller on the PC

At the time of this writing, the Xbox 360 is roughly one month away from general release, but luckily for me, I'm developing one of the first games for the Xbox for my employer. Interestingly, for the first time in console history, Microsoft has decided to make its controller compatible with the PC. You'll notice that the wired Xbox 360 controller comes with a standard USB connection cable that can also attach to the PC.

Microsoft has released the drivers and the same API for the controllers as that used on the console. So you can learn advanced console development right on your PC! Because the 360 also runs Direct3D (although modified quite a bit), if you learn everything in this book well enough, you'll not only be a highly qualified DirectX developer but also an Xbox 360 developer!

Figure 14.1 shows the Xbox 360 controller.

Figure 14.1
The Xbox 360 controller.

> **Caution**
>
> One note of caution: I'm writing this book before the Xbox 360 has been released, and Microsoft might make some small changes to the content of this chapter in later releases. I already know some, and I'll point them out along the way. Also, all updates and errata for the book are available on the book's Web site at www.courseptr.com. Just enter the title of the book, and you'll be able to get the latest info.

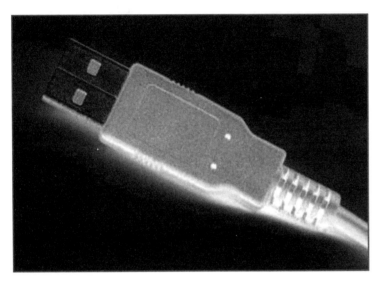

Figure 14.2
The Xbox 360 controller has a standard PC-compatible USB connection.

If you've ever done console programming work, you know how incredibly over-complicated and annoying it can be just to get the controllers working. Amazingly, the Xbox 360 controllers are incredibly easy to work with. They don't use the DirectInput API, which is part of previous releases of DirectX. Instead, they use a new API called *XInput*, which only ships with DirectX SDK versions dated October 2005 and later.

At the time of this writing, the drivers are shipped separately. Microsoft tells me the drivers will be available via Windows Update, among other places. They currently don't work with the Xbox 360 wireless controllers with wired extension, but it's my hope that Microsoft will patch this one day. The XInput API works exclusively with Xbox 360 controllers. It's not a general API like DirectInput. However, you can use both at the same time, as I'll show you in this chapter.

The Xbox 360 controller has a lot of functionality for such a small package. It has ten digital buttons, two analog 2D thumbsticks, and two 1D triggers. It comes in wired and wireless versions, and it has two rumble packs for tactile feedback. You'll see how to control all of this in this chapter.

The XInput API

By this stage in your programming career, you know that Microsoft has a penchant for over-engineering APIs. However, you probably will be pleasantly surprised (or shocked into coma) to hear that only *three* function calls make up XInput! It doesn't even use COM, which is even more fantastic. You might be wondering how you could possibly manage four controllers with 16+ buttons and multiple axes with only three functions. The truth is that after you see this API, you'll wonder why there were so many function calls in the past.

An important thing to note is that XInput supports a maximum of four connected Xbox 360 controllers at any one time to maintain compliance with the Xbox 360. You can connect more, but XInput only addresses controllers 0 to 3, so you're just wasting USB slots if you try more!

To work with this chapter, you must download the DirectX SDK October 2005 or later. You also need an Xbox 360 wired controller (not wireless with wired extension) and drivers to make it work. If you bought this book soon after publication, you might need to wait a week or two for the drivers to show up on Windows Update. Then simply set up your `include` and `lib` directories where you have installed the XInput SDK. Link to `xinput.lib` and `#include winxinput.h`.

The three functions deal with the three actions you need to do with a controller:

1. Figure out the capabilities of the device.
2. Get the current state of the controller.
3. Set the tactile feedback.

Let's look at these in more detail now.

The Device Capabilities

In the future, there will be many types of controllers, and XInput will no doubt expand. However, for now, only one controller is worth mentioning: the standard

game pad. This function is not really used at the moment, but it is great for discovering whether a device is connected. The function has the following prototype:

```
DWORD XInputGetCapabilities(
  DWORD dwPort,
  XINPUT_CAPABILITIES*
);
```

dwPort is the index of the controller that you want to get the capabilities of. This can be 0, 1, 2, or 3. pCapabilities is a pointer to the structure that will be filled with capability data.

The function returns the amazingly double-think value of ERROR_SUCCESS if everything goes all right. Only one error could occur: If XInput can't detect the controller, it returns ERROR_DEVICE_NOT_CONNECTED. You can call this function if you want and check the return status on each controller to see how many are connected.

The XINPUT_CAPABILITIES structure looks like this:

```
typedef struct _XINPUT_CAPABILITIES
{
    BYTE     SubType;
    WORD     Reserved;
    union
    {
      XINPUT_GAMEPAD Gamepad;
    } In;
} XINPUT_CAPABILITIES, *PXINPUT_CAPABILITIES;
```

It contains an XINPUT_GAMEPAD substructure. Well, it wouldn't be Microsoft without nest structures, would it? The structure looks like this:

```
typedef struct _XINPUT_GAMEPAD
{
    WORD                            wButtons;
    BYTE                             bLeftTrigger;
    BYTE                             bRightTrigger;
    SHORT                           sThumbLX;
    SHORT                           sThumbLY;
    SHORT                           sThumbRX;
    SHORT                           sThumbRY;
} XINPUT_GAMEPAD, *PXINPUT_GAMEPAD;
```

As you can see, it's a pretty basic structure containing information about what buttons are active. You'll probably never use this function, so I won't spend too much time on it.

Getting the Device State

The most important thing you'll be doing with XInput is getting the state of the controllers. Getting the state means reading all the values for what the buttons are doing for the controller. This allows you to know when to fire weapons, move the camera, pause, and so on, just like with the original DirectInput. You generally read the state of the controller once per frame. The function to do this is simple and looks like this:

```
DWORD XInputGetState(
  DWORD dwPort,
  XINPUT_STATE* pState
);
```

dwPort is the index of the controller to read data from, which can be 0, 1, 2, or 3. pState is the pointer to an XINPUT_STATE structure to receive the current state of the device.

Typically, you would call this function once every tick to update your input code with new information. I'll show you this function in action shortly. Notice that it takes the same parameter structure as XInputGetCapabilities().

Rumble Effects

The Xbox 360 controller contains two rumble motors: one on the left and one on the right. The two motors are different and can create distinct effects. The left motor is for low-frequency effects, whereas the right is for high-frequency effects. You could use low-frequency effects for things like gunshots from a large bore shotgun. The high-frequency motor could be used for the RPM gauge on a highly revved motor bike.

You control the speed at which the motors spin to create various effects. You alter the speed by passing the controller two WORD values, which are, of course, 16-bit unsigned integers that range from 0 to 65535. 0 is off and 65535 is full speed.

Unlike with DirectInput, you don't need to worry about the number of times you send instructions to the controller. The controller will never run out of memory or buffer space. You can even set the frequency to change every frame if you want! In my experience, the motors are quick to change frequency, moving from one full extreme to another in roughly 200 milliseconds. Shorter changes are much quicker.

You set the controller rumble effects with this function:

```
DWORD XInputSetState(
  DWORD dwPort,
  XINPUT_FEEDBACK * pFeedback
);
```

dwPort is the index of the controller to set the rumble effect for, which can be 0, 1, 2, or 3. pFeedback is a pointer to the feedback structure that contains the new rumble effects.

I have a funny feeling that this structure will have a different name in later versions of DirectX because it has a different name on the Xbox 360. If you get compile errors here, check that XINPUT_FEEDBACK isn't called something else. The structure is simple and looks like this:

```
typedef struct _XINPUT_FEEDBACK
{
    union
    {
        XINPUT_RUMBLE Rumble;
    };
} XINPUT_FEEDBACK, *PXINPUT_FEEDBACK;
```

The preceding structure contains a single nested structure. Why? That's a good question that I don't have the answer for. However, the nested structure looks like this:

```
typedef struct _XINPUT_RUMBLE
{
    WORD   wLeftMotorSpeed;
    WORD   wRightMotorSpeed;
} XINPUT_RUMBLE, *PXINPUT_RUMBLE;
```

Set these two values to something between 0 and 65535 and fire the structure off the controller with XInputSetState(). Your controller will rumble away happily.

Coding an XInput Controller Class

Obviously, dealing with those three functions is a little clunky in practice compared to having a real input system for your game. With that in mind, I coded a simple class that plugs into the `cInputManager` discussed in Chapter 2. Each controller is represented by one of these classes. So, in practice, you would do something like create an array of four of them to represent each controller. Here's the class definition:

```
#pragma once

#include <winxinput.h>

namespace Input
{
    class cXInputController
    {
    public:
        cXInputController(UINT index = 0);
        ~cXInputController(void);

        // Data
    public:

    private:
        int m_ControllerIndex;
        XINPUT_STATE m_ControllerState;
        XINPUT_FEEDBACK m_CurrentVibration;
        // Functions
    public:
        bool Run();
        void GetState(XINPUT_STATE* pState);
        void SetFeedback(float leftMotor, float rightMotor);
        void GetCurrentFeedbackValues(float& leftMotor, float& rightMotor);

    private:


    };
}
```

Now let's look more closely at how this class works. The constructor takes an index of the controller that you want it to represent. If you don't specify one, it defaults to representing the first controller:

```cpp
cXInputController::cXInputController(UINT index /*=0*/)
{
    m_ControllerIndex = index;
    ZeroMemory(&m_ControllerState, sizeof(XINPUT_STATE));
    ZeroMemory(&m_CurrentVibration, sizeof(XINPUT_FEEDBACK));
}
```

The constructor zeroes out the structures that control the state and vibration, so you don't get insane values the first time you read or write to the controller. Now check out the destructor, which does something very important:

```cpp
cXInputController::~cXInputController(void)
{
    SetFeedback(0.0f, 0.0f);
}
```

The destructor sets the controller feedback to 0.0 on the left and right motors. XInput should do this automatically, but it fails sometimes. This leaves you in the annoying role of have a noisy controller bouncing around your desk until you start up your game again to reset it. By forcing the controller to stop vibrating on shutdown, you shouldn't have this problem.

The class also has a Run() method that is called every frame. This is where the controller's data is read. Here's the code:

```cpp
bool cXInputController::Run()
{
    if(SUCCEEDED(XInputGetState(m_ControllerIndex, &m_ControllerState)))
        return true;

    return false;
}
```

If this function returns false, the controller has become disconnected. You might want to warn the user at this point if the primary controller becomes missing.

To get the state of the device, call this function:

```cpp
void cXInputController::GetState(XINPUT_STATE* pState)
{
    *pState = m_ControllerState;
}
```

As you can see, the function copies the contents of the device state into the pointer passed to the function. This is a good place to add functionality to the class so that the caller doesn't have to root through the XInput structures manually.

To set the actual feedback, you call this function, which takes two floats as parameters:

```
void cXInputController::SetFeedback(float leftMotor, float rightMotor)
{
    UINT leftSpeed = (WORD)(leftMotor * 65535.0f);
    UINT rightSpeed = (WORD)(rightMotor * 65535.0f);

    m_CurrentVibration.Rumble.wLeftMotorSpeed = leftSpeed;
    m_CurrentVibration.Rumble.wRightMotorSpeed = rightSpeed;

    XInputSetState(0, &m_CurrentVibration);
}
```

This function takes two `float` parameters, ranging from 0.0 to 1.0. These are converted inside the function to unsigned integers ranging from 0 to 65535, ready to be passed to the controller. Just to reiterate, unlike DirectInput Force feedback, you can call this function as often as you like without slowing down the system or filling up the controller's buffer.

If you need to get the vibration back, the following function can handle it:

```
void cXInputController::GetCurrentFeedbackValues(float& leftMotor, float& rightMotor)
{
    leftMotor = (float)m_CurrentVibration.Rumble.wLeftMotorSpeed / 65535.0f;
    rightMotor = (float)m_CurrentVibration.Rumble.wRightMotorSpeed / 65535.0f;
}
```

This function returns floats ranging from 0.0 to 1.0, just like how you set them. Here's the full class to make it clearer:

```
        class cXInputController
    {
    public:
        cXInputController(UINT index = 0);
        ~cXInputController(void);

        // Data
    public:
```

```cpp
private:
    int m_ControllerIndex;
    XINPUT_STATE m_ControllerState;
    XINPUT_FEEDBACK m_CurrentVibration;
    // Functions
public:
    bool Run();
    void GetState(XINPUT_STATE* pState);
    void SetFeedback(float leftMotor, float rightMotor);
    void GetCurrentFeedbackValues(float& leftMotor, float& rightMotor);

private:


};

    cXInputController::cXInputController(UINT index /*=0*/)
{
    m_ControllerIndex = index;
    ZeroMemory(&m_ControllerState, sizeof(XINPUT_STATE));
    ZeroMemory(&m_CurrentVibration, sizeof(XINPUT_FEEDBACK));
}

cXInputController::~cXInputController(void)
{
    SetFeedback(0.0f, 0.0f);
}

bool cXInputController::Run()
{
    if(SUCCEEDED(XInputGetState(m_ControllerIndex, &m_ControllerState)))
        return true;

    return false;
}

void cXInputController::GetState(XINPUT_STATE* pState)
{
    *pState = m_ControllerState;
}
```

```cpp
void cXInputController::SetFeedback(float leftMotor, float rightMotor)
{
    UINT leftSpeed = (WORD)(leftMotor * 65535.0f);
    UINT rightSpeed = (WORD)(rightMotor * 65535.0f);

    m_CurrentVibration.Rumble.wLeftMotorSpeed = leftSpeed;
    m_CurrentVibration.Rumble.wRightMotorSpeed = rightSpeed;

    XInputSetState(0, &m_CurrentVibration);
}

void cXInputController::GetCurrentFeedbackValues(float& leftMotor, float& rightMotor)
{
    leftMotor = (float)m_CurrentVibration.Rumble.wLeftMotorSpeed / 65535.0f;
    rightMotor = (float)m_CurrentVibration.Rumble.wRightMotorSpeed / 65535.0f;
}
```

Connecting the Input Manager

The XInput controllers aren't going to be much use if you can't use them with the manager, so let's see how to do that now. Check out the new cInputManager class, with the new additions in bold:

```cpp
class cInputManager
{
private:
    cInputManager(void);
public:
    ~cInputManager(void);

// Functions
public:
    static cInputManager* getInstance();
    indBool Start();
    indBool Run();
    indBool Shutdown();

    indBool isMouseButtonDown(indUInt buttonIndex)
    {
        return (m_MouseData.rgbButtons[buttonIndex] & 0x80) ? true : false;
    }
```

```cpp
        indBool isKeyDown(indUInt buttonIndex)
        {
            return (m_KeyboardBuffer[buttonIndex] & 0x80) ? true : false;
        }
protected:
    indBool StartKeyboard();
    indBool StartMouse();
    indBool StartJoystick();
    void ProcessInput();

// Variables
public:
    enum mouseButtons
    {
        PRIMARY_BUTTON = 0,         // usually left
        SECONDARY_BUTTON = 1,       // usually right
        TERTIARY_BUTTON = 2         // usually middle scroll button
    };

    static DestroySingleton()
    {
        if(ms_pInputManager)
        {
            delete ms_pInputManager;
            ms_pInputManager = 0;
        }
    }

protected:
    static cInputManager *ms_pInputManager;
    static bool           ms_InstanceFlag;

    LPDIRECTINPUT8        m_pDirectInput;
    LPDIRECTINPUTDEVICE8  m_pKeyboardDevice;
    LPDIRECTINPUTDEVICE8  m_pMouseDevice;
    LPDIRECTINPUTDEVICE8  m_pJoystickDevice;

    indByte               m_KeyboardBuffer[256];
    DIMOUSESTATE          m_MouseData;

    cXInputController     m_XInputController1;
    cXInputController     m_XInputController2;
```

```
        cXInputController    m_XInputController3;
        cXInputController    m_XInputController4;

};
```

The new controller objects are added as four member classes. Now let's look at the implementation of the input manager, where I've done something kind of cool to show off two parts of the controller at once. During the input processing, the code reads the current state of controller 0, in particular the left and right analog triggers. Then it massages these values slightly and sends them straight back to the controller's rumble motors. With this example, you can control the speed of the motors using the triggers. It's a neat way to get a feel for how they work. Here's the manager's code, with the changes in bold:

```
        cInputManager* cInputManager::getInstance()
{
    if(!ms_InstanceFlag)
    {
        ms_pInputManager = new cInputManager();
        ms_InstanceFlag = true;
        return ms_pInputManager;
    }
    else
    {
        return ms_pInputManager;
    }
}

cInputManager::cInputManager(void)
    : m_XInputController1(0),
      m_XInputController2(1),
      m_XInputController3(2),
      m_XInputController4(3)
{
    // Private constructor
    m_pDirectInput = 0;
    m_pKeyboardDevice = 0;
    m_pMouseDevice = 0;
    m_pJoystickDevice = 0;
    ZeroMemory(&m_KeyboardBuffer, sizeof(m_KeyboardBuffer));
    ZeroMemory(&m_MouseData, sizeof(m_MouseData));

}
```

```cpp
cInputManager::~cInputManager(void)
{
    Shutdown();
}

indBool cInputManager::StartKeyboard()
{
    assert(m_pDirectInput);

    HRESULT hr = S_OK;
    hr = m_pDirectInput->CreateDevice(GUID_SysKeyboard, &m_pKeyboardDevice, 0);
    if(FAILED(hr))
    {
        OutputDebugString("Failed to create keyboard input device\n");
        assert(0);
        return false;
    }

    assert(m_pKeyboardDevice);

    hr = m_pKeyboardDevice->SetDataFormat(&c_dfDIKeyboard);
    if(FAILED(hr))
    {
        OutputDebugString("Failed to set keyboard data format\n");
        assert(0);
        return false;
    }

    hr = m_pKeyboardDevice->SetCooperativeLevel(GAMEENGINE->GetMainWnd(),
        DISCL_BACKGROUND | DISCL_NONEXCLUSIVE);
    if(FAILED(hr))
    {
        OutputDebugString("Failed to set keyboard cooperative level\n");
        assert(0);
        return false;
    }

    hr = m_pKeyboardDevice->Acquire();
    if(FAILED(hr))
    {
        OutputDebugString("Failed to acquire keyboard\n");
        assert(0);
```

```
            return false;
        }

        return true;
    }

    indBool cInputManager::StartMouse()
    {
        assert(m_pDirectInput);

        HRESULT hr = S_OK;

        hr = m_pDirectInput->CreateDevice(GUID_SysMouse, &m_pMouseDevice, NULL);
        if(FAILED(hr))
        {
            OutputDebugString("Failed to create mouse device\n");
            return false;
        }

        hr = m_pMouseDevice->SetDataFormat(&c_dfDIMouse);
        if(FAILED(hr))
        {
            OutputDebugString("Failed to set mouse data format\n");
            return false;
        }

        hr = m_pMouseDevice->SetCooperativeLevel(GAMEENGINE->GetMainWnd(),
                DISCL_NONEXCLUSIVE | DISCL_FOREGROUND);
        if(FAILED(hr))
        {
            OutputDebugString("Failed to set mouse cooperative level\n");
            return false;
        }

        hr = m_pMouseDevice->Acquire();
        if(FAILED(hr))
        {
            OutputDebugString("Unable to acquire mouse\n");
            return false;
        }

        return true;
```

```cpp
}

indBool cInputManager::StartJoystick()
{
    return true;
}

indBool cInputManager::Start()
{
    HRESULT hr = S_OK;

    hr = DirectInput8Create(GAMEENGINE->GetInstanceHandle(), 0x0800,
            IID_IDirectInput8, (void**)&m_pDirectInput, NULL);
    if(FAILED(hr))
    {
        OutputDebugString("Failed to start DirectInput");
        assert(0);
        return false;
    }

    assert(m_pDirectInput);

    if(!StartKeyboard())
    {
        OutputDebugString("Failed to start Keyboard device");
        assert(0);
        return false;
    }

    if(!StartMouse())
    {
        OutputDebugString("No mouse found\n");
        return true;
    }

    if(!StartJoystick())
    {
        OutputDebugString("No Joysticks found\n");
        return true;
    }

    ShowCursor(true);
```

```cpp
            return true;
}

indBool cInputManager::Run()
{
    HRESULT hr = S_OK;

    assert(m_pKeyboardDevice);
    assert(m_pMouseDevice);

    m_XInputController1.Run();
    m_XInputController2.Run();
    m_XInputController3.Run();
    m_XInputController4.Run();

    // XInput sample code... triggers control rumble effect
    {
        XINPUT_STATE currentState;
        m_XInputController1.GetState(&currentState);
        float curLeftValue = (float)currentState.Gamepad.bLeftTrigger / 255.0f;
        float curRightValue = (float)currentState.Gamepad.bRightTrigger / 255.0f;
        m_XInputController1.SetFeedback(curLeftValue, curRightValue);
    }

    hr = m_pKeyboardDevice->GetDeviceState(
                sizeof(m_KeyboardBuffer), &m_KeyboardBuffer);
    if(FAILED(hr))
    {
        m_pKeyboardDevice->Acquire();
    }

    hr = m_pMouseDevice->Poll();
    if(FAILED(hr))
    {
        m_pMouseDevice->Acquire();
        m_pMouseDevice->Poll();
    }

    hr = m_pMouseDevice->GetDeviceState(sizeof(m_MouseData), &m_MouseData);

    ProcessInput();
```

```cpp
        return true;
}

void cInputManager::ProcessInput()
{
    assert(m_KeyboardBuffer);

    if(isKeyDown(DIK_ESCAPE))
        GAMEENGINE->Quit();

    if(isKeyDown(DIK_C))
        CAMERA->Reset();

    if(isKeyDown(DIK_W))
        GAMEENGINE->ToggleWireframe();

    if(isKeyDown(DIK_R))
        PARTICLEMANAGER->ReparseAll();

    indReal32 movementScale = 1.0f;
    indReal32 rotationScale = 300.0f;

    indReal32 xTrans = (indReal32)(m_MouseData.lX) / movementScale;
    indReal32 yTrans = (indReal32)(m_MouseData.lY) / movementScale;
    indReal32 xRot = (indReal32)(m_MouseData.lX) / rotationScale;

    if(isMouseButtonDown(SECONDARY_BUTTON))
    {
        CAMERA->SetVelocity(D3DXVECTOR3(xTrans,-yTrans,0));
        CAMERA->SetAngularVelocity(D3DXVECTOR3(0,0,0));
    }
    else if(isMouseButtonDown(PRIMARY_BUTTON))
    {
        CAMERA->SetVelocity(D3DXVECTOR3(0,0,-yTrans));
        CAMERA->SetAngularVelocity(D3DXVECTOR3(0,xRot,0));
    }
    else
    {
        CAMERA->SetVelocity(D3DXVECTOR3(0,0,0));
        CAMERA->SetAngularVelocity(D3DXVECTOR3(0,0,0));
    }
}
```

```
indBool cInputManager::Shutdown()
{
    SAFE_RELEASE(m_pKeyboardDevice);
    SAFE_RELEASE(m_pMouseDevice);
    SAFE_RELEASE(m_pJoystickDevice);
    SAFE_RELEASE(m_pDirectInput);

    return true;
}
```

Pretty cool, huh? It shouldn't take much extra work to connect the other controller buttons to things like the camera. I leave that as an exercise for you!

Video Output with DirectShow

Video playback has always been notoriously difficult. In the past few years, PCs have finally acquired a decent amount of processing power, which means playing videos doesn't cause them to break into a sweat. It used to be that computers would fall over at the sight of a tiny 160×160 compress video. Today we are left with a legacy of solutions from yesteryear to play back videos in thousands of different ways, each claiming to be slightly faster than the other.

Microsoft, of course, has attempted to come up with an answer that masks all the different encoding, decoding, reading, writing, and other kitchen sink code behind a single interface. Naturally, because it's Microsoft, this new interface is possibly the most abstracted, obscure, and complicated interface ever devised to run on a PC. Its name is DirectShow. (Thunder snaps and lighting flashes as a black cat jumps through your window. Yes... it's evil.)

If you just want to play videos, you can ignore most of the truly evil DirectShow code, close your eyes, and be very happy that it works. Working with DirectShow is like walking across a field of land mines. To avoid most of those, I'll keep the coverage to standard playback, and you can expand on it later if you're feeling like a walk on the wild side.

DirectShow is at times shipped with the DirectX SDK and at other times not. The runtime is always available on end users PCs because it is part of Windows. However, actually tracking down DirectShow can be tricky if you don't have it as part of the main DirectX SDK. Searching for "DirectShow SDK" in various parts of MSDN (http://msdn.microsoft.com) should help you find it. I would provide a link, but it changes so often that the link would be out of date within weeks of publication.

The Theory of DirectShow

DirectPlay is programmed to be similar to a physical system where you can just wire bits and pieces of it together in various ways and it will work just fine. In fact, if you get past the evil obscurity of it all, it's an elegant system. DirectShow is designed to work with playback components. Each component has a job to do, such as loading a file, stripping a file into audio and video portions, decoding video, decoding audio, rendering video, playing audio, and so on. There are components for all these tasks and more, all made by different vendors depending on which codec you are using to encode your video.

Each of these components is programmed to strict guidelines to ensure that it works well with all the other components. Therefore, all the components operate through *pins* to continue the physical abstraction. Components have input pins and output pins, which connect one component to another. For example, an audio component has an input pin that takes in compressed audio and an output pin that sends out decompressed audio. This is the same for all DirectShow components.

Setting up all these components can be messy in the best of times. Luckily, when working with standard playback, there is not much to do, and all the components and their connections are done for us. When all the components are ready and wired together, they are called a graph. A *graph* is simply a collection of connected components that you can pass data through. If the components are connected correctly, you should just have to specify a file name to play and an output destination, and everything will work out perfectly.

You need to go through five steps to play back standard video with DirectShow in your game. The first is to initialize COM and let it know your thread will be using COM with a call to `CoInitialize()`. On shutdown, you need to call the opposite of this function to free all the COM resources with the function `CoUninitialize()`.

When that is complete, you can create a *graph builder object*. A graph builder connects all the COM components to a graph that's capable of playing back video. When the graph builder is set up, you can move on to create a *media controller*, which controls the playback of video, just like Windows Media Player.

The penultimate step is to create a *video window* that keeps your video playback in sync with your rendering window. This is important because if the game's window is dragged around the screen, you want the movie to move with it!

Finally, you create a *media event controller*, which notifies you of events such as the user aborting video playback (if there are controls available for him to do this) or the video finishing play.

At this point, you are ready to play a video file, which is where the graph is created behind the scenes by DirectShow. You can start playback by passing a video file name to DirectShow. You then tell DirectShow to *render* the file, which basically means to construct a graph that's capable of turning the file into moving images and sound. After that, you attach the file to your rendering window and start to play.

You can watch for events to figure out when things like end of playback occur. Let's turn this theory into practice and see some code.

The cVideoRenderer Class

This class encapsulates all the interesting functionality of DirectShow into a nice, easy-to-use class that you can expand later if you wish. Check out the definition, where you will see all the parts I was talking about previously:

```
#include <dshow.h>

namespace Video
{

    class cVideoRenderer
    {
    public:
        cVideoRenderer(void);
        ~cVideoRenderer(void);

        // Data
    public:
        bool IsComplete()
        {
            return m_bPlayComplete;
        }

    private:
        IGraphBuilder *m_pGraphBuilder;
        IMediaControl* m_pMediaControl;
        IVideoWindow* m_pVideoWindow;
        IMediaEventEx* m_pMediaEvent;
```

```
        RECT m_PreviousClientRect;
        bool m_bPlayComplete;

        // Functions
    public:
        bool Start();
        bool Run();
        bool Shutdown();

        bool PlayVideoFile(WCHAR* filename);
    private:


    };
}
```

Notice all the member variables that I was discussing in the theory section, which you will see in action shortly. One variable that I didn't mention was m_PreviousClientRect. The video tends to flicker even if the position has not changed. I use this member variable to track the window position and only update DirectShow if the position actually changes. This ensures flicker-free playback. The m_bPlayComplete variable tracks whether the current video has finished playing.

Now let's examine the code in more detail. The constructor looks like this:

```
        cVideoRenderer::cVideoRenderer(void)
    {
        m_pGraphBuilder = 0;
        m_pMediaControl = 0;
        m_pVideoWindow = 0;
        ZeroMemory(&m_PreviousClientRect, sizeof(RECT));
        m_pMediaEvent = 0;
        m_bPlayComplete = false;
    }
```

There's nothing complicated here. The code just zeroes out all the member variables to prevent surprises later on. Similarly, the destructor calls the shutdown code:

```
        cVideoRenderer::~cVideoRenderer(void)
        {
         Shutdown();
        }
```

Now we get to the interesting code—the initialization. This is burdened with all the usual COM nonsense, but try not to let that block you from seeing what is going on:

```
bool cVideoRenderer::Start()
{
    CoInitialize(NULL);

    CoCreateInstance(CLSID_FilterGraph, NULL,
                CLSCTX_INPROC, IID_IGraphBuilder, (void **)&m_pGraph-
        Builder);
    if(!m_pGraphBuilder)
    {
        assert(0);
        OutputDebugString("Failed to create video graph builder\n");
        return false;
    }

    m_pGraphBuilder->QueryInterface(IID_IMediaControl, (void **)&m_pMediaControl);
    if(!m_pMediaControl)
    {
        assert(0);
        OutputDebugString("Failed to create video media controller\n");
        return false;
    }

    m_pGraphBuilder->QueryInterface(IID_IVideoWindow, (void **)&m_pVideoWindow);
    if(!m_pVideoWindow)
    {
        assert(0);
        OutputDebugString("Failed to create video window\n");
        return false;
    }

    m_pGraphBuilder->QueryInterface(IID_IMediaEventEx, (void **)&m_pMediaEvent);
    if(!m_pMediaEvent)
    {
        assert(0);
        OutputDebugString("Failed to create video event\n");
        return false;
    }

    return true;
}
```

As you can see, the code starts by initializing COM with CoInitialize(). This lets Windows know we will be using all those hefty COM DLLs in our process. The next step uses COM to create the graph builder. If you forget to put in the call to CoInitialize(), as I did on the first pass of this code, this call fails miserably without explanation. Next, the code creates the media controller, which manages the playback of the video. Finally, the video window and media event controller are created.

Now let's check out the code that is called every frame while the video is playing:

```
bool cVideoRenderer::Run()
{
    if(m_pVideoWindow)
    {
        RECT clientRect;
        GetClientRect(GAMEENGINE->GetMainWnd(), &clientRect);

        if(clientRect.left   != m_PreviousClientRect.left   ||
           clientRect.top    != m_PreviousClientRect.top    ||
           clientRect.right  != m_PreviousClientRect.right  ||
           clientRect.bottom != m_PreviousClientRect.bottom)
        {
            m_pVideoWindow->SetWindowPosition(
            clientRect.left, clientRect.top,
            clientRect.right, clientRect.bottom);
        }

        m_PreviousClientRect = clientRect;
    }

    long code, parameter1, parameter2;
    while(SUCCEEDED(m_pMediaEvent->GetEvent(&code, &parameter1, &parameter2, 0)))
    {
        HRESULT hr = m_pMediaEvent->FreeEventParams(
                                        code, parameter1, parameter2);

        switch(code)
        {
        case EC_COMPLETE:
            {
                m_bPlayComplete = true;
                break;
```

```
            }
            default:
                continue;
        }
        break;
    }


    return true;
}
```

This function is called every frame. It begins by checking for the existence of the video window and then getting the current client rect of the render window. If the rectangle has changed since the last frame, DirectShow is updated so that it knows to render the video in the new location.

The function then checks whether any events have been passed through. The only one we are interested in at the moment is whether the video has finished playing. Next up is the code that is called when we request that a video be played:

```
bool cVideoRenderer::PlayVideoFile(WCHAR* filename)
{
    m_bPlayComplete = false;

    if(!m_pGraphBuilder)
    {
        assert(0);
        OutputDebugString("Attempt to play video file with invalid graph builder\n");
        return false;
    }

    HRESULT hr = m_pGraphBuilder->RenderFile(filename, 0);
    if(FAILED(hr))
    {
        assert(0);
        OutputDebugString("Failed to play video file\n");
        return false;
    }

    hr = m_pVideoWindow->put_Owner((OAHWND)GAMEENGINE->GetMainWnd());
    if(FAILED(hr))
    {
```

```
        assert(0);
        OutputDebugString("Failed to set player window\n");
        return false;
    }

    hr = m_pMediaControl->Run();
    if(FAILED(hr))
    {
        assert(0);
        OutputDebugString("Failed to run media player\n");
        return false;
    }
    return true;
}
```

You call this function with the file name of the video that you want to play. DirectShow deals only with wide character strings, so if your file names are in plain ASCII, you can convert them with a utility function. The function starts by checking whether a valid graph builder was created. Nothing can happen without this.

Then the function calls RenderFile(), which constructs the graph for us. If this fails, it's usually because the video file was not found or because it is encoded in an unsupported format. You probably want to notify an error here. It's pretty bad if you can't play your intro videos!

Next, the put_Owner() function is called, which sets the window to use as a render target. Annoyingly, it takes a window handle as an OAHWND. I don't know why this is, but it's irritating because an unneeded cast is required. Finally, if all went according to plan, we can tell the media controller to Run(), which actually plays the file to the screen with audio.

Shutting down is pretty simple. We just need to make the video invisible and remove its association with our rendering window. Then we can release all the resources and uninitialize COM. And that is all there is to playing video files! Here's the complete code:

```
#include <dshow.h>

namespace Video
{
```

```cpp
class cVideoRenderer
{
public:
    cVideoRenderer(void);
    ~cVideoRenderer(void);

    // Data
public:
    bool IsComplete()
    {
        return m_bPlayComplete;
    }

private:
    IGraphBuilder *m_pGraphBuilder;
    IMediaControl* m_pMediaControl;
    IVideoWindow* m_pVideoWindow;
    IMediaEventEx* m_pMediaEvent;

    RECT m_PreviousClientRect;
    bool m_bPlayComplete;

    // Functions
public:
    bool Start();
    bool Run();
    bool Shutdown();

    bool PlayVideoFile(WCHAR* filename);
private:


};

}
//////////////////////////////////////////////////////////////
#include "stdafx.h"

#include "cGameEngine.h"

#include ".\cvideorenderer.h"
```

```cpp
namespace Video
{

    cVideoRenderer::cVideoRenderer(void)
    {
        m_pGraphBuilder = 0;
        m_pMediaControl = 0;
        m_pVideoWindow = 0;
        ZeroMemory(&m_PreviousClientRect, sizeof(RECT));
        m_pMediaEvent = 0;
        m_bPlayComplete = false;
    }

    cVideoRenderer::~cVideoRenderer(void)
    {
        Shutdown();
    }

    bool cVideoRenderer::Start()
    {
        CoInitialize(NULL);

        CoCreateInstance(CLSID_FilterGraph, NULL, CLSCTX_INPROC,
                IID_IGraphBuilder, (void **)&m_pGraphBuilder);
        if(!m_pGraphBuilder)
        {
            assert(0);
            OutputDebugString("Failed to create video graph builder\n");
            return false;
        }

        m_pGraphBuilder->QueryInterface(IID_IMediaControl, (void **)&m_pMediaControl);
        if(!m_pMediaControl)
        {
            assert(0);
            OutputDebugString("Failed to create video media controller\n");
            return false;
        }

        m_pGraphBuilder->QueryInterface(IID_IVideoWindow, (void **)&m_pVideoWindow);
        if(!m_pVideoWindow)
        {
```

```cpp
            assert(0);
            OutputDebugString("Failed to create video window\n");
            return false;
        }

        m_pGraphBuilder->QueryInterface(IID_IMediaEventEx, (void **)&m_pMediaEvent);
        if(!m_pMediaEvent)
        {
            assert(0);
            OutputDebugString("Failed to create video event\n");
            return false;
        }

        return true;
    }

    bool cVideoRenderer::Run()
    {
        if(m_pVideoWindow)
        {
            RECT clientRect;
            GetClientRect(GAMEENGINE->GetMainWnd(), &clientRect);

            if(clientRect.left   != m_PreviousClientRect.left   ||
               clientRect.top    != m_PreviousClientRect.top    ||
               clientRect.right  != m_PreviousClientRect.right  ||
               clientRect.bottom != m_PreviousClientRect.bottom)
            {
                m_pVideoWindow->SetWindowPosition(
                    clientRect.left, clientRect.top,
                    clientRect.right, clientRect.bottom);
            }

            m_PreviousClientRect = clientRect;
        }

        long code, parameter1, parameter2;
        while(SUCCEEDED(m_pMediaEvent->GetEvent(&code,
                                        &parameter1, &parameter2, 0)))
        {
            HRESULT hr = m_pMediaEvent->FreeEventParams(code,
                                        parameter1, parameter2);
```

```
            switch(code)
            {
            case EC_COMPLETE:
                {
                    m_bPlayComplete = true;
                    break;
                }
            default:
                continue;
            }
            break;
        }


        return true;
    }

    bool cVideoRenderer::PlayVideoFile(WCHAR* filename)
    {
        m_bPlayComplete = false;

        if(!m_pGraphBuilder)
        {
            assert(0);
            OutputDebugString("Attempt to play video file with invalid graph builder\n");
            return false;
        }

        HRESULT hr = m_pGraphBuilder->RenderFile(filename, 0);
        if(FAILED(hr))
        {
            assert(0);
            OutputDebugString("Failed to play video file\n");
            return false;
        }

        hr = m_pVideoWindow->put_Owner((OAHWND)GAMEENGINE->GetMainWnd());
        if(FAILED(hr))
        {
            assert(0);
            OutputDebugString("Failed to set player window\n");
```

```
            return false;
        }

        hr = m_pMediaControl->Run();
        if(FAILED(hr))
        {
            assert(0);
            OutputDebugString("Failed to run media player\n");
            return false;
        }
        return true;
    }

    bool cVideoRenderer::Shutdown()
    {
        if(m_pVideoWindow)
        {
            m_pVideoWindow->put_Visible(false);
            m_pVideoWindow->put_Owner(0);
        }

        SAFE_RELEASE(m_pGraphBuilder);
        SAFE_RELEASE(m_pMediaControl);
        SAFE_RELEASE(m_pVideoWindow);
        SAFE_RELEASE(m_pMediaEvent);

        CoUninitialize();

        return true;
    }
}
```

With a little bit of extra work, you can easily attach the renderer to a Direct3D surface and use that as a texture for 3D models if you want to expand the video playback to your game. A new exciting use for videos is as Heads Up Display (HUD) components in games. Play beautifully swirling graphics that display in the background while rendering the dynamic content on top. The effect is fantastic.

Conclusion

You now have two interesting technologies you can add to your engine. XInput allows you to use the ergonomic and familiar controller from your Xbox 360 on your PC, which for a lot of games is an intuitive way of playing. You can also play back video for your intro movies with DirectShow. In this chapter, you learned about the following:

- How to get your PC to recognize an Xbox 360 controller
- How to retrieve the states of the buttons, triggers, and sticks
- How to control force feedback effects on the controller
- What DirectShow and video playback can do
- How to use graphs and media controllers
- How to detect and respond to DirectShow events
- How to play a video file

In the next chapter, I'll show you a sample application that brings together almost everything covered in the book so far.

CHAPTER 15

PUTTING IT ALL TOGETHER

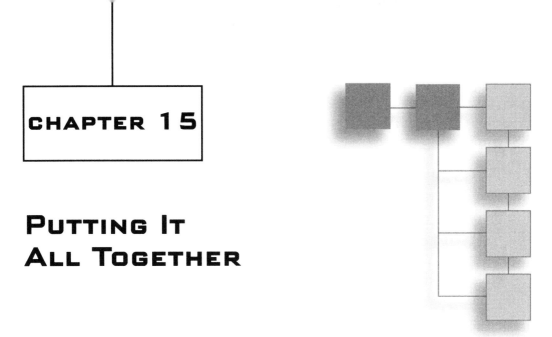

You've come a long way if you've read this book cover to cover. Your eyes must be nearly as worn as my poor strained hands after all this typing. This chapter is all about putting everything you've learned in this book into a single sample application so that you can see how it can all fit together. Mix everything you have in this book with a little bit of information from other books on Artificial Intelligence (AI), collision detection, physics, and sound effects, and you have the basis of an impressive game engine that's capable of impressing employers and universities.

The sample code in this chapter contains only changes to the main `cGameEngine` class, which is where everything is coordinated from. In particular, you will see the following demonstrated:

- The game engine coordinating the initialization, shutdown, rendering, and updating of all game managers and resources
- DirectInput used to control the camera around the scene
- Effect files and shaders used to render every object in the scene
- Particle systems used in a variety of different ways, including a waterfall, volumetric fog, snow, and as a crazy flying fire effect running around a route
- An exported Maya character
- Water effects
- Various skinned animated characters running around the scene in a variety of animation sequences
- The script being called to print text to the screen
- Dynamically generated terrain with per-pixel blended textures
- A cubic texture sky box that moves with the camera
- The camera and particle system following advanced routes

Wow! That's a lot of stuff. In fact, thinking briefly of the various other game development books, I hope you'll find that this is one of the most advanced 3D game engines developed from start to finish compared with any other game programming book currently available (although I might be proven wrong on that one). Nonetheless, everything you've learned in this book is directly applicable to the games industry. The reason I chose these topics was because in my experience, everyone in the game industry is expected to know this stuff, but there is no decent source of information with it all in one place. Hopefully, you believe this book was a wise investment, and it will save you a lot of time in the future.

Here is a selection of screen shots from the sample program for this chapter if you don't have it open.

Putting It All Together 461

Figure 15.1
A close-up of the evil dwarf shooting his water spell.

Figure 15.2
The Tiny model in a variety of animated poses, with the water effect in the foreground.

462   Chapter 15 ■ Putting It All Together

Figure 15.3
A close-up of the animated models: one waving, one walking, and one running.

Figure 15.4
If you look closely, you can see the volumetric fog slowly rolling through the hills.

Putting It All Together 463

Figure 15.5
The insane fire particle system hurtling along its route.

Figure 15.6
She's been running so long she's seeing stars. Or is that snow?

Figure 15.7
The dwarf casting a volumetric shadow across the landscape.

Let's check out the code currently used in the game engine to create the example for the book. I won't give you the entire source because it has grown pretty large by this stage, but I *really* recommend that you download it just to see how cool everything looks. Here is the `cGameEngine` class definition:

```
// cGameEngine.h: interface for the cGameEngine class.
//
//////////////////////////////////////////////////////////////////////

#if !defined(AFX_CGAMEENGINE_H__438EB04C_1B1E_4BEA_ACDD_AA03EE7EAEE8__INCLUDED_)
#define AFX_CGAMEENGINE_H__438EB04C_1B1E_4BEA_ACDD_AA03EE7EAEE8__INCLUDED_

#if _MSC_VER > 1000
#pragma once
#endif // _MSC_VER > 1000

#include <d3d9.h>
#include "cParticleSystem.h"
#include "cThread.h"
#include "cSkinnedAnimationMesh.h"
```

```cpp
#include "cTerrainGenerator.h"
#include "cSkyBox.h"
#include "cRouteManager.h"

namespace Graphics
{
    const indUInt DEFAULT_SCREEN_WIDTH = 640;
    const indUInt DEFAULT_SCREEN_HEIGHT = 480;
    const indReal32 DEFAULT_GAME_FPS = 60.0f;

    class cGameEngine : public cThread
    {

    // Functions
    public:
        virtual ~cGameEngine();


    private:
        cGameEngine();

    public:
        bool        Start();
        int         Run();
        bool        Shutdown();

        static cGameEngine* getInstance();

        static DestroySingleton()
        {
            if(ms_pEngine)
            {
                delete ms_pEngine;
                ms_pEngine = 0;
            }
        }

        void Quit()
        {
            m_bQuit = true;
        }
```

```cpp
HWND        GetMainWnd()
{
    return m_hMainWnd;
}

HINSTANCE   GetInstanceHandle()
{
    return m_hInstance;
}

LPDIRECT3DDEVICE9 GetDeviceAddRef()
{
    assert(m_pDevice);
    m_pDevice->AddRef();
    return m_pDevice;
}

LPDIRECT3DDEVICE9 GetDevice()
{
    assert(m_pDevice);
    return m_pDevice;
}

inline float GetTimeDelta()
{
    return m_TimeDelta;
}

void ForceFrameRate(bool bForce, indUInt rate = DEFAULT_GAME_FPS)
{
    m_bForceFrameRate = bForce;
    m_ForcedFrameRate = rate;
}

void ToggleWireframe()
{
    m_bRenderWireframe = !m_bRenderWireframe;
}

bool IsWireframe()
{
    return m_bRenderWireframe;
}
```

```cpp
virtual void EndThread();

float GetLastFrameDurationMS()
{
    return m_LastFrameDurationMS;
}

UINT GetEngineRunTime()
{
    // Time game has run in milliseconds
    UINT time = timeGetTime();
    return time - m_EngineStartTime;
}

LPDIRECT3DTEXTURE9 GetDefaultTexture()
{
    assert(m_pDefaultTexture);
    return m_pDefaultTexture;
}

void GetGlobalLightPosition(D3DXVECTOR3& lightPos)
{
    lightPos = m_GlobalLightPosition;
}

void GetLightDirectionToPosition(D3DXVECTOR3 position, D3DXVECTOR3& lightDir)
{
    lightDir = position - m_GlobalLightPosition;
    D3DXVec3Normalize(&lightDir, &lightDir);
}

void GetLightDirection(D3DXVECTOR3& lightDir)
{
    // Get light direction to origin
    lightDir = -m_GlobalLightPosition;
    D3DXVec3Normalize(&lightDir, &lightDir);
}

void SetSkyColor(D3DXCOLOR& newColor)
{
    m_SkyColor = newColor;
}
```

```cpp
        D3DXCOLOR& GetSkyColor()
        {
            return m_SkyColor;
        }
    protected:
        indBool InitializeGraphics();
        indBool LoadAssets();
        indBool ValidateDevice();
        indBool CreateDevice();

        void Synchronization();

        indBool PreRender();
        indBool Render();
        indBool PostRender();

        indBool InitGrid();
        indBool RenderGrid();
        void    UpdateGlobalLight();
        virtual DWORD ThreadProcedure();

    // Variables
    public:

    protected:
        HWND                m_hMainWnd;
        HINSTANCE           m_hInstance;
        static bool         ms_InstanceFlag;
        static              cGameEngine *ms_pEngine;

        D3DPRESENT_PARAMETERS m_D3DPresentParams;

        LPDIRECT3DDEVICE9   m_pDevice;
        LPDIRECT3D9         m_pDirect3D;
        indUInt                 m_DefaultEffectID;
        indUInt                 m_GridEffectID;
        LPDIRECT3DVERTEXBUFFER9 m_pGridVB;

        indReal32           m_FrameRate;
        indReal32           m_TimeDelta;
        bool                m_bForceFrameRate;
        indUInt             m_ForcedFrameRate;
```

```
    indString              m_AppName;

    indUInt                m_ScreenWidth;
    indUInt                m_ScreenHeight;
    indBool                m_bFullscreen;

    D3DXMATRIX      m_matIdentity;

    indInt64               m_CounterFrequency;
    indInt64               m_LastCount;
    double                 m_LastRateUpdate;
    float                    m_LastFrameDurationMS;

    indInt64               m_AvgFrameRateAccum;
    UINT                   m_NumSamples;

    bool                    m_bRenderWireframe;
    bool                    m_bQuit;

    UINT                   m_EngineStartTime;
private:
    LPDIRECT3DTEXTURE9   m_pDefaultTexture;
    D3DXVECTOR3                 m_GlobalLightPosition;
    Terrain::cTerrainGenerator m_TerrainGenerator;
    D3DXCOLOR                   m_SkyColor;

    D3DXVECTOR3            m_PlayerStartPoint;

    SkyBox::cSkyBox        m_SkyBox;
};

} // end namespace

#endif //
!defined(AFX_CGAMEENGINE_H__438EB04C_1B1E_4BEA_ACDD_AA03EE7EAEE8__INCLUDED_)
```

And the implementation that goes with it looks like this. I've bolded the important code:

```
// cGameEngine.cpp: implementation of the cGameEngine class.
//
//////////////////////////////////////////////////////////////////////
```

Chapter 15 ■ Putting It All Together

```cpp
#include "stdafx.h"

#include "cEffectManager.h"
#include "cGameEngine.h"
#include "cInputManager.h"
#include "cCamera.h"
#include "cVisualResource.h"
#include "cResourceManager.h"
#include "cParticleSystemManager.h"
#include "cSkinnedAnimationManager.h"
#include "cScriptInterface.h"
#include "cTerrainGenerator.h"

//////////////////////////////////////////////////////////////////////
// Construction/Destruction
//////////////////////////////////////////////////////////////////////

extern HWND g_hWndMain;
extern HINSTANCE g_hInstanceMain;


Resources::cVisualResource* g_pResource = 0;


namespace Graphics
{
    struct GRID_VERTEX
    {
        D3DXVECTOR3 position;
        DWORD color;
    };

    const DWORD GRID_VERTEXFORMAT = D3DFVF_XYZ | D3DFVF_DIFFUSE;

    bool cGameEngine::ms_InstanceFlag = false;
    cGameEngine* cGameEngine::ms_pEngine = NULL;

    cGameEngine* cGameEngine::getInstance()
    {
        if(!ms_InstanceFlag)
        {
            ms_pEngine = new cGameEngine();
```

```cpp
            ms_InstanceFlag = true;
            return ms_pEngine;
        }
        else
        {
            return ms_pEngine;
        }
    }

    cGameEngine::cGameEngine()
        : cThread()
    {
        _CrtSetDbgFlag ( _CRTDBG_ALLOC_MEM_DF | _CRTDBG_LEAK_CHECK_DF );
        //private constructor
        D3DXMatrixIdentity(&m_matIdentity);

        m_pDevice = 0;
        m_pDirect3D = 0;
        m_TimeDelta = 1.0f;
        m_LastRateUpdate = 0;
        m_LastFrameDurationMS = 0.0f;

        m_PlayerStartPoint = D3DXVECTOR3(0,100,0);

        m_EngineStartTime = timeGetTime();
        m_GlobalLightPosition = D3DXVECTOR3(20, 100, 20);
        m_pGridVB = 0;

        m_AppName = "Engine";

        m_ScreenWidth = DEFAULT_SCREEN_WIDTH;
        m_ScreenHeight = DEFAULT_SCREEN_HEIGHT;
        m_bFullscreen = false;

        m_bQuit = false;
        m_bRenderWireframe = false;

        m_FrameRate = DEFAULT_GAME_FPS;
        m_bForceFrameRate = false;
        m_ForcedFrameRate = (indUInt)DEFAULT_GAME_FPS;

        ZeroMemory(&m_D3DPresentParams, sizeof(m_D3DPresentParams));
```

472 Chapter 15 ■ Putting It All Together

```cpp
        m_LastCount = 0;
        m_CounterFrequency = 0;
        m_AvgFrameRateAccum = 0;
        m_NumSamples = 0;

        m_pDefaultTexture = 0;

        m_SkyColor = D3DXCOLOR(0.1f, 0.1f, 0.4f, 1.0f);
    }

    cGameEngine::~cGameEngine()
    {
        EndThread();
    }

    indBool cGameEngine::InitializeGraphics()
    {
        if(NULL == (m_pDirect3D = Direct3DCreate9(D3D_SDK_VERSION)))
            return false;

        if(m_bFullscreen)
        {
            m_D3DPresentParams.BackBufferWidth = m_ScreenWidth;
            m_D3DPresentParams.BackBufferHeight = m_ScreenHeight;
            m_D3DPresentParams.BackBufferFormat = D3DFMT_A8R8G8B8;
            m_D3DPresentParams.BackBufferCount = 1;
            m_D3DPresentParams.MultiSampleType = D3DMULTISAMPLE_NONE;
            m_D3DPresentParams.MultiSampleQuality = 0;
            m_D3DPresentParams.SwapEffect = D3DSWAPEFFECT_DISCARD;
            m_D3DPresentParams.hDeviceWindow = m_hMainWnd;
            m_D3DPresentParams.Windowed = FALSE;
            m_D3DPresentParams.EnableAutoDepthStencil = 1;
            m_D3DPresentParams.AutoDepthStencilFormat = D3DFMT_D24S8;
            m_D3DPresentParams.Flags =
                        D3DPRESENTFLAG_DISCARD_DEPTHSTENCIL |
                        D3DPRESENTFLAG_LOCKABLE_BACKBUFFER;
            m_D3DPresentParams.FullScreen_RefreshRateInHz = 0;
            m_D3DPresentParams.PresentationInterval =
                        D3DPRESENT_INTERVAL_IMMEDIATE;
        }
        else
        {
```

```cpp
            m_D3DPresentParams.BackBufferWidth = m_ScreenWidth;
            m_D3DPresentParams.BackBufferHeight = m_ScreenHeight;
            m_D3DPresentParams.BackBufferFormat = D3DFMT_UNKNOWN;
            m_D3DPresentParams.BackBufferCount = 1;
            m_D3DPresentParams.MultiSampleType = D3DMULTISAMPLE_NONE;
            m_D3DPresentParams.MultiSampleQuality = 0;
            m_D3DPresentParams.SwapEffect = D3DSWAPEFFECT_DISCARD;
            m_D3DPresentParams.hDeviceWindow = m_hMainWnd;
            m_D3DPresentParams.Windowed = TRUE;
            m_D3DPresentParams.EnableAutoDepthStencil = 1;
            m_D3DPresentParams.AutoDepthStencilFormat = D3DFMT_D24S8;
            m_D3DPresentParams.Flags =
                            D3DPRESENTFLAG_DISCARD_DEPTHSTENCIL |
                            D3DPRESENTFLAG_LOCKABLE_BACKBUFFER;
            m_D3DPresentParams.FullScreen_RefreshRateInHz = 0;
            m_D3DPresentParams.PresentationInterval =
                            D3DPRESENT_INTERVAL_IMMEDIATE;
        }

        CreateDevice();

        // Init render states
        m_pDevice->SetRenderState(D3DRS_LIGHTING, 0);
        m_pDevice->SetSamplerState(0, D3DSAMP_MINFILTER, D3DTEXF_LINEAR);
        m_pDevice->SetSamplerState(0, D3DSAMP_MAGFILTER, D3DTEXF_LINEAR);
        m_pDevice->SetSamplerState(0, D3DSAMP_MIPFILTER, D3DTEXF_LINEAR);

        HRESULT hr =
            D3DXCreateTextureFromFileEx(m_pDevice, "media\\DefaultTexture.bmp",
                D3DX_DEFAULT, D3DX_DEFAULT,
                D3DX_DEFAULT, 0, D3DFMT_FROM_FILE, D3DPOOL_MANAGED,
                D3DX_FILTER_TRIANGLE,
                D3DX_FILTER_TRIANGLE, 0, 0, 0, &m_pDefaultTexture);
        if(FAILED(hr))
        {
            assert(0);
            OutputDebugString("Failed to load default texture");
            m_pDefaultTexture = NULL;
        }

        return true;
    }
```

```cpp
indBool cGameEngine::CreateDevice()
{
    HRESULT hr = m_pDirect3D->CreateDevice(
        D3DADAPTER_DEFAULT, D3DDEVTYPE_HAL, m_hMainWnd,
        D3DCREATE_HARDWARE_VERTEXPROCESSING | D3DCREATE_MULTITHREADED,
        &m_D3DPresentParams, &m_pDevice);
    if(FAILED(hr))
    {
        OutputDebugString("Failed to create hardware direct3d device");
        HRESULT hr = m_pDirect3D->CreateDevice(
            D3DADAPTER_DEFAULT, D3DDEVTYPE_HAL, m_hMainWnd,
            D3DCREATE_MIXED_VERTEXPROCESSING | D3DCREATE_MULTITHREADED,
            &m_D3DPresentParams, &m_pDevice);
        if(FAILED(hr))
        {
            OutputDebugString("Failed to create mixed direct3d device");
            HRESULT hr = m_pDirect3D->CreateDevice(
                D3DADAPTER_DEFAULT, D3DDEVTYPE_HAL, m_hMainWnd,
                D3DCREATE_SOFTWARE_VERTEXPROCESSING | D3DCREATE_MULTI-
THREADED,
                &m_D3DPresentParams, &m_pDevice);
            if(FAILED(hr))
            {
                OutputDebugString("Failed to create software direct3d device");
                assert(0);
                Quit();
                return false;
            }
        }
    }

    return true;
}



indBool cGameEngine::LoadAssets()
{
    Resources::cVisualResource* pNewResource =
        new Resources::cVisualResource("bigplane.x",
RESOURCEMANAGER->GenerateUniqueID());
```

Putting It All Together 475

```cpp
        //pNewResource->ChangeEffect("water.fx");
        //pNewResource->OverrideTexture("media\\water.bmp");
        //pNewResource->SetEnvironmentMap("media\\skybox02.dds");

        //RESOURCEMANAGER->AddVisualResource(pNewResource);


        Resources::cVisualResource* pNewItem =
            new Resources::cVisualResource("dwarf.x",
RESOURCEMANAGER->GenerateUniqueID());
        g_pResource = pNewItem;
        pNewItem->SetPosition(D3DXVECTOR3(500.0f, 220.0f, 700.0f));
        pNewItem->SetShadowed(true);
        pNewItem->SetScale(100.0f);
        RESOURCEMANAGER->AddVisualResource(pNewItem);


        PARTICLEMANAGER->SpawnSystemInstance("fire");
        PARTICLEMANAGER->SpawnSystemInstance("clouds");
        PARTICLEMANAGER->SpawnSystemInstance("rain");
        PARTICLEMANAGER->SpawnSystemInstance("waterfall");

        ROUTEMANAGER->FindRoute("camRoute.route")->SetCameraAttach(true);
        ROUTEMANAGER->FindRoute("fireRoute.route")->
            AttachToParticleSystem(PARTICLEMANAGER->FindSystemInstance("fire"));

        ANIMATIONMANAGER->AddAnimatedMesh("media\\tiny_4animb.x");
        ANIMATIONMANAGER->AddAnimatedMesh("media\\tiny_4animb.x");
        ANIMATIONMANAGER->AddAnimatedMesh("media\\tiny_4animb.x");
        ANIMATIONMANAGER->GetAnimatedMesh(1)->SetCurrentAnimationByIndex(2);
        ANIMATIONMANAGER->GetAnimatedMesh(0)->SetCurrentAnimationByIndex(1);
        ANIMATIONMANAGER->GetAnimatedMesh(2)->SetCurrentAnimationByIndex(0);

        return true;
    }

    indBool cGameEngine::Start()
    {
        m_hMainWnd = g_hWndMain;
        m_hInstance = g_hInstanceMain;

        QueryPerformanceFrequency((LARGE_INTEGER*)&m_CounterFrequency);
```

Chapter 15 ■ Putting It All Together

```
        InitializeGraphics();
        INPUT->Start();
        EFFECTMANAGER->Start();

        m_DefaultEffectID = EFFECTMANAGER->FindEffect("default.fx");
        m_GridEffectID = EFFECTMANAGER->FindEffect("grid.fx");

        CAMERA->Start();
        CAMERA->SetPosition(m_PlayerStartPoint);
        RESOURCEMANAGER->Start();
        PARTICLEMANAGER->Start();
        SCRIPTMANAGER->Start();
        ROUTEMANAGER->Start();

        InitGrid();

        LoadAssets();

        ANIMATIONMANAGER->Start();

        m_TerrainGenerator.Start();
        m_SkyBox.Start();

        Script::cScriptTestObject testObject("scripts\\enginetest.lua");

        testObject.Run();

        return true;
    }

    indBool cGameEngine::ValidateDevice()
    {
        assert(m_pDevice);
        HRESULT deviceState = m_pDevice->TestCooperativeLevel();

        if(deviceState == D3D_OK)
            return true;

        if(deviceState == D3DERR_DRIVERINTERNALERROR)
        {
            assert(0);
            Quit();
        }
```

Putting It All Together

```cpp
        if(deviceState == D3DERR_DEVICENOTRESET)
        {
            SAFE_RELEASE(m_pDevice);
            CreateDevice();
            return true;
        }

        return false;
    }

    void cGameEngine::Synchronization()
    {
        if(m_LastCount == 0)
        {
            QueryPerformanceCounter((LARGE_INTEGER*)&m_LastCount);
            return;
        }

        indInt64 currentCount=0, timeDiff=0;
        QueryPerformanceCounter((LARGE_INTEGER*)&currentCount);
        timeDiff = currentCount - m_LastCount;
        double milliSecsPassed = (double)(long double)(timeDiff) /
                                                    (long double)
(m_CounterFrequency) * 1000.0;

        m_FrameRate = (float)(1000.0 / (double)milliSecsPassed);
        m_TimeDelta = (float)m_FrameRate / DEFAULT_GAME_FPS;

        if(m_LastRateUpdate > 250.0)
        {
            m_NumSamples++;
            m_AvgFrameRateAccum += (indInt64)m_FrameRate;

            if(m_NumSamples > 60)
            {
                m_NumSamples = 1;
                m_AvgFrameRateAccum = (indInt64)m_FrameRate;
            }

            indChar newWindowText[256];
            sprintf(newWindowText, "%s - [%f, %f, Avg:%i] FPS",
                m_AppName, m_FrameRate, m_TimeDelta, UINT(m_AvgFrameRateAccum /
m_NumSamples));
```

```
                SetWindowText(m_hMainWnd, newWindowText);

                m_LastRateUpdate = 0;
        }

        m_LastRateUpdate += milliSecsPassed;
        m_LastFrameDurationMS = (float)milliSecsPassed;

        QueryPerformanceCounter((LARGE_INTEGER*)&m_LastCount);

}

indBool cGameEngine::PreRender()
{
        m_pDevice->BeginScene();

        m_pDevice->Clear(0,
                NULL, D3DCLEAR_TARGET | D3DCLEAR_ZBUFFER | D3DCLEAR_STENCIL,
                (D3DCOLOR)m_SkyColor, 1.0f, 0 );

        return true;
}

indBool cGameEngine::Render()
{
        m_SkyBox.Render();

        m_TerrainGenerator.Render();

        ROUTEMANAGER->Render();
        RESOURCEMANAGER->RenderAll();

        ANIMATIONMANAGER->Render();
        PARTICLEMANAGER->Run();
        return true;
}

indBool cGameEngine::PostRender()
{
        m_pDevice->EndScene();
        m_pDevice->Present(0,0,0,0);
```

```
        return true;
}

DWORD cGameEngine::ThreadProcedure()
{
    Start();

    while(!m_bQuit)
        Run();

    Shutdown();

    return 0;
}


indInt cGameEngine::Run()
{
    if(!ValidateDevice())
        return 0;

    Synchronization();

    ROUTEMANAGER->Run();
    UpdateGlobalLight();
            INPUT->Run();
    SCRIPTMANAGER->Run();
    CAMERA->Run();

    m_TerrainGenerator.Run();
    PreRender();

    RenderGrid();
    m_SkyBox.Run();

    UINT runTime = GetEngineRunTime();

    float value = (float)runTime / 1000;
    float x1 = sin(value) * 100;
    float y1 = cos(value) * 100;
    float x2 = sin(-value) * 200;
    float y2 = cos(-value) * 200;
```

```
        ANIMATIONMANAGER->GetAnimatedMesh(0)->SetRotation(0, 0, -(value - 1.57f));
        ANIMATIONMANAGER->GetAnimatedMesh(1)->SetRotation(0, 0, (value - 1.57f));
        ANIMATIONMANAGER->GetAnimatedMesh(0)->SetPosition(D3DXVECTOR3(x1,y1,50));
        ANIMATIONMANAGER->GetAnimatedMesh(1)->SetPosition(D3DXVECTOR3(x2,y2,50));
        ANIMATIONMANAGER->GetAnimatedMesh(2)->SetPosition(D3DXVECTOR3(0,0,50));

        ANIMATIONMANAGER->Run();

        Render();
        PostRender();

        return true;
}

indBool cGameEngine::InitGrid()
{
    UINT length = sizeof(GRID_VERTEX) * 206;

    m_pDevice->CreateVertexBuffer(
        length, D3DUSAGE_WRITEONLY,
        GRID_VERTEXFORMAT, D3DPOOL_MANAGED, &m_pGridVB, 0);
    if(!m_pGridVB)
        return false;

    GRID_VERTEX* pGridData = 0;
    m_pGridVB->Lock(0,0, (void**)&pGridData, 0);

    D3DXCOLOR currentColor;
    D3DXCOLOR smallGridColor(0.4f, 0.4f, 0.4f, 1.0f);
    D3DXCOLOR largeGridColor(0.2f, 0.2f, 0.2f, 1.0f);
    D3DXCOLOR originColorX(1.0f, 0.0f, 0.0f, 1.0f);
    D3DXCOLOR originColorY(0.0f, 1.0f, 0.0f, 1.0f);
    D3DXCOLOR originColorZ(0.0f, 0.0f, 1.0f, 1.0f);

    int gridSize = 100;
    int halfGrid = gridSize / 2;
    float gridExtent = (float)halfGrid;

    UINT vertexCount = 0;

    // Fill in the X Axis
    for(int i = 0 ; i < 101 ; i+=2)
    {
```

```cpp
        float x;

        x = (float)i - 50.0f;

        if(i == halfGrid)
            currentColor = originColorX;
        else if(i % 5)
            currentColor = largeGridColor;
        else
            currentColor = smallGridColor;

        pGridData[vertexCount].color = (DWORD)currentColor;
        pGridData[vertexCount].position = D3DXVECTOR3(-gridExtent, 0.0f, x);

        ++vertexCount;

        pGridData[vertexCount].color = (DWORD)currentColor;
        pGridData[vertexCount].position = D3DXVECTOR3(gridExtent, 0.0f, x);

        ++vertexCount;
}

// Fill in the y axis
for(int i = 0 ; i < 101 ; i+=2)
{
        float y;

        y = (float)i - 50.0f;

        if(i == halfGrid)
            currentColor = originColorZ;
        else if(i % 5)
            currentColor = largeGridColor;
        else
            currentColor = smallGridColor;

        pGridData[vertexCount].color = (DWORD)currentColor;
        pGridData[vertexCount].position = D3DXVECTOR3(y, 0.0f, -gridExtent);

        ++vertexCount;

        pGridData[vertexCount].color = (DWORD)currentColor;
        pGridData[vertexCount].position = D3DXVECTOR3(y, 0.0f, gridExtent);
```

```
            ++vertexCount;
        }

        pGridData[vertexCount].color = originColorY;
        pGridData[vertexCount].position = D3DXVECTOR3(0.0f, -gridExtent, 0.0f);

        ++vertexCount;

        pGridData[vertexCount].color = originColorY;
        pGridData[vertexCount].position = D3DXVECTOR3(0.0f, gridExtent, 0.0f);

        m_pGridVB->Unlock();

        return true;
    }

    indBool cGameEngine::RenderGrid()
    {
        D3DXMATRIX worldMat;
        D3DXMatrixIdentity(&worldMat);

        GAMEENGINE->GetDevice()->SetStreamSource(0, m_pGridVB, 0, sizeof(GRID_VERTEX));

        VisualEffects::cEffect* pCurrentEffect =
EFFECTMANAGER->GetEffect(m_GridEffectID);

        pCurrentEffect->SetTransforms(
            worldMat, CAMERA->GetViewMatrix(), CAMERA->GetProjectionMatrix());
        pCurrentEffect->Dispatch();

        indUInt numPasses = 0;
        pCurrentEffect->Begin(numPasses);

        GAMEENGINE->GetDevice()->SetFVF(GRID_VERTEXFORMAT);

        for(indUInt passCount = 0 ; passCount < numPasses ; passCount++)
        {
            pCurrentEffect->BeginPass(passCount);

            GAMEENGINE->GetDevice()->SetTexture(0, 0);
            m_pDevice->DrawPrimitive(D3DPT_LINELIST, 0, 103);
```

```
            pCurrentEffect->EndPass();
        }

        pCurrentEffect->End();

        GAMEENGINE->GetDevice()->SetTexture(0, 0);

        return true;
}

indBool cGameEngine::Shutdown()
{
    m_SkyBox.Shutdown();
    m_TerrainGenerator.Shutdown();

    ROUTEMANAGER->Shutdown();
    EFFECTMANAGER->Shutdown();
    INPUT->Shutdown();
    CAMERA->Shutdown();
    RESOURCEMANAGER->Shutdown();
    PARTICLEMANAGER->Shutdown();
    ANIMATIONMANAGER->Shutdown();
    SCRIPTMANAGER->Shutdown();

    SAFE_RELEASE(m_pGridVB);
    SAFE_RELEASE(m_pDevice);
    SAFE_RELEASE(m_pDirect3D);
    SAFE_RELEASE(m_pDefaultTexture);

    EFFECTMANAGER->DestroySingleton();
    INPUT->DestroySingleton();
    RESOURCEMANAGER->DestroySingleton();
    PARTICLEMANAGER->DestroySingleton();
    CAMERA->DestroySingleton();
    ANIMATIONMANAGER->DestroySingleton();
    SCRIPTMANAGER->DestroySingleton();
    ROUTEMANAGER->DestroySingleton();


    PostMessage(m_hMainWnd, WM_DESTROY, 0, 0);
    return true;
```

```
    }
    void cGameEngine::EndThread()
    {
        // Called from destructor
        cThread::EndThread();
    }

    void cGameEngine::UpdateGlobalLight()
    {
        float secondsElapsed = (float)GetEngineRunTime() / 1000.0f;
        m_GlobalLightPosition.x = sin(secondsElapsed) * 100;
        m_GlobalLightPosition.z = cos(secondsElapsed) * 100;
    }

} // end namespace
```

The best way to learn from the sample is to open it and change the code around. Try studying the components and see if you can re-create them in your own engine. The best way to learn is by doing!

I would love to hear from you if you end up using this code or the ideas from it to create a really cool engine. You can contact me at mrzen@msn.com, which I finally got up and running again after a period of downtime caused by an error at MSN. You are free to redistribute the *compiled* code from this book in any commercial or noncommercial projects. However, remember that the source code is copyrighted, so you cannot distribute it in uncompiled form. If you end up making millions, feel free to make a donation if you would like books like these to continue coming out.

If you have any questions about this book or good or bad comments, please let me know. And if you find any bugs, tell me so that I can post updated code to the book's Web site.

Happy coding!

Peter Walsh
October 2, 2005
Dundee, Scotland

Now where's that beer...

INDEX

Symbols
: (colon), 36
__ (double underscore), 118
identifier, particle systems, 148
:: (resolution operator), 405

A
acceleration, particle systems, 136
ActiveLuaMethod() function, 316
AddRef() function, 222
Alias Maya program
    coding conventions, 192–194
    DAG (Directed Acyclic Graph), 190
    dependency nodes, 190
    described, 181
    DG (Dependency Graph), 190
    export formats, 198–201
    function sets, 191
    naming conventions, 191–192
    paths, 203
    Plug-In Manager, 196–198
    Plug-in Wizard
        confirmation page, 186
        Dependency Graph Node option, 184–185
        discussed, 182
        Empty option, 184
        library file addition, 187
        location configuration, 189
        MEL command option, 184–185
alignment, cache, particle systems, 116–119
alpha blending, 99–100
ambient color, vertex shaders, 41–42
angular velocity, 80
animals and birds, particle objects, 111

animation
    animation controller, 277
    animation manager creation, 285–288
    animation mesh, rendering, 269–272
    D3DXLoadMeshHierarchyFromX() function, 243
    frames
        CreateFrame() function, 251, 258
        creating and destroying, 251–252
        mesh containers and, 244–249
    loading, 263–267
    mesh containers, creating and destroying
    multiple animated meshes, 289–290
    sequences
        blending between, 282–285
        character movements, 276
        code, 279
        initialization, 281
        multiple instances, 282
        Start() function, 280
    skinned animation example
        base pose model, 236
        bone, 237
        discussed, 233
        motion capture data, 238–239
        skinned mesh example, 240–242
        weights and indices, 240
applications, windowed, 9, 15
assert() function, 7
Auto Load check box, Maya Plug-In Manager, 197
automatic techniques, 34

B
BeginPass() function, 91
bFlipflop variable, 412
bilinear filtering, 44

486 Index

billboarding, particle systems, 122–126
birds and animals, particle objects, 111
BlendIn() function, 282
blending, between animation sequences, 282–285
bone, skinned animation example, 237
branching, optimization techniques, 112–113
breakpoints, 7

C

cache alignment, particle systems, 116–119
calling functions, Lua scripting language, 315–318
camera creation
    declaration, 77–79
    movement and position, 79–80
    rotation control, 80–81
    view matrix, 81–84
cEffect class
    code, 48–49
    description, 47
    file name parameters, 49–50
    ID parameters, 49–51
cEffectManager class
    description, 55
    effects, loading from disks, 58–59
    finding effects, 57–58
    ID creation, 58
    initialization, 56
    shutdown, 57
ceil() function, 415
cEngine class
    CreateDevice() function, 17
    discussed, 10
    InitializeGraphics() function, 17
    Start() function, 17
cGameEngine class
    implementation code, 469–484
    interface definition code, 464–469
char member, 117
characters
    character movements, animation sequences, 276
    NPCs (Non-Player Characters), 304
cInputManager class, 60–62
class functions, Lua scripting language, 310–312
classes
    cEffect
        code, 48–49
        description, 47
        file name parameters, 49–50
        ID parameters, 49–51

cEffectManager
    description, 55
    effects, loading from disks, 58–59
    finding effects, 57–58
    ID creation, 58
    initialization, 56
    shutdown, 57
cEngine
    CreateDevice() function, 17
    discussed, 10
    InitializeGraphics() function, 17
    Start() function, 17
cGameEngine
    implementation code, 469–484
    interface definition code, 464–469
cInputManager, 60–62
cParticle
    code, 136–139
    description, 134–135
    members, list of, 135–136
cScriptableObject, 304–308
cSkinnedAnimationMesh, 263
cVolumetricShadow, 344
ID3DAllocateHierarchy, 250
CloneMeshFVF() function, 259
code
    animation
        animated mesh, rendering, 269–272
        animation manager creation, 285–288
        D3DXLoadMeshHierarchyFromX() function, 243
        frames and mesh containers, 244
        frames, creating and destroying, 251–252
        loading, 263, 265–267
        mesh containers, creating and destroying, 253–263
        multiple animated meshes, 289–290
        sequences, 280–285
    BlendIn() function, 282–283
    camera creation
        declaration, 77–79
        movement and position, 80
        rotation control, 80
        view matrix, 81–84
    cEffect class, 48–49
    cGameEngine class
        implementation code, 469–484
        interface definition code, 464–469
    CreateDevice() function, 18–19

Index

cubic environment mapping, 220–222
cVideoRenderer class, 446–447, 452–456, 488
D3DXColorLerp() function, 120
__declspec align, 118–119
Dispatch() function, 54
effect files, 28–34
    cEffect class, 50
    cEffectManager class, 55–59
    shutdown, 52
frame rate calculation and display, 72–73
game execution speed control, 74
GetEngineRunTime() function, 216
glow effects, 96–100, 102–106
InitializeGraphics() function, 17–18
InitInstance() function, 14–15
input polling, DeviceInput, 67–68
InputManager class, 60–62
joystick support, DirectInput, 67
LoadAssets() function, 222
Maya program coding conventions, 192
message pump, 12
mouse device, DirectInput, 66–68
MyRegisterClass() function, 15
particle systems
    billboarding example, 124–126
    branching techniques, 112–113
    color linear interpolation, 120–121
    cParticle class, 134–139
    float-to-integer conversions, 114–115
    function inlining, 115–116
    grid rendering, 127–130
    linear interpolation, 119–120
    NumParticle command, 145, 147
    particle creation, 154–155
    resetting particles, 162–163
    storage, 153–154
    system manager and library creation, 170–174
    updating code, 139–141
    velocity, 165–166
pixel shaders, 33–34
PostRender() function, 23
PreRender() function, 22
ProcessInput(), 68
rand() function, 121
register keyword, 36
Render() function, 23
rendering functions, 22–23
routes
    linear interpolation, 413–416
    loading, 408–410
    rendering process, 410–412
    route class creation, 403–407
    route manager code, 418–421
SAFE_RELEASE() function, 20
shadows
    function conversion, 348–364
    global light, 327–328
    occluded vertices, 328–331
    rendering to frame buffer, 335–339
    self-shadowing, 345–346
    stencil buffers, rendering process, 332–333
sky box
    generation code, 392–396
    rendering process, 396–397
    shaders, 398–399
Sleep() function, 75
static member, 7
techniques, 35
terrain
    creating, 372–380
    fog effects, 387–388
    rendering, 381
    shaders, 383–386
textures, overriding, 217–219
timeGetTime() function, 75, 215
ValidateDevice() function, 21
vertex shaders, 33
    ambient color, 41–42
    colors, 41–42
    diffuse color, 41
    function declaration, 39–40
    view direction, 41
visual resources
    initialization, 85–86
    loading, 86–90
    multiple onscreen objects, 93
    rendering, 90–92
    shutting down, 92
water effects, 227–231
WinMain() function, 11–13
Xbox 360 controllers
    class definition, 432–436
    device capabilities, 429
    device state, 430
    feedback, 434
    input manager connection, 436–444
    rumble effects, 431

Index

coding conventions, Maya program, 192–194
CoInitialize() function, 445
colon (:), 36
color
    ambient color, vertex shaders, 41–42
    particle systems, 135
    water effects example, 224
color linear interpolation, 120–121
COM objects, SAFE_RELEASE() function, 20
configurable particle systems, 142
confirmation page, Maya Plug-in Wizard, 186
cos function, 225
cParticle class
    code, 136–139
    description, 134–135
    members, list of, 135–136
CreateDevice() function, 17, 19
CreateFrame() function, 251, 258
creation function, particle systems, 152
cScriptableObject class, 304–308
cSkinnedAnimationMesh class, 263
cubemap texture, 397
cubic environment mapping, 220–222
culling, 168
cVideoRenderer class, 446–447
cVolumetricShadow class, 344

D

D3DLoadMeshFromX() function, 88
D3DLoadMeshHierarchyFromX() function, 263
D3DMatrixRotationAxis() function, 84
D3DXColorLerp() function, 120
D3DXComputeNormals() function, 259
D3DXCreateEffectFromFile() function, 51
D3DXCreateTextureFromFileEX() function, 89
D3DXLoadMeshHierarchyFromX() function, 243
D3DXMATERIAL structures, 88
D3DXMESHCONTAINER structure, 249
D3DXVec3Lerp() function, 416
DAG (Directed Acyclic Graph), Maya program, 190
__declspec align, 118–119
#defines *versus* constants, 5
Dependency Graph (DG), Maya program, 190
dependency nodes, Maya program, 190
DestroyFrame() function, 251
device creation, Direct3D API setup, 19–21
device reacquisition, DirectInput, 67–69

device state, Xbox 360 controllers, 430
device validation, Direct3D API setup, 21
DG (Dependency Graph), Maya program, 190
DIMOUSESTATE structure, 66
Direct3D API setup
    device creation, 19–21
    device validation, 21
    initialization, 17–19
    shutdown code, 20–21
    Visual Studio .NET setup, for DirectX, 16–17
Directed Acyclic Graph (DAG), Maya program, 190
DirectInput
    cInputManager class, 60–62
    device reacquisition, 67–69
    input polling, 67–69
    joystick support, 67
    keyboard device, 63–64
    mouse device, 65–67
    ProcessInput() function, 68–69
    starting, 62
DirectInput8Create() function, 63
directories, adding to Lua scripting language, 300
DirectShow, video playback, 444–446
disks, loading effects from, 58–59
Dispatch() function, 50, 54
doIt() function, 196
double underscore (__), 118
do...while loop, 299
DrawPrimitive() function, 382
DrawPrimitiveUP() function, 382, 410
Duke Nukem 3D, 234
dwPort variable, 429
dynamic configuration, particle systems, 169–174

E

effect files
    cEffect class
        discussed, 47–48
        file name parameters, 49–50
        ID parameters, 49–51
    cEffectManager class
        description, 55
        effects, loading from disks, 58–59
        finding effects, 57–58
        ID creation, 58
        initialization, 56
        shutdown, 57
    code, 28–34

D3DXCreateEffectFromFile() function, 51
EffectEdit tool, 46–47
glow effects, 96–100
ID3DXEffect::SetMatrix() function, 55
rendering with, 53–54
shutting down, 52
emergent behavior, particle systems, 107
Empty option, Maya Plug-in Wizard, 184
environment generation
    sky box
        cubemap texture, 397
        described, 389
        generating, 392–396
        properties, 390
        rendering process, 396–397
        shaders, 398–399
        sphere generation, 393
    terrain
        coordinates, 375
        creating, 372–380
        description, 368
        DrawPrimitive() function, 382
        DrawPrimitiveUP() function, 382
        fog effects, 387–388
        heightmap texture, 369, 373
        LoadTerrainTextures() function, 370–372
        loops, 376
        rendering process, 380–381
        segmentWidth variable, 372
        shaders, 383–386
        texture size, 375
environment mapping, cubic, 220–222
error handling, 8–9
example code. *See* **code**
execution function, particle systems, 152
explosions, particle systems, 109–110
export formats, Maya program, 198–201
external design, particle systems, 142

F

feature files, particle systems, 142–144
feedback, Xbox 360 controllers, 434
file name parameters, cEffect class, 49–50
Filename component, 244
filtering, bilinear and linear, 44
FindFirstFile() function, 58–59
FindNextFile() function, 58–59
fire example, particle systems, 178

float values, generating with limited range, particle systems, 121–122
float-to-integer conversions, optimization techniques, 113–115
floor() function, 415
fluidity of movement, water effects, 226
fog effects, 387–388
fopen() function, 410
for loop, 299
FPS (Frames per Second), 73–74
frame buffer, rendering shadows to, 335–339
frame rates
    calculation and display, 72–73
    forcing, 74–76
frames
    CreateFrame() function, 251, 258
    creating and destroying, 251–252
Frames per Second (FPS), 73–74
full-screen development, windowed applications, 15
function pointers, 311–312
function sets, Maya program, 191
functions
    ActiveLuaMethod(), 316
    AddRef(), 222
    assert(), 7
    BeginPass(), 91
    BlendIn(), 282
    calling, Lua scripting language, 315–318
    ceil(), 415
    CloneMeshFVF(), 259
    CoInitialize(), 445
    cos, 225
    CreateDevice(), 17, 19
    CreateFrame(), 251, 258
    D3DLoadMeshFromX(), 88
    D3DLoadMeshHierarchyFromX(), 243, 263
    D3DMatrixRotationAxis(), 84
    D3DXColorLerp(), 120
    D3DXComputeNormals(), 259
    D3DXCreateEffectFromFile(), 51
    D3DXCreateTextureFromFileEx() function, 89
    D3DXVec3Lerp(), 416
    declaration, vertex shaders, 39–40
    DestroyFrame(), 251
    DirectInput8Create(), 63
    Dispatch(), 50, 54
    doIt(), 196
    DrawPrimitive(), 382

functions *(continued)*
   DrawPrimitiveUP(), 382, 410
   FindFirstFile(), 58–59
   FindNextFile(), 58–59
   floor(), 415
   fopen(), 410
   GetDesktopWindow(), 195
   GetEngineRunTime(), 216
   GetInstance(), 7
   ID3DXEffect::SetMatrix(), 55
   InitGrid(), 126
   InitializeGraphics(), 17
   InitInstance(), 14–15
   inlining, 115–116
   Interpolate(), 120
   LoadAssets(), 222
   LoadTerrainTextures(), 370–372
   LockRect(), 374
   Lua scripting language, 299, 310–312
   lua_getglobal(), 308
   lua_isfunction(), 316, 319
   LuaLocalMethodHandler(), 312
   luaL_ref(), 307
   lua_newtable(), 307
   lua_pcall(), 319
   lua_pushclosure(), 312
   lua_rawgeti(), 308
   MyRegisterClass(), 15
   PostRender(), 22
   PreRender(), 22
   ProcessInput(), 68–69
   PS(), 43
   public static, 7
   put_Owner(), 451
   QueryPerformanceCounter(), 75
   rand(), 121
   Render(), 22
   RenderFile(), 451
   RenderGrid(), 126
   RenderResource(), 344
   ResetParticle(), 159, 162
   Run()
      description, 11
      linear interpolation, 413
      particle system execution, 155–158, 162
      rendering functions, 22
   SAFE_RELEASE(), 20, 52
   SetupBoneMatrixPointers(), 265
   SetupBoneMatrixPointersOnMesh(), 266
   SetWindowText(), 73
   Shutdown(), 11
   sin, 225
   Sleep(), 75
   Start()
      animation sequences, 280
      cEngine class, 17
      cParticleSystem class, 154
      description, 11
      routes, loading, 408
      sky box generation, 392
   strings, 311
   Synchronization(), 72–73
   text2D(), 43
   timeGetTime(), 75, 215
   UpdateBoneMatrices(), 268
   UpdatePosition(), 158
   ValidateDevice(), 21
   VS(), 39
   WinMain(), 11
.fx extension. *See* effect files

G

game engine, placeholder
   high-performance window creation, 14–16
   Win32 API connecting, 11–14
GetDesktopWindow() function, 195
GetEngineRunTime() function, 216
GetInstance() function, 7
global light, shadowing, 326–328
glow effects, 96–100
glowing cloud example, particle systems, 175
glue code, 297, 301–303
GPU (Graphics Processing Unit), 26–27
grid rendering, particle systems, 126–130

H

Heads Up Display (HUD), 456
heightmap texture, terrain, 369, 373
HLSL (High Level Shader Language)
   defined, 27–28
   variables, 37
HUD (Heads Up Display), 456

I–J

ID parameter
    cEffect class, 49–51
    cEffectManager class, 58
ID3DAllocateHierarchy class, 250
ID3DXEffect::SetMatrix() function, 55
IDirect3D9 interface, 194
if statement, 112
if/then/else statements, 300
indices, skinned animation example, 240
InitGrid() function, 126
initialization
    animation sequences, 281
    cEffectManager class, 56
    cVideoRenderer class, 446–447
    visual resources, 85–86
InitializeGraphics() function, 17
InitInstance() function, 14–15
inlining, functions, 115–116
input manager connection, Xbox 360 controllers, 436–444
input parameters, pixel shaders, 43
input polling, DirectInput, 67–69
integers, float-to-integer conversion, 113–115
interface creation, Windows, 9
Interpolate() function, 120
interpolation, linear, 119–121, 413–416
intersection, shadows, 325

joystick support, DirectInput, 67

K–L

keyboard device, DirectInput, 63–64

libraries
    Maya Plug-in Wizard, 187
    particle systems, 170–174
light direction, water effects, 224
linear filtering, 44
linear interpolation, 119–121, 413–416
LoadAssets() function, 222
loading
    animation, 263–267
    routes, 408–410
LoadTerrainTextures() function, 370–372
location configuration, Maya Plug-in Wizard, 189

LockRect() function, 374
loops
    do...while, 299
    for, 299
    Lua scripting language, 299–300
Lua scripting language
    ActiveLuaMethod() function, 316
    class functions, 310–312
    directories, adding, 300
    downloading source code to, 300
    functions, 299, 315–318
    history of, 296
    libraries, downloading, 300
    loop structures, 299–300
    lua_getglobal() function, 308
    lua_isfunction() function, 316, 319
    LuaLocalMethodHandler() function, 312
    luaL_ref() function, 307
    lua_newtable() function, 307
    lua_pcall() function, 319
    lua_pushclosure() function, 312
    lua_rawgeti() function, 308
    nil statements, 300
    overview, 298
    parameters, 299
    popularity of, 295–296
    variable declaration, 299
    Web site, 297

M

m_Acceleration member, cParticle class, 136
mass, particle systems, 136
matrix
    D3DMatrixRotationAxis() function, 84
    ID3DXEffect::SetMatrix() function, 55
Maya program
    coding conventions, 192–194
    DAG (Directed Acyclic Graph), 190
    dependency nodes, 190
    described, 181
    DG (Dependency Graph), 190
    export formats, 198–201
    function sets, 191
    naming conventions, 191–192
    paths, 203
    Plug-In Manager, 196–198

Maya program *(continued)*
   Plug-in Wizard
      confirmation page, 186
      Dependency Graph Node option, 184–185
      discussed, 182
      Empty option, 184
      library file addition, 187
      location configuration, 189
      MEL command option, 184–185
m_bShadowed member, 344
m_CombineTransformationMatrix member, 245
m_ComputePoints member, 405–406
m_CurrentColor member, cParticle class, 135
m_CurrentSize member, cParticle class, 136
m_CurrentTime member, 406
MEL Command option, Maya Plug-in Wizard, 184–185
m_EndColor member, cParticle class, 135
mesh containers, creating and destroying, 253–262
MeshData structure, 246
meshes
   animation mesh, rendering, 269–272
   CloneMeshFVF() function, 259
   D3DLoadMeshFromX() function, 88
   multiple animated, 289–290
MeshOptions component, 244
message pump code, 12
m_HeightModifier member, 392
milliseconds elapsed, particle systems, 136
MinFilter filter, 44
m_InterpolationMode member, 407
MipFilter filter, 44
m_LifeSpan member, cParticle class, 136
m_LifeTimeElapsed member, cParticle class, 136
m_Mass member, cParticle class, 136
m_NumAttributeGroup member, 249
m_NumBoneInfluencesPerVertex member, 249
m_NumLusCallableMethods member, 307
m_NumPaletteEntries member, 249
m_NumPushedArguments member, 307
m_NumVertices member, 392
models, base pose, 236
motion capture data, skinned animation example, 238–239
mouse device, DirectInput, 65–67
movement and position, camera creation, 79–80
m_pAttributeTable member, 248
m_pBoneCombinationBuffer member, 249
m_pOriginalMesh member, 248
m_Position member, cParticle class, 135
m_ppBoneMatrixPtrs member, 249
m_ppTextures member, 248
m_pRoutePoints member, 406, 410
m_pRouteVertsRender member, 406
m_pTerrainVB member, 371
m_pVertices member, 392
m_SizeEnd member, cParticle class, 136
m_SizeStart member, cParticle class, 136
m_StartColor member, cParticle class, 135
multi-vertex polygons, 199
m_vAnimatedMeshes member, 287
m_Velocity member, cParticle class, 135
MyRegisterClass() function, 15

N

namespaces
   code readability, 5
   polluting the global namespace problem, 4
   scope resolution operator, 4
naming conventions, Maya program, 191–192
New Project dialog box (Visual Studio), 9
nil statements, Lua scripting language, 300
Non-Uniform Rational B-Splines (NURBS), 198, 214
NPCs (Non-Player Characters), 304
NumMaterials parameter, 246
NumParticles command, particle systems, 144–147
numTextureTiles variable, 375
NURBS (Non-Uniform Rational B-Splines), 198, 214

O

object existence, singletons, 6–7
objects, manual creation, 7
occlusion, shadowing, 324–325, 328
once-per-frame scene initialization, 22
optimization techniques, particle systems
   branching, 112–113
   cache alignment, 116–119
   float-to-integer conversions, 113–115
   function inlining, 115–116
overriding textures, 217–219

P

pAdjacency parameter, 246
pAlloc component, 244

parameters, Lua scripting language, 299
particle systems
    acceleration, 136
    billboarding, 122–126
    color linear interpolation, 120–121
    colors, 135
    configurable, 142
    cParticle class, 134–135
    creation function, 152
    dynamic configuration, 169–174
    emergent behavior, 107
    execution function, 152
    explosions, 109–110
    external design, 142
    feature files, 142–144
    fire example, 178
    glowing cloud example, 175
    grid rendering, 126–130
    ## identifier, 148
    instanciable, 109
    linear interpolation, 119–121
    mass, 136
    milliseconds elapsed, 136
    NumParticles command, 144–147
    optimization techniques
        branching, 112–113
        cache alignment, 116–119
        float-to-integer conversions, 113–115
        function inlining, 115–116
    particle creation, 154–155
    particle objects, 111
    point sprites, 110–111
    random float values, generating with limited range, 121–122
    rendering, 110–111, 167–169
    rendering function, 152
    ResetParticle() function, 159, 162
    routes and, 422
    shutdown function, 152
    storage, 153–154
    system execution, 155–158
    system manager and library creation, 169–174
    textured quads, 111
    theory of, 108–109
    untextured primitives, 110
    updating code, 139–141
    velocity, 135
    VelocityFinalHigh command, 165
    VelocityFinalLow command, 165
    VelocityInitialHigh command, 165
    VelocityInitialLow command, 165
    water stream example, 176–177
paths, defined, 203
pDevice component, 244
pFrameFirstChild parameter, 245
pFrameSibling parameter, 245
pixel shaders
    code, 33–34
    defined, 27
    description, 42
    filtering techniques, 44–45
    input parameters, 43
    sampler states, 43–44
platform-independent variables, 5–6
Plug-In Manager, Maya program, 196–198
Plug-in Wizard, Maya
    confirmation page, 186
    Dependency Graph Node option, 184–185
    discussed, 182
    Empty option, 184
    library file addition, 187
    location configuration, 189
    MEL Command option, 184–185
pMaterials structure, 246
pMeshContainer parameter, 245
pNextMeshContainer parameter, 247
point sprites, 110–111
points on routes, moving between, 403
polygons
    multi-vertex, 199
    triangles, 200
position and movement, camera creation, 79–80
PostRender() function, 22
ppAnimController component, 244
ppFrameHierarchy component, 244
PreRender() function, 22
primary mouse buttons, 67
primitives, untextured, 110
Prince of Persia, 234
private constructors, 7
ProcessInput() function, 68–69
PS() function, 43
public static function, 7
put_Owner() function, 451

Q–R

Quake, 295, 346
Quake 1, 110–111, 234
QueryPerformanceCounter() function, 75

rain, untextured primitives, 110
rand() function, 121
random float values, generating with limited range, particle systems, 121–122
readability, namespaces, 5
reflection, water effects example, 220–222
register keyword, 36–37
Render() function, 22
RenderFile() function, 451
RenderGrid() function, 126
rendering
    animated mesh, 269–272
    with effect files, 53–54
    grid rendering, particle systems, 126–130
    particle systems, 110–111, 167–169
    PostRender() function, 22
    PreRender() function, 22
    Render() function, 22
    routes, 410–412
    shadows to frame buffer, 335–339
    sky box, 396–397
    stencil buffers, 332–335
    terrain, 380–381
    visual resources, 90–92
RenderResource() function, 344
ResetParticle() function, 159, 162
resolution operator (::), 405
rotation
    rotation control, camera creation, 80–81
    textured quads, 111
routes
    described, 402
    linear interpolation, 413–416
    loading, 408–410
    m_ComputePoints member, 405–406
    m_CurrentTime member, 406
    m_InterpolationMode member, 407
    moving between points on, 403
    m_pRoutePoints member, 406, 410
    m_pRouteVertsRender member, 406
    particle systems and, 422
    rendering, 410–412
    route class creation, 403–408
    route manager code, 418–421

rumble effects, Xbox 360 controllers, 430–431
Run() function
    description, 11
    linear interpolation, 413
    particle system execution, 155–158, 162
    rendering functions, 22

S

SAFE_RELEASE() function, 20, 52
sampler states, pixel shaders, 43–44
scaling, textured quads, 111
scene initialization, once-per frame, 22
scope resolution operator, 4
scripts
    cScriptableObject class, 304–308
    discussed, 293
    glue code, 297, 301–303
    Lua scripting language
        ActiveLuaMethod() function, 316
        class functions, 310–312
        directories, adding, 300
        downloading source code to, 300
        functions, 299
        functions, calling, 315–318
        history of, 296
        libraries, downloading, 300
        loop structures, 299–300
        lua_getglobal() function, 308
        lua_isfunction() function, 316, 319
        LuaLocalMethodHandler() function, 312
        luaL_ref() function, 307
        lua_newtable() function, 307
        lua_pcall() function, 319
        lua_pushclosure() function, 312
        lua_rawgeti() function, 308
        nil statements, 300
        overview, 298
        parameters, 299
        popularity of, 295–296
        variable declaration, 299
        Web site, 297
    scriptable object implementation, 319–320
    uses for, 294
    when to use, 295
SDK (Software Development Kit), 28
secondary mouse buttons, 67
segmentWidth variable, 372
self-shadowing, 344–346

semantics
  defined, 33
  register constants and, 36–37
sequences, 279
  blending between, 282–285
  character movements, 276
  initialization, 281
  multiple instances, 282
  Start() function, 280
SetupBoneMatrixPointers() function, 265
SetupBoneMatrixPointersOnMesh() function, 266
SetWindowText() function, 73
shaders
  defined, 26
  effect files, 28–34
  glow effects, 96–100
  HLSL (High Level Shader Language), 27–28
  pixel
    code, 33–34
    defined, 27
    description, 42
    filtering techniques, 44–45
    input parameters, 43
    sampler states, 43–44
  semantics, 33
  sending data to, 54–55
  sky box, 398–399
  surfaceShader attribute, 206
  terrain, 383–386
  vertex
    ambient color, 41–42
    code, 33
    defined, 27
    descriptions, 37–38
    diffuse color, 41
    function declaration, 39–40
    minimal use, 38–39
    specular color, 42
    time tracking techniques, water effects example, 214–217
    view direction, 41
shadows
  discussed, 323
  global light, 326–328
  intersection, 325
  occlusion, 324–325, 328
  rendering to frame buffer, 335–339
  restrictions, 346–348

  self-shadowing, 344–346
  stencil buffers
    description, 325–326
    rendering process, 332–335
shutdown
  cEffectManager class, 57
  effect files, 52
  particle systems, 152
  shutdown code, Direct3D API setup, 20–21
  visual resources, 92
Shutdown() function, 11
sin function, 225
singletons, 6–7
skinned animation example
  base pose model, 236
  bone, 237
  discussed, 233
  motion capture data, 238–239
  skinned mesh example, 240–242
  weights and indices, 240
sky box
  cubemap texture, 397
  described, 389
  generating, 392–396
  properties, 390
  rendering process, 396–397
  shaders, 398–399
  sphere generation, 393
Sleep() function, 75
Software Development Kit (SDK), 28
source code, downloading to Lua scripting language, 300
sparks, untextured primitives, 110
speed control, synchronization, 73–74
sphere generation, sky box example, 393
stack order, function inlining, 115
Start() function
  animation sequences, 280
  cEngine class, 17
  cParticleSystem class, 154
  cSkinnedAnimationMesh class, 263
  description, 11
  routes, loading, 408
  sky box generation, 392
startX variable, 372
startZ variable, 372
static flags, 7
static members, 7

static variable declarations, updating particle systems, 140
stencil buffers
    description, 325–326
    rendering process, 332–335
storage, particle systems, 153–154
strings, 311
surfaceShader attribute, 206
synchronization
    frame rate calculation and display, 72–73
    frame rates, forcing, 74–76
    game execution speed control, 73–74
Synchronization() function, 72–73
system execution, particle systems, 155–158
system manager, particle systems, 170–174

T

Taylor, Phil, 253
techniques
    automatic fallback, 34
    code, 35
    defined, 34
terrain
    coordinates, 375
    creating, 372–380
    description, 368
    DrawPrimitive() function, 382
    DrawPrimitiveUP() function, 382
    fog effects, 387–388
    heightmap texture, 369, 373
    LoadTerrainTextures() function, 370–372
    loops, 376
    rendering process, 380–381
    segmentWidth variable, 372
    shaders, 383–386
    texture size, 375
text2D() function, 43
textures
    cubemap, 397
    overriding, 217–219
    textured quads, 111
time delta, 73–74
time tracking in vertex shaders, water effects example, 214–217
time variable, 216
timeGetTime() function, 75, 215
Tomb Raider, 235–236

transformations, 237
triangles, polygons, 200
truncation, 114
type-checked values, 5
typedef parameter, 311

U

Unreal, 295
untextured primitives, 110
UpdateBoneMatrices() function, 268
UpdatePosition() function, 158
updating code, particle systems, 139–141
USB connection cables, Xbox 360 controllers, 426

V

ValidateDevice() function, 21
validation, device, Direct3D API setup, 21
variables
    declaring, 299
    HLSL (High Level Shader Language), 37
    platform-independent, 5–6
velocity
    angular, 80
    particle systems, 135
VelocityFinalHigh command, particle systems, 165
VelocityFinalLow command, particle systems, 165
VelocityInitialHigh command, particle systems, 165
VelocityInitialLow command, particle systems, 165
vertex shaders
    ambient color, 41–42
    code, 33
    defined, 27
    descriptions, 37–38
    diffuse color, 41
    function declaration, 39–40
    minimal use, 38–39
    specular color, 42
    time tracking techniques, water effects example, 214–217
    view direction, 41
video playback
    cVideoRenderer class, 446–447
    DirectShow, 444–445

view matrix, camera creation, 81–84
visual resources
    initialization, 85–86
    loading, 86–90
    managing, 93–95
    multiple onscreen objects, 93
    rendering, 90–92
    shutting down, 92
Visual Studio
    New Project dialog box, 9
    Visual Studio .NET setup, for DirectX, 16–17
volumetric shadowing. *See* **shadows**
VS () function, 39

W

water effects
    color, 224
    fluidity of movement, 226
    full effect code, 227–231
    light direction, 224
    NURBS plane, 214
    particle systems, 176–177
    reflection, 220–222
    textures, overriding, 217–219
    wave changes, time tracking, 214–217
weights, skinned animation example, 240
Win32 API, connecting to game engine, 11–14
windowed applications, 9, 15
Windows interface creation, 9
WinMain() function
    description, 11
    WM_QUIT message, 14
wizards, Maya Plug-in
    confirmation page, 186
    Dependency Graph Node option, 184–185
    discussed, 182
    Empty option, 184
    library file addition, 187
    location configuration, 189
    MEL Command option, 184–185
WM_PAINT messages, 16
WM_QUIT message, 14

X–Z

Xbox 360 controllers
    input manager connection, 436–444
    USB connection cables, 426
    XInput API
        class definition, 432–436
        device capabilities, 428–430
        device state, 430
        feedback, 434
        rumble effects, 430–431

Bonus Easter Egg for Reader:

0100100101100110001000000111100101101111011101010010000001100011011000010111011
1000100000011100100110010101100001011001000110000011101000110100001101001011
100110010000001111001011011110111010100100000011000010111001001100101001000001
1000010010000001110100001110010011101010110010100100000011001110110000101101101
0110010100100000011100000111001001101111011001110111001001100001011011010110
1010110100101101110011001110010000001100111011101010101110010011101010100100001

CREATE AMAZING GRAPHICS AND COMPELLING STORYLINES FOR YOUR GAMES!

THOMSON COURSE TECHNOLOGY

Professional ■ Technical ■ Reference

Beginning Game Graphics
ISBN: 1-59200-430-X ■ $29.99

This step-by-step guide begins with the most basic modeling techniques and wraps up with advanced workflows used by professional game artists. It provides powerful and easy-to-use tools to get you started, and it covers many of the methods, philosophies, and proven techniques that can improve your game demos and help separate you from the crowd in the rapidly growing interactive entertainment industry.

The Dark Side of Game Texturing
ISBN: 1-59200-350-8 ■ $39.99

Get ready to analyze—and re-create—the textures and graphics used in your favorite 3D first-person shooter games. Not a born artist? That's okay. You'll learn how to let Photoshop do most of the work. Begin with texturing basics, including pixel sizes, color modes, and alpha channels. Then jump right into hearty texture tutorials as you create everything from sci-fi backgrounds and molten lava to medieval castle walls and dragon skin.

Shaders for Game Programmers and Artists
ISBN: 1-59200-092-4 ■ $39.99

Master the fine points of shader creation by using ATI's RenderMonkey platform. This easy-to-use framework allows you to focus your energy on shader development as you cover simple techniques, from the basics of color filters to more advanced topics, such as depth of field, heat shimmer, and high-dynamic range rendering. Extensive exercises at the end of each chapter allow you to test your skills by expanding upon the shader you've just developed.

Character Development and Storytelling for Games
ISBN: 1-59200-353-2 ■ $39.99

This is a book of ideas and of choices. Knowing which choices to make is not teachable. It's part of that creative instinct we call talent whose secret voice guides us every time we sit down at the keyboard. All stories are not identical. They are shaped by all those unique facets of the human beings who write them. [This book] is meant to inform, to instruct, and maybe even inspire. [It] has been designed as a quest. We are all of us on a journey toward a destination for which there is no single road. —**Lee Sheldon, Author**

THOMSON COURSE TECHNOLOGY
Professional ■ Technical ■ Reference

Call 1.800.354.9706 to order
Order online at www.courseptr.com

THOMSON
＊
COURSE TECHNOLOGY

Professional ■ Technical ■ Reference

GOT GAME?

Game Testing All in One
1-59200-373-7 ■ $49.99

Game Design, Second Edition
1-59200-493-8 ■ $39.99

Game Interface Design
1-59200-593-4 ■ $39.99

The Game Producer's
Handbook
1-59200-617-5 ■ $39.99

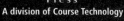

Call **1.800.354.9706** to order
Order online at **www.courseptr.com**

Don't just play the game.
Rule the game!

Game Guru: Strategy Games
1-59200-253-6 ■ U.S. $19.99, CAN. $27.95

Cover the origins of strategy games—both turn-based and realtime—as you master the balance between the core gameplay factors such as empire-building, resource management, defense, and offense. With hundreds of examples and in-depth interviews with the experts, this book reveals the secrets of what makes great games compelling and successful. Whether you are a professional or a hobbyist, you'll enjoy the comprehensive coverage and the clear analysis of play balance, character and level design, learning curves, risk versus reward, puzzles, scale and scope, catch-up effects, symmetry, and many other aspects of game theory.

Game Guru: Role-Playing Games
1-59200-254-4 ■ $19.99, CAN. $27.95

Role-playing games almost meticulously evoke a parallel life for the player—sometimes down to the detail of what kind of wine is in their hip flask. This book examines not only the gameplay and simulation aspects of role-playing games, but also the conventions that underlie it—the threat of evil, the archetypal playground of the sword-and-sorcery setting, and so on. It includes hundreds of examples and in-depth interviews with the experts, revealing the secrets to what makes great games com-pelling and successful. It offers clear analysis of play balance, character and level design, learning curves, risk versus reward, puzzles, scale and scope, catch-up effects, symmetry, and more.

Call 1.800.354.9706 to order
Order online at www.courseptr.com